Religious Festive Practices
in Boston's North End

SUNY series in Italian/American Culture

Fred L. Gardaphe, editor

Religious Festive Practices in Boston's North End

Ephemeral Identities in an Italian American Community

Augusto Ferraiuolo

Cover photo by William Albert Allard / National Geographic Image Collection

Published by State University of New York Press, Albany

For information, contact State University of New York Press, Albany, NY
www.sunypress.edu

Production by Ryan Morris
Marketing by Michael Campochiaro

Library of Congress Cataloging-in-Publication Data

Ferraiuolo, Augusto.
   Religious festive practices in Boston's North End : ephemeral identities in an Italian
American Community / Augusto Ferraiuolo.
       p. cm. — (SUNY series in Italian/American culture)
   Includes bibliographical references and index.
   ISBN 978-1-4384-2809-3 (hardcover : alk. paper) — ISBN 978-1-4384-2810-9
(pbk. : alk. paper)   1. Fasts and feasts—Massachusetts—Boston.   2. Festivals—
Massachusetts—Boston.   3. Italian Americans—Massachusetts—Boston—Religion.
4. Italian Americans—Massachusetts—Boston—Ethnic identity.   5. North End
(Boston, Mass.)—Religious life and customs.   6. North End (Boston, Mass.)—
Social life and customs.   I. Title.
   BX1418.B7F47   2009
   263'.908828274461—dc22
                                                                                  2008054156

10 9 8 7 6 5 4 3 2 1

This work is dedicated to whatever God or Goddess allows me to wake up every morning and to see your eyes continuously bringing joy, serenity, and love into my life.

Buíochas le Dia, tá grá agam duit!

And it is dedicated to all the people that crossed the Atlantic to make a new village but never forgetting the old one, generation after generation. To them, and to me, the North End is not a state of mind surrounded by water, but a place we could call home in spite of nostalgia.

Contents

Illustrations

All photos were taken by the author between June 2002 and September 2005.

Figures

Map

Table

Acknowledgments

Writing a page of acknowledgments is a very poor way to thank all the people who supported me through this exciting journey of a new research, a new challenge, a new twist in my life.

My research in the North End would not have been possible without the generosity of Boston University–University Professors Program sponsoring my studies and my fieldwork.

I met so many scholars throughout these years during formal meetings, lessons and seminars, coffee breaks, or just chat, and I received from them important comments, contributions, and insights. I am particularly grateful to Anthony Barrand, Fredrik Barth, Marilyn Halter, Michael Herzfeld, Frank Korom, Charles Lindholm, and Corky White for the kindness and patience in reading my pages, and for always encouraging me with refined and precious suggestions. Also, I want to thank the two anonymous readers of my manuscript for their invaluable ideas and advice.

Furthermore, some sections of this volume reelaborate and develop part of the contents of a previous essay of mine: "Boston's North End: Negotiating Identity in an Italian-American Neighborhood," *Western Folklore*, 65, no. 3 (Summer 2006).

Many people in the United States and in Europe have helped me. Thank you Robert Adams, Gerri and Ricky Bellitti, Jennifer Caputo, Donald and Henrietta Cosentino, Luisa Del Giudice, Elvira Di Fabio, Alan Follows, J. P. Hennessey, Nea Herzfeld, Scott McElveen, Bernice Poloniak, Sal Primeggia, Gayle Rae, Warren Rhodes, Joe Sciorra, Arthur Snyder, Hugh Wattenberg, my American friends. And thank you Gianluca and Leandro Ferraiuolo, Enzo Battarra, Paolo Favero, Andrea and Brilli Giuntini, Felice and Pina Imperato, Aldo Mariano, Gerardo and Rosaria Masciandaro, Paola Rossi, Antonio Sarno, Giuseppe Venditto, and Lina Zanni: I think of you as my kin. I also thank Tim Messick for his friendship and for helping me in my struggle with a new language and rhetoric: mistakes and accents are my own fault, despite his wonderful support.

There are so many people of the North End I would love to thank individually; however, the list is too long to include here. I do need to thank at least Jason and Vivian Aluia, Joe Di Girolamo, Jerry Di Prizio, and all the friends of Saint Anthony and Saint Lucy Societies; Dale Palma, John Norris and Elio LoRusso, and the Madonna di Anzano Society, Salvi Puglisi and the Roma

Band; as well as Pasquale Luise, Pasqualino Colombaro, Bob D'Attilio, and Lia Tota. But without Guild Nichols and his invaluable help during every moment of my fieldwork, as well as his continuous support, critique, and dialogue, I would not know anything about the North End.

Finally, special gratitude is what I feel for Sal and Therese Diecidue of the Madonna del Soccorso Society; they were and they are my North End family.

Introduction

Caffè Graffiti is a bar on Hanover Street,[1] the central artery of the North End, the Italian American neighborhood of Boston.[2] It is an "Italian" bar,[3] where people sit, especially in the morning for an "Italian" breakfast, (usually coffee—or cappuccino—and pastry). Or they might order an aperitif, probably a Campari Soda. People do not stay long, just the time to drink their coffee and eat their pastry. Sometimes they do not even have their pastry there, but nearby, at Mickey's Place. People gather around the Caffè Graffiti, because there are tables inside and benches outside. It is possible to sit for a while, every morning, talking with friends, or waiting for other friends who may be coming. Patrons also chat with the owner or the waiters. They speak Italian, loudly, so, I think, everybody can recognize the place as an "Italian" place.

One morning after three weeks of fieldwork before returning to Italy I wanted to meet my friends in the North End.[4] We were drinking a cup of coffee, a very nice "Italian" espresso. There were four or five old men talking, sitting on a bench outside, enjoying that sunny July 3. At the end of their conversation one of the group said good-bye to the others in this way: "Compa', facite nu buone fourth of July." A simple sentence I am sure is heard frequently in the United States. At least for me, as an Italian anthropologist working on the cultural identity of Italian Americans, this sentence had and still has a special meaning: a blend of languages and cultures, of tradition and modernity. It contained a complex manipulation of symbols such as feasts, dialects, and kinship where the boundaries between Italy and America were continuously crossed and where ethnic identity showed itself as a cultural construct, absolutely malleable and negotiable.[5] And it encapsulates the objective of my research: to find out how the Italian Americans of Boston's North End negotiate identities by manipulating symbols.

If we analyze the sentence we can find several things. First, the use of the Italian term *Compa'*, (short for the Italian *Compare*, female *Comare*). This term can be translated as "godfather," evoking a kind of kinship that still exists in Italy, above all in southern Italy. In fact, the *comparaggio*, the way of becoming and to be *compari*, is a very complex cultural institution, as Campbell (1964) has demonstrated in his analysis of ritual kinship in Greece.[6] The term relates to a man or a woman who, often during religious ceremonies such as baptism, confirmation of first communion, becomes a kind of mentor for the young boy or girl. The comparaggio can even be established between men (or women) and a saint. For instance, in southern Italy the comparaggio with Saint Michael is used as a protection against the devil. In a more general way the term compare is used between close friends, and to show respect. Second, the saying *facite nu buone*, in southern Italian (Neapolitan) dialect. It can be translated as "Have a nice." Perhaps this is the phrase that got my attention—evidently I was still surprised to hear my dialect so far away from my city—and maybe this is why I could fully understand the conversation. It is sufficient to note that the man did not use only English and Italian, but English, Italian, and Neapolitan, and this has to do with the idea of cultural enclaves and cultural identities, as I will discuss in this book. Finally, we have the phrase *fourth of July*. Here we see the man switching language to English when using fourth of July and we note that he is talking about a very important American holiday, the American Independence Day. Along with Thanksgiving Day, this holiday elicits, more than any other, a feeling of cultural identity for the American people. Thus, in this one brief sentence the man manipulates symbols such as language and kinship to show himself as an "Italian," actually as a "Neapolitan," while at the same time using the symbol of a holiday to negotiate his cultural identity as an "American." He shows us directly how the Italian Americans of Boston's North End negotiate identities by manipulating symbols.

In this book I will discuss one of these symbols: the religious festivals.[7] These festivals occur with weekly regularity in Boston's North End during the summertime and are organized by voluntary religious societies venerating different Madonnas (delle Grazie, del Soccorso, etc.) and various other Catholic saints. The festivals I study are multidimensional phenomena, where individual and collective manifestations reveal and reinforce not only a religious identity but also a complex ethnic belonging. What religion? And what ethnic identity? The answers "Catholic" and "Italian American" are certainly not enough. Those general labels miss the complexity and multiple dimensions of such an event.

I approach the festivals as symbols and as an aggregation of symbols, as dramatic demonstrations and confirmations of group identity organized around the display of central religious statues. I will demonstrate how the festivals declare communities and ethnic identities. I call these complex social negotiations "ephemeral identities." But as a starting point I propose an analysis of the territorial and symbolic boundaries of the neighborhood, characterized by ambiguities and persistences, changes and maintenances. Defining this territory is not an easy task. Over time the North End, once a peninsula connected with the coast through a narrow strip of land (appropriately called the "Neck") became the "Island of Boston," separated from the city by a creek and accessible only from two small bridges. This was the time of the North End as a wealthy, desirable area, in need of physical separation and defense from possibly dangerous "others." But the others finally came, in the form of waves of immigrants, transforming the neighborhood into a slum. The symbolic border of marginalization was consequently erected and the creek, no longer necessary, was filled in. Other physical boundaries were built after an initial gentrification of the slum: the Fitzgerald Expressway and, above all, the Big Dig, separating but also defending the North End from the rest of the city. This complex process is analyzed in chapter 1, with specific attention to the social consequences in terms of political, cultural, and ethnic identities.

The aim of chapter 2 is to provide a historical perspective on the immigration movements first from Ireland, then from eastern and southern Europe. The perception of the North End as an "Italian" neighborhood started at the beginning of the twentieth century and not without reason: previous settlers moved out of the area as they moved up the social ladder. But the North End was far from a homogeneous place, spangled as it was with numerous ethnic enclaves, referring to the various Italian villages of origin.

The ethnic enclaves, sustained by the mechanism of chain migration, conjugal strategies, job niches, and selective clustering, found their highest symbolic expression in the festive practices, organized not by the clergy but by religious societies symbolically carrying both the name of the patron saint and of the village and physically carrying the religious icons, thus maintaining the original tradition of sanctifying the space in procession. This peculiar form of voluntary association is analyzed in chapter 3, between tradition and modernity, where "Italian" memories blend into "American" models of social life.

The festive practices are the subject of chapter 4. I explore the ethnographic data concerning all the religious festivals. There are two reasons for this repetition: first, I want to respect what the fieldwork told me, and second, and no less important, it is precisely in these repetitions that the reader will find, as I did, the interpretative level. In fact, the festive practices in the North End seem focused not on the correct belief, the orthodoxy, as it is still visible in the feasts celebrated in the Italian village of origin,[8] but rather on the correct performance of practices, the orthopraxy, respecting a local pattern developed in the North End.

In chapter 5 I will provide analytical reflections on ritual, festive practices and performances, often seen as breaks in time. Arguing about distinctions between ordinary and extraordinary times, I propose the more blurred concept of "discrete locations" with different degrees of localizability, suggesting the pervasiveness of the feasts in the daily life of the neighborhood. From this perspective it is important to analyze the relationship of the actual festive practice with the mythical and historical past, as well as with the contemporary forms of other festivals, in order to confirm the tendency to orthopraxy, possible through a process I will call "stylization." Notions of tradition, modernity, authenticity, and transgression are carefully examined in order to understand the festive practices in the North End. Essential ethnicities and identities are strategically displayed and claimed through the performance of the feasts: these identities are economic resources, which are now definitively scarce. Here I argue that hybridity and creolization, metaphors usually utilized by scholars, are only partially helpful. Therefore I read ethnic identity also as a form of technologies of the self, situationally and intentionally performed following the model of ephemeral identities in which it seems possible to find analogies with hypertextual theories.

Inevitably I will deal with methodological issues: the rhetoric of anthropological writing presupposes the treatment of this topic. And I will respect this narrative tradition, choosing a reflexive approach that will allow me to talk about myself as an anthropologist trained first in conformity to the Italian tradition (mostly Gramscian and Demartinian) then in the United States, under the influence of social anthropology and ethnic studies.

This is the challenge I have accepted, and these chapters are the response to this challenge. I am the last person to claim "authenticity," "originality," and "truth," convinced as I am of the ambiguities embodied in these terms. Therefore I will not claim any kind of general effectiveness of my arguments. If I answer just some of the many questions that arise from the fieldwork, I will have reached a satisfactory result. And if I provoke further questions about ethnic identities, I will consider my task accomplished. But, more simply, I am going to narrate the histories and, above all, the stories of the people from Boston's North End.

Thus, I identify, in a way, with the narrator of Chaucer's *Canterbury Tales*:

> He seyde, "Syn I shal bigynne the game,
> What, welcome be the cut, a goddes name
> Now lat us ryde, and herkneth what I seye."
> And with that word we ryden forth oure weye,
> And he bigan with right a myrie cheere
> His tale anon, and seyde as ye may heere.[9]

1

The North End

❊

The North End is a state of mind surrounded by waters.

—*A Bostonian proverb*

The first time I went to the North End I followed the Freedom Trail, a tiny red line painted on the streets that goes through downtown Boston in order to facilitate the tourist enterprise of visiting the historical sites of the city. Exiting the subway, I led myself all the way to Downtown Crossing, not lingering enough at the Old State House, giving a quick look at the window of the Old Corner Bookstore, rapidly crossing the courtyard at Faneuil Hall, while still taking long enough to pay due homage to Sam Adams's statue (I am not a proper or improper Bostonian, I am not even an American, but I do like a good beer), and of course stopping at the Union Oyster House for a ritual cup of clam chowder. Even though I was late, I allowed myself to stop at the Holocaust monument for what soon became another personal ritual of respect. It was Saturday morning, therefore Haymarket Square was crowded with people shopping for fruit and seafood but I found my way through the multitude and finally reached my final destination, the gateway to Boston's North End. The small entrance led to a concrete winding tunnel overlooking the Big Dig, the gigantic construction project for the subterranean Central Artery. Every passerby could see the unceasing and endless work in progress from Plexiglass windows, viewing what seemed to be a supernatural—at least from the economic point of view—effort to make a more livable city. Nowhere along the walls of the tunnel were advertisements of any kind posted, but rather historical maps of the city and municipal coats of arms of many Italian cities: Napoli, Parma, and Roma, to name but a few.

I moved from my initial surprise and astonishment at these seemingly odd urban decorations to arrive at a logical and economic explanation of them. They were advertisements of the two most appealing and marketable resources of the neighborhood: history and ethnicity. After all, I was entering the oldest residential district of the city, that "for the last half century . . . has been known as "Little Italy." Its streets are lined with espresso bars, old-fashioned grocery stores, and Italian restaurants housed in 100-year-old brick buildings. Today, a sizable chunk of the neighborhood's residents bear Italian last names. It's not unusual to hear Italian being spoken on the streets, or, in some cases, yelled from upper-story windows."[1] This is what I will explore in this work—the two fundamental categories: history and ethnicity.

On Boundaries and Changes

Boston's North End is a peninsula of almost one hundred acres, half a mile long and wide, confined by the ocean on the north, east, and west sides. The ocean can be considered, above all, a physical frontier, even if it is embedded with different symbolic meanings. For instance, the feeling of territoriality and belonging connected to the ocean is certainly not the same between a North Ender born in the mountain of Montefalcione and working in a factory or holding a local, terra firma, business and a neighbor from Sciacca, a fisherman from generation to generation, who expands the idea of territoriality beyond streets and buildings, including ships, waters, and courses.[2] Another physical as well as symbolic border was the Big Dig project separating the North End from the rest of the city on the south and southwest sides. Despite all the problems connected with this almost endless work, the North End, protected by the Big Dig, became more and more a sort of exotic secret place to protect and discover, favoring a sort of strategic essentialism of the "Italian" neighborhood (Spivak 1989, 1993).

   It is important to state immediately that these boundaries are historically and culturally determined, changing over time. I will explore in the following paragraphs some of the ambiguities and persistences, changes and maintenances, of these elusive and exclusive boundaries that have delimited, and above all defined, the North End in the past and into the present. Shaping and naming an area should be seen not only as a process of drawing down physical borders, but also, and not surprisingly, as a process of building symbolic boundaries, declaring and reinforcing situational and ephemeral identities. Following Fredrick Barth's seminal work (1969), any discussion concerning ethnicity must involve boundaries. Boundaries inevitably influence the life of both the insiders and the outsiders, they dichotomize "we" and "the others," giving a sense of ascriptive identity for exclusive groups. Mainly, scholars' investigations of ethnicity focus on the construction and maintenance of social and symbolic boundaries, and my study will be the same. But along with this sort of analysis, I will look also at the geographical markers of territories: It is quite evident that they carry symbolic implications too.[3] Territorial boundaries, in other words, should be considered as important variables in the discussion about the complexity of identity negotiations. This idea of boundaries is a heuristic tool that can help unfold the ambiguities, contradictions, and dynamics of an ambiguous, contradictory, and dynamic space. Therefore, the discussion of territorial boundaries will allow me to suggest the idea of a conflicted space, in which a society, hierarchically structured, struggles. The metaphor of a territorial border delimiting a group from my point of view is restrictive and misleading. But a territorial border that incites social dynamics is a useful metonymy in order to reconceptualize groups and identities.

In my argument I am critically questioning the postmodern concept of "deterritorialization" in a globalized world, in which territory supposedly becomes increasingly less significant. I am very much in favor of a notion of "reterritorialization," as proposed by David Newman:

> Globalization does not lead to a reduction in the significance of territory per se, but it does lead to a new, more complex, understanding of the multi-dimensional, and dynamic, components of territory as a mechanism through which society is bordered, ordered and controlled. . . . Reterritorialization, as contrasted with deterritorialization, is the process through which territorial configurations of power are continually ordered and reordered. (2004, 6)

This concept, not new as Newman points out, refers to the creation of new states and the disappearance of others.[4] Scholarship focuses mainly on international borders and borderlands, border-crossing and narratives of nation-states, territorial conflicts and transnational communities. In other terms scholars privilege territorial borders on a macroscale. My argument demonstrates that analyses of these types of boundaries at the microlevel raise important epistemological questions: such as in the specific case of Boston's North End such analysis is fundamental for understanding social conflicts and ethnic behavior.

Another aim of this work is to bring into consideration historical perspectives. Most of the anthropological work on territorial borders, according to Alvarez, has been ahistorical:

> History is more than context, yet we have not incorporated historical interpretation into our border studies. In our quest to expose and illustrate the importance of difference and contrasts, the role of the border in people's creation of bonds and social networks over time has been neglected. (1995: 466)

The historical perspective I suggest allows me to introduce a more theoretical argument about constituting, modifying, and maintaining these boundaries.

The question therefore becomes: if boundaries, every sort of boundary, canalize social life, what kind of social dynamics correlate with borders, bridges, expressways, or the Big Dig?

I propose the concepts of "instability," "negotiability," and "permeability" of the border to illustrate the processes of continuous definition and redefinition of Boston's North End boundaries. This particular idea of boundaries allows me to avoid the major risks that occur when studying a bounded territory. Boundaries often are taken to imply essentialism and primordialism, containing unchanging cultures. According to this approach, boundaries delimit sorts of innate, fixed, unmodifiable characteristics (the Geertzian assumed "givens"),[5] persisting over time because they are fundamental for group and personal identity. My idea of borders, any kind of borders, is more instrumentalist, because I approach them as developing in a dialectical and historically determined relationship to social requirements.

In conclusion what defines a boundary are the social dynamics excited by them and around them. In other words, I am not looking for any territorial integrity, but for social negotiations, conflicts and crossing processes, that arise around the borders.

Instability: Physical and Symbolic Borders

Instability of boundaries seems to be the fundamental characteristic of Boston's North End. Over time the neighborhood negotiated its own geographical dimension with the rest of the city and, subsequently, the specific assumption of territory and territoriality. Physical and symbolic boundaries concur to define the identity of the group settled in the neighborhood, therefore the endless negotiation of these boundaries inevitably implies an endless negotiation of identity, especially in terms of ethnicity. The boundaries of the North End, being elusive and unstable, continuously changing over time, inevitably carry an ephemeral and more synchronic dimension into the present: historical changes lead to contemporary ambiguity.

The starting point for my analysis is a definition of the North End, made by Robert Woods in 1902:

> The North End is less than half a mile in any of its dimensions. It is a "tight little island," hemmed in by continuous and ever-encroaching currents of commercial activity. The station thoroughfares lead to the markets. The markets extend to the docks. The docks reach around from the markets to the railroads again. (1902: 2–4)

A century later the boundaries so clearly delineated by Woods are obsolete, as they were hardly predictable centuries before.

At the beginning of the seventeenth century, this land was a hilly peninsula, called by the local Native Americans "Shawmut." According to Whitehill and

Kennedy (2000, 3), Reverend William Blaxton (or Blackstone) was the first European settler in the area. He arrived in New England as a chaplain following the expedition of Robert Gorges in 1623. The failure of Gorges's plantation in Wessagusset (now Weymouth, Massachusetts) did not discourage Blaxton, who moved north to the Shawmut peninsula in 1625. The solitary reverend settled in the vicinity of what is now Beacon and Spruce streets, slightly southwest of the North End, until the arrival of the Puritans led by John Winthrop in 1630. The Puritans first settled in Charlestown, on the mainland, but soon moved, apparently for lack of fresh water, to the Shawmut peninsula (now called Trimountain, for its geographical characteristics). On September 7, 1630, they renamed the area Boston. Winthrop's first settlement was near the present Dock Square, back then certainly part of the North End. As the toponym suggests, Dock Square derived its name from the town dock that was, in Whitehill and Kennedy's words, "at the head of Town Cove, which, jutting in from the harbor, divided Boston into North and South Ends" (2000, 5). Dock Square is now well inland but it is important to remember that the actual geographical limits of Boston now exceed by more than half the land available in 1630.[6] Over the years, the marshy lands surrounding the Neck, a narrow area along the line of Washington Street, were reclaimed with dams, excavations, and fillings.

It is possible to get an idea of the human settlement in Boston from the data contained in the *Book of Possessions*, presumably compiled in 1643.[7] According to these data, householders had established themselves primarily along the shore in the North End. The Town Cove—developed by Valentine Hill and his associates after which the city granted in 1641 the land of Bendalls Cove, now Faneuil Hall Square—at this time was considered part of the North End. The other side of the peninsula, the marshy north cove facing Charlestown, was granted in 1643 to Henry Symons, George Burden, John Button, John Hill, and their partners

> on condition that within three years they "erect and make upon or neere some part of the premises, one or more corne mills, and maynteyne the same for ever." They were to make a flood gate ten feet wide for the passage of boats into the cove, and were to have the right of cutting through the mars from the cove to a creek on the line of present Blakstone Street, and to dig trenches in the highway or waste grounds provided they "make and mainteyne sufficient, passable and safe wayes over the same for horse and Cart." (Whitehill and Kennedy 2000, 11)

The cove was partially separated from the Charles River by a narrow ridge "that had been used by the Indians as a footpath over the flats" (Rutan 1902, 15).[8] This natural boundary was reinforced into a dam, with possibilities of waterpower. The marshy cove was therefore transformed into Mill Pond, with grist mills using the tidal power. The beneficiaries of the grant also exploited the right to dig a trench connecting Mill Pond and the Town Cove, and bridging it. It was known, as Rutan reminds us, "for a century and a half as the Mill Creek" (1902, 15). The erection of the dam and the construction of the trench had two important effects on the landscape of the North End: first, the shallow water of Mill Pond covered a large section of the peninsula (presently Salem and North Margin streets); and second, Mill Creek divided Boston in two, shaping the North End as the "Island of Boston." The North End was physically separated from the rest of the city, connected through the bridges at North and Hanover streets. Dock Square and Bendalls Cove are, at this point, outside the North End, now completely surrounded by water: the harbor, the Charles River, Mill Pond, and Mill Creek. At this time the North End was the most populous neighborhood of the town. According to Rutan (1902, 16), the growing population can be inferred from the building of the Second Church (also called Old North Church), in 1650, in North Square which decades later became the center of the area.[9]

The need for protection against attackers from the sea (Todisco 1976, 7), who were feared by the newly successful community, led to the erection of a fortification—the natural boundary of the seashore was strengthened with an artificial battery: the North Battery, also called the Battery Wharf. If North Battery is definitely a protective artificial boundary, built not to be crossed, on the other side of the island (former peninsula) from Hudson's Point the natural border of the Charles River was continuously and increasingly crossed by ferries to Charlestown.[10]

The time of the Puritans concluded with two catastrophic fires: one in 1676 and one in 1679. The rebuilding of the neighborhood marked a profound change in the social conditions of the population, as witnessed in their dwellings. If the early seventeenth century is denoted by the presence of skilled artisans living in wooden hovels, the late period of the century (the colonial or Queen's time) saw the rise of rich merchants, living in brick and cement houses, elegant and prosperous.[11] According to Rutan the difference between the two periods can be seen in the varying names of the neighborhood streets:

> In the early Puritan times, the titles given to the streets [of the North End] are mostly of a cumbrous, descriptive character, as "The street leading up to the house of Sir Williams Phips, Knight." In Garden Court Street there still lingers a pleasant flavor of the descriptive custom; but most of the old names that survive chronicle events rather than characteristics, and show the difference between the simple expedients of a hamlet and the exacting demands of a growing town. The more formal and permanent names of the streets appear in the complete list already mentioned as having been made in 1708. At that time Black Horse Lane ceased to be called after the tavern at its head and was known as Prince Street, while Fleet Street became the recognized title of Scarlet's Wharf Lane. (1902, 23)

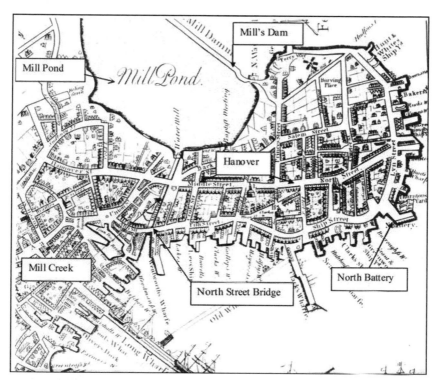

MAP 1.1 Map of Boston by Captain John Bonner, 1722

The first detailed and contemporary map of the city is Captain John Bonner's map of 1722 (map 1.1). It shows many topographical aspects.

Although Mill Creek can be considered an important boundary between the North End and the rest of the city, nevertheless new topographical transformations suggest the ambiguity of the southern border. In 1742, Peter Faneuil built a two-story brick structure.[12] According to Rutan (1902, 28), Faneuil Hall established the gateway to the North End for the remainder of the century as the heart of Boston business. Naturally the question I am raising is not about a more or less formal identification of a landmark of separation between two or more components of an urban landscape; rather, it concerns how the identity of the contained or excluded social group is shaped through a process of boundary-making and boundary-maintenance. Symbolically, but also pragmatically, Faneuil Hall refers to the mercantile, business-oriented bourgeoisie. Including this building inside the North End borders denotes the neighborhood as a wealthy place for wealthy business.[13] Excluding Faneuil Hall from the North End is a consequence of a drastically modified economy and a prelude to the creation of a slum. This process culminates in 1805 with the filling of the Town

Dock and the construction of North and South Market streets, as desired by Mayor Quincy. The boundaries' modification, combined with the evacuation of tradesmen after the War of Independence, led to progressive abandonment of the North End by businessmen and the bourgeoisie, subsequently creating room for the poor and marginal and, also for, immigrants.

According to Whitehill and Kennedy (2000, 46), the years preceding the Revolution were turbulent under the political point of view, but from a topographical perspective they did not see significant modification: few changes on streets, the Clark's Wharf now called Hancock's Wharf, and the new religious buildings, such as the Old South Meeting House (replacing the Old South Church's wooden building) and the King's Chapel (rebuilt in 1750 on the site of the original church).

The eighteenth century witnessed the publication of many maps, showing the growth of the city. In these maps, Boston is no longer the Puritan hamlet established by Winthrop and it is not even the town by the sea, with a harbor of scarce importance. At this point drawing maps is not just a bureaucratic tool to track the evolution of the city, and it is not even just a functional tool utilized for topographical, economic, or tourist reasons. It is a symbol of importance. It is a declaration, in both directions, to the city itself and to the outside, that the area is rising to an important level, that it has reached the dignity of a city. In other words, the rising middle class, the merchants, and the bourgeoisie need visible signs of identification and recognition. Maps are one of these signs.

The maps of the end of eighteenth century certainly show the crowded and narrow streets in the North End, anticipating a troubled urban expansion, ready to redirect itself toward the south. A couple of factors can account for this topographical and social change. One is the evacuation following the War of Independence. "When General Howe left Boston, on the eight of March 1776, he took with him nearly one thousand of the residents of the town.[14] Such wealthy and important families as the North End had held were among these refuges" (Rutan 1902, 30). Another factor is the rebuilding of the city caused by the evacuation of the loyalists and the arrival of newcomers, mostly wealthy country families from Essex County, attracted by the economic opportunities. The North End, because of its topographical characteristic, was already crowded and, at that time, town planning concerning the area such as the filling in of Mill Pond was not yet approved.[15] Therefore, the newcomers built their mansions on Fort Hill, Beacon Hill, and Bowling Green, relocating the social center of the city out of the congested North End.

I suggest that the construction of a series of buildings on North and South Market streets, completed in 1826 following a city planning meeting led by Mayor Quincy, marked the climax of this double process and a new negotiation of the symbolic boundaries of the North End.

Mayor Quincy undertook a major piece of city planning that involved filling the Town Dock and building over the wharves between it and the Long Wharf, thus creating space for a new two-story granite market house, 555 feet long and 50 wide, that was flanked by harmonious granite warehouses, fronting on the newly created North and South Market Streets.[16] The whole series of buildings, which were designed by Alexander Parris, provided Faneuil Hall with an approach from the harbor of extraordinary dignity and beauty. (Whitehill and Kennedy 2000, 96)

As shown by the contemporary maps, in 1829 important changes in Boston's urban landscape can be observed: Quincy Markets and the already filled Mill Pond, and the two new bridges (the Charles River Bridge completed in 1786 and the Warren Bridge, inaugurated on Christmas Day 1828). The two bridges run on two major arteries delimiting Mill Pond: Charlestown and Causeway streets. The boundaries surrounding the North End became more and more artificial and the new and improved transportation, made possible by bridges and highways, modified the characteristic of the neighborhood: for the newcomers there is no longer a need to live there, they can move out to more desirable locations.

Another important change concerns the Mill Creek. In 1828 water was cut off from the canal. The North End was no longer an island and, as Runan (1902, 35) suggests, no longer a peninsula, because the filling of the Mill Pond now directly connects the North End with the West End, leading to unstable and blurred boundaries.[17] All the area is now an ambiguous place. Therefore, despite the possibilities offered by filling Mill Pond and the new lines of communication resulting from the new bridges and thoroughfares, the North End never again, in the nineteenth century, reached the status of wealthy neighborhood. It was necessary to wait another century.

The landscape of Boston has been completely transformed in less than four centuries, and of course not without consequences to the social dimensions of life in the city. Coming back to the specifics of the North End, it is important to state that the modification of its boundaries, with the consequent dislocation of the economic center, determined the progressive decay of the North End. The economy in the neighborhood was completely based on shipping and merchant business, which means the incessant growth of dockyards and warehouses. Sailors, immigrants, and, generally, unskilled workers became the biggest components of the North End's population. From its earlier wealth, the North End was degenerating into a slum. The paradox of the North End at this time is exactly this: topographically the North End was being reabsorbed by the city. The natural borders were so profoundly modified and the new artificial ones were continuously negotiated, suggesting an ambiguous territory and an even more ambiguous territoriality. The Island of Boston became a memory. But simultaneously, social boundaries were erected, establishing the neighborhood as a dangerous place to live—a slum—comprised of immigrants.

Negotiability

The question I am raising here is about who defines a specific territory, in other words, who draws maps, builds bridges and trenches, expressways or endless tunnels, and so on, that make a territory so specific.[18] A first answer about "who traces the borders" is that technicians such as urban planners, architects, and cartographers are responsible for this process of boundary-definition. While correct, this is quite a naif answer. For the moment I will simply note that technical agents are situated in complex social dynamics at the structural level such as economic trends, ethnic segregation, political discourses, or a combination of all three. They are at the same time the products and the producers of social changes. But technicians are not alone, of course; we must ask who commissions the urban planning and the maps, and why. An answer such as the city's mayor or the Massachusetts Turnpike Authority's Board is situated on a different level of naivety, adding a bureaucratic dimension but leaving the question substantially unaltered. In this complex dialectic we must discover the influences and the possibilities of negotiation that the inhabitants can bring to bear. Even in this more participatory situation, anonymous agencies occupy important roles influencing the structural level, and vice versa. The mirroring game between structures and agencies is endless. I will analyze a few examples in order to illustrate the complexity of the problem.

Mill Creek

The digging of Mill Creek, and the consequent isolation of the North End in the middle of the seventeenth century, ought to be framed in a more general situation. From the *Book of Possessions* it is possible to notice first a relevant concentration of householders' residences along the shore of the North End. The reasons were, on one hand, the proximity to the sea, a more suitable location for an economy based on trades with England necessarily supported by wharves and ships, and on the other hand, the marshy ground along the shorefront (the *Book of Possessions* indicates no settlements on Fort Hill, Copp's Hill, and the Trimountain). The economy of the town was rapidly increasing. Thus, the need for more wharves and warehouses led to the Town Council's decision on November 29, 1641, to grant merchants such as Valentine Hill (see Whitehill and Kennedy 2000, 11) the wasteland in Bendall's Cove (now Faneuil Hall Square) with the purpose of building a great and ordered cove: the Town Cove. A similar decision was made a year and a half later for another cove, Shelter Cove, near State and Milk streets. And on July 31, 1643, the merchants Henry Simons, George Burden, John Button, and John Hill were granted the marshland of the North Cove. The town was expanding on the northern side, facing Charlestown, an area not suitable for wharves but perfect for building mills, therefore allowing a differentiated economy, supporting but also expanding the sea-based contemporary markets. In a few years the North Cove was converted into a mill pond, maintaining a grist mill, a saw mill, and a chocolate mill. A system of tidal flow was necessary for the operation of the mill's water, made possible by the digging of Mill Creek, connecting the Town Cove and Mill Pond. The result, as I have said, was the creation of the North End as the "Island of Boston," the center of the town's life.

What kind of negotiability is possible in this situation? The answer lies inevitably in what kind of social tensions between groups can be individuated. It is important to state that this is the time of the settlement of the Puritans, a basically homogenous group.[19] Class relations in preindustrial time and eighteenth-century towns were profoundly different than they later became. Instead of being based on the capitalist mode of production, social relations were contextualized within a face-to-face community. Economic and social factors were important, but not as significant as ideology and intimate social relations. According to Nash, this social organization was familially organized. The family was a little commonwealth and the town, as a larger collection of families, was a larger commonwealth "recognizing the common good as the highest goal. . . . The corporate whole, not the individual, was the basic conceptual unit" (1986, 2). In this relatively stable and homogenous situation, where the indispensability of social hierarchy was unquestionable (Nash 1986, 3), the level of negotiability of the borders was situated in the relationship between the Town Council and prominent members such as merchants, who sought a convenient, functional distribution of lands and the consequent allocation of economic resources. Stability did not mean equality. Indeed Nash's analysis of the distribution of wealth in Boston suggests that at the end of the seventeenth century 10 percent of the populace was in control of 40 percent of the community's assets, but this "was entirely normal, especially in urban centers, where the division of material goods and property was always less even than in the countryside" (1986, 10). Nonetheless unemployment was virtually unknown and poverty was an almost irrelevant factor except for widows, the disabled, and orphans. Stability did not mean that protest was impossible, but it was limited. Tager (2000, 25–40) notes a small number of riots, but they were rare. There were some riots for food, such as the sabotage of a grain ship owned by Andrew Belcher, the second largest shipowner in Boston, and the market riot of 1737, motivated by taxes and rising prices. Protests against the elite also occurred in Puritan society where formally every church member could vote but where in fact only those with a taxable property of £80 were allowed to, with the result that only twenty-four men (out of more than four hundred members of the congregation) could vote in 1687. "In 1690, the authorities extended the right of freemanship to all those paying taxes of at least four shillings, or holding houses or land in the value of £6. The new British charter abolished religion as a criterion for the franchise" (ibid., 20). But still, in 1692, only 350 people could vote in the Boston town meeting. A century later, in 1760, the number of people eligible to vote was estimated at 3,750, in a population of 15,000, but only 1,500 had the financial requirements to vote in the town meeting. According to Tager:

> A better indication of the disposition of political power is not over eligibility, but how many people actually voted. In the early 1730s, for example, 650 or .04 percent of Boston's 15,000 people voted. While the population rose in the 1740s, thereafter it rapidly declined to just over 15,000 by 1763. In that year, 1,809 or .07 percent of the population voted, a sign of slightly increased participation by eligible voters. (ibid., 21)

The first evidence of antielite riots dates from 1720. A pamphlet was circulated against the rich and protested their custom of sending empty carriages out of the town neck to meet farmers coming to the market and buying farm goods during food shortages. As a result, the common people could not purchase food. Vandalism against Governor William Dummer's carriages occurring for the same reason is dated in 1725; and in 1755 "there was an attack upon a group of upper-class Bostonians returning from a Harvard commencement by ferry" (ibid.). The small number of antielite riots seems to confirm what I already stated, that in this society social hierarchy was considered to be an unquestionable right.

In stable and homogenous social groups characterized by social relations of taken-for-granted hierarchy, the development of Mill Creek, desired by Henry Simons and associates and granted by a Town Council decision, has to be seen as the consequence of the economic trend of a town experiencing rapid and dramatic growth. In its turn, this new, artificial border influenced the social landscape of the neighborhood.[20]

An early example of group identity, shaped by the creation of boundaries between the North End and the South End, can be seen in the seventeenth to eighteenth centuries' boisterous ritual celebrating November 5, the "Pope Day:"

> On the eve of the Revolution, North and South End would organize rival processions, each with the effigies of the Pope, the Devil and the Pretender. When they met a free-for-all ensued, with broken heads and broken noses. A North End triumph meant the burning of the Southenders' effigies on Copp's Hill. A southern success led to the burning of the Northenders' Pope, Devil and Pretender on the Common. (Whitehill and Kennedy 2000, 29)

The Pope Day in Boston was always characterized by the violence of the celebration. According to Tager:

> At some point in the century, a rivalry developed between lower classes of the North and the South Ends. . . . The fighting was often quite

furious, resulting in many injuries. Vandalism was rampant, and property destroyed and stolen. (2000, 46)

The ritual celebrated the anniversary of the failure of the Catholic conspiracy in England, when on November 5, 1605, Guy Fawkes and a group of conspirators attempted to blow up the House of Parliament. Not surprisingly the Pope Day was one of the few English holidays that the Puritans brought with them across the Atlantic. According to Nash:

In the 1730's or earlier, Boston's artisans began to commemorate the day with a parade and elaborate dramaturgical performances that mocked popery and the Catholic Stuart pretender. For several years artisans from the North End dominated the elaborate mummery. But South Enders soon began competing with them, parading through the streets with their own stage. What started out as friendly competition soon turned into gang battles. The victorious party won the right to carry the opposition's pageantry to the top of a hill and to burn it at night along with their own stage. As the years passed, artisans from both areas formed paramilitary organizations with elaborate preparation preceding the annual event. (1986, 165)

The festival was not only a claim for identity but, as often happens for carnivalesque celebrations, a moment of status reversal

when youth and the lower class ruled, not only in controlling the streets of the town but also in going from house to house to collect money from the affluent for financing the prodigious feasting and drinking that went on from morning to night. (ibid., 165)

According to Cogliano, the festival was also a way to redirect repressed antiauthoritarian feelings toward an external subject:

The elite appreciated the stabilizing impact of anti-papal rhetoric which unified and bound a socially disparate people together. The pope was thought to be a good lightning [sic] rod to direct anger away from them. (1995: 24)

The temporary suspension of any kind of social hierarchy is the basic characteristic of carnivalesque events, or, using Bakhtin's terms (1968, 9), the carnivalization of the everyday lives suggests the undermining of the hegemony of dominant ideology, proposing an alternate and alternative conceptualization of reality. But, as in this case, the narcotizing function of the festival is evident. It is a form of social control, allowing ritualized transgressions in specific, clearly circumscribed, times of the year. The social tensions can be named and even violently mocked but at the end of the ritual the dominant social order is reassembled. Paradoxically therefore the ritual performance of destruction of the hegemonical authorities becomes the confirmation of authority itself.

The Pope Day was a public display for claimed identities (the North End and the South End). Interestingly, the identities are reaffirmed by the locations of the eventual burning of the effigies: on Copp's Hill, in case of a victory of the North Enders or in the Common, in case of South Ender's triumph. At that time both places were situated clearly inside the respective neighborhoods. Burning the opponent in effigy in the winner's territory is a sign of reinforced identity.

In conclusion, if it is true that the forming of Mill Creek as a boundary involved a negotiation inside relatively stable and homogenous groups, and affirmed the identification of the specific area (in this case as the economic center of the town), it is also true that the possible social tensions were canalized through the claim for a specific local identity. Mill Creek, desired for economic purposes, separated the town and generated differentiations and exclusive groups.

The discussion about this artificial border cannot be considered concluded if I do not analyze the complementary aspect of its creation, that is, its disappearance. Economic growth in the North End during the last part of the seventeenth century and most of the eighteenth was impressive. North Square, with the adjacent harbor in continuous expansion, was the social center of the neighborhood, characterized by the flourishing of all kinds of commercial activity, especially by skilled artisans. Once the external boundaries were established, the negotiations for a group identity turned inward. This process can be seen in the proliferation of differentiated religions and in the consequent building of churches. The Puritan times were over and the new social landscape had to satisfy different religious observances. This demand was mainly expressed by the new English merchants. It is no accident that in 1723 the Anglican Christ Church was built in Salem Street, which is famous for Paul Revere's enterprise. After the Second Church, which was founded in 1650 and for sixty-four years was the only church in the North End, a so-called New North Church, at the corner of Clark and Hanover streets, was formed in 1714. But in 1719 an important part of this congregation departed and founded the New Brick Church, also known as the "Revenge" (Todisco 1976, 8). Later, in 1741, Samuel Mather, and almost one third of the parishioners of the Second Church, founded a Congregational Church on a corner of North Bennett and Hanover streets. More significantly, in 1679, a place for worship was established by the Baptists on Salem Street, and in 1796, the Methodists also built a church on a corner of Hanover and North Bennett streets.

Another important element structuring the group was the development of the marketplaces. The need for a specific market was due to the expansion of small business activities but also of the sea-based economy all along the wharves. As a town of increased size, both economic and geographical, Boston erected three temporary structures for markets in North Square, Liberty Tree, and at the

Town Dock. In 1742, as already noted, Faneuil Hall was finally built as a market, but also as the place for town meetings. Quoting Rutan, it "established the gateway to the North End for the remainder of the century as the business heart of Boston" (1902, 28).

But the economic expansion of the North End was the reason for its growth as well as its decay. The area remained the center of the sea-based economy: beside the many wharves for ship landings and departures were built an increasing number of dockyards for recovery and warehouses for stocks. This brought an increasing number of sailors and transients to the area, therefore, according to Todisco:

> This created a less desirable neighborhood for the citizen who could afford to live elsewhere. Those who could afford to maintain the great mansion built by previous generations no longer wished to own them. (1976, 19)

The unoccupied mansions rapidly deteriorated because they were too expensive to rent and maintain. The centrifugal movement that coincided with the centripetal movement of immigration was pushed also by other factors. Thomas Pemberton in 1794 wrote that "the town is capable of great increase, as many large spaces of land still remain vacant."[21] This trend was even more evident after the Revolution and the subsequent evacuation of the loyalists and wealthy families above all from the North End. Newcomers—the bourgeoisie largely from Essex County—moved in, attracted to the economic advantages of the town. They soon became a prominent part of Boston's business life. But the crowded North End could not allow any new building, especially of the luxurious kind described by Pemberton. The wealthy business families as well as the enriched merchants moved westward to Fort Hill, Beacon Hill, and Bowling Green (now Bowdoin Square), but also to Roxbury, facilitated by the improvement of transportation. For many years, according to Rutan, the social development of the West End was at an inverse ratio to the decay of the North End. A signal of this trend was that even clergymen abandoned the neighborhood. Rutan quotes an old chronicler: "There are six large congregations to the northward of the canal, and only one of their ministers resides there" (1902, 33). The progressive decay of the neighborhood was slow but inexorable and at the turn of the century the narrow streets of the North End were no longer the core of economic life of the town; the old houses became tenements and retail businesses. The economic business center for the new industrial and financial economy was now downtown. The neighborhood was still a crowded center of social life but progressively was losing the quality of an attractive area.

This is the kind of social circumstance that promoted the filling of Mill Pond. The water was cut off from Mill Creek in 1828. The North End was no longer the Island of Boston. The disappearance of this artificial border should be seen as one of the symbols of a fading identity of an original group, spreading in different areas and no longer in need of any kind of territorial boundary protecting the North End. Significantly, the Pope Day was abolished immediately after, in 1833.[22] Now the North End was becoming a slum, a place for all the emigrants. The new identity of the neighborhood was then shaped by more symbolic boundaries such as ethnicity and social class.

As a preliminary conclusion it seems evident that an important dimension of this territorial boundary was the product of bourgeois social actors who materially negotiated the forming and destroying of Mill Creek. Negotiations about the borders first occurred inside a relatively homogeneous group of Puritans and, later on, within the context of an increasingly differentiated social order of wealthy merchants and businessmen.

With the westward movement of the dominant group, the territorial and symbolic boundaries disappeared as well as their territorial-based identity. The question therefore becomes: in the absence of a hegemonic pressure for a common identity, with the concomitant redirection of antiauthoritarism toward public rituals, and the assertion of an imagined homogeneity, what kind of new identity was possible for the subaltern classes left behind after the flight of the elite? Territorial boundaries and old symbolic borders seem to have eroded, but this was just the prologue for different claims for different identities, ethnically enforced.

The Central Artery Project

For more than a century the North End was identified as a slum and isolated not by territorial boundaries but by even stronger symbolic borders, based on ethnicity and class. These are the effects of an impressive movement of emigration, involving the Irish, Jewish, Portuguese, and finally Italian immigrants.

I have suggested that territorial boundaries are made or at least are rendered more evident when the social class that inhabits the area is an economically strong one. A slum does not need to be geographically isolated, bounded as it is by symbols and representations of ethnic and class identities. The two terms were, in this era, almost coincident since immigrants were situated at the lower level of the social scale, and belonged almost without exception to the working, unskilled, class.

The first modern attempt to again divide the city can be considered the Central Artery Project. Modern urban planners were expecting that car traffic in the city would reach an unbearable level for the dimension of streets that had been built for another era.[23] An early project for "a Central Artery cutting through the heart of the city" (O'Connor 1993, 82) had been suggested in 1930, after three years of an extensive traffic survey, by the Boston Planning Board in the *Report on a Thoroughfare Plan for Boston*. Robert Whitten, president of the American City Planning Institute and the main consultant of the Boston Planning Board, had the vision of an upper-level roadway as a practical way to provide for the through traffic and also for the traffic going to and from the Central District. The solution, revolutionary at that time, was delayed because of the Great Depression. Nevertheless, all the following reports of the board "continued to urge implementation of the project in much the same terms as the original project" (O'Connor 1993, 83). In 1948 the construction of the Central Artery became a fundamental point in the political agenda of Governor Bradford, but still it was impossible to start the construction. According to O'Connor (1993, 83), even if several contracts were already defined in 1951 (with a completion date at the end of the 1953), a number of problems arose: from the steel strike in April 1952 to the discovery of hordes of rats infesting the area and the consequent need for an extermination program; from the meat handlers of Haymarket ready to move to the new quarters only after the full completion of the refrigeration system to Chinatown residents who were against the cutting of a large swath through their area to the opposition of the Italians of the North End who feared the closing of many business and other important places. Eventually the final project, as designed by the state's Department of Public Works, led by the former chairman of the Massachusetts Turnpike Authority William F. Callahan, to build an elevated highway (the "Highway in the Sky") through downtown Boston began to be realized.

Like early protests, other controversies immediately emerged with the construction of the Central Artery. On one hand, in 1954, the dream of the Highway in the Sky sank with the decision of the Department of Public Works to build a tunnel from Congress Street to Kneeland Street, better known as the Dewey Square or South Station Tunnel. This last elevated portion of the highway was considered "too obtrusive and disruptive in the midst of downtown life."[24] On the other hand, according to the Massachusetts Turnpike Authority: [25]

> And even as it was being built from the Mystic Bridge south, the new artery, which displaced more than 20,000 people and demolished more than 1,000 structures, was seen as ugly and divisive of city neighborhoods. Its construction spurred citizen groups and others to successfully oppose the building of the Inner Belt.[26]

The Central Artery, or Fitzgerald Expressway, was concluded in 1959, again with controversy. According to the Massachusetts Turnpike Authority, the original project expected the amount of traffic to be 75,000 vehicles a day, but because of structural problems such as the twenty-seven exits and the lack of merge and breakdown lanes, inadequate for this level, it never reached the target, consequently causing slow and chaotic commuting.[27] Without any doubt the Central Artery brought about a deep change in the landscape of the city, creating an artificial border between the city and the North End. The North End became, again, the Island of Boston, separated not by water but by asphalt. The Central Artery did not solve the traffic problems; furthermore, it added the eyesore of an elevated highway, an evident demarcation signal.

Negotiability of this artificial border can be seen in the protests of neighbors. These protests were against the urban planners, politicians, bureaucrats, or technicians who were pushing for public support based on a supposed common good. Their solution for an increasing traffic problem seemed, at least in part, a reflection of economic interests. On the other side, clustered local groups were expressing their point of view. The controversies were multicentered

> but perhaps the most vehement objections to the proposed Central Artery came from the residents of the North End, one of Boston's oldest and most historical neighborhoods, which had been home to a succession of different immigrant nationalities including Africans, Anglo-Saxons, Irish, Jews, and finally Italians. Not only was the new expressway scheduled to destroy more than one hundred dwellings and uproot some nine hundred businesses, but its projected route would clearly slice off the historic community from the main part of the downtown area, thus isolating the North End from the rest of Boston. During the spring of 1950 store owners, restaurateurs, and food wholesalers organized a "Save Boston Business" to protest the coming disaster, while longtime residents formed a Committee to Save the North End of Boston to head off what they felt would be the complete obliteration of their old, colorful, and distinctively Italian neighborhood. (O'Connor 1993, 84)

The protests were not enough to stop the construction, not even after some buildings were torn down in November 1950. In October 1951, when it became clear that Hanover Street, the center of the North End, would be cut off, the inhabitants held another protest, but it again produced no positive results.

> The old post office, where so many old-time residents had deposited their money, was also threatened with demolition, and local pushcart peddlers on Blakstone Street faced the possibility of eviction. All their protests were ineffective, however as the central artery expressway became a reality and slowly began snaking its way through the city. (O'Connor 1993, 85)[28]

The Fitzgerald Expressway was finally finished in 1959. The history of this project is probably a history of continuous negotiations, which sometimes had positive results for protestors, as in the case of the opposition for the Inner Belt, but more often resulted in frustration and failures, as occurred in the North End protests. This process of boundary-making provoked, inevitably, profound changes in the neighborhood. The most important being the North End was again an island, separated from the rest of the city. However, an observation is possible regarding the capability of the North Enders to take part in negotiation about boundaries. The Fitzgerald Expressway controversy now reaffirmed the North Ender's power to negotiate a decision as an opposing party.[29] It was an important success to achieve a claim for self-expression, even if the political battle was lost. A few years later this capability (or power) led to success in other cases, as I will demonstrate with the Waterfront project and the North Ender Frank Langone's political work. The capacity to protest and negotiate is a signal of a radical change in the political relationship between the North End and City Hall: after years of Irish leadership in the political life the Italians slowly became influential as well. Not surprisingly the negotiations about the Fitzgerald Expressway were destined to fail. But in these negotiations the hegemonic, omnipervasive, decisions about boundary-making were finally contested.

The Waterfront

I analyzed the territorial boundaries of the North End paying attention almost exclusively to the southern border. This is the border that makes the neighborhood an island or a peninsula, where important urban renewal projects were proposed and made. But it is not the only border. The waters of Boston Harbor is the other frontier. I briefly talked about the construction of the North Battery, and surely the changes provoked by building and modifying wharves as well as by filling in coves needs better attention, but it seems to me that they affect the hypothetical group identity in a minor way, where economic interests and power tensions can be individuated but still not immediately and directly involving a supposed "others." However, in 1964 the Boston Redevelopment Authority (BRA) proposed the North End/Waterfront Urban Renewal Plan. It is important to keep in mind that the late 1950s and the 1960s were characterized by urban renewal systematically directed toward working-class people and their neighborhoods, such as the West End, the East End, and Charlestown. Boston's urban renewal was aimed at the revitalization of downtown business districts, creation of new residences, and the rehabilitation of old working-class areas for the middle and upper classes. The strategic indifference for the lower social groups, provoking their expulsion from the center of the city and the creation of ghettos in peripheral areas (Mattapan, north Dorchester, Roxbury), eventually produced an intense reaction. According to Tager (2000, 190), the widespread discontent resulted in political expressions and negotiations; for instance, it was the basis of Gabriel Piemonte's political platform while running for mayor in 1963. Furthermore, in 1967, a populist candidate, Louise Day Hicks (chairperson of the Boston School Committee and an opponent of racial desegregation), challenged Kevin White for the mayoral post. Kevin White should be seen as a mediator between the economic interests of downtown businessmen and neighborhoods' needs. "Between 1968 and 1975, the White administration spent over $500 million on neighborhood capital improvements, a vastly greater sum than that spent by the previous administration" (ibid., 191).

The original North End/Waterfront Urban Renewal Plan "would have taken from the Callahan Tunnel, the entire right hand of North Street to Commercial Street" (Langone 1995, 43), including Fulton, Richmond, Langdon Place, Lewis, Fleet, and Clark all the way to the corner of North Street and Commercial Street. According to Langone, BRA director, Ed Logue,

> wanted to take Cross Street where Martignetti Liquors and the fruit stands, as well as Joe Pace and Purity Cheese now stands, for a ramp to be built across the top of the tunnel over Cross Street to Haymarket Square. This would have killed the North End shopping area and pedestrian access into Boston. (1995, 43)

Langone is a primary source, being involved in the political negotiation as a city representative. Solicited by residents primarily living on North Street, Langone began a controversy with City Hall on two fronts: the political arena and in the courts. The negotiation with Mayor White resulted in scrapping the idea of taking half of North Street and of making the ramp over Cross Street. The BRA accepted the reduction of the new Atlantic Avenue from one hundred to forty feet. After a long trial for federal housing subsidies the gained land was available for affordable housing and in 1975 construction of new buildings—the first new housing in the North End's recent history—began. The Christopher Columbus Senior Citizen Housing Development on Commercial Street and Ausonia Housing at the corner of Commercial and Lewis streets were built and Langone found an agreement for affordable housing for senior citizens in the Mercantile block (30 percent of the personal income). Langone (1995, 44) refers to a public meeting in Faneuil Hall held by the BRA which debated the division of eight and a half acres of land between the North End and the Waterfront. Langone was accused of being personally interested in this housing project because of the possible applications of his sons. He answered in the following way:

> It didn't matter because my first aim was to preserve the North End and its atmosphere and characteristics. I didn't want the same thing that happened to the West End.[30] As a result, our senior citizens were fortunate enough to have the opportunity to move to the waterfront at a much lower rent than the private condos and apartments. I planned this elderly housing to keep North End Italians here at an affordable rent. They, in turn, would preserve the aesthetics of our neighborhood. (ibid.)

Personal interests or not, the political action of Frank Langone could have a double interpretation. First, he can be considered an attentive leader of his community, acknowledging the request of the North End's inhabitants. Second, he can be considered as another agent of hegemonic power.

The negotiation he proposed, at the end, surely stopped the original BRA project; therefore the waterfront border was saved. And Langone rightly could be proud to have obtained affordable housing for North Enders. But the price of this negotiation was to consent to the impressive property speculation that started from the waterfront and gradually spread through the whole neighborhood. Through Langone, whether he was aware of it or not, the urban renewal of the waterfront in the North End became possible with the fundamental consent of the inhabitants.

The Big Dig

From many perspectives the Fitzgerald Expressway Project was a failure. In order to fix some of its many problems, urban planners proposed the replacement of the expressway with a Central Artery/Tunnel Project (CA/T), better known as the "Big Dig," which would replace the elevated highway with an underground expressway. The final goal of the CA/T was not only to solve the traffic problems caused by an obsolete highway but also to reconnect neighborhoods drastically separated from the city. At the beginning of the 1970s, Governor Frank Sargent organized a multidisciplinary study group composed of engineers, lawyers, architects, economists, and ecologists.[31] After two years the group presented a proposal of first depressing the Central Artery. In the report entitled *Boston Transportation Planning Review* it was stated:

> The long-term depress and widen alternative would demolish the existing viaduct and reconstruct the artery below ground from Congress street to the Sumner/Callahan tunnel portals. A new surface street would be constructed over the depressed highway to service local traffic. The major objectives of this alternative would be to increase the core-bound and through traffic capacity of the artery, to improve connections to the Sumner/Callahan Tunnels, to improve safety, and to reduce congestion due to bottlenecks on local service ramps providing access to the core and the airport.[32]

Along with the traffic problem, the study was particularly concerned about the effects on the Downtown Waterfront Renewal Plan: depressing the Central Artery could allow additional housing development sites, without the visual and psychological barrier of the expressway and the consequent "real or perceived problems of security" because of the dark spaces underneath. Another expected benefic effect was

> optimizing interaction of visitors among the numerous visitor attractions such as Faneuil Hall, the proposed New Market Street market, the Waterfront Visitor Center complex and the North End shopping

district. Obviously the ease of pedestrian and vehicular movement among these areas enhances exposure to the visitor and increases expenditure potential representing sales, income and tax revenue to the operators and city. Such benefits would extend from such visitor-oriented activity operations as hotels, restaurants and gift shops to bonus patronage for grocery, apparel and other outlets which derive most of their business from the resident population. (ibid.)

In the middle of the 1980s federal funds allowed the realization of the project for a depressed Central Artery, the Big Dig, in order to solve the traffic problem of handling 190,000 vehicles per day in the 1990s. According to the Massachusetts Turnpike Authority:

> After more than a decade of heavy construction, the Big Dig began paying dividends in 2003, with the completion of the I-90 connector to Logan International Airport in January. That new connection to the Ted Williams Tunnel meant the Massachusetts Turnpike had reached its final, 138-mile length. And within months, the new I-93 underground artery and the Leonard P. Zakim Bunker Hill Bridge also opened to traffic. The new Central Artery has the capacity to carry 250,000 vehicles per day. With the demolition of the old elevated highway, local traffic will travel along newly reconfigured surface streets, which will further facilitate traffic flow since far fewer vehicles will be using the underground artery for intra-city trips. Meanwhile, the Ted Williams Tunnel allows westbound traffic from the Massachusetts Turnpike to go directly to Logan Airport and the North Shore without having to use I-93. By carrying an estimated 90,000 vehicles per day, the Ted Williams Tunnel reduces the amount of traffic using the Sumner and Callahan Tunnels.[33]

The impact of the Big Dig's construction on the city landscape was enormous. The elevated Central Artery again divided the city in two, running aboveground with its intricate ramp system and the overcrowded traffic, as a sort of wall, at the same time physical and symbolic. The Big Dig construction works literally traced a deep trench that may be crossed only at a few points through winding and narrow tunnels. In spite of the final goal—to knit the separation between the North End and downtown—it was a greater physical and symbolic wound on the ground, a sort of amputation, cutting the city even more into two parts. The controversies concerning the Big Dig were, are, and will be endless: too expensive, taking too much time, with continuous delays, and so on. The urban planners and the political authorities were forced by law and social pressures into continuous negotiation with a plethora of associations defending lands and neighborhoods. In the North End formal and informal groups also worked and still work to negotiate this boundary.

The main issue, at least for the North End neighbors, has been the use of the public land (the parcels) when the Central Artery finally goes underground. This concern was negotiated between the city's urban planners, all sorts of authorities, spontaneous associations, simple residents, political leaders, and electors, during many meetings held in the North End, beginning in 1998 and continuing through the present. A specific account of this confrontation, surely possible, should be a matter of specific research about not only negotiability but also leadership formation, voluntary associations, political power, community activism, and technical hegemony. As an example, I recount here an interview with Guild Nichols, webmaster of northendboston.com, who attended the meetings as a longtime North End resident and journalist.

Guild: I attended almost all of the meetings to follow the process by which the community as a group could make suggestions into the process of defining what could be built on top of the Big Dig. Initially the community reacted to the parcels that were closest to the majority of the North End, which are parcel 8 and parcel 10 which are directly at the exit of Hanover Street and Salem Street, which are the center of the North End. And once that process got on the way and started to move forward another issue concerning a further parcel which is called parcel 12 which is at the southern extremity of the North End, where the North End comes up against what is currently called the Christopher Columbus Park. That parcel became a very hot issue largely because of the interest of a number of residents that live there, that have properties there, that were absolutely deeply worries about another building being built on this parcel. There are four parcels that touch the North End directly: parcel 6 is a parcel that covers the exit and entrance to the Big Dig and because that's an exit and ingress whatever the words are in this parcel they had the right to be built upon and the reason for that was they felt the BRA and the Massachusetts Transit Authority considered a building on that parcel would help for ventilation purposes, covering the ugliness of the entrance and exit. There is another entrance and exit to the system and is parcel 12. . . . A lot of the concerns in the North End were what buildings should be built. With regards to parcel 8 and 10 those were always being determined to be park parcels which nothing was gonna be built on except plants and grass. So to a certain extent parcels 8 and 10 were far from the concern of the North End, something could be designed and certainly it could be possible an impact on the design, but the biggest concerns were parcel 6 and 12, because those were building areas. . . . The difficulty with parcel 6 and parcel 12 as building areas is they have a number of constraints on, you are not allowed a lot of weight on, they are physical constraints. . . . Parcel 6 from the very beginning was determined . . .

something should be built to benefit the community. Consequently the only proposal that really came further was the YMCA and the Boston Museum Project. The Boston Museum Project did not get the green light and the YMCA is going to be built on parcel 6. On parcel 12 it is not very clear what is going to be built however the Boston Museum Project has put a bid on that parcel. Many people think that they bid on parcel 6 even if they knew they were going to lose because they really wanted parcel 12. But the people down on parcel 12 have their own ideas and their own idea was . . . they wanted a park on top of that. So two years ago when there was a very angry debate going on the people from the BRA decided to make money available to the citizen groups who were formerly against parcel 12 to bring in some experts to help them decide what are the technical possibilities and some landscape designers and city planners came together, and they came up with their proposal supported by that group to build a park there and they called themselves the "Homestead."

Augusto: I want come back to a term you use, rightly I guess, very often: community. But, physically who were these people? Who could participate to these meetings?

Guild: A number of people came to the planning meetings that took place at the City Square in Charlestown, but at the end just six or seven people really participate regurarly. Consequently in the North End when the question came up on what we can put on parcel 6 and 12 there was a large amount of people showing up. In 2000 and 2001 attending these meetings were very vociferous and angry people but they represented just themselves not the community. The leader was this lady Nancy Caruso who was from the North End. There was a very open discussion. After the decisions were made the general community involvement disappeared and then the professional meeting attenders came in. These were people that had special interests in landscaping, real estate, urban planning and the meetings became much more focused. The attendance was more professional. . . . The "complain period" was probably late '99 through 2002 up to the point that three things happened. One thing was that the requested proposal for parcel 6 was completed and the design team was selected, this changed the tenor of the meetings. Point number two, when the people that organized the North End Central Artery Committee saw that there was still a lot of unresolved issues in parcel 12. The urban planners very rudely put this argument out of discussion. And the third element was that people got tired.

Augusto: What is the real power of negotiation that the Committee and the people that represent the neighborhood really have?

Guild: The most revealing part of this process was the total absence of involvement of the political elected figures. De Masi, Scapicchio, Travaglini they paid attention to the community but they were not leading the community. The things went out very nicely without them. They were cast aside. The committee was able to negotiate by itself.

Augusto: If some kind of real negotiation was possible this is a great success. But it was really possible? Or the decisions were already made somewhere else?

Guild: I tend to be very cynical about these processes, but it was not in that way. Actually they did listen. This is an example: the designer team was led by a designer from Seattle. She showed up for the first meeting ... very disrespectful to the other people. It was so palpable that Nancy Caruso never invited her back again and she went back to Seattle, the head of all design and never came back again. Her assistant, her name was Nicole I forgot the last name, was much more available for listening, taking notes, changing the plan. The decision probably was already made but still a negotiation was possible. They were very open to explore different options. Maybe they got what they wanted but the people were able to negotiate. I feel strong about this, the process by which the North End was involved and was listened to by the power can be a case study of participation. The issue of the Big Dig and what to put on these parcels cut to the core of the North End in a certain way even more than the Sacred Heart Church.

Negotiation of the border was historically crucial and can be seen as a metonymy of the complex social dynamics. The trend seems to be toward a progressive increment of participation and even conflicting dialogue with a counterpart that moved from monolithic decisions and hegemonic proposals to, finally, debates and dialogues, still unbalanced but real and significant.

Permeability

In political geography and, generally, in economic and social sciences, the concept of permeability of a border designates the ability of a border to prevent illegal crossing (Langer 1999, 29). This general approach is again modeled on a macrolevel and relates to international relations. Instead, I am assuming permeability as a set of social practices implemented to cross the territorial boundaries at a microlevel, the city and its neighborhood. Therefore I am not looking for any illegal practices punishable by law. The North End is not a sort of Warsaw ghetto even if social stigma can be equally effective, but in spite of this it is still possible to find patterns of crossing, changing over time and connected again with ethnicity, social classes, and economy.

Permeability thus becomes a reflection of social dynamics such as segregation, creolization, and assimilation, as well as expulsive/inclusive processes between subaltern and hegemonic dominant groups. And permeability is a multidimensional phenomenon having dimensions, directions, times, and intensities. From my perspective, permeability can be centripetal or centrifugal, temporary or definitive, individual or collective, voluntary or forced. But despite the appearances I am not proposing any sort of structural approach and the categories should be seen not as rigid or exclusive, and surely not as clusters of opposite terms. In many cases they may cluster together in different ways; for instance an individual, temporary, centripetal case of permeability may occur at the same time of a centrifugal, definitive, and collective situation, or a temporary crossing can be followed by a more definitive one or vice versa. Furthermore, the borders of these categories should be read as blurred and malleable, like the territorial boundaries involved: for instance, did the unskilled Italian worker digging the subway in Downtown Boston or the Back Bay cross the boundary voluntarily? Or did the economic pressure of a specific niche market, one of the few available for immigrants, force the crossing? Probably they occurred at the same time. The list therefore should be seen as more of a suggestion of possible dynamic adjectives rather than as a model based on opposition.

As examples of centripetal dynamics I suggest the initial Puritan settlement populating the area. The progressive implementation was mainly due to economic reasons, since the harbor and the waterfront were the center of business life. The permeability of the border was fundamental at that time: the economic growth of the town pushed for a transient border. Mostly voluntary and collective, this dynamic also should be considered as definitive, at least in the intentions of the settlers. Again, a basic reason is a social group that was relatively homogeneous, where a social hierarchy is believed to be natural and not discussed. At the end of this process, when the settlement is configured, the permeability of the border became even more important, but as an instrument of regulation and limitation. Mill Creek was formed and only two bridges connected the North End to the rest of the town. The historical perspective, while suggesting a logical pattern of alternation of centripetal/centrifugal dynamics, also relates this pattern to economic phases and a more or less transient border. An economically stable and wealthy neighborhood needs a less transient and permeable border, and vice versa. In other terms the centripetal movement toward the North End, based on the growth of the economy reached its climax with the symbolic and material construction of a border (the Mill Creek). The centrifugal movement toward other sites of the town (or, in the specific case of the postrevolution loyalist, toward Nova Scotia) coincided with the abolition of the territorial border, which at the same time allowed the centripetal movement of lower classes of immigrants to settle in the now-designated slum. But a close look at this centripetal movement shows its heterogeneity, presenting overlapping phases. The subsequent immigrant settlements, ethnically different, construct a permeable border connected again with economic variables. For instance the centripetal permeability of the border at the end of nineteenth century was certainly different for an Irish immigrant, probably second or third generation and already assimilated, than for an Italian newcomer. The latter, for a combination of factors such as the ethnic enclaves based on chain migration and family/village strategies of settlement could plan to cross the border with difficulty, while the first was already on his or her way to more attractive places. On a different scale of the different waves of the Italian migrations, I can argue different degrees of permeability: the centrifugal movement of the immigrant, starting as individual crossing, soon becomes a more collective phenomenon due to the already mentioned chain migration process, characterized by a recall mechanism. This means a relatively easy dynamics of centripetal permeability if the migrant belonged to the same village and, vice versa, a very difficult crossing in the opposite case.

Another example of centrifugal/centripetal movement can be seen in the urban renewal of the 1960s and 1970s. In order to facilitate the creation of new residences or rehabilitate old working-class areas for the middle and the upper classes, first the Waterfront and later the North End was the object of a complex strategy: the old settlers were urged, with economic pressure such as relevant offers for the old tenements, to move out to the suburban areas, so the change became possible in real estate values and renewal, allowing a new generation of "yuppies" to enter the neighborhood. This is the historical moment when a striking territorial border, the Fitzgerald Expressway, in need of change, was replaced by an even more striking border, the Big Dig, which is almost impermeable.

A peculiar form of permeability of the border can be seen on the Freedom Trail. Definitely a centripetal dynamic, the Freedom Trail cannot be otherwise, since it is basically a tourist attraction and therefore fundamentally an individual (or small group) choice, absolutely voluntary. It is interesting to note that the red line a tourist follows that connects the sixteen more important historical sites of the city (most of them in the North End) was created in 1958,[34] in a moment of a positive economic trend.[34] The permeability of the border is possible for the tourist who is perfectly integrated in the contemporary economic market.

Not surprisingly, permeability of the border appears to be associated with social and economic factors. Ethnicity, also associated with economic trends, is one of these variables. But again the pattern is not rigid and changes with different ethnicities. Continuing the Irish/Italian example, the centrifugal movement characterizing the social climbing of Irish groups can be compared to the late centripetal movement of the Italians, and the consequent reinforcement of the border for the same economic reasons.

Instability, permeability and negotiability highlight not only the nature of the territorial border but the complex social processes and dynamics that surround it.

Conclusion

The aspects of instability, negotiability, and permeability of the borders and the historical dynamics allow me, in conclusion, to argue that the boundaries of the North End are an ambiguous, contradictory, and dynamic space. Like the identities that these borders supposedly contain, they are blurred, malleable, and situationally negotiable. Because of these borders, I am suggesting the North End can be conceptualized as an ephemeral place, where ethnic ephemeral identities are continuously negotiated. At least since Barth's seminal work on ethnic boundaries (1969) and Herbert Gans's description of low-level ethnic identification based on symbolic structures (1979), identity and specifically ethnic identity has always been presented along with adjectives such as situational (see Cohen and Kennedy 2000; Okamura 1981), portable (O'Sullivan 1999), convenient or part-time (see Halter 2000, and her works on the marketing of ethnicity), voluntary or tourist (Wood 1998), and optional (Waters 1990), to name just a few examples. All these overlapping definitions not only illustrate the multivocal dimension of ethnic identity and the voluntary aspects of the choices but they also imply a vanishing temporality. From this perspective, I will use the term "ephemeral identities," which makes a claim not for substantial differences with the previous terms, because every ethnic identity is basically ephemeral, but for some differences in degrees and shades. I choose this term because (1) the ethnic identities I am analyzing are intensively performed during the day of the religious feast.[35] Therefore the term *ephemeral*, seems more philologically accurate, describing a phenomenon lasting one day.[36] It seems also in conformity with some interviews I made during the festivals. For instance, during the procession of the *Little Saint Anthony*,[37] Mr. Greco referring to the "Italianess" showed everywhere, ironically told me "Ogge è accussi, ma rimane turnamme a essere Ammericane tutte quante" [Today it goes in this way, but tomorrow we turn again Americans].[38] (2) An offshoot of the adjective ephemeral is the noun *ephemeris*. Traditionally it refers to a table providing the predictable positions of heavenly bodies for every day during a given period of time. It is also related to calendar, diary, journal, or almanac, in general a record of daily occurrences.[39] The complex festive practices I am studying, and therefore the ethnic identities related to them, occur following a precise and predictable calendar, a sort of ephemeredes, a day-by-day listing of religious performances. (3) Another derivate term is *ephemera*, referring to written and printed matter published with a short intended lifespan, such as letters, greeting cards, tickets, posters, and so on, that now have become everyday memorabilia. They can be seen, according to Maurice Rickards, curator of *The Encyclopedia of Ephemera*,[40] as the minor transient documents of everyday life. Ephemera collectables related to the experience of migration are now an important market. For instance, the official Web site of Ellis Island (www.ellisisland.org) sells manifests and pictures of the ships, reproductions of the journals of arrivals, tickets, and so on. In my fieldwork experience probably every family in the North End, somehow involved in the migration experience preserves, if not collects, similar ephemera. They are now important icons of ethnicity.

Ironically, as well as interestingly, the semantic halo evoked by ephemeral and its derivatives[41] includes predictability and evanescence, transient aspects of everyday life and annual performed rituals, memories, and fragments of the past as well as ethnic claims. Like the festivals I am studying.

2

Diasporas, Ethnic Enclaves, and Transnational Perspectives

✠

The transformation of Boston's North End from a desirable place to a slum suitable only for the social outcasts of the city was certainly slow and heterogeneous, traumatic and yet expected, and also aided by different economic factors.[1] A new industrialism caused the economic crisis of the small artisans and craftsmen of the area, and the persistence of a sea-based mercantile economy turned the North End into an increasingly crowded and noisy place, where sailors and transients could live, even if only temporarily.

The decay of the neighborhood can be seen, therefore, as a function of the transformation of a society from preindustrial to capitalist. The need for unskilled and cheap workers ought to be considered as a fundamental pull factor for the impressive waves of emigrants beginning in the nineteenth century. Creating a slum for immigrants was an urban necessity, the only suitable settlement close to the industrial area but at the same time marginalized by social if not territorial boundaries. In other terms, stigmatized people were forced to occupy stigmatized places (Krase 2006). From this perspective, the study of what can be called "vernacular landscape,"[2] the peculiar organization of space of these subaltern communities, can offer an initial insight. Vernacular landscape, for instance, can be considered as territorial histories, that is, "the history of bounded spaces, with some enforcement of the boundary, used as a way of defining political and economic power. It is the political and temporal complement of the cognitive map; it is an account of both inclusion and exclusion" (Hayden 1991, 11). Furthermore, according to Harvey, "successful control presumes a power to exclude unwanted elements. Fine-tuned ethnic, religious, racial, and status discrimination are frequently called into play within such a process of community construction" (1989, 266).

On the other hand, as noted by Portes (1995, 12), the need for ethnic concentrations, in the contemporary world as well as in the past, is correlated with a lack of social capital. Individuals can control scarce resources in a better way if integrated in networks. Creating a slum is always a complex social dynamic, involving continuous internal and external negotiations.

An important element of the vernacular landscape, illustrating the conditions of this slum, its change and the underlying social dynamics, can be considered the housing characteristic. The deteriorated mansions, which remained unoccupied after the loyalist escape or after the relocation of wealthy families, were not destroyed but were inhabited by the newcomers, the immigrants from Ireland, Germany, and England. Often the same mansions were replaced by four- and five-story tenements, generally cheaply made, with the resultant overpopulation in a small area.

The municipal concern about housing conditions and the consequent sanitary problem of the neighborhood has to be seen in a more complex frame. Even Chandler recognized this in 1902:

> There all four well-defined periods in the history and housing problems of the North and West Ends. These may be designated as the period of epidemics, until the last outbreak of smallpox in 1872; the period of constructive effort, from the clearing away of Fort Hill in 1867 to 1889; the period of detailed investigation from 1889 to 1897; and the present period, with its enlarged municipal powers, beginning in 1898. (75)

The overcrowded and filthy tenements could be defined without any doubt as the local cause of the spread of contagious disease such as smallpox in 1824 and Asiatic cholera in 1832. In 1845, the ratio of inhabitants to houses for the North End was 17.79 (the eastern part, belonging to Ward 2) and 19.15 (the Fort Hill district, belonging to Ward 8), with many houses not connected with the city sewage system. Despite an average ratio for the city of 10.57, it was fairly predictable where the next epidemic could spread. In 1849, Asiatic cholera exploded for the second time: 611 people died in Boston, and 114 deaths were in the North End. In 1854, cholera appeared for the third time and the smallpox epidemic spread throughout the city in 1872, with a total of 3,700 cases and 1,040 deaths (Chandler 1902, 76-80). The sanitary situation of the tenements was considered urgent and fundamental.

In 1885, a municipal decree defined the tenements as buildings where more than three families lived separately. According to a report written by Dwight Porter in 1889,[3] a tenement in the North End was occupied by four to fifteen families— almost sixty to seventy tenants. The rent was definitely cheap (Porter found out an average of $1.85 a week). But despite the Boston Health Act of 1885, prescribing the sanitary conditions to be respected in all the buildings of the city, with special concern for the sewer system, dumping rules, crowding index, and so on, the tenements in the North End were nonetheless very far from healthy.[4]

The structural problems of a tenement usually were due to the lack of a rubbish dump (or even a yard to deposit the garbage). Therefore, according to Martellone, garbage:

> pertanto venivano ammucchiate, in attesa di essere prelevate, al piano terreno, ammorbando scale d'ingresso ed abitazioni

> [was accumulated at the first floor, waiting for the withdrawal, consequently infecting entrances and houses] (1973, 238)

Another problem was the sweatshops, present almost everywhere in the North End. One must keep in mind a sort of paradox: the rising price of the urban land, even in the North End, did not allow for the building of big factories, therefore leaving room for many small factories and shops, mostly identifiable in the sweatshops system.[5] But the main concern was overcrowding: Porter reports a tenement in the North End where nine Italian families were living, almost sixty people, with only one lavatory, filthy and in bad condition, located in the basement, also accessible to everybody from the street.

In 1891, in the wake of Porter's report, City Hall provided a census of the tenements. Again, many tenements were found dilapidated, and the crowding index was impressive. More than half of the 259 families, living in a small area of the neighborhood, were forced to live an entire family to a room (Martellone 1973, 241). But, according to Bushee, the worst conditions were found in the tenements where immigrants were living without families. There, ten or twelve men used to live in a single room, paying a rent of twenty-five to thirty cents per week (1902, 29).

In 1892, the Massachusetts Bureau of Statistics of Labor,[6] under the direction of H. G. Wadlin, reported the population density and the overcrowding. The average number of people to a house, in the precinct bounded by North Street, North Square, Prince Street, and Hanover Street, was 17.91, but in the northern and eastern part of the neighborhood the situation was even worse: 259 families were reported as living in one-room tenements (with an average of 2.67 persons to a family) and 1,154 families in two-room tenements (with an average of 3.74 persons to a family). For the whole city the statistics were: 1.96 persons per family, for 1053 families in one-room tenements and 2.87 per family for 5,695 families in two-room tenements.

In 1919, the Common Council entrusted a commission to study the possibility of improvement for the Boston neighborhoods. The survey reached the following conclusions:[7]

1. The tenement situation in the North End was almost the same as in 1895, with a potential enormous risk for the public health.

2. The death rate was decreasing, reaching 1.6%. But these data were less significant when one takes into account that the inhabitants of the North End were immigrants, mostly young workers. Therefore their age was lower than inhabitants of other neighborhoods. More importantly, the birthrate was very high: 50/1000, twice the average birthrate of the city: 25/1000.

3. Even after the acquisition of the North End Park, the North End Beach, the Coop's Hill Terraces and the Prince Street Playground, 7.7 acres assigned for public activities in the neighborhood constituting 1.1% of the overall area, was sensibly inadequate for the population needs.

4. The last one-family houses, concentrated around the Old North Church, on Hull and Salem Streets, were sold and other tenements took their place.

5. The density of population in the Ward 6 was 3% higher than the worst conditions in New York City.

6. The land value was increasing ($4-5 a square foot). Therefore the rent for a tenement of 300 square feet, three rooms, was almost $12 a month. Generally this kind of apartment was rented by a family which sub-rented some space to another 3-4 people, paying $1 a week.[8] Therefore 6-7 people could live practically in promiscuity in a small area. Some rooms were without windows and the kitchen was used at night as a bedroom for at least two people. The lavatory was outside and shared with three families, almost 20 people.

7. The Italians increasingly owned the property of the real estate and they exploited it as rented tenements (to fellow countrymen) or as boarding houses.

At the time of the City Planning Board's survey, in spite of the Irish escape from the North End's slum to more agreeable places, the population density of the neighborhood continuously increased. The main factor was the endless influx of migrants mainly from southern Italy, a mass movement that slowed down only during the fascist era.[9]

This was the North End, a slum for the social drift constituted by immigrants landing from different parts of the world. And I will argue in this chapter that ethnicity plays a fundamental role in the community construction as an exclusionary agent favoring claimed identities, but also as an inclusive factor favoring the manufacture of social relationships and connections. This is to say that interethnic struggles are based not on essential qualities but on boundaries, both symbolic and territorial. These boundaries are sometimes strategically impassable but, as I demonstrated in the first chapter, in general they are characterized by negotiability and permeability. The exclusive ethnic group gives way to strategic alliances and convenient dynamics, historically determined and therefore understandable through historical investigations.

I will suggest, furthermore, that ethnicity evolves over time from strictly territory-based to a diffused territoriality-based community, variously imagined and variously manipulated. In this dynamic situation the ethnic enclave of Boston's North End changed again: from a forced destination and a marginalized slum to an exclusive and desirable neighborhood, where a strategic essentialism became necessary in order to preserve an identity, now transformed into a scarce resource.

The Irish Diasporas

The Italians were just one of the many immigrant groups landing in Boston's North End. And they were the last. First came the Irish.

In 1636, 140 passengers set sail from Carrickfergus for the Merrimack area, but because of adverse weather conditions, they could not land in America.[10] The project was not abandoned, and in 1719, the Londonderry settlement was formed in the Merrimack area, with sixteen Presbyterian families, and soon they spread, some of them reaching Boston. They were not the first settlers in New England. According to Griffith (1971, 2–28), in 1640 Darby Field, an Irishman, was ordered by Governor Winthrop to explore northern New England and he discovered the White Mountains. The same year Michael Bacon, from Dublin, first settled in Boston and then was granted land in Woburn, Massachusetts. In 1644, Daniel Gookin the Younger, "son of an early settler in Virginia, moved to Massachusetts where he became a member of the governor's council, Major General of militia and Superintendent of Indian affairs." In 1645, Teague Jones, an Irishman, became a freeholder and resident of Yarmouth, Massachusetts. In 1653, James Butler settled in Massachusetts, soon becoming the largest landowner in Worcester. In 1654, four hundred Irish indentured servants arrived in Boston on the ship *Goodfellow*. They were kidnapped from Kinsale, County Cork, and sold at Ipswich.[11]

It seems impossible to find a general pattern in the early years, since the migration was basically an individual decision, but definitely a trend toward growth became evident in the following years. From the very beginning Irish migration seems to be indissolubly connected to prejudices.

In 1688, Mary Glover, a native of Ireland, who was "sold as a salve in Barbados and subsequently brought to Massachusetts,"[12] was hanged as a witch in Boston. The same year Cotton Mather, the Puritan preacher and judge of the Salem trials, published *Memorable Providences, Relating to Witchcrafts and Possessions*, and in 1702, published the more important *Magnalia Christi*, concerning the trial of Mary Glover, responsible for the affliction of the Goodwin Children of Boston.[13] For Robert Calef, the author of *More Wonders of the Invisible World* in 1700, the real reason was the anti-Catholicism of Mather. Besides looking like a rehearsal for the Salem trial of 1692, the trial offers a clear example of Puritan discrimination against this woman, who was guilty of being Catholic, Irish, and poor. Not yet content, in 1700, Mather defined the Irish colonies as "formidable attempts of Satan and his Sons to Unsettle us," probably referring to the Goodfellow's episode (see Cullen 1889, 23).

In 1720, the governor of Massachusetts noted that in the previous three years twenty-six hundred Irishmen had arrived in Boston. He complained "of the public burden imposed by the coming of so many poor people from abroad, especially those that come from Ireland. The general Court of Massachusetts warned immigrants from Ireland to leave the colony within seven months" (ibid., 29). It does not seem that this happened and there is no evidence of any further decision by the court.

In 1723, Boston authorities complained because of the considerable number of Irish immigrants entering the city, without any sort of regulation. On May 4, the town meeting passed the following order:

> Whereas great numbers of Persons have very lately bin Transported from Ireland into this Province, many of which by Reason of the Present Indian war and other Accedents befalling them, Are now Resident in this Town whose Circumstances and Conditions are not known, Some of which if due care be not taken may become a Town Charge or be otherwise prejuditial to the well fair & Prosperity of the place.
>
> For remedy whereof Ordered That Every Person now Resident here, that hath within the space of three years last past bin brought from Ireland, or for the future shal come from thence hither, Shal come and Enter his name and Occupation with the Town Clerck and if married the number and Age of his Children and Servants, within the space of five days, on pain of forfeiting and paying the sum of twenty Shillings for each offence, And the Sum of the Shilling for every one that Shal continue in the neglect or non-Observance of this order, for and During the term of forty-Eight hours after the expiration of the fiue dayes afore-said So often as the Persons offending Shal be complained of and Convict before any Justice of the Peace within the Said County.
>
> And be it further Ordered that whoever Shall Receive and Entertain and keep in his family any Person or Person Transported from Ireland as aforesaid, Shal within the space of forty-Eight hours after Such Receipt and Entertainment Return the Names of all Such Persons with their circumstances as far as they are able to the Town Clerck. On penalty of Twenty Shillings fine for the first forty-Eight hours and Ten Shilling for every twenty-four houres he Shal be convict after the first forty-Eight hours and so toties quoties. (quoted in Cullen 1889, 67–68)

But because at this time Irish migrants were mostly Presbyterians from Ulster who had already abandoned the Gaelic language, their integration was slow but possible.[14] Bridenbaugh (1955a, 123–136) described an episode of acceptance when in September 1750 almost two hundred Irish immigrants were welcomed at their landing in Boston. This process was accelerated by the participation of the so-called Ulster-Americans or Scotch-Irish at the American Revolution, but in no way can it be considered a complete assimilation to the predominant Anglo-Saxons. Personal success and social mobility of a small part of the Irish immigrant group still was exceptional.

The general scenario of prejudice was probably the reason for the constitution of the Charitable Society for the relief of the poor and indigent countrymen. In 1737, twenty-six persons of Irish nationality, residing in Boston, founded the society—the oldest Irish society in the United States—because of their "affectionate and compassionate concern for their countrymen in these parts" (D'arcy McGee 1852, 35).

At the end of eighteenth century, the number of Irish Catholics in Boston increased significantly. This fact can be seen as both the cause and the effect of changes in religious attitude. In September 1799, the Massachusetts delegates for the State Constitution composed a Bill of Rights ending discrimination against Catholics.[15] The same year Michael Burns, Owen Callahan, Patrick Campbell, Edmund Conner, John Duggan, and John Magner bought land on Franklin Street for the construction of a new church. The project was entrusted to Charles Bulfinch, and in September 29, 1803, the church was dedicated to the Holy Cross. This moment can be considered the affirmation of Irish Catholics,[16] the aftermath of the French departure, already relocated out of Boston, in spite of the very poor economic condition of the Irish parishioners. O'Connor quoted Father John S. Tisserant, a clergyman from Connecticut visiting Boston, who observed that the Irish folk "were drawn here by the miserable condition that existed in their native country" (1995, 25).

Handlin (1941, 242) reports passengers entering Boston by sea, for the period 1821 to 1865. In the five years from 1831 to 1835 2,361 Irish landed in Boston. This figure, even if far from the impressive number of the Famine time (65,556 Irish immigrants arrived in Boston in 1846 and 63,831 in 1851), still represents a fourfold increase from the previous five years (1826–1830) and three times the 1821–1825 period. This was enough to be considered or, better, to be felt, as a threat.

A preliminary question arises: how many of the migrants, coming by sea (or by land from Canada or different ports), settled in the city? A first suggestion come again from Handlin (1941, 35-37): Boston was an important port of entry to the United States, but few decided to stay, during the first period of nineteenth-century immigration. This is a diffuse pattern, valid in general for the European migrants. For these people, mostly ordinary peasants and laborers, the city was not a first choice. If agricultural people, they were looking for better climatic conditions and cheap land, farther west; if they were artisans, the few that remained did so to supply the needs of all the transient immigrants. But the situation changed and by the 1830s, the Irish were an impressive labor force, cheaper, and therefore preferable to the locals.

Thus, not surprisingly, prejudices against the Irish, and immigrants in general, climaxed in the nativist actions against immigrants, which a few years later enflamed the United States, and in particular Boston. This is the experience of the Know-Nothing Movement. This political party, which originated in 1853 in New York State, was also known as the Order of the Star-Spangled Banner or simply the American Party.[17] In 1854, the organization was present in Massachusetts. It was not the first nativist organization, at least in Boston, where people were anxious about the impressively increasing number of migrants, and where a variety of secret societies had already been founded. Societies such as the Sons of '76, the Druids, the Sons of Sires, and the Order of United Americans were founded in order to preserve the economic and cultural supremacy of the Anglo-Saxon Protestants.

In 1854, the Know-Nothing Party, by and large, won the election and Henry Gradner was elected governor of Massachusetts and in the same year Jerome Van Crowninshield Smith became mayor of Boston.[18] All the most important offices until 1857 were in the hands of the Know-Nothing Movement. Their first action against the Irish was to dismantle the Irish militia companies, then "the new legislature made the reading of the Protestant version of the Bible (the King James version) compulsory in all the public schools and deprived diocesan officials of all control over church property" (O'Connor 1995, 77). According to Handlin (1941, 202–206), even though the Know-Nothing Movement acquired the power to restrict the influence of immigrants through absolute control of the government, they failed to pass permanent restrictions.[19] Nonetheless, they proposed a "Twenty One Year Law," with the purpose of preventing any immigrant from voting until he had been a resident for twenty-one years, and they proposed a literacy amendment to the Constitution, as well as a bill to exclude paupers from politics.

The Know-Nothing Party dissolved as fast as it appeared. But the feeling against the Irish remained. In 1857, a referendum concerning a literary test was approved by 63 percent of the voters, which was directed at everyone but with the intentional purpose to affect the Irish, based on the presumption that they could not read or write. In 1859, a law preventing the immigrants from voting until two years after their naturalization was passed.

The nativist fear, regardless of the form it assumed, was a defense against the unrestrainable influx of migrants landing in the United States. Denying basic electoral rights was meant to preserve the supremacy of the old Anglo-Saxon establishment. It was at the same time the cause and effect of an endless mirroring game of ethnic prejudices and discrimination.

The Boston anti-Irish feeling—or, better, the feeling about this anti-Irish feeling—is also expressed by the slogan "No Irish Need Apply." In the middle of the nineteenth century, advertisements such as the following one could be found in the Boston newspapers:

> Wanted—A good, reliable woman to take the care of a boy two years old, in a small family in Brookline. Good wages and a permanent situation given. No washing or ironing will be required, but good recommendations as to character and capacity demanded. Positively no Irish need apply. Call at 224 Washington Street, corner of Summer Street.[20]

The slogan seems to appear for the first time in Europe, probably after the 1798 Irish Rebellion. It was used by the English at least until 1820 to discriminate against the Irish.[21]

Besides stereotypes and prejudices, it is possible to assume that an overwhelming number of Irish immigrants in Boston were unskilled workers, traumatically transplanted from a social and cultural rural landscape, characterized by extreme poverty and abuse, to an urban center in a phase of industrial and commercial explosion. Therefore, according to Handlin:

> the absence of other opportunities forced the vast majority into the ranks of an unemployed resourceless proletariat, whose cheap labor and abundant numbers ultimately created a new industrialism in Boston. But for a long time they were fated to remain a massive lump in the community, undigested, undigestible. (1941, 55)

In 1850, with a population of 35,287 Irish natives, only 14,595 were employed (41.4 percent). The distribution of occupations by nativity, as reported by Oliver Warner in *Abstract of the Census of Massachusetts, 1865: With Remarks on the Same, and Supplementary Tables*, published in 1867 (quoted in Handlin 1941, 250–251), in the Irish case demonstrates a clustering of a few unskilled occupations. Besides a relatively small number of artisans (356 are listed as carpenters, 307 as smiths, 1,045 as tailors), the two larger concentrations (representing 63.7 percent of the Irish working population) are 2,292 servants (representing 70.5 percent of a total of 3,249 servants in Boston and 15.3 percent of the Irish working population) and 7,007 generic laborers (representing 81.9 percent of a total of 8,552, and 48.01 percent of the Irish working population).

This social class literally landed on the North End and East Boston shores in the preponderant case and simply could not move anywhere else. In a situation of an overstocked job market, with barely enough money "to keep them fed and sheltered for a week or two" (Handlin 1941, 59), with the charitable association that could help only a small percentage of them, without the possibility to return to Ireland or to find transportation to go elsewhere, they simply were stuck in the city. Under the pressure of the need for basic survival they could rely only on occasional, day-by-day, labor. Often a first, sporadic, heavy-labor job could be obtained at the docks, without the additional cost of urban transportation.

This pattern of settlement in the city can be seen by analyzing data such as a list of passengers, wages, cost of local transportation, and housing expenses. For example, here I focus on the *Alexina* and *Oregon* passenger list, both landing in Boston in 1840.[22] One hundred and fifty-three passengers are listed as having sailed on the *Alexina*. First, the almost similar number of males (eighty-three) and females (seventy) seems to confirm the pattern that Irish migration was not gender differentiated. The list suggests also that not only young single males or females (the average migrant was 21.3 years old) but families too migrated from Ireland.[23] With the exception of a teacher (John Kylfoyle) and a blacksmith (John McNamara), the other listed occupations are farmer (thirty-one) and generic laborer (twenty-four). Twenty-four children and infants were listed along with four matrons, thirteen housewives, thirty-five spinsters, four servants, and sixteen listed as unknown. This data confirms the pattern of unskilled workers migrating to the United States. Michael Ryan had $26.50 for him and his large family; James Shannon had $16.40 for him, his wife, and their three children. Not surprisingly John Kilfoyle, a teacher, declared the possession of $20.65. But in general the Irish migrants carried with them an average of $3.50 per person.

On the *Oregon*, 146 persons left Europe but it was a hard trip: eighteen people died during the crossing of the Atlantic. Of the 128 people who landed in Boston, there were fifty-three women and seventy-five men; the average age was 20.5. Families too were traveling on the *Oregon*, like the Leachman family who were tragically affected by the hard trip, with William, the father, Charlotte, the wife, and Elizabeth, the oldest daughter, dying at the sea, leaving the other six children on the ship: Harriet (ten), Mary (eight), Richard (six), Frederick (four), and twins Charlotte and William (only eight months old). Besides four merchants and two mechanics, the others were again unskilled laborers: farmers (fifteen) and generic laborers (fifty-three). Females were listed as wife (sixteen), spinsters (sixteen), twenty children, and two unknown. The money carried on the *Oregon* was $13.12 per person, but the average in this case is misleading because the four merchants by themselves carried $1,105 (66 percent of the entire sum). Excluding the merchants, the average money drops to $4.70 per capita.

Irish migrants landing in Boston, confirming Handlin's suggestion, had only enough money to survive for a week or two. The average day's wage for a dock laborer was $0.90, reaching from $0.95 to $1.10 if the job involved heavy lifting, as in the case of construction work on Fort Hill. Twenty years later the situation was still the same with an average week's wage of $4.50 to $5.50 (Handlin 1941, 77).[24]

Of course there were better paying jobs but these were practically unreachable for Irish migrants, who were unskilled and stuck near the harbor (the North End and Fort Hill), because of the cost of transportation. From the North End the costs could be as follows:[25]

FROM	TO	$/RT	MIN/RT	MEANS
North End	Watertown	$0.85	120	horse
North End	Somerville	$0.65	30	horse
North End	Cambridge	$0.60	50	horse
North End	Dorchester	$0.55	10	horse
North End	Charlestown	$0.45	20	horse
North End	West End	$0.30	15	horse
North End	Docks	$0.00	15	foot
North End	Downtown	$0.00	9	foot
North End	Garment District	$0.00	8	foot

It is quite evident that the only choice that Irish migrants had after settling in the North End (or in Fort Hill) was to find a job nearby. Other chances were economically impossible. The Irish migrants were isolated in the slum, with very few opportunities to move.

In 1840, the housing cost was another important factor of marginalization in a few neighborhoods, as the following listing highlights:[26]

LOCATION	TYPE	ROOMS	$/WEEK	NOTES
North End	Rooming House	1	$1.10	Small, no plumbing
Fort Hill	Rooming House	1	$1.25	Share with other family
North End	Converted Factory	1	$1.25	No plumbing
South Cove	Rooming House	1	$1.25	Share with other family
Fort Hill	Converted Factory	1	$1.35	Share kitchen, bath
North End	Converted Factory	1	$1.35	Over blacksmith shop
North End	Converted Factory	1	$1.45	Share with other family
North End	Rooming House	1	$1.50	Share with Irish family
Fort Hill	Converted Factory	1	$1.65	Single woman only
South Cove	Converted Factory	1	$1.65	Single woman only
Fort Hill	Converted Factory	1	$1.75	Share with other family
Fort Hill	Rooming House	1	$1.75	Cellar room
South Cove	Rooming House	1	$1.75	Cellar room
South Cove	Converted Factory	1	$1.75	Share with other family
North End	Rooming House	1	$1.80	Cellar room
North End	Tenement	2	$2.50	Outside plumbing

* This list, partial and presented in order of increasing expense, suggests at first glance that affordable rent was concentrated in the North End and Fort Hill areas but also gives information about the quality of living. The cheap rents were available for small rooming houses, with no plumbing. In some cases the room was in the cellar or in a tenement, to be shared with an Irish family. Tenements and rooming houses are the only affordable houses for the migrants. Certainly uncomfortable but with a very important prerogative: they were near the wharfs, near a possible job.

The North End and, in a less evident way, Fort Hill were, before the arrival of the migrants, fashionable neighborhoods with elegant mansions. Therefore a process of refunctionalization of the old real estate was necessary. In general, the old houses and warehouses were converted into tenements or boardinghouses to host more people in response to an increasing demand. According to Handlin:

> a sub-lease system developed, whereby a contractor, usually Irish himself and frequently a neighborhood tradesman, leased an old building at an annual rental, subdivided it into immigrant flats, and sub-rented it at weekly rates. (1941, 101)

The great number of immigrants looking for any kind of cheap, affordable housing for their almost nonexistent resources, and the consequent property speculation that aimed at the maximum profit with the minimum expense turned out not to be only the cause of deteriorated living conditions, but also of very precarious hygienic conditions. The main problems were the absence of a sewage system, the need for a pure water supply, and the cleaning of the streets. As Chandler (1902, 71–99) suggests, it is important to note that in the eighteenth century the town of Boston had few sanitary regulations and only with Mayor Quincy, in 1822, did the sanitary problems of the now incorporated city begin to be faced, but still for a long time the city suffered from frequent epidemics. Inevitably, the epicenters were always the overcrowded and unclean slums, the North End and Fort Hill, where the Irish settled down.

As I already mentioned, in 1845 the city average was 10.57 inhabitants to a house, the North End had 17.79 and Fort Hill had 19.15. Again, this was a product of extreme needs on the one hand and, on the other hand, of an extreme lack of scruples. Not surprisingly, in 1865, in the North End where the Irish population was predominant, the correlation between tuberculosis and housing were impressive. In the North End, the Irish population was 33.5 percent, with an average of 14.39 persons per dwelling. The death rate by phthisis was 4.57 per thousand, and the death rate by all diseases was 23.2 per thousand.[27]

Another index of the situation of extreme poverty characterizing the social marginalization constituted by Irish migration is statistics about the nationality of inmates in Boston's jails.[28] In the Deer Island House of Industry, the Irish inmates, including also the second-generation migrants, were in the following percentages:

1855	1856	1857	1859	1860
48.3	55.59	55.59	67.86	75.21

In the House of Correction the data were the following:

1858	1859	1860	1861	1862	1863
48.52	47,80	40.14	58.87	67.85	50.00

The trend is also confirmed by another statistic regarding the national identity of people arrested and of detentions by the Boston Police Department in 1864. In a total of 12,914 arrests, 9,791 (75.82 percent) were Irish, and in a total of 23,638 inmates 17,293 (73.16 percent) were Irish.

This sort of data fueled the stereotype of the Irish as violent and alcoholic. In 1846, there were 850 liquor dealers in the city, increasing to 1,200 in three years. The great majority of the dealers were Irish and almost half were concentrated in the North End and Fort Hill. Even more important: "In addition, numerous Irish families sold gin as a sideline, without license, to cater to the demands of their countrymen" (Handlin 1941, 121), probably in order to increase their very low income. The correlation between alcohol intoxication and crime in the Irish case is impressively strong. But the relevant numerical data are misleading, since these crimes were mostly minor misdemeanors, which, as Handlin (1948, 121) suggested, not even punishable or at least more tolerated in the case of more affluent offenders.

The endless game of stereotyped labeling, with its counterpart of self-ascriptive cultural intimacy, can be seen through the vicissitudes of Bernard "Barney" McGinniskin (Galvin 1975, 52–55). In September 29, 1851, McGinniskin, an Irish North Ender, was unanimously appointed to the police force. He was the first Irishman (born in Galway, Ireland) to become a police officer in Boston. Nativist intolerance, based on the idea that an Irishman could not properly act against his fellow countrymen was expressed through protest meetings, and in January 5, 1852, McGinniskin was fired.[29] He was formally accused of being "noisy, quarrelsome, meddlesome (all common insults hurled against the Irish)" (Todisco 1976, 24).

In the Irish settling in Boston's North End in the middle of the nineteenth century, another fundamental expression of cultural intimacy and self ascription as an ethnic group was gathering together in places of Catholic worship. Belonging to a Catholic Church in a still predominant Protestant world was a form of external embarrassment and at the same time a shared assurance of common sociality. When the Irish landed in the North End, there was no

Catholic Church there. St. Mary's Church was the second Catholic Church in Boston and the first in the North End. In 1834, a building on Endicott Street was purchased and two years later the structure was completed and dedicated to Saint Mary of the Sacred Heart, an Irish church. The importance of this church as an icon of identity is illustrated by the following quotation:

> [T]hough serving as a parish church, its ministry is not restricted to those living within its parochial bounds. Visual evidence of this is given by the throngs that pour through the doors of its sacred edifice after a Sunday morning mass and scatter the other parts of the city. The procession of these returning worshipers going over the new Charlestown bridge presents a truly impressive sight, extending from one end [of] the bridge to the other, a compact moving column, and occupying a considerable time in passing. Indeed, the non-resident following of St. Mary's offsets more or less the shrinkage in its local consistency caused by the removal of the Irish from the North End. (Cole 1902, 268)[30]

Another Irish Catholic Church was St. Stephen on Hanover Street. St. Stephen was a more local parish and was definitely affected by the exodus of the Irish parishioners, above all the more prosperous families. In 1902, according to Cole, St. Stephen was still a distinctive and influential parish, attracting local politicians for consent issues (1902, 269).[31]

Besides the church in the nineteenth century, another form of group consciousness, based on a declared ethnic identity, was the voluntary association. Around the middle of the century, many Irish societies were founded. As I already mentioned, the first was the Charitable Irish Society, established in 1737. More than one hundred years later, by 1845, it had lost its original characteristics. It was no longer a benevolent society helping the poor escaping Ireland. Instead, it focused on organizing a grand dinner for St. Patrick's Day, which every year became more magnificent, to the point that very few Irish could join the association. The Friends of Ireland Society was founded on October 6, 1840, with the purpose of raising funds for the Irish fighting against Britain. Also important were social organizations such as The Shamrock Society, founded in 1844, and the militia companies—the Montgomery Guards, the Bay State Artillery, the Sarsfield Guard, and the Columbian Artillery—were popular in Boston. They were dismantled by the Know-Nothing regime but they continued social activity under different names and apparently with different purposes. The Columbian Artillery became the Columbian Literary Association and the Sarsfield Guard became the Sarsfield Union Association, for instance.

But the question remains as to how many of these societies were directly or even indirectly involved with the Irish migrant life in the North End. All the mentioned societies were a product of middle-class, bourgeois groups that were very far, geographically and economically, from the struggling social outcasts of the North

End. Occasionally, poor Irish could turn to these associations for financial help and support and surely they could address them in a trial of hegemonic consent for nationalistic purposes.[32] But they did not belong to the slum. Social classes and economic barriers are not only boundaries between ethnic groups but also within ethnic groups. I am not proposing here any sort of essentialist perspective of the Irish migrants in Boston as a whole. The life trajectory of Charles Weir, a thirty-year-old merchant landing in Boston in 1844 on the *Oregon*, with $525 in his pocket, was not the same, neither in Ireland nor in the United States, as James Froste, the fifty-year-old farmer traveling on the *Alexina* the same year, with his wife and eight children and $6.35. No more data are necessary to hypothesize that Weir was not trapped in the slums, while inevitably this was Froste's destiny. Weir, anticipating a further debate, was already "white," probably not completely accepted in the Protestant world of the Boston Brahmins but hardly considered an outcast. On the other hand, the destiny of Froste was almost certainly to be an outcast: his process of racial desegregation was still long and uncertain.

This differentiation is also evident in the social activities of the associations.[33] The Charitable Irish Society commemorated St. Patrick's Day in 1856 with a grand dinner in the magnificent, recently opened, Parker House.[34] This was simultaneously a signal of the loss of an original ethnic character and the achievement of social dignity. The Shamrock Society celebrated the event not in quite such grand style but nonetheless taverns such as Dooley's, the Mansion House, or Jameson's were not affordable for the average North Ender. Hibernian Hall was the place for the balls organized by the Erina Association, and Waverly's Grove and Beacon's Grove were the location for enjoyable picnics.

But this was not the life of the Irish migrants of the North End. The gathering places in the neighborhood, besides the churches, were dance halls, saloons, gambling dens, bistros, and brothels, and even these places mostly attracted transient costumers from outside what was then called "Black Sea" or the "Murder District."[35] The customary activities of these "jilt shops" were to entice the costumer for robbery (Cole 1902, 192). And while the activities of the more elite Irish social clubs were boat races modeled after fashionable regattas, the "fashion" game in the North End's jilt shops was the rat pit or rat baiting. These shops were strewn all along Ann Street (now North Street) since the beginning of the nineteenth century. In 1825, the Beehive brothel was raided by a mob of incensed citizens, but despite the general annoyance places such as the Beehive still existed throughout the entire nineteenth century. In 1851, on Ann Street, 165 persons were apprehended during a police blitz.

The last of the dance halls, ostensibly selling only nonalcoholic drinks and therefore without need of any license, but directly involved in prostitution, was closed in the spring of 1900. According to Cole:

> the closing of the dance halls really registered the moral change that had taken place in the North End within the last quarter of a century.

The conditions out of which their continuance really depended, had ceased to exist. During their later years the dance halls had been more and more of an anachronism . . . for the changed moral situation has been due, for the most part, to the change of the population. The moral decadence began with the incoming of the vicious and criminal of all races to take the places left vacant by the departure of the people of the better grades; with the coming of self-respecting and industrious foreign immigrant began the moral revival. In other words, the history of morals at the North End is at the bottom little more than the history of the social changes that have taken place here. (1902, 194–195)

The nonnamed people responsible for the moral decay of the neighborhood—defined as "vicious and criminal of all races"—were, inevitably, Irish.[36]

Otherwise an attentive scholar, Cole made a historical mistake when he considered as a causative variable the evident but misleading relationship between ethnic groups and morality and crime. Instead, he identified an intervening variable; that is, the existent relation between ethnic groups and morality and crime that is mediated by economic and social class factors. From this point of view, ethnicity became the hegemonic label covering the complex phenomenon of the making of a social and geographical slum. In other words, what is important is to understand the forming, the maintenance and the changes, even the need for, social outcasts in a specific, selected, and marginalized area of the city. The historical perspective, combined with the social anthropological one, is therefore fundamental.

The impressive wave of Irish migrants in the North End was continuously growing until the 1880s when a second wave of immigrants, from different parts of Europe, began landing on the shore of the neighborhood. This was the beginning of the process that in fifty years gradually transformed the neighborhood from an Irish to an Italian enclave. This process is at the same time centrifugal and directly connected with increasing economic and social conditions, and centripetal and directly connected to the new migrants coming and fueling the unskilled, low-wage labor reserve.

But before the Italians another important ethnic group settled in the North End for a relatively short period of time, although they became an important factor in the change of the social landscape of the neighborhood. These were the Jews, mostly from Russia and other eastern European countries.

The Jewish Diasporas

The Jewish immigrants settled in a triangular area nearly one-quarter mile on each side, extending roughly from Hanover Street to Endicott Street and back to Prince Street, Salem, Cross, Stillman, North Margin,

and Parmenter Streets, Baldwin, Salem, Noyes, and Bartlett Place were
included. There were other earlier Jewish settlements in Boston, but they
were composed mainly of German Jews. . . . Regarded as outsider by the
more westernized German Jews, they formed a separate settlement in
the North End. (Todisco 1976, 30)

In less than twenty years the Jewish population in the North End almost doubled,
increasing from thirty-five hundred in 1880 to sixty-two hundred in 1895, constituting 26 percent of the local inhabitants. According to Wieder (1962, 18),[37]
the Jews settling in the North End should not be considered an amorphous whole.
There were not only distinctions between German Jews and Jews coming from
the Russian empire but also even inside the latter many divisions existed based on
locality and different Yiddish dialects, Hebrew pronunciation, and religious traditions. Settlers in the North End, even if from mixed origins, seemed to have
more of a *Litvak* character, while the West End, for instance, was more *Russiche*.

The pattern of Jewish migration is very much different from the Irish and
also from the Italian. While the Irish and Italians were, in general, extremely
poor and unskilled peasants, the Jewish were more oriented to small trades. They
landed in Boston with more resources. Therefore they were not stuck in the
North End but could choose to stay and to start a business that was not immediately connected with the neighborhood. Jewish peddlers traveled to sell their
goods; they were not forced by economic reasons to stay and work in the area.

The main reasons why they chose the North End were first because they
were not welcome in other Jewish neighborhoods by German Jews (for instance,
the South End or the West End), and second because of the cheap housing and
the possibility of commuting by ferry or by land to different parts of the city or
even different towns. In other words, what for the Irish was an extreme difficulty became a basic resource for the Jews.

According to Wieder (1962, 25–26), it is true that the Jewish migrants
moved away from conditions similar to the Irish or the Italians but their economic background was different: in Europe they were tradesmen, not peasants.
Therefore, in America they maintained the same economic activity. The tradition of small trade could be continued because of the economic demand of the
city and because of the support of the ethnic community.

Around the end of the century, a large percentage of Jews in the North End
were peddlers. As soon as they landed in the North End they "took the basket,"
filling it with needles, shoelaces, ribbons, and yarns or the "pack on the back,"[38]
containing more valuable goods such as pillowcases, sheets, towels, dresses, and
so forth. Interestingly, one of Wieder's consultants reported that one of the first
sentences in English learned by the peddlers was "Look in the basket."

The opportunity to start peddling immediately after landing was the result
of the credit arrangements available in the community. As Wieder reported
from an interview:

When an immigrant arrived and wanted merchandise for peddling, they would talk to [the owner of a peddlers' supply store] and if he appeared honest they would give him fifty dollars credit. When he paid the amount, he would get more credit. (1962, 27)

The peddler's system was complex: the new peddler was aided by other peddlers in order to find a "new" area for new customers, and profit was possible because of the installment plans affordable for the average customer. The peddler could sell an item and collect a small amount of money for it every week. This plan increased clients and, consequently, the profit. The profit, a few dollars for an entire week of strenuous work, was divided basically into three parts: living expense, reinvestment in new merchandise, and collecting enough money to bring some loved one to the United States.

Because peddling was a very hard job, as soon as a peddler accumulated enough funds he would tend to open a store or even a peddlers' supply store in the North End. This also shows the perceived social strata inside the Jewish community. The leading group was constituted by the owners of peddlers' supply stores, followed by the owners of retail stores. The peddlers were considered below the storekeepers but above people working manually, such as tailors and shoemakers.

Because of the ambition and aggressiveness of the Jewish newcomers, in a few years the North End became one of the most active shopping districts,[39] filled with Kosher butchers, bakers, delicatessens, clothiers, tailors, and food markets, mostly concentrated on Salem Street and in the adjacent blocks.

Using again the perspective of vernacular landscapes analysis, the transformation of the neighborhood can also be seen in the change of real estate ownership and, consequently, in the architecture. I have already described the condition of the tenements at the end of the nineteenth century. At the time of the Jewish settlement, the old houses were already transformed into tenements and boardinghouses to receive the expanding demand for housing related to Irish migration. Despite decay, the houses were still solid and sturdy, so Jewish real estate businessmen found them convenient to refurbish, making them more livable. They started building "apartment houses" in the North End, which were more comfortable and livable than the "tenement houses." Again, this was possible because of the entrepreneurial ability, based on a complex mortgage system available to acquire many of the decayed tenement buildings left by Irish heading to South Boston.

In many instances, 100% of the purchase money was available through Jewish mortgage brokers representing first mortgage financiers. By requiring that these brokers place second mortgages in their own name, first mortgage holders were secure enough to offer 5–6% mortgage rates. Utilizing such readily available financing, Jews soon owned substantial portions of the North End housing and commercial space by the 1890s. Capitalizing on their ownership, they often either gutted whole buildings and subdivided them into apartments or they tore them down, replacing them with new construction.[40]

Besides the economic ties among the Jewish community of the North End, religion had a central, even if controversial, role. According to Wieder (1962, 45–52, 67), the orthodox approach of first-generation settlers, which recapitulated patterns of European Jewish religious life, was contrasted to a strong Reform movement, more "liberal" and, in the long run, more accepted by second and following generations. Cole reported a Jewish North Ender saying: "'My father prays every day; I pray once a week; my son never prays'" (1902, 277). But at least at the beginning of the twentieth century the attendance at religious services was still remarkably high. The description offered by Cole of religious services during the Atonement season is characteristic:[41]

> Within the Baldwin Place synagogue the scene is strange and impressive. The entire floor of the place is a solid mass of men and boys, while the galleries are crowded with women and girls. All heads are covered, and in addition every male has over his shoulders a "prayer shawl"— a scarf of silk or linen with curiously knotted fringe at the ends. The older men are clad also in long garments of white linen, the robes of their burial. Upon a raised platform around the reading-desk are grouped the readers who have been called up from the congregation, the cantor in his raiment of white and gold, and the members of the choir, wearing black robes and turbans. At the right and left of the "ark," in the "chief seats," sit the president and other officials, or "rulers," of the synagogue. An ever-burning lamp, symbol of Jehovah's presence, hangs high over all. (279)

In general, the Jewish community prospered and, in an accelerated centrifugal process, soon moved out of the neighborhood toward Roxbury, Chelsea, Revere, Dorchester, and Brookline. By 1920, only a few signs of the Jewish presence were still evident in the North End. And what remains to this day is a pale Mogen David at Baldwin Place, a few discernible letters of the sign "Hebrew School" on Jerusalem Place off Salem Street, and the impalpable but extraordinary heritage of the social change in the neighborhood.

The Italian Diasporas

It is possible to trace early Italian settlers in the Irish enclave, anticipating the migrants' wave at the end of the nineteenth century. With high probability, the first Italian immigrant in the North End, Marquis Niccolò Reggio from Genova, arrived in the North End in 1832. This Italian businessman was a shipowner who contributed to the expansion of the shipping trade in the city, and who settled in the neighborhood probably to be close to his business. He served as consul in Boston for the Papal States, Spain, and the kingdoms of Sardinia and of the two Sicilies. Reggio, even if an atypical immigrant, is representative of the early examples of Italians in the United States.[42] In Boston, Reggio and "exotic" migrants like him were well accepted. The same thing cannot be said about the Italians who fifty years later started to populate the area.

By the 1860s, a first and atypical Italian settlement was developing in the area around Ferry Court and North Street, and by the 1880s also on Cross Street and North Bennet Street. This first Italian ethnic enclave was relatively small in number: almost two hundred Genoese (De Marco 1981, 21) were residents in the North End. Not exotic like Marquis Reggio but also profoundly different from the generally unskilled peasants from southern Italy of the following decades, the Genoese were mostly merchants, trading fruit, such as Alessandro Badaracco, owner of the largest fruit business in Boston, or wine, oil, and so on.[43] Food shops were opened by Genoese migrants such as Luigi and Pietro Pastene.[44]

Data concerning Italian immigration to Boston in the 1880s is generic and relatively reliable. A general idea is provided by a report written by the Italian vice-consul in Boston at that time, Vittorio Thaon di Revel.[45] The Italian colony in the Boston area, almost eleven thousand people from 1885 to 1886,[46] was largely composed of Genoese (45 percent). Other northern Italians were listed, from Lombardia and Piemonte (7 percent) and Toscana (5.45 percent), but also the southern Italians were represented: from Avellino (27.3 percent), Calabria (7.3 percent), Campobasso (2.7 percent), and from Caserta, Abruzzo, and Benevento (3.6 percent). Interestingly, the Italian source also provides information about fields of work: northern Italians were mostly traders and artisans, therefore more oriented to a definitive, permanent stay; southern Italians, with few exceptions such as barbers (mostly Neapolitans), tailors, and masons (in general from Toscana), were unskilled farm laborers (so-called *braccianti*) and more oriented to seasonal emigration, to be the birds-of-passage depicted in the usual pattern. The large percentage of unskilled workers is a major reason for ethnic tension with the Irish. Competition in a relatively small, specific job market, above all construction work, often led to fights that are still preserved in the memory of the social groups. It is important to state that the Irish, after more than fifty years of immigration, were starting a centrifugal movement to more attractive residential areas because of their social expansion.

Thaon di Revel's report also provides data regarding economic condition and perspectives of the Italian colony: on one hand, the Genoese, the wealthy part of the Italian population oriented to trade, saving, and reinvestment; and on the other hand, the southern Italian immigrants, unskilled, illiterate, non-English-speaking, but still preferable to the Irish because they were said to be sober and respectful. Thaon di Revel remarked that, aside from seamstresses, laborers, some peddlers, and a few artisans, in the North End many people earned their living picking rags in the dumps or even by searching through the street's garbage. The difference between northern and southern Italians also could be noted through other economic and, more generally, social data. As observed by Sherman (1904, 671) at the end of the nineteenth century a northern Italian entered the United States with an average of $21.70 *pro capite*, a southern Italian only had $9.25. Southern Italians were more birds-of-passage, as already noted, therefore the tendency to save for a better economic condition in Italy for the migrant and the family led also to a very low standard of living. Sherman (ibid.) also noted that southern Italian migrants were willing to pay no more than $0.30 for weekly rent, and no more than $1.00 for living expenses. This trend was associated with poverty and criminality. According to Martellone unlike the Genoese who were basically not involved in any sort of crime, the increasing southern Italian population had a high crime rate. This was said to be because the southern Italians were "especially licentious and passionate" and easily broke the law due to their jealousy and inclination to quarrel (1973, 211)[47]. This data is misleading and, like in the case of the Irish mentioned before, can cause confusion between causative variables and intervening variables. It bears an implicit essentialism, defining "characters" and "inclinations" of an ethnic group. Specifically, this data does not say anything about the class opposition between laborers for the market of unskilled jobs, a clash because it maintained low wages by the replacement of long-standing immigrant workers with new and cheaper immigrants. I am arguing here that being and/or becoming Italian (and how and why this is accomplished) must be an object of discussion,[48] no matter what side of the Atlantic we are on; similarly being and/or becoming white is a complex historical journey, as Roediger (1991) and Jacobson (1997; 2006) have demonstrated. Southern Italians for a long time were considered "in-between" categories (Orsi 1992, 314). People from southern Italy had little identification with the new Italian nation-state, and racial categories, such as "Africans" or "Turks," were used against them by northern Italians. Also notable American politicians such as Henry Cabot Lodge distinguished the "Teutonic Italians" (northern Italians) from the dark-skinned southern Italians.[49]

The Italian settlements in the North End, featuring ethnic enclaves based on the village of origin in Italy, chain migration based on kinship and friendship, familial strategies modeled on an almost endogamic pattern, seem to encourage the notion of inner separations, but again we have to analyze the historical and social dynamics that produced and reinforced the racial idea and the discrimination of the ethnic group, which build symbolic and territorial boundaries in a twofold (self-ascriptive and ascriptive by others) process of the constitution of ethnicity.

Italian Ethnic Enclaves

The 1880s were an important turning point in the ethnic fabric of the North End. For the first time after years of massive migration of the Irish the population began declining.[50] From a population of almost twenty-six thousand inhabitants of the neighborhood, sixteen thousand were Irish (see table 2.1).

The centrifugal shift of the Irish was combined with the arrival of new immigrants from eastern Europe (the Russian Jews) and eouthern Europe (the southern Italians). As we have seen, for them the North End was the area where they were allowed to land, because of cheap rent, the proximity to workplaces for unskilled workers, or, as in the Jews' case, because of close and affordable lines of communication and trade. Important general push factors, that resemble the general patterns of emigration to the United States for the two groups, are immediately recognizable: in the case of Russian Jews, the end of the nineteenth century was characterized by pogroms and persecutions by the Russian government. In the case of the southern Italians the unification of the country did not bring the expected social changes but instead increased taxation and unfavorable government politics.

The census of 1895 reported that the number of Italians in the North End reached seventy-seven hundred, while the Jewish numbered sixty-two hundred. This is a considerable increase from the almost one thousand Italians and the few hundred Jews present in the neighborhood in the 1880s.

The Genoese community still lived in the Ferry Court area and on North Bennet Street until the first decade of the twentieth century, when, according to De Marco, they "felt uncomfortable living in a now predominantly southern Italian neighborhood" (1981, 24). When they left they were replaced not by other northern Italians, who already preferred to emigrate to South America, but by other southern Italians.

Another ethnic enclave can be found in the area bounded by Prince, Salem, Tileston, and Hanover streets, which was inhabited by *Abruzzesi* and a few *Napoletani* (De Marco 1981, 23) The area bounded by Hanover Street, North Square, and Fulton Street saw the growth of *Avellinesi*, coming from Taurasi, Chiusano San Domenico, and Mirabella Eclano, as well as from Montemarano and Montefalcione. The Sicilians, with an important community from Sciacca, came to Boston at a later time, populating the area around North Street, and also taking the place of the Genoese group in Ferry Court. The settlement pattern is well known and self-evident: the Italians tended to cluster together on the basis of the village of origin, in relatively small enclaves.

To better understand this phenomenon it is necessary to analyze the Italian scenario at the end of the nineteenth century and the patterns of settlements in the United States. I will argue the necessity of deconstructing the idea of Italianness (see Vecoli 1964) and proposing, according to Gabaccia (1999), Italy as a place of many diasporas, suggesting that migrants became Italians only on arrival in the receiving country. In reference to this transformation, I

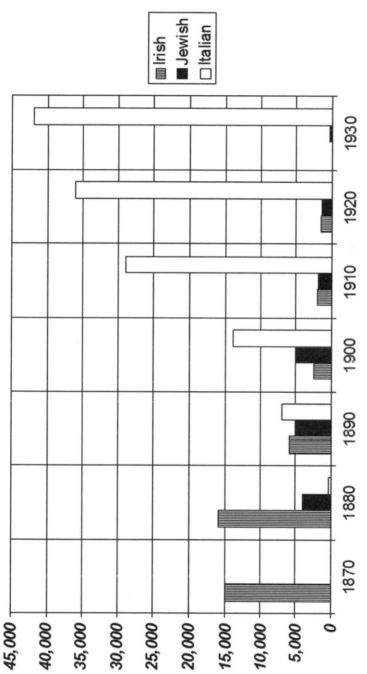

TABLE 2.1 Ethnic Variations in the North End, 1870–1930

want to repeat the famous sentence of the Italian political leader Massimo D'Azeglio immediately after the military unity of the country: "Abbiamo fatto l'Italia, adesso dobbiamo fare gli Italiani" ("We made Italy, now we must make Italians"). This was exactly the scenario of Italy at the end of the nineteenth century. It was a country politically united but profoundly divided in terms of history, culture, and economics. Behind the myth of the Roman Empire (consciously used in the fascist times to build the sense of the nation) and Dante's language, the new country was united after centuries of Spanish, Austrian, and French domination. Each region had a different dialect, very far from the officially imposed Tuscan-Italian, which generally was spoken only in that region or between intellectuals. In terms of identity and belonging, people used to define themselves, for instance, as *Napoletani, Siciliani, Lombardi, Sciaccatani*, and *Montefalcionesi*. Self-definition was based on a local, sometimes a regional, perspective. It is ironic that individuals leaving Italy during the time of mass migration from the late nineteenth century to the early twentieth century had no concept of being Italian.

According to historian Rudolph Vecoli, for instance, the sentiment of regionalism (or, better, *campanilismo*—the overwhelming spirit of local, parochial belonging, symbolically expressed by the *campanile*, the bell tower of the parish) undermined any sense of unity of Italians:

> [E]ach regional group regarded those from other regions with their strange dialects and customs not as fellow Italians, but as distinct and inferior ethnic types. . . . The experience did not create a sense of nationality among the Italians strong enough to submerge their parochialism. (1964, 413)

They became Italians in America, when confronting other immigrants.[51] Finally, according to Gabaccia, Italy is a place of many diasporas:

> Without clear national identities in the nineteenth century, Italy's migrants could scarcely form a single Italian Diaspora. They did, however, form many village- and region-based Diasporas that overlapped and intersected in particular neighborhoods and workplaces in many receiving countries around the world. . . . Italy's Diasporas were Diasporas of residents of a single town, such the *biellesi* from Biella, or of a region, such the *siciliani* from Sicily. (1999, 1124)

Combining the situation of the sending country with the most important mechanisms from the host society—that is chain migration and the chain occupation processes—the urban landscape of the immigrants almost inevitably became a sort of kaleidoscope of ethnic enclaves, defined as functional equivalents for the villages and family networks.

What is important to observe is the dichotomy of perception: on the one hand a sort of etic perspective, from the observer-outsider point of view, recognizing the general and totalizing characteristic of the enclaves as Italians. On the other hand, instead, lays a more emic concern, from the observed-insider point of view, where it is possible to recognize the many facets of different origin. Therefore, I prefer not to speak about the North End as an "Italian neighborhood," as it is usually identified by the outsider, but about the "Sicilian section" or "Neapolitan settlement" in the neighborhood, as the insiders prefer.

But when and how were the ethnic enclaves in Boston's North End made? Through what sort of mechanisms? If a village-based campanilismo is the cultural reference point carried from the sending country, chain migration is the principal engine of constitution of ethnic enclaves in the receiving country. Synthetically, these mechanisms occur when earlier migrants encouraged other family members or members of the same village to migrate and helped locate employment for them. The pattern of these mechanisms can vary. For instance, it is important to analyze not only individual behavior but also the role of societies, such as the religious society and/or society for mutual aid in the context of migration.

First, I will analyze chain migration mainly through the words of actual North Enders who carry on the group memory, as it in this interview with Jerry D. P.:

Augusto: The people from Montefalcione they all lived in the same area?

Jerry: Right here, they lived around here.

Augusto: How did they come here?

Jerry: My father came here, his uncle was living down on Cooper Street, he holds the house. He came over in the late nineteenth century, he came here and he brought his wife and his kids, and the next thing he brought my father with them. And he went to work and all started to work. They all came here as laborers. A lot of them worked digging the subways, a lot of them worked doing longshore works, just all kind of things, someone was, you know . . . all kind of jobs. I remember my father went out with few people, all saying the story they went to Canada for construction work. Then they still weren't citizens, they were illegitimate, had to sneak back to get back to the United States through the Vermont border, because they worked up there and they came back. And the next thing they met the girlfriends and their wives here, like my father. He married here, he married the girlfriend from the paese he was born and a lot of them started to make money so they moved to East Boston, some moved to the West End, some moved to Somerville.

Jerry's narrative highlights many characteristics of the chain migration: recall mechanism (Jerry's uncle was already here with his wife and kids and he brought Jerry's father), job niches (Jerry's father and uncle were able to find a job for him as an unskilled laborer as construction worker), conjugal strategies (Jerry's father was married in the United States, but with a girlfriend from the *paese*), and group solidarity (the financing of the trip was not only an exclusive matter of individuals but of societies and groups of mutual aid).

Besides campanilismo, vaguely referring to a general and shared cultural frame, another possible and more specific reason for ethnic differentiation can be seen in terms of language: with few exceptions, at the end of the century, migrants as well as the people in the village of origin did not speak the Italian language, which was the Tuscan dialect imposed after the unification of the country and spoken previously between intellectuals and the upper classes. Dialect was very often the only language known, and communication was not easy. This is so even today, as I know from a personal experience in the North End. One Saturday morning I was at the Fishermen's Club, where the Sciaccatani gather together to play cards, chat, or just enjoy the company of friends. An old man came close to me asking if it was true that I was doing research on the club and the migrants. As soon as I told him that this was the reason why I was at the club, he asked me to interview him because he could tell me a lot of things since he was one of the older emigrants, having come to Boston at the end of the 1920s as a child. I immediately asked him if we could tape the conversation and he answered me affirmatively but also said that he wanted to be interviewed in Italian. Of course I agreed; but with great embarrassment a few minutes later, I asked him to switch to English. The reason was that he was using a very old form of Sicilian dialect. I am fluent in Roman and Neapolitan dialects and I can understand the "modern" Sicilian and other southern Italian dialects, but I was not prepared for the Sciaccatano from the end of the 1920s.

The importance of dialect as a social boundary is often underestimated by scholars but it is a strong identifying and unifying tool as well as force for separating. The following interview with Pietro and Salvatore, two old sailors and members of the Madonna del Soccorso Society, shows the same pattern of chain migration but also of the importance of the dialect for the Sciaccatani:

Augusto: All the people in this area were Sciaccatani?

Pietro: Yes, all Sciaccatani, provincia di Agrigento, Sicily. Tutti erano, you know, li parenti nostri che conoscevano a tutti pecchè erano de lu stesso paise. E cà in America niuno parlava Americano tutti parlavano Sciaccatano. Io sognu nato cà, down on these streets, ma nuie parlaveme sciaccatano, pecchè mio padre e mia madre parlavano sciaccatano a casa. My father and mother also spoke Italian. We went to school over here, when eravamo piccoli and that's the way it was. I genitori nostri, padri, madri . . . mia mamma nun ha mai lavurato, stava a la casa. Sulo o patre, chesta era la tradizione siciliana. Patreme era piscatore e sto giuvinotto cà (*tapping on Pietro's shoulder*) (Pietro: giuvinotto? ma che giuvino', io sugno Cristiano[52]) faceva 'o macchinista pe la barca de mio patre. Then he bought my father's barca. And the fishermen here were all Sicilian. Do you see all the boats over here (*pointing to a picture on the wall*)? You can't see anymore, are all gone.

[Yes, all Sciaccatani, from Agrigento, Sicily. Everybody, you know, our relatives they knew everybody because they came from the same village. And here in America nobody could speak English, they used to speak Sciaccatano. I was born here, down on these streets, but we were talking Sciaccatano, because my father and my mother were talking Sciaccatano at home. My father and mother also spoke Italian. We went to school over here, when we were kids and that's the way it was. Our relatives, fathers, mothers . . . my mother never worked, she took care of home. Only my father, this is the sicilian tradition. My father was a fisherman and this young man here (*tapping on Pietro's shoulder*) (Pietro: Young man? What young man? I am Christian) was the engineer for my father's ship. Then he bought my father's ship. And the fishermen here were all Sicilian. Do you see all the boats over here (*pointing to a picture on the wall*)? You can't see anymore, are all gone.]

Pietro and Salvatore again suggest the importance of chain migration, in this case based on work niches, pointing out the Sciaccatani as fishermen.

The structure of the ethnic enclaves is also highlighted in the following interview with Sal "Bosco" Dieciduc, then president of the Fishermens' Society. He pointed out not only the reason for the settlement in the specific area, but also the difficulties of leaving the ethnic enclaves, even if only to move a few blocks away.

Augusto: It seems to me the structure of the village. So if I understood, Sal, the Sciaccatani used to live almost on the same street—

Sal: Primarily they lived in North Street, Fleet Street, Clark Street, any way where they could face the water, because they were fishermen. When my mother was born they all lived in one building. My mother was the last one to get married, she was the youngest, and the sisters they all got married but they all lived close to one another. His grandmother (*looking at Dominic*) was one of the first move-away, from North Street, she moved four block down, and they all wear black, they cried, because she has a bad heart and she couldn't climb the stairs so the apartment the daughter told to go to was only a couple of step up but all the sisters were crying because she left the neighborhood and they were only a couple of streets, it was near the fire station.

Augusto: So it was very close.

Sal: Yes, but they were not Sciaccatani. And they drove! Joe, his poor grandfather has to pick up all the sisters, putting in the car and drive them there. They won't walk. And then he dropped them off and when he dropped them off he waited, look out the window, and then they go home.

The growth of the Italian ethnic enclaves, of course, brought changes in the social dynamics of the neighborhood. An important arena of these dynamics was the development of local Catholic churches. Two important Irish churches were already established in the North End: St. Mary's, run by the Jesuits, and St. Stephen's, on Hanover Street, built by Bulfinch. In the last quarter of the nineteenth century two other Catholic churches were inaugurated in the North End to assist Italian immigrants: St. Leonard's, on Prince Street, opened in 1874 and the Sacred Heart, in North Square, opened in 1890.[53] Despite the growing presence of Italians, Saint Leonard's Church still was predominantly for Irish settlers, who economically sustained the new worship place. This was a partial, yet not completely satisfying, answer to the needs of the Italian community. Therefore the Genoese settlers organized the San Marco Society,[54] with the specific purpose of building an exclusively Italian church, to be conducted according to the system of the *fabbriceria*.[55] In 1884, the newly constituted society bought Father Taylor's Seamen's Bethel, a Protestant church, in North Square.[56] One year later, the San Marco Society asked Bishop Williams for formal recognition as a religious society and to consecrate the church as an Italian parish.[57] Bishop Williams denied the requests, probably following the advice of some opponents worried about the possible transgressive spirit of the society, as Martellone (1973, 269) points out. Or perhaps this struggle should be considered in the more general framework of the difficult relationship between the Irish Catholic hierarchy and the Italian settlers in the United States. But it seems evident that the main obstacle was the proposed organization of the church by the fabbriceria system. The San Marco Society sent Tommaso Brichetto as emissary to the Vatican, just to obtain the necessary documents to proceed following the hierarchical line. In a letter sent by Cardinal Simeoni,[58] a member of the Sacra Congregazione De Propaganda Fide, to Bishop Scalabrini, dated September 8, 1888, he wrote:

Non so se l'E.V. sappia, che a Boston havvi una congregazione di Italiani, la quale ha chiesa propria, ma che non vuole dipendere, non so perchè, dal clero locale. Quella povera gente, che ascende a parecchie migliaia, si raduna tutte le feste nella chiesa stessa; vi canta il Kirie, il Gloria, il Credo, ecc. e vi recita il Rosario. Vi ritorna poi la sera per il canto dei Vespri e per la seconda recita del Rosario, il tutto e sempre senza alcun prete. Non vuol saperne di usare alle chiese loro destinate da quell'Arcivescovo. Io pertanto, dietro ripetute istanze di quei coloni, ho creduto bene di inviare colà P. Zaboglio Segretario Generale della nostra Congregazione, per vedere se e come si potrebbe rimediare al grave disordine: speriamo, qualora l'Arcivescovo vi consenta, mi affretterò a spedire colà anche due missionari con qualche catechista. Ma di ciò non mancherò di scriverle altra volta.

[I do not know if Your Eminence knows that in Boston there is a congregation of Italians, having their own church, but that they do not want to relate with the local clergy, I do not know for what reason. These poor people, several thousand, for every feast gather at the church, singing the Kirie, the Gloria, the Credo, etc. and reciting the Rosary. They come back in the evening for the Vespers and the second Rosary, always without a priest. They do not want to use the churches indicated by the Archbishop. Therefore, after the continuous suggestions of the settlers, I thought to send there F. Zaboglio, General Secretary of our Congregation, to see if and how it would be possible to solve the disorder: I hope, if the Archbishop will agree, that I will quickly send two missionaries and some catechists. But I will write to you about it another time.]

The letter highlights two fundamental points in the evolution of the Italian religious assistance in the United States: first, the fear of transgressive, even heretical, behaviors;[59] and second, the attention that the new organized congregation of Scalabrini fathers devoted to the problem of the immigrants.[60]

The controversy was finally concluded thanks to the mediation of father Francesco Zaboglio. The church was formally sold to the archdioceses with the specific condition that it be dedicated to the needs of the Italian community. The Scalabrini fathers would be appointed as overseers. On May 25, 1890, the church was consecrated and dedicated to the Sacred Heart.

The evolution of ethnic expression can be seen also in social tensions between different ethnic groups, especially the Irish and the Italians. The Irish were leaving the neighborhood to the new southern Italian settlers, but still they were fighting for supremacy in the North End, a battle that later moved on political fields but in the late 1800s was fought in the streets, every day. Since 1860, according to Whyte (1939, 626), Ferry Court, the southeast side of North Street, basically all the area around Ferry Street, was a stage for this sort of ethnic tension. Gangs of young Irish gathered outside the many bars and dance halls, sometimes hidden in dark alleys, to assault drunks and the easily recognizable Italians. Twenty years later the second-generation Italians still had a controversial coexistence with the Irish. The reason was conflicts about the sexual lives of the young generation. Italian boys hoped to meet Irish girls in the local ballrooms (or even in the West End the South End, East Boston, and Charlestown), rather than Italians, who were rigidly controlled by the family.

This led almost inevitably to fights and aggression. Whyte reported the following interview with an Italian describing this atmosphere:

> We could dance better than the Irish, so we could take their girls. . . .
> But always before the evening was over, we would run into a fight. The
> Irish would get after us. Some one would whistle, and we would all
> get together and have it out. We were prepared with black jacks and
> brass knuckles. . . . We had to expect a fight, but that way we got to
> know the girls, and then we would make dates with them. Sometimes
> they would come down to the North End, and we would treat them to
> a plate of spaghetti or some Italian food. . . . They seemed to like us
> better than the Irish fellows, because we spent more money on them.
> It wasn't that we had more money, but we saved more than the Irish
> fellows, so we could afford it. (1939, 627)

This ethnic tension between the Irish and the Italians continued even after the Irish moved out of the North End. The memory of the fights in the 1930s and 1940s on the Charlestown Bridge is even now still alive, and it is an important element of negotiation and construction of identities. Jason A., a member of the Saint Anthony Society, talking about his own perceived ethnic identities, once told me:

> . . . I feel Italian when I fight against the Irish or when we watch the
> soccer games on TV . . . . [61]

Quite interestingly Jason used the present, even if this kind of events belongs more to the narrated group memory rather than to the historical present.

Relations between the Italians and the Jews were different, probably because they were based more on commercial trades. Lia Tota, director of the ABCD social program in the North End, talking about the relationship between Italians and Jews, reported:

> Molti degli ebrei avevano dei negozietti, erano persone d'affari, e così
> dunque quando son vissuti insieme quel che è successo è che l'ebreo ha
> imparato a parlare l'italiano. E così c'erano molti ebrei che parlavano
> l'italiano qui.

> [Mostly the Jews held little shops, they were businessmen, therefore
> when they lived together what happened is that the Jew learned to
> speak Italian. There were many Jews speaking Italian here.]

Salvatore, a member of the Fishermen's Society, told me this anecdote, confirming the importance of speaking "Italian":

And now I tell you a short story, there was a Jewish butcher, Julius, one of the best guys I met, he was a very handsome man, but he was very respectful. He could speak at least eight dialects in Italian. Notably in this area there were Sicilians but also *Genoesi, Abruzzesi, Avellinesi,* even *Calabresi.* There was a lot of mix. And there were Portuguese, Spanish, we all got along good. So this guy, Julius, "How much do you owe me? Don't worry about it" he got a piece of paper, you bought soup meat with the bones, he didn't charge for the bones. He said, "Give me twenty-five cents for the meat and the bones" and you could feed six or seven of us. This is the way we grew up.

Sense of community and/or sense of business can be easily seen in this tale: Julius is a good guy. He does not need to charge even for the bones. He is a member of this community. He is respected and respectful. And he knows that this community is fragmented, therefore he learns how to speak eight different dialects. He shows a sense of business but also a sense of community. The question is and will remain, What kind of community? Of course, in the first place I am talking about a growing community that in 1925 had more than forty thousand people, of which about 90 percent were Italians or of Italian descent. But within this community social changes and internal divisions were evident in the neighborhood: from an area populated almost exclusively by unskilled workers it became a place where prominent professionals began to appear at the turn of the century so that there were a large number of lawyers and medical doctors. The progressive change can be seen through the pages of *La Gazzetta del Massachusetts*, which contained numerous advertisements offering these services. And this leads to another important signal of the need for and the making of self-representation of the area: the newspaper. In 1896, *La Gazzetta del Massachusetts*, the first newspaper of the neighborhood,[62] initially written in Italian, was first published by James Donnarumma. The *Gazzetta* (and the following *Post-Gazette*, still published) is definitely the oldest and the more important local newspaper, but it was not the only one. Emanuele Lo Presti was the founder of *La Notizia*, with an initial socialist spirit. In 1921, the *Italian News* was issued, interested in local news but also in national and international events. Other newspapers or magazines, directly or indirectly involved with the social life of the North End, were the satiric *Il Rigoletto*, from 1916; the weekly *Il Moscone*, from the beginning of the twentieth century; and the *Vita Italiana*, from 1907, but with a very short life. In this journalistic landscape the figure of Aldino Felicani stands out. Felicani was a Tuscan anarchist forced to leave Italy in 1914. In 1918, he settled in Boston's North End as a printer. Felicani is probably better known for organizing the support group for the defense of Bartolomeo Sacco and Nicola Vanzetti in the 1920s but certainly he was the preeminent antifascist in Boston's area.[63] He founded the *Agitazione* (1920–1925) and the *Lantern* (1927–1929) in order to support the two anarchists; and, in 1938, he founded the *Controcorrente*, published first in Italian, then, in 1939, in Italian and English, with the purpose of denouncing fascist politics and its development in Boston.

The differentiation of the newspapers in the North End shows inner social differences in a heterogeneous social group: if at that time the *Gazzetta del Massachusetts* can be considered, with some exception, the voice of middle-class Italians such as *notabili* (professionals and/or intellectual elite) or *prominenti* (businessmen, owning real estate) (Martellone 1973, 309), the *Lantern* is a political newspaper targeting workers who were still mostly unskilled. If the first supported the moderated American Federation of Labor, exalting the Italian participation at Labor Day parades, the second sided with the socialist International Workers of the Word, commemorating the First of May and the anarchists killed in Chicago. And if, on one hand, the *Gazzetta*, in 1905,[64] trying to downsize the importance of the local anarchist movement, wrote

> È avvenuto in Boston un piccolissimo e ridicolo movimento conciona-torio che ha sbrigato la fervida fantasia della polizia metropolitana. Una quindicina di buoni e pacifici lavoratori, riuniti in North Square intorno a quattro giovanotti predicanti l'anarchismo, furono la causa di tanto subbuglio.

> [In Boston a small and ridiculous movement awakened the fervid fantasy of the local police. The cause of the turmoil was the gathering together in North Square of some fifteen good and peaceful workers, combined with a few young anarchist agitators.]

then on the other hand, the *Lantern* later publicly declared its support of the movement. In the North End the anarchists found a fertile ground for their ideas and this is connected with a specific pattern: the male serial migration. According to Robert Pascoe this type

> contained the most anarchists, the Vanzetti type. These men were "serial" in the sense of being part of long threads of kinship and camaraderie which stretched around the globe. Their eventual aim was to settle down back in their own province, but for the time being circulated around the world, learning and developing their individualist critique of social and industrial relations. (1983, 11)

Unskilled workers, mostly young bachelors who, as in the Sacco and Vanzetti case, lacked strong linkages to the local ethnic enclaves because they did not come from well-represented *paesi* were the ideal types of anarchists in Boston. With Buenos Aires, Boston was the principal center of anarchism in the Western world. In 1912, the *Cronaca Sovversiva*, probably the most popular anarchist journal of the area, was published in Lynn by Luigi Galleani. The organization to which Sacco and Vanzetti belonged was based in East Boston. In the North

End, according to Pascoe (1983, 11), the Hod Carriers' Union kept up a fierce antiwar campaign in the 1910s. It is well known how these supposedly political subversive activities were repressed. After the first strike in Lawrence in 1912, which had a very strong ethnic component,[65] almost one thousand people were arrested in New England with the accusation of being anarchists. After the second strike in 1919, the "red scare" was widely diffused, so that when in January 1919 the molasses tank on Commercial Street collapsed, forming a wave fifteen feet high with two million gallons flooding the North End and killing twenty-one people, the owners of the tank blamed the anarchists.

It is interesting to note that the Sacco and Vanzetti execution and the following funeral in the North End turned into a moment of ethnic solidarity, with little if any reference to their political ideas, but revealing contradictory, even schizoid, feelings. As Pascoe (1983, 16) highlights, using the now bilingual *Gazzetta* as an example,[66] the section written in English said one thing, assuring the English reader about the loyalty of the Italians and emphasizing no rash behavior in response to the imminent death of the two anarchists. But the Italian section said quite the opposite, emphasizing ethnic values for the Italian reader.

In the late 1920s, for the first time in its recent history, the North End's population saw a negative trend of growth. The basic reasons were the absolute necessity for open areas in the neighborhood and the consequent tearing down of old tenements as well as the slowing down of the immigration waves from southern Italy,[67] basically caused by the restrictive quota laws of the time and by the negative fascist attitude toward emigration. And, for the first time, it became possible to see a centrifugal movement of successful Italian immigrants and second-generation Italian Americans to suburban areas. This is also the time of a new centripetal movement, where nonimmigrants and non-Italians, attracted by low rent but also by the peculiar sense of community that the North End (at least superficially) seemed to offer, moved into the neighborhood. According to Todisco (1976, 45) several artists moved into the North End, including the painter and decorator Robert S. Chase, looking for a sort of Bohemian style of life. According to the 1930s census the population in the neighborhood dropped to twenty-one thousand.

The 1930s was the time, as I already demonstrated, of the dislocation of ethnic rivalry between the Irish and the Italians from the streets to the political arena. The connection between this world and the world of local criminality is explored by the sociological classic *Street Corner Society*, published by William F. Whyte in 1943. The importance of this book is unquestionable, but it is also clear that some of Whyte's hypotheses are objects of contention. As Boelen suggested, a first question is about the importance of the racket and the gangs in the life of the neighborhood:

> When interviewing the various "gang" members on the racket organization, I feared that I would meet with a flat denial to my questions

on racketeers because the stereotype of Italians suggests that they cover up, disavow, or trivialize their criminal activities, and adhere to the law of *omertà*, or total silence. Amazingly, everyone admitted that in Whyte's time, as much as in 1970 or 1988, there was a certain element of racketeers hanging about in Cornerville but that they were a small and secluded group. We are therefore confronted with two opposite opinions on the issue of racketeers in Cornerville. Whyte considered them a dominant group manipulating the neighborhood, whereas the inhabitants referred to racketeers as an isolated small group having no influence on their day-to-day activities. Who is one to believe in a follow-up study almost 50 years post factum? One is inclined to assume that the Italians did not like it that Whyte walked into their "backyard and saw the dirty laundry hanging," but Gans (1962), who studied an adjacent Italian neighborhood (some streets of Cornerville ran also into the area studied by Gans) only 14 years after SCS was published, mentioned that he encountered little evidence of delinquency while he lived there. Although he comprehensively analyzed the social structure of this community, he did not address racketeering in any detail. Gans mentioned that illegal work activities, such as gambling and even racketeering, were condoned, as long as their activities did not hurt the peer group society but were aimed at the outside world. Tolerance was further based on the restriction of their violence to their own associates and competitors. (1992, 11–12)

Quite interestingly, Sal Diecidue, then the president of the Fishermen Society from Sciacca, used the term "mystique" to describe this stereotypical idea of the North End's gangs considered by Whyte to be "the building blocks of the community-wide organization of the rackets:"

Way back twenty years ago there were certain people in the neighborhood they watched the neighborhood and they say you know you don't shit where you eat. And they watched the neighborhood too. If a guy from the neighborhood got out of hand could be a neighbor a guy that was a little crazy they talk to him first and after that you know they could convince him so you respected your neighborhood much more and people knew people all over the city knew don't come to the North End and do anything because they were some certain people on the corners they watch you. And people still believe that's happening still today. People have the perception that it is still happening today. The way I see people always were intrigued about it you know if they needed a favor they always came here, they don't know the boss they come to you because you are from the neighborhood so you may be an associate so they look at you if they need a favor there is a kind of mystique still today. There was no drugs, illegal activities were bookmaking, numbers, a lot of stuff falling off some trucks, you know the doors are open or . . . they drove on bumpy roads.

What Sal calls "mystique" is a practice of stereotypes demonstrating, on the one hand, from the point of view of the insider, the disemic process of a moment of cultural intimacy. In fact the description of Mafia—the "certain people watching the neighborhood"—widely considered as a denigrating Sicilian phenomenon (and Sal is a third-generation Sicilian American) is implicitly a reframing of a positive local moral response to an absence of local authorities (not the Italian state, of course, but local and general authorities in the United States). It is at the same time a defensive posture against these authorities and, being a sort of "interior ethnomyms," it promotes a sense of local cultural and moral autonomy and dignity (Herzfeld 1997a, 16). For instance, in the same interview, Therese Diecidue, Sal's wife, declared:

The perception of even nowadays is . . . envious because even now we still have a neighborhood that is contained by itself, we still practice our culture, we still have a sort of unity. I don't wanna say they are jealous because jealous is bad, but they are envious. A neighborhood that we know that if somebody is sick somebody will bring a bowl of soup.

And Sal:

The North End was not as wealthy [a place] but it was always safe. It was safe because everybody knew everybody. If a stranger walked by and my mother, his mother, someone looks out the window they don't know who that person was, they call up each other: "There is a stranger walking by." And everybody watch for everybody's children at the window. They were their own police force. We did have a police, you know, but the crime was very very low because like I said everybody watched everybody. In the building itself were mostly all family, cousins, aunts, everybody. We didn't hold the property but in my particular family all the sisters lived together, they were all married, and I ironically when my mother sister . . . was his grandmother? And his grandmother (*Sal point[s] to other people—Dominic, Joe, and Kevin—in the room. Therese is also in the room*), and as I said everybody is related but in the building . . . everybody . . . I lived in the first floor, my aunt lived in the second, another aunt lived in the third, another one lived across the streets, a cousins lived over here. We all watched each other.

Self-ascription in this case is clearly built on what Herzfeld (1997a, 22) called structural nostalgia, claiming for primordial characteristics evident also to the outsiders, even if easily misunderstood. How this process constitutes a strategic essentialism will be the object of discussion later, but it is worth noting the complex dialectical process. The disemic dynamic, in other words, belongs not only to the self-abscriptive construction of the local identity, but influences also the perception from the outside, by the others. Stereotypes are widely used not only to interpret the neighborhood, but even to relate with local representatives.

My critique of *Street Corner Society* therefore is mainly that Whyte's lack of knowledge of the Italian language and the Italian culture led him to hasty interpretations of local phenomena. The examples are again the corner boys, whom he saw as gangs gathering together, controlled by racketeers and politicians. In Whyte, there is no attention to the cultural background, to the preexisting social rules in the village of origin brought with the migrants to the North End. Rather, it is his lack of anthropological sensitivity that kept him from understanding the complex game of stereotype-making and using. He did not realize that he was moving on the sophisticated field of cultural intimacy. He did not pay attention to the dynamics of the disemic process that unveiled a complex negotiation of identities. And he made the crucial mistake by underestimating the peculiar social poetic emerging in—and from—the daily life of the community. Paradoxically, the participant observation method followed by Whyte only partially reveals the actors and their actions, and reveals even more projections from the author.

The 1930s saw another issue that again shows the Italian migrants in Boston to be a heterogeneous group: the degrees of support for the fascist regime in Italy. It is not enough to say that this support demonstrates the conservative approach to politics by the Italians. This is not confirmed by the local trend toward democratic candidates that is a historical characteristic of the neighborhood, from the Irish era up to recent years. Rather, support for Mussolini is not from a distaste for democracy, but has to be seen basically as a matter of cultural identification and ethnic declaration.[68] The principal center of fascist support was East Boston: in 1936, a parade took place where almost fifty thousand Italians rallied to support fascism. Interestingly, in Cambridge, many antifascist intellectuals, first of all Gaetano Salvemini, tried to bridge the gap with the Italian American community, with enormous difficulties. Pascoe reports Salvemini's statement illustrating the problematic of survival of the community:

> Most Italians of recent immigration have other problems on their hands than studying the constitution of either the United States, Italy or any other country. They have to earn their living. Not long ago one of these immigrants in Boston applied for citizenship. The judge asked him who was the President of the United States, who was the Governor of the Commonwealth, how many States form the Union, etc. The answer was a consistent: "I don't know." "Then, you don't know

anything?" "Mister Judge, do you know how many bananas they are to a bunch?" "No I don't." "Do you know how many bananas I have to sell every day to make a living?" "No, I don't." "Well, this is my business and that is your business." (1983, 19)

This is not an apolitical statement, rather it seems more an antipolitical one. From this point of view I agree with Pascoe in considering the local and administrative election to be more a business matter, an economic imperative. Moving onto the level of national elections or international politics then an ethnic identity, even an imaginary one, accentuated by the hegemonic fascist rhetoric, offered Italian immigrants a sense of ethnic pride and self-esteem. Naturally, an antipolitical statement such as the one reported by Salvemini does not only indicate the gap between community and intellectuals but also the defeat of the latter as capable of directing or at least influencing the local groups.

In the 1930s, a new trend became evident that later—and nowadays—can be considered one of the fundamental characteristics of the neighborhood: the food business. The North End, as a self-contained and marginalized area, always offered to the inhabitants bars, saloons, and restaurants, sometimes trying to attract people from outside but mostly for criminal purposes. At the end of the nineteenth century, the North End was already filled by very cheap little restaurants or *pizzerie*: it was possible to eat at La Bella Napoli, Il Garden Turin, La Stella, ristorante napoletano, or La Cucina della casareccia, for five, ten, or fifteen cents (Martellone 1973, 284). In 1909, according to the Boston City Directory, eight restaurants were active in the North End: Café Marliave (on Bosworth Street), Leverone and Porcella (on North Street), Parker House Restaurant (on School Street), Ponticelli and Palumbo (on Parmenter Street), and four others with no name: one in North Square, one in Garden Center, and two on North Street. In the 1930s, restaurants such as the Grotto Azura or Posillipo were renowned, attracting not only local customers but also outsiders. The food business, with a general appreciation for Italian cuisine and cookery, became important, then fundamental, for the local economy, with a deep influence on actual negotiations of ethnic identities, as I will demonstrate further.

This was the beginning of a social, cultural, and economic change, but still the neighborhood is a sort of slum, called, as Firey (1947, 171) reminds us, Boston's land of poverty. According to the 1940 census,[69] the North End was still overcrowded. Even if population declined from 21,111 in 1930 to 17,598 in 1940, the percentage of households with over 1.5 persons per room was 15.8 percent in the North End (as opposed to a 3.9 percent in Boston as a whole) and the population density was 924.3 persons per inhabited acre, impressively far from the 94.5 of Boston in general and even from other crowded neighborhoods such as the West End (369.7), the South End (349.3), Charlestown (255.1), or East Boston (203.4). The structural deterioration of the North End was shown by the 16.46 percent of the dwelling units defined by the census as in need of major repairs (compared with 9.32 percent for Boston in general). This seems somehow inevitable since 60 percent of the buildings in the North End were forty or more years old and 18 percent of them were eighty or more years old. In the 1940s the North End was still Italian: 93.77 percent of foreign-born white persons were Italians (5,940 of 6,335), and the overwhelming majority of native white residents were second- or third-generation Italians.

Applying George Simmel's ecological theory of space as an element of group persistence,[70] Firey (1947, 179), for the first time, theorized the residence in the district was based on distinctive values regarding occupation, family, pier's group choice, group membership, etc. In other words the North End could no longer be seen as the area of minimum choice or as a product of compulsion rather than design, such as was the case of the first settlement of the newcomers. Rather, it is "only by invoking once again the cultural component that space acquires its symbolic property as an instrumentality of value-consensus" (Firey 1947, 179). Therefore the social structure of the North End in the 1940s was the result of interactions of at least three patterns of association: the mutual aid societies, with a peculiar importance of the religious societies, the less or more structured groups of *paesani*—people coming from the same area of origin, and extended kinship, familiar and symbolic,[71] which can be seen as a product but also as a cause, since the mechanism of chain migration through familiar lines is fundamental for the specific migration phenomenon of the ethnic enclaves. Church, political and extralegal organizations contributed to the peculiar community life organization of the North End at that time.

Another important phenomenon became very evident in this era: the emigration from the North End. The centrifugal movement, starting in the 1930s, involved above all the second generation, the Italian Americans. The first generation, the Italian-born, constituted the 40.54 percent of the population, yet only 1,049 people moved out from the North End in the decade 1930–1940, the 23.58 percent. The second generation represented the 59.46 percent but they contributed 76.42 percent of people relocating outside the neighborhood. In other terms the second generation lost the 27.08 percent of their members, in contrast to 12.26 percent of their number for the first generation. The centrifugal movement was definitely an Italian American phenomenon. But this centrifugal movement, while demonstrating, according to Firey (1947, 179), no apparent affective attachment to the neighborhood as spatial area and assimilation into American values, nevertheless, the symbolic ties such as the return to the neighborhood for gathering with old friends, for specific foods, for attending the Sunday mass at Sacred Heart or Saint Leonard, and for the religious feast, confirms the importance of the North End as icon of the Italian community. Federico, a retired clerk, who emigrated in the United States in 1934 and in 1942 was enrolled in the American Army in Japan, offers an interesting narrative of this centrifugal movement during the World War II:

Durante la guerra nel 1942–43 gli italiani qua si hanno messo paura, tutta questa gente, che andavano a bombardare qui e allora sono andati fuori dal North End, perchè la Germania poteva venire a bombardare questo quartiere che era italiano.

[During the war in 1942–43 the Italians here were scared, all these people, that they could bomb here, then they went out from the North End, because the Germany could come here and bomb this neighborhood because it was Italian.]

Naturally the point is not the credibility of the tale or its historical foundation, but that through this tale the movement of the North Enders out of the neighborhood find a logic. It seems possible to see a moment of declared national identity, if—with my consultant—I interpret the fear of a possible German bombardment of the North End as a reaction to the fall of the fascist regime and the alliance of the new Badoglio's government in September 1943 with the United States against the German occupation.

After World War II immigration from Italy was still present but far from the mass phenomenon of the early decades of the century. It is a well-known stereotype that the Italian, above all southern Italian emigration, was direct, especially toward the United States. Mangione and Morreale (1993) have deconstructed this stereotype demonstrating how Argentina, France and other European countries were privileged destination as well as the United States. In the 1950s migration was still widely practiced in Italy but the trend was now internal, toward northern Italy where the postwar industrial reconstruction took place. Patterns of emigration to the United States at this time remained along the lines of chain migration, as family or friends sponsored the trip and assured the first job for unskilled or low skilled workers moving to the North End.

The process of change from a slum to a desirable area was slow. Using housing conditions as a variable in the 1960s the census still considered 30 percent of the dwellings to be deteriorated and 5 percent as dilapidated. But, even if the neighborhood was recognized as poor, other variables determined an increase in a now continuous centripetal movement of new settlers, mainly young urban professionals. A first factor of attraction was surely the low rent, but the perceived safety of the area became important as well: in 1958 (Todisco 1976, 51) the North End accounted for less than 1 percent of the juvenile delinquency figures in Boston.[72] For the first time in many years the neighborhood was described not as a slum but as a "model of city life" (Jacobs 1961), opposing the "ambience of the Italian way of life" to the hectic American way. This led to another pull factor: an appreciation for a community style life that was now evident in the area even for the outsiders. Hanover Street began to be populated by several Italian-style restaurants and other ethnic business, attracting tourists walking along the Freedom Trial and customers from the city at large. An overall economic prosperity became evident with the increasing value of real estate, even before the dramatic change of the 1970s. According to Todisco,"individual North Enders took advantage of the rising property of the 60s to undertake their own renewal projects to upgrade private property" (1976, 53). Both private and public buildings were restored in the North End: Cardinal Cushing approved the restoration of Saint Stephen in 1965, and the North End Branch Library designed by Carl Koch Associates was built in the same year. For the first time in the history of the North End ethnicity became an economic value, introducing an incentive for the local businesses to show themselves and the neighborhood to be Italian.

This phenomenon is not peculiar of Boston's North End. According to Krase (2006) a process of gentrification of socially marginal and working-class areas of central cities began in the 1960s. Space (and time) are used in the social and material construction of an urban middle class (Zukin 1987, 130): the Yuppie "invasion" of Boston's North End is just an example of this more general trend, when ethnic identity became a scarce resource as outsiders moved into the area during the 1970s. What is interesting is the dynamic between this social change and a strategic essentialism, claiming an authentic ethnic identity and reinforcing or even inventing whatever could symbolize Italian ethnicity, crucial for the economic prosperity of the North End.

According to the *1970 Census of Populations and Housing*, the residents of the North End numbered approximately ten thousand, with 63 percent declaring Italian descent. In 1980, with a decreased number of residents, now eight thousand, people declaring Italian descent were less than 50 percent of the entire population, with 3 percent native-born Italians. In the 1990s, people from Italian ancestry represented only the 43 percent of the local population. The last consistent moment of Italian immigration to the North End occurred in the late 1960s and early 1970s, mostly as a result of changes in immigration laws. The Immigrant Act (1965) eliminated immigration quotas, establishing new criteria for immigrants. The Hart-Celler Act in 1965, framed as an amendment to the 1952 McCarran-Walter Act, abolished national origin quotas, specifying preferences for quotas immigrants. Specifically they regarded: unmarried adult sons and daughters of citizens; spouses and unmarried sons and daughters of permanent residents; professionals, scientists, and artists of exceptional ability; married adult sons and daughters of U.S. citizens; siblings of adult citizens and/or workers, skilled and unskilled, in occupations for which labor was in short supply in the United States.

An example of immigration during this period, not exceptional but emblematic, is Pasquale Luise, president of the COMITES (Comitato Italiani all'Estero— Committee for Italians Abroad) and trade unionist for the Italian CGIL.

> Io faccio parte dell'ultima ondata di emigrazione, uno degli ultimi arrivati negli anni settanta col famoso visto della quarta quota, era una quota particolare per gli emigrati che si mettevano in lista di attesa che durava per anni. Un fratello o una sorella facevano un atto di richiamo cioè questa

petizione per i parenti in Italia e c'era una specie di lista di attesa e quando poi si arrivava ad essere convocati si veniva chiamati dal consolato locale, nel caso mio a Napoli. Tutta la famiglia. Oltre ad una intervista, la richiesta di certificati c'era anche un esame medico. La mia famiglia, come in genere le famiglie di questa ondata, venivano in America non tanto per un bisogno economico ma più che altro per un'esperienza diversa e una sistemazione per i propri figli. Infatti i miei genitori sono venuti poi se ne sono ritornati in Italia sono rimasto solo io qui. Quindi era da un lato la curiosità e dall'altra parte per cercare un avvenire per i figli. Nelle nostre zone se non sei raccomandato, se non appartiene ad una parrocchia particolare, i problemi sono tanti. Qui c'era una zia, la sorella di mia madre che aveva fatto questa petizione e poi c'era la sorella di mio padre a Chicago che insomma era una persona che ha avuto successo in America, la creatrice dell'azienda la pizza Celeste. Mio padre pensava che venendo qui avrebbe potuto avviare qualche attività con la sorella, ma poi fu impossibile anche perchè mio padre si ammalò. Rimanemmo qui a Boston, perchè mia zia abitava qui a Boston. Per me era interessante per la possibilità di studiare, con tutte le università.

[I belong to the last emigration wave, I am one of the last migrants coming in the 1970s with the so called Fourth Quotas visa, it was a specific quota for emigrant who were listed in a waiting list that could be long, years long. Brothers or sisters made a petition for the relatives in Italy and you had a waiting list and when your turn came the local consulate called you, in my case in Naples. The whole family. They interviewed you, asking for certification and there was a medical visit. My family, like the families of this wave, came in America not because of an economic need but above all for a different experience and in order to look for a future for their sons. On one hand there was the curiosity and on the other hand the future for the children. In our country if you have not connection, if you don't belong to a specific 'parish', you can have many problems. Here used to live my aunt, my mother's sister, who made the petition and also my father's sister in Chicago, a person quite famous here, she created the Pizza Celeste factory. My father though he could make some business here with his sister but he went sick. We settled here in Boston, because of my aunt. To me it was interesting for the possibility of keeping on studying, with all the universities.]

In comparison to the mass migration at the beginning of the century, the newcomers in the 1970s faced a different problem. The unskilled and illiterate people from southern Italy dealt with stigmas and negative stereotypes largely from the Bostonian mainstream culture, where class belonging was inseparable from ethnicity or even the idea of race. Their process of becoming white, from an initial position of people in-between (Orsi 1992),[73] was long and difficult, and fought against the middle-class-oriented American society. In contrast, the new immigrants did not have to deal with the Bostonian WASPs but mainly with the Italian Americans of second, third, or even fourth generation. This is for at least three reasons: (1) the economic prosperity of the North End reflected a diffused new image of Italy and Italians, and vice versa, in a sort of mirror's game reflecting the now different status of the ethnic community. The process of becoming white could be considered concluded in the 1970s. Lia Tota, the already mentioned director of the ABCD social program in the North End, expressed this change with the following words: "L'ambiente è italo americano, adesso la gente viene e partecipa a questa cultura perchè la ragione per cui vuole vivere qui al North End è proprio per questo. La gente percepisce l'Italia come qualcosa da apprezzare una cosa che una volta non c'era, assolutamente" [The ambience is Italian American, now people come here and participate to this culture because this is the reason why they want to live here. People perceive Italy as something to appreciate, and this is something than was not in this way before, absolutely]; (2) Class-proximity, since the newcomers were mostly skilled and cultured. Pasquale Luise, talking about this new generation of immigrants who are closer to an American way of life said: "Gli ambienti che bazzicavamo noi erano si i caffè però anche le università" [Yes, we used to frequent the caffè but also the universities]; and (3) The contrast between an imagined home country, supported by the symbolic expressions of the old immigrants (and the feasts are just one of these symbolic manifestations), and the image inevitably carried by the newcomers of a different, modernized Italian society. This is not only a matter of declared or implicit cultural differences but a social threat for the North End if we consider that the economic prosperity of the neighborhood was—and still is—founded on a stereotypical rhetoric of primal ethnic identity as represented through strategic essentialist mechanisms. The newcomers basically constituted a contradictory image to this image rather than a confirmation of it. Again Pasquale Luise, talking about the feasts, illustrates this difference:

> Per noi le feste all'inizio erano una curiosità, forse noi ci aspettavamo la festa del paese ed era tutta un'altra cosa. Comunque ci si divertiva ad ascoltare la banda Roma ma ci rendevamo conto che non era una festa nostra ma delle generazioni precedenti, degli italo-americani, che in qualche modo gestivano queste feste, in un modo . . . loro, specialmente per quanto riguarda il lato economico, bancarelle, food stand.

> [For us the feasts at the beginning were a curiosity, perhaps we were expecting the village feast and it was a totally different thing. Anyway we used to have good time listening to the Roma Band but we were aware that it was not our feast but a feast of previous generations, of Italian Americans, who somehow held these feasts, in a way . . . their way, especially in terms of the economic aspect, such as stalls and food stands.]

The contrast between Italians and Italian Americans, with an important role played by the street corner gangs made famous, maybe too much famous, by Whyte, is well demonstrated by the narrative of Pasquale Luise:

> Devo dire che i nostri problemi, i primi problemi sono stati non con gli americani ma con gli italo-americani in questo quartiere. Nel senso che vedevano in noi qualcosa di diverso dai loro genitori, non vestivamo come loro, non eravamo come loro immaginavano dovessimo essere. Poi allora c'erano queste famose gangs che in qualche modo cercavano di aggredire i nuovi emigranti, chiedevano soldi ti minacciavano che so 'portami qua in macchina ci sono state delle minacce, anche dei diversi incontri anche a livello fisico comunque c'è stato sempre qualcuno che ci ha protetti nel senso che.. persone più grandi di noi anche gli italo-americani più sensibili. C'è stato un problema con queste piccole gang fino alla fine degli anni settanta.

> [I have to say that our problems, the first problems were not with the Americans but with the Italian Americans in this neighborhood. I mean that they saw us as something different from their parents, we did not dress as them, we were not like they imagined we should be. And then they were these famous gangs that somehow tried to assail the new emigrants, they asked for money, they threatened what I can say 'bring me there with the car' there were threats, even some physical fight anyway there was always somebody who protect us I mean older people and also Italian Americans more sensible. The problem with this little gangs continued until the end of the 1970s.]

The social change represented by the new economic prosperity of the North End is also revealed in the massively increasing values in real estates. I will analyze this phenomenon through examples of narratives of the neighbors, privileging again the point of view of the insider. Pietro (a fishermen from Sciacca) said about the renewal of the North End in the 1970s:

> You mean on the Waterfront? You know why? Somebody visualized in their mind that people in the North End love the water, they love to live by the seashore, somebody got the idea in their minds 'Let's buy up that property' for cheap money, money again involved! And we will build condos. And now they charge half a million dollars and people buy it! And what happened to the old people living in this area? Now they are living in the nursing home, they have no more property.

Pasquale Luise pointed out:

> Il North End dopo la speculazione edilizia ha perso la sua italianità

nel senso che la maggior parte degli emigranti hanno lasciato il North End. Durante gli anni della speculazione edilizia c'è da dire che in alcune parti del North End non ci si poteva neanche andare, i palazzi erano abbandonati le strade lo stesso Waterfront era una discarica. Fu data anche l'opportunità ai residenti di comprare i palazzi malandati e non lo fecero perchè pensarono che investire in vecchi palazzi no era un buon investimento. Hanno fatto male i conti, preferivano andare fuori e comprare la casetta a Medford. E d'altra parte per allora la casetta a Medford era una conquista sociale. Alcuni però avevano intuito e si buttarono e adesso sono milionari.

[The North End after the renewal has lost its Italianità meaning that the majority of the emigrants left the North End. I have to say that during the renewal you could not even go in some parts of the North End, buildings were abandoned and the Waterfront was a dump, They gave the opportunity to the residents to buy the deteriorated buildings but they didn't because they thought the old buildings were not good business. They made a mistake, they preferred to buy a little house out of the city, in Medford. And I have to say that buying a house in Medford was a social symbol. Some of them took the risk and now they are millionaires.]

Lia Tota described the change and the new group's dynamics in this way:

Nel 70 hanno convertito tutti questi caseggiati di 3, 4 o 5 famiglie in condomini. Per cui quel che è successo è che c'è stato un boom di questi condomini che sono stati sviluppati tutti nel 70 e nell'80 perchè l'emigrante italiano venuto qui 50 e più anni fa aveva comprato queste case per pochissimo che so 3.000 dollari anche di meno. Quando è venuto il momento del cambiamento questi developers cercavano di comprare questi condomini che so per quelli che un tempo costavano 2000-3000 dollari ora venivano offerti che so 250.000. e quindi per la gente che aveva comprato questa proprietà era un grande affare. È cominciato più o meno nel 70 quando hanno fatto questa conversione dei condomini e quando la gente ha dovuto o ha scelto di andare fuori e nello stesso tempo c'e stato questo cambiamento della prossima generazione che voleva vivere in città che poteva pagare gli affitti molto alti. Quindi questa generazione ha cambiato un po' tutto non è più italiano o Italo-Americano ma il giovane professionista che vuole stare in città. Il North End essendo un rione ancora abbastanza sicuro non è pericoloso il ne è anche perchè c'è ancora un po' di quella atmosfera etnica italiana per i ristoranti nel modo che ci sono ancora gli anziani. Adesso c'è due culture, due gruppi completamente diversi ed è l'italiano o l'italo americano anziano che sta per andar via poco alla volta e il nuovo arrivato il ragazzo o la ragazza professionista che è venuta ad abitate qui perchè vuole vivere in città e l'uno non ha niente a che fare con l'altro, sono completamente separati sono due culture completamente separate e totalmente diverse.

[In the 1970s they converted the tenements of three, four, or five families into condos. Therefore what happened is that a boom of these condos developed in the 1970s and in the 1980s because the Italian emigrant who came here fifty years ago bought houses for nothing. What can I say? 2,000–3,000 dollars and now they could receive offers for 250,000, so for the people holding the property was a great deal. Everything started more or less in the 1970s when the made the condos and when the people by need or by choice went out of the neighborhood and at the same time the next generation changed, they wanted to live in the city and they could afford the very high rents. Therefore this generation changed almost everything; it is no longer Italian or Italian American but the young professionals who want to live in the city. Since the North End is a neighborhood that is still safe enough and also because there is still the Italian ethnic atmosphere due to the restaurants and because the elders still live here. Now there are two cultures, two totally different groups and the Italian or the old Italian American is slowly going away and the newcomers, the young man or woman professionals, came here to live in the city and the one has nothing to do with the other, they are completely separated, they are two cultures completely separated and totally different.]

Narratives like these are widespread in the North End and they always carry on one hand the feeling of an ethnic identity irremediably lost, and, on the other hand an awareness of economic prosperity, with dramatic consequences concerning the unaffordable cost of living of the neighborhood.

According to the 2000 census[74]—and it is important to recall that formally now there is no longer any marking Italian ethnicity in census results, which is a clear sign of change of perception—in the central area of Boston (North End, Downtown and Chinatown) the ethnic composition is:

Race and Ethnicity, 2000 Number and Percentages (U.S. Bureau of the Census)

White	17,516 (70%)	291,561 (50%)
Black	1,024 (4%)	140,305 (24%)
Hispanic	941 (4%)	85,089 (14%)
Asian or Pacific Islander	5,280 (21%)	44,280 (8%)
Native American	29 (<1%)	1,517 (<1%)
Other	48 (<1%)	8,215 (1%)
Multiracial	335 (1%)	18,174 (3%)

The process of assimilation, the process of becoming white or, according to Alba (1985), the twilight of an ethnicity, is formally completed. The Italians are included—again, formally—in the wide category "white."

The paradox of the North End seems now clear: the prosperity is intimately connected to a declared ethnicity (the perceived safety and good condition of life of the neighborhood, seen as a community Italian-style village). Therefore, the North End must keep on being Italian, even if the Italians are gone. The need for identity, above all because now identity can be considered a scarce resource, is central for the economy of the North End. And every symbol declaring a sort of *Italianità* must be used to maintain this scarce resource. The North End ought to be an Italian neighborhood in the general perception, and it is necessary to reinforce the now necessary Italian stereotypes, as exemplified in this publicity quote put out by real estate interests:

> Boston's most livable neighborhood: The North End is arguably the safest neighborhood in Boston in which to live. There is definitely no other place quite like it anywhere else in Massachusetts. In fact, it is probably one of the most vibrant and thriving neighborhoods of its kind left in the United States. And quite frankly, where else can you get a *caffe latte*, a newspaper, a date, a dinner, and a moonlit serenade all in the same evening, just steps from your front door? Nowhere else but in Boston's North End. There is simply no place quite like it on earth, unless you're willing to travel 3,000 miles across the Atlantic to Italy itself. Welcome to Boston's Little Italy, where friends are *amici*, desserts are *dolci*, and Visa is the preferred method of payment since the card name ends in a vowel![75]

This is the North End, an imagined community, a state of mind surrounded by water, a declared gemeinshaft, where identity and authenticity have become economic values and exchange goods.

Italians Do Not Live Here Anymore: The Case of the Sacred Heart

On September 1, 2004, the Sacred Heart Church in Boston's North End was closed as official parish of the Archdiocese of Boston as a result of the reconfiguration project that Archbishop Sean O'Malley approved at the beginning of the spring. Here I will summarize some of problems and factors that induced the Archdiocese to take this unpopular decision. Symbolically, the closure of the Sacred Heart represents the scaling down or, better, the displacing of an ethnic rationale, no matter how it has been declared or possessed, how contingently it has been displayed in ephemeral situations or sanctioned by a passport. In other words, it is a later, and probably definitive, moment of renegotiating identities and belonging where self-perception of ethnicity clash against ascription by others who are socially stronger.[76]

The Italians, for Boston's Catholic hierarchies, do not live here anymore, meaning that they are no longer the humble peasants destined to the mills in Lawrence or Lowell, employed to dig the local subway, receive starvation wages, a blessing for their family and their saints, and the promise to become, in the future, white. This dream (and for those people it was really the American dream) has come true: they are all white now, even the kinky-haired, dark-skinned Sicilian, for whom so many perjorative names were coined. They now own business and have moved to the suburban area; if they come back to the neighborhood, that really means a successful life. Who else but a success can afford the afford the expensive cost of real estate here in Boston's North end, now?

Therefore, from the point of view of the local Catholic leadership, it is better to try to not sink in the economic disaster generated by the settlements with sexual abuse victims and it is absolutely necessary to manage the scarce resources in a new way. And it is necessary to pay attention to the needs of new immigrants.

The Franciscan Sean P. O'Malley assumed the leadership as Archbishop of Boston's Catholic Church, the fourth-largest Catholic community in the United States, at the end of 2003, sent by Pope John Paul II in order to deal with the profound crisis occurred to the community as a consequence of the sex abuse scandal. The nature of this crisis was not only of an economic nature, but more general, involving vocation, the change on patterns of religious behavior, and the relations between church and faithful, threatened by the polity of the last period. O'Malley faced a dramatic economic situation: according to him,[77] for the settlement with the victims and the insurance companies the local church took out three loans for a total of $97.5 million. The loans, according to the economic project of the Archdiocese, should have basically two sources of repayment: recoveries from insurance companies and the sale of almost 27.6 acres of the Brighton campus.

Father Vincenzo Romano, the pastor of Sacred Heart's Church, probably the last priest in the area entitled to celebrate mass in the Italian language, was worried about the future of his church and the neighborhood's other church, St. Leonard's, as can be seen in Sam Allis's article for the *Boston Globe*, dated December 26. Naturally Father Romano was informed about the recent decision of the Archbishop, and he said: "This is it. After this, we'd have to say that we don't have an Italian church for the people anymore." Allis closed the article with hope, quoting the archdiocese spokesman, Rev. Christopher Coyne: "Not necessarily. You could easily find that both parishes stay."

O'Malley's process of reconfiguration did not stop and a few months later, on February 4, 2004, he made his point more clear.[78] His document suggested three reasons for this reconfiguration: first changes in demographics. The trend characterized by building churches and opening parishes in order to accommodate the immigrants from overseas, from 1860 to 1960, is now outdated.

Neighborhoods have changed, as immigrants have moved to the suburban areas and new immigrants have arrived in the city. In old immigrant settlement such as Dorchester (mostly Irish) the parishes suffered, in over fifteen years, a drop of four hundred baptisms. At the same time in other neighborhoods, such as East Boston, with a strong increase of Latino immigrants, baptism went from 163 to 436 in the same time. This is the first clear sign of the necessity for a relocation of resources. Secondly, the decline of number of clergy. Since 1988 in Boston there has been a loss of 341 diocesan priests, with a decline of more than the 37 percent. Furthermore, the median age of priests is fifty-nine, with 132 priests over seventy. Third, the overwhelming economic problems of many parishes. Parishes and schools owed $26.6 million to the Archdiocese at the beginning of 2000. After three years not only were they not able to pay back the debt but they accumulated another debt of $7.4 million; the maintenance charges for the Archdiocese's properties (just in the city of Boston) were estimated in about $140 million, simply to make them safe and suitable.

The process of reconfiguration started on January 9, 2004,[79] with the call to pastors to gather in cluster meetings with the lay leadership of their parishes.[80] On March 16,[81] Boston's central cluster held a meeting to recommend two churches for closure.[82] It was a late meeting, postponed due to scheduling conflicts. Prior to the meeting, the priests of the clusters met three times and also had meetings with their own parishioners, but this was the first meeting involving priests and lay representatives of each church. The decision seemed very complex, as Father Rosato declared during the interview. Speaking about the specific situation of Sacred Heart, Father Rosato said: "We are doing very well. We are in good physical situation. We are very financially stable." The greater risk for Sacred Heart parish was probably its proximity to another parish, Saint Leonard, in Hanover Street, a few steps farther from North End Square. Hope was founded on the fact that Sacred Heart could be considered a "national Italian church" for the Italians, not specifically for those residing in the North End, but for those from anywhere in the area. It could therefore claim a sort of ethnic privilege, whereas Saint Leonard was considered to be just a neighborhood parish. Nevertheless, the central cluster final meeting suggested the closure of Sacred Heart's Parish and Saint Anne's Church.

Over Our Dead Bodies

On March 24, 2004, Father Vincenzo Romano called a meeting with the parishioners to inform them about the central cluster decision.[83] This was the starting point for a series of initiatives involving the North End communities in order to prevent what they considered an abuse perpetrated by the Archdiocese. The leadership of the protest was soon taken by community leaders such as Bennett and Richard Molinari, of Saint Mark's Society.[84] According to Donna Scire,[85]

Sacred Heart was facing a twofold dilemma: being considered a National Italian Immigrant Church for Italians everywhere it was not a neighborhood parish and it was staffed by the Scalabrini Fathers who are not dependent directly on the Archdiocese, but who follow the hierarchy of their own order.[86]

It is necessary to remember that the mission of Scalabrini's order was and still is to assist Italian immigrants in new lands. In the summer 2003 the local Province of Scalabrini made a decision to remove their priests from eight churches (one of them was Sacred Heart) if the Archdiocese asked. The reason seems to be to relocate their scarce resources in different areas with more evident needs for Italian immigrant populations. In other words, the Scalabrini's mission to assist the Italian immigrants in Boston's North End, began in the 1880s, was considered accomplished. This is a central point of the discussion, and it can be surely considered as a central moment in the negotiation of ethnic identity: on the one hand, there is a social group claiming the ethnic privilege of being Italian through a process of self ascription, on the other hand, a formal social group, holding a specific power, declares the end of this privilege. This dialectical tension characterized the Sacred Heart conflict, at least from the native point of view. In April 2, 2004, the *Post-Gazette* published an article by Bennett and Richard Molinari (*Save Sacred Heart*) that can be considered a programmatic document for the protest against the archdiocese's decision to close Sacred Heart.[87] The document was made after two meetings, the one of March 24, called by Father Romano, and another one on March 29, which perhaps two hundred parishioners attended.

Analyzing the contents as well as the rethorical mechanisms used by the authors in this documents the conflicting polls are portrayed in the following way:

North Enders	Catholic Hierarchy
Personal (*We*, as collective persona)	Impersonal (Archdiocese–Scalabrini)
Passive addressee of decisions	Active agents of decisions
Minded of historical processes (purchasing of the Church, bringing the Scalabrini here, paying the Community Center)	Careless of historical processes (closing the Church, moving the priests somewhere else, selling the Community Center)
Family oriented	Economically oriented
Emotionally involved in the process	Clinically impersonalizing the process
Claiming for ethnic privilege	Not recognizing the ethnic privilege

The last aspect becomes the critical feature, involving the previous contradictions characteristic of self-ascription and ascription by others (Barth 1969, 13). The authors of the article build their "agendas of popular mobilization and leadership consolidation" (preface to 1998 ed., 6) by declaring self-ascribed categories, making possible a process of ethnic identification through the rhetorical constitution of a dichotomy. Again, it is not simply a matter of listing categories but listing categories against an outsider who bears *other* categories, often oppositional, sometimes inflated in order to underline dissimilarities. The pivot of the dichotomy is the boundary and the continuity of the ethnic groups which, according to Barth (ibid., 14), depend on the maintenance of the boundary. The Sacred Heart event shows this dynamic clearly: preserving the boundary allows the ethnic group to preserve an ethnic identity that is in danger. Sacred Heart is the boundary marker to be preserved. It is, of course, a social boundary but also has a territorial counterpart. The basic importance of Sacred Heart is not only to be a parish of a neighborhood but also to be the symbol of an Italian community, not necessarily included inside the geographical borders of the neighborhood. I am using here the singular (community), because *hic et nunc* the claim is not for a local, regional identity but for a more general one. This an important point, above all taking into consideration what usually in the North End religious icons constitute symbols of local aggregation, bearing therefore implicitly and explicitly inner differentiations, indicating at the same time a mythical different origin (the village from whence the immigrants, and the statue of the Saint, came) and different ethnic enclaves in the neighborhood (the Montefalcionesi of Endicott Street, the Sciaccatani of North Street, etc).

This symbolic unity also includes, as the metaphor of the wheel strongly indicates, the Italians who over the time moved away from the North End, toward the suburban area, following a middle-class oriented project of life, very common in the metropolitan areas of the United States.[88] Therefore we are dealing with a boundary that is definitely social, but does not require any deterritorialization of the boundary. While it is true, on one hand, that the community (again, using the singular) is widespread, it is also true that the territory to be preserved is geographically well determined. The North End is, quoting the subtitle of Fred Langone's book (1995), "where it all began."

Territory and Territoriality

This case demonstrates that ethnic groups and territories are not necessarily immediately connected, meaning that ethnic groups can be based on territory, with geographical boundaries, but can also have a more complex relationship, which it is necessary to conceptualize. According to Krase:

> [I]n the post-modern society, although stereotypically ethnic neighborhoods may admittedly be of less immediate and practical importance to assimilated individuals, new, often ymbolic, functions for them have evolved. Many ex urban-villagers periodically return from the suburbs to thei own and other's old neighborhood to visit, shop and recharge their "soul." They mat attend celebrations, buy things, like freshly made mozzarella, unavailable in their own homogenized

settlements, visit old relatives, occasionally demonstrate ethnic pride, and increasingly to re-discover ones roots. (2006, 10)

I suggest a distinction between territory, the geographical area per se, and territoriality, as a notion that entails territories but also the social process of establishing resources and access to resources. According to Barth, "ethnic groups are not merely or necessarily based on the occupation of exclusive territories; and the different ways in which they are maintained, not only by a once-and-for-all recruitment but by continual expression and validation, need to be analyzed" (1969, 15). Within this continual expression and validation of maintaining territories the idea of territoriality becomes a useful analytic tool.

I suggest a definition of territoriality as social practices for the maintenance of an area within which residents or legitimate members manage one or more economic, symbolic and/or environmental resources. Furthermore, ethnic territoriality assumes the specificity of indispensable social practices to declare, protect and impose an inalienable ethnic identity, defined and experienced as a scarce resource. Closing the Sacred Heart implies not only the acceptance of a decision taken in a different place by different people, but also the acceptance of the presupposition for this decision: (1) that they are no longer enough Italian immigrants here (as declared by the Scalabrini), and (2) that there is no longer the need for an official Italian church (the archdiocese's choice in preserving as parish Saint Leonard).

This is the "true" danger. Or, to be precise, this is the danger that the authors of the pamphlet bring to the audience. The Sacred Heart event also shows a social dynamic related to mobilization of powers, to contrasting leaderships, to traditional and organic intellectuals facing each others. To be more explicit, the article is not an antiseptic chronicle of an event. It is a call to enter the lists against a threat; it is a political agenda declared by situational leaders; it is an attempt to fight what it is seen as an hegemonic imposition.

Certainly the protestors are aware that there is a risk not only for the church, but also for the connected School, certainly they know that people can lose their jobs, that Sacred Heart is the target of a complex economic maneuvering about lucrative real estate, but these reasons are not easy to support with the necessary evidences, and are not so involving as the issue of a threatened identity. Certainly they also feel excluded from a decision taken over their heads about something that they feel belongs to them: Sacred Heart is owned by Saint Mark's Society (Bennett and Richard Molinari belong to this society) and given in trust to the archdiocese. But even this is not a shared feeling with the rest of the community.

Certainly they know that the decision of the archbishop is unpopular because it can be seen as an insult to the North Enders. O'Malley is Irish, and as I suggested in a different section, the Italians in the North End still remember the struggle against the Irish for the territory. There is also a difference in religious attitude. O'Malley is a Franciscan, and Saint Leonard, the church that was chosen to survive is staffed by Franciscans. However, these issues cannot be declared so publically. They can be said only in whispers, not loudly as political slogans. Therefore the choice to stress ethnic privilege, including identity and belonging, shared feeling and memories, and potentially a conflict with the church's power is the best and most convincing one for the North Enders, if not the only one. But for the archdioceses, Italians do not live here anymore.

Identity as Scarce Resource and Strategic Eessentialism

The closure of Sacred Heart symbolically declares the end of a perceived ethnicity, at least by outsiders with an opportunistic interest in denying possible privileges. Naturally, and realistically, the situation is much more complex, as I demonstrated. Tensions and dynamics characterize the social process of self-ascriptive ethnicity and boundary-making. But what seems to be indisputable is, on one hand, the necessity to reaffirm an ethnic identity, even if ephemeral, mostly for economic reasons.[89] From this perspective identity assumes the peculiarity of a scare resource, a concept mediated from economy. Consequently the process of declaration and confirmation of this ephemeral identity will be characterized by fundamentally strategic intentional essentialism, claiming authenticity, history and tradition.

As I mentioned, the concept of identity as scarce resource was first proposed by Simon Harrison (1999) employing the analytical perspective suggested by Annette Weiner (1992) in her work about the symbolism of exchange in Melanesia. Her economic anthropological contribution of studying the norms of reciprocity appears to be very helpful as well when exploring ethnic relations.

Harrison extended Wiener's argument concerning inalienable possessions, goods representing the identities of the transactors themselves, to symbolic practices by which social groups and categories represent their identities, called "identity symbols" (1999, 240). If for Wiener identity depends on maintaining an exclusive association with a distinctive set of symbolic objects and preventing others from acquiring them, according to Harrison identity, particularly collective identity,

> can rest also on maintaining an exclusive association with a distinctive
> set of symbolic practices, and thus, crucially, on the power to prevent those
> defined as outsiders from reproducing these markers of identity. (243)

A similar concept of culture as property was also found among West Indians in London, by Abner Cohen (1993). Identity, from this perspective, assumes, or it is at least perceived, as having to be protected, since it is a limited good or a scarce resource.

Harrison suggested four distinct sorts of conflicts about ownership, control or possession of icons (and symbolic practices) of ethnic identity:

> Firstly, as we have seen, social actors may be relatively powerful or powerless in relation to those group whose symbolic practices they are seeking to adopt. Secondly, they may be aiming to diminish or even eliminate the differences between themselves and those groups—put loosely, they may be trying to unify two groups or at least reduce the social barriers between them—or their aim may be the reverse: to create social barriers, or deepen existing divisions, between themselves and those from whom they are borrowing. In short, the four prototypical situations I have identified seem to be generated by the intersection of two axes, one concerning degrees of power and the other having to do with degrees of intended social exclusion or inclusion. (1999, 249)

Harrison's general model is an important heuristic tool in a more broad and general sense. Applying the model to the North End case, while useful to represent social dynamics and unbalanced relations of power between ethnic groups (especially the extended hyphenated Italian Americans and a supposed Main Stream group, such the labeled WASP, for instance) does not represent the historical erosion of a supposed authentic Italian identity, in all its aspects. On one hand, symbolic practices can be threatened by "others," even other Italian Americans (see for instance the feasts in the greater Boston area, having the North End as archetypical model). On the other hand, the threat arises from the increasing "cultural distance" from the historical, now mythical, ethnic identity.

Harrison's model rightly stresses dialogical and synchronic situations of contact between ethnic groups but it lacks the diachronic perspective: the inalienable good of identity and the related icons and symbolic practices are deteriorating over time. Without any essentialist intention it is possible to state for instance that Italian language (and the different dialects) are no longer spoken in the North End, that the orthodoxy of religious rituals is gradually replaced by an orthopraxy of performances, and even the Italian presence (meaning people claiming an Italian heritage) is more and more a blurred memory. This erosion of self-ascriptive ethnicity or ethnicity that is ascribed to and by others is happening in a time when ethnicity is economically relevant for the whole neighborhood. As a matter of economic survival the North End cannot allow itself not to be Italian or at least not to represent and perform itself as Italian. Therefore, in this time when identity is more than ever a scarce resource, strategies are vital to support the North End. Inevitably these strategies continuously use essentialist traits to declare a supposed authentic ethnic identity.

The concept of strategic essentialism was proposed by Gayatry Spivak (1989). She suggested that under particular circumstances it can be advantageous for social groups to propose essentialist traits. Circumstances can be different but they are always related to oppressed groups, such as women who essentialize female identity for immediate feminist gain, or as Stuart Hall (1996) pointed out, colonial groups who essentialize an originary unity to which they wish to return. Strategic essentialism implies that groups have cultural traits self-definable as essential, but at the same time which can be strategically chosen by the group itself (even if this involves paying attention to what others think are the group's specific essential traits). The paradox is that while declaring authenticity the declaration of essential traits becomes an opportunistic tool, useful for political and economic reasons, so that basically the traits become an oxymoron. Strategic essentialism thus is very close to role-playing or, according to Bailey (1993), a fictional essence.

Therefore the crux of the matter is not about," "essentialism," already deconstructed by post-colonial critics, but about "strategy," which needs to be better analyzed. According to Parkin, strategy presupposes choice but the term ought to be used in a neo-Durkheimian manner, and not as a rationalist concept. Strategy, from this perspective,

> rests on collective understanding of their predicament, or their opportunity, that induces members of a polity to seek specific means to attain desired ends. An acceptable cultural idiom, backed up by the appropriate forms of performance and belief, become the means, and political and economic security the goal. (1995, xix)

More than directly determining social action, strategic essentialism seems to be the indirect product of pushing and pulling forces. Strategy does not necessarily mean a coherently organized political practice, in the broad sense, but more often is a consequence of unbalanced power, and is performed by necessity.

In conclusion, identity as scarce resource and strategic essentialism seem to be the product of the processes of ethnic negotiations in Boston's North End.

3

The Societies of Saints

⚛

The Italians settling in the North End also brought their symbolic imaginary: all of their religion, devotions and rituals. Patron saints were literally and symbolically carried out from the original village to the streets of the new ethnic enclaves as icons of identity. Around and beyond the patron saints many social processes were (and are) expressed: from the associative levels to the controversial relationship with the formal ecclesiastic hierarchy, from the dialectic tradition/modernization to processes of absorption in a more general cultural frame characterized by the logical/global tension, with suggestion of hyphenated ethnicities and strategic essentialisms.

In this chapter I will analyze the role of particular religious devotions to Catholic saints and these related voluntary associations in the dynamic of social relationships in the North End.[1] As I shall show, each specific religious society claims a specific identity, recreating the campanilismo and the campanile in the ethnic enclaves of the North End. Through the rituals that they enact the societies manufacture the distinctiveness of their neighborhoods, while also strategically constituting the entire North End as an ethnic area.

I will also contextualize the religious societies in the broader scenario of voluntary associations developed in the North End by the Italians, historically tracing changes and tracts of stability. I will argue that these religious societies evolve from their original function as mutual aid groups for members of the village of origin and the ethnic enclave and become complex cultural institutions where tradition and modernity face each other in a dynamic relation. Finally, I will suggest that the religious societies can help us to understand the so called "Italian Problem of American Catholicism," and to explore processes where ethnic identities finally can be negotiated by local agents, and not merely externally imposed.

This negotiation also implies social changes in the perception of the others, and it is strongly connected with a transformation toward a more familiar middle-class and mainstream pattern. The Italians (and in this case of external perception a generalization is not only possible but necessary) have become white after a long period of marginalization and ambiguity. They can finally claim situational, convenient, and ephemeral ethnic identities through a continuous process of negotiation.

Devotions to the Saints

Worship of saints is central in Italian religiosity but it is important to separate the formal doctrine about the cult of saints from what the people believe and practice, in other terms what Robert Orsi (1984; 1992; 1996) calls "religion of the streets." A saint is a special example, a sort of mythical figure who embodies special virtues and can be proposed as a model for believers. Combining these characteristics with the very large number of official saints (roughly ten thousand) it is quite possible to suppose a form of hegemonic social control on the populace perpetrated by the Catholic Church through the mechanism of sainthood. Saintliness is formally accepted after a long process of investigating doctrinal purity, heroic virtue and evidence of miraculous intercession after death. But for the layman, sainthood is all about miracles, where curing illness and saving a village from a natural disaster occupy a central importance (Primeggia 1999, 82).

The distance between official and popular religion can be expressed by the emblematic position of Carlo Levi:[2]

> Nel mondo dei contadini non c'è posto per la ragione, per la religione e per la storia. Non c'è posto per la religione appunto perchè tutto partecipa della divinità, perchè tutto è, realmente e non simbolicamente, divino, il cielo come gli animali, Cristo come la capra. Tutto è magia naturale. Anche le cerimonie della chiesa rientrano nei riti pagani, celebratori della indifferenziata esistenza delle cose, degli infiniti terrestri dei del villaggio. (1945, 102)

> [There is no place for reason, for religion and for history in the farmer's world. There is no place for religion just because everything participates in the divine, everything is, realistically and symbolically, divine, the sky like the animals, Christ like the goat. Everything is natural magic. Even church ceremonies are pagan rituals, celebrating the undifferentiated existence of things, and the infinity of village deities.]

Levi's approach, while important from a political point of view because it underlies the subalternity of the peasant masses in southern Italy, does not distinguish itself from the traditional way of studying folklore. This approach revolves around four main concepts: (1) the "irrational" and magic mark of a basically primitive religion; (2) ancientness, privileging the idea of "relics" or vestige indebted with the nineteenth-century folkloric survivalism (Hodgen 1936); (3) the syncretic character of subaltern religion, combining Catholicism with previous religions; and (4) the familistic relationship with the divine, based on pragmatic exchanges: "the southerner instituted a custom of making all manner of up-front bargains with saints or the Madonna." (Primeggia 1999, 83) Paradoxically this approach does not fully take into consideration the importance of the official doctrine, expressed by formal institutions like the church and diffused by priests, organic intellectuals of this institution. This approach misses the dynamic between a hegemonic group and a subaltern one engaged in continuous dialogue and influencing each other, even if in different measures. Subaltern religion does not stand by itself. Following Gramsci's perspective (1929–1959), folklore (therefore popular religion) contrasts with the official, dominant and hegemonic culture (and religion) because of its position in the social dynamic, but they are both defined by this dialectic. In other words, doctrinal and local religion are interdependent, as Stewart (1989) suggests. Stewart argues persuasively that dichotomy folk/official distinction does not unfold the breadth and coherence, in his case, of contemporary Greek cosmology, and, in general, of religiosity of the street. A dynamic approach should be suggested not only by looking at comparisons with the hegemonic level but also by analyzing the subaltern itself. In other words, alongside the idea of vestige and relics comes an archeological vision that is basically static. According to Natalie Zemon Davis, "religious cultures are not merely inherited or imposed; they are also made and remade by people who live them." (1980, 331)[3]

Devotion to the saints is a fundamental aspect of the Italian, above all southern Italian, style of Catholicism. Not surprisingly, therefore, saints became a crucial aspect of the religious life of Italian Americans. Saints are imagined as intermediaries in transactions with God, the supreme divine.[4] This theory stresses the syncretism between Catholicism and preexisting pagan polytheism, blending with the southern Italian precarious conditions of life, a belief in saints

> professed through pagan style worshiping and Catholic devotion, must be understood as a need to anchor one's faith in the concrete, in the palpable, to be accessible. Being human [yet] having the superhuman power of miracles, saints abolished the distance between the cosmic grandiosity of God and his human earthly manifestations. Therefore, saints were not just viewed as intercessors, but as the most important religious agents in favor of the needy. In a word, where life was very precarious, man-made evils abounded, and natural disasters (droughts, floods, earthquakes) and diseases struck without warning and without logic, the causes were attributed to forces and powers of superhuman agents. In making sense of senseless and dangerous world, the undeserving affliction brought on by superhuman powers could only be mitigated or even prevented with the protection of superhuman benevolent agents. (Varacalli, Primeggia, Lagumina, and D'Elia 1999, vi–vii).

According to Rudolph Vecoli the southern Italian folk religion seems to favor personal aspects of magic behaviour which is associated with a kind of amoral familistic practical sense, and communality belonging.

> The religion of the *contadini* was enclosed within the spirit of *campanilismo*. Each village had its own array of Madonnas, saints, and assorted spirits to be venerated, propitiated, or exorcized. There was no turn of fortune, for good or for ill that was not due to the benevolence or malevolence of these supernatural being. God, like the King, was a distant, unapproachable figure, but the local saints and Madonnas, like the landlords, were real personages whose favor was of vital importance. With a mixture of piety and shrewdness, the supplicants bargained with their patrons, offering gifts, sacrifices, and praise, if their petitions were granted. The feast day of the patron saint or Madonna was the highpoint in the life of the village. With panegyrics, processions, brass band, and fireworks, these communal celebrations exalted the miraculous powers of the patron and invoked his protection upon the village. (1969, 228–229)

This perspective, while describing correctly the campanilismo and the personal, individual relationship with the saints, especially during the important festive days, missed one important point: the relationship of powers that are expressed in the feast of the patron saint. It is not enough to ignore this issue by saying that God and the King are unapproachable figures because they are so far away. Nor is this actually true. God and King are actually indirectly present exercising their power through local cultural brokers, such as the priests, who are organic intellectuals connected with the social class to which they belong. Gramsci's analysis of hegemony and social control through consent (1971, 1984) demonstrates the dynamic of powers by which the hypothetically oppositional subaltern classes were controlled. Religion and rituals play an important role in this ancient hegemonic game. It is possible to trace the importance of the hegemonic use of the feast to Roman times: this can be seen in the so-called *panem et circenses* (bread and circuses) the policy to assure a minimum level of food for all the people (starvation can be a powerful cause for mass revolts) and to furnish amusements as a form of social control. In southern Italy, during the Regno delle Due Sicilie, the Borboni pushed this idea further: social control was assured by the policy of "Festa, Farina, Forca" [Feast, Bread and Gallows], the last seen not only as public demonstration of force and justice but also as entertainment. Religious feasts were not only a moment of declared religious and communal belonging, but also a place and a time where hegemonic power relationships were unfolded and revealed. If this is true, the main question remains, what happened to this display of authority after migration? This is the so called Italian problem.[5] And even where Catholics did exist, we should remember that at the time of the mass migration from Italy, the American Catholic church hierarchy was almost entirely Irish, whose larger concern was the assimilation of Catholics into the Protestant-dominated mainstream America. According to sociologist Salvatore Primeggia, Settling in a new and often incomprehensible world, the

> Italian immigrants turned to chose security and defense mechanisms that had served them so well in their homeland or *paese*. . . . The newcomers were all more convinced that the best way to survive was to hold onto the convoluted belief structure that had protect them against misfortunc in Italy. (1999, 79)

However, the Catholic Church in America did not understand their practices, seeing them as unorthodox and embarrassing. Therefore, the solution was to place Italian or at least Italian speaking priests in United States. This allowed the immigrants to have their own parishes, and hold their own feasts.

But, as ever, the situation is much more complex than what appears at first glance. Two factors seem to be very important at this point. On the one hand the flourishing of associations in the North End, often related to political and economic purposes, which seems to follow an American pattern of social life. On the other hand, the North End was the theater of the constitution of several religious societies, organized around the icon and the celebration of the patron saint of the village of origin, in a sort of sanctification of the ethnic enclaves.

Associations in the North End

The Societies of Saints are not the only kind of association existing formally or informally in the North End. Even when the neighborhood was a slum, many associations formed there and other associations came to the area, with many different purposes and goals. I am not going to trace the history of voluntary associations in the North End, but I will write a short summary of some of them, directly related to the Italian settlement at the end of the nineteenth and the beginning of the twentieth centuries.

At that time, philanthropic activities were organized in order to help the new comers. Many associations, mostly religious, began working in the Italian slum at the end of the nineteenth century. Most Catholic associations, for instance the San Raffaele supported by the Scalabrini fathers, were centered around the Italian parishes of Saint Leonard and Sacred Heart, but other groups, with different religious orientations were also present in the historically Catholic North End. For instance, in 1890 a group of students from the School of Theology of Boston University, headed by Edgar J. Helms, opened a Methodist mission on Charter Street with the purpose of helping immigrants find jobs and housing. The mission was a success and for this reason in 1893 the Methodist Church asked the Conference in Rome for a missionary. In August 1893 Gaetano Conte,[6] from Sessa Aurunca, Campania, an interesting and controversial figure, arrived in Boston. According to Martellone (1973, 354), Conte was well aware of the Bostonian hostility toward the Italian immigrants and immediately started working to increase the material and spiritual condition of life in the neighborhood.[7]

Supporting the immigrants against those trying to take advantage of them, Conte gained the attention of Bostonian reformists and, after a meeting held in Faneuil Hall, he founded, along with other Italian and American members, the Società di Protezione degli Emigrati Italiani, organized for job assistance, money remittance, legal assistance and education. Later, from 1895 to 1897, he was involved in a similar society called the Società Giorgio Washington, and in 1902 he founded the Società per la Protezione degli Immigrati Italiani, also called Boston Society for the Protection of Italian Immigrants,[8] on Hanover Street. But Conte's social activity was not without ambiguity. Martellone (1973, 365) noted that even if the mission of the association was to help the unskilled immigrants, the members of the society were almost exclusively Americans, with only two Italian members, Conte and the Italian consul. Therefore Conte was not well accepted by the wider Italian community first, because he was not Catholic, second, because of his preference for working with and advising the lower social strata of the southern Italian immigrants, and third, because he preferred to associate with Americans rather than Italians. Because of this approach he was stigmatized by other Italian associations in Boston. On February 28, 1903, after a meeting involving most of the Italian associations a document was produced that founded the Lega Protettiva degli Italiani, and criticizing Conte:

> [N]on sappiamo niente e non crediamo niente di quanto ha operato il signor Gaetano Conte in riguardo alla protezione italiana. . . . Con ciò avvertiamo il signor Conte che la finisca una buona volta di illustrarci sui giornali americani a sembianza di scimmie, danneggiando e demoralizzando il prestigio e l'onore della patria.

> [[W]e do not know and we do not trust what Mister Gaetano Conte has done about protection to the Italians. . . . We warn Mister Conte to finally stop depicting us like monkeys in the American newspapers, damaging and demoralizing the prestige and the honor of the homeland.]

The "crusade" against Conte, accusing him of being non patriotic and inimical to ethnic interests was a success and in 1903 a new pastor, Salvatore Musso, began to lead the Methodist mission in the North End.[9]

Conte and the Methodists were not the only non Catholic association in the North End. For example, the Boston Baptist of Bethel City Mission Society, took the place of an American church established before the Italians, the First Mariner's Baptist Church, which was founded on Hanover Street in 1852. Another example is the Boston Italian Mission, a Congregationalist mission, which started in 1902.

Martellone (1973, 467) rightly suggested that this sort of association was a replica of the settlement houses,[10] such as the Circolo Italo-Americano, the Italian section of the Denison House, located in the South End, which was harshly criticized by the Italian newspapers. The mission of the settlement houses was motivated by a social utopist Christianity, with a mandate to help workers and migrants to assimilate into the United States. These claims for assimilation and Americanization, framed in utopist socialism and seeking an external recognition of ethnic peculiarity, were a threat to the local Italian notabili (prominent citizens). The notabili feared losing economic control and social authority over the mass of emigrants in the presence of alternative agencies supporting the new settlers. Not surprisingly a local newspaper labeled the Denison House's social workers as *mucciose zitellone* (snotty old maids).[11] In the North End settlement houses in general had varying degrees of success in terms of admission, popularity and the number of activities involving migrants. Moderately successful was the Civic Service House, founded in 1901 which had the mission of assisting immigrants to prepare petitions for citizenship, and the Settlement Home, supported by the Episcopalian Church.

The pattern of these philanthropic associations can be seen in the membership, which was sometimes voluntary but more often professionally based, involving mainly middle-class Italians and Americans who had a mission of secular and/or religious "evangelization," in order to convert the immigrants to a new religion (Methodist, Congregationalist, Episcopalian) or to the new American way of life (settlement houses). They were associations for Italians not of Italians, and did not include, even in Conte's case, the unskilled, lower class, birds-of-passage Italians who were the main settlers in the North End.

A different kind of association can be discerned in the professional organizations, such in the Società dei Barbieri Italiani, or the Unione degli Scavatori, and the Hod Carriers' Union. Gathering together entrepreneurs and workers, these professional organizations can be characterized as charitable associations, motivated by solidarity, but also as a mechanism of social control over possible subversive syndicalism through asserting a hegemonic claim for an ethnic belonging.[12] Again, with few exceptions like the socialist Unioni di Mestieri organized by Domenico Bonanno and Costantino Ciampa, the pattern seems to be a mixed membership instrumentally organized by middle and upper class Italians and Bostonians to manage large numbers of the North End settlers through a mechanism of declared work, class and ethnic solidarity.

In contrast to these externally organized settlement houses and professional associations of different sorts, the Societies of Saints were organized, at least at the beginning, on a geographical bases: the villages of origin in the home country and the ethnic enclaves in the receiving one. They claimed to be solely religious in function, and the most visible events conducted by them were and are the religious festivals, which I shall describe below.

The Societies of Saints

In the summertime, every weekend Boston's North End is the stage for Italian American festivals, dedicated to different Catholic saints, patrons of different Italian villages. All these festivals are organized by private and voluntary associations, designated by the name of the saint and of the village in the home country, which seem to be independent from Catholic religious hierarchy, and which have scarce and even negligible contacts with the local parish churches.

I will start with a narrative suggested by Jerry, from the Saint Anthony of Padua of Montefalcione Society. He described the making of ethnic enclaves and the constitution of societies in the following way:

> They were (the montefalcionesi) all within a walking distance, they can meet. So every Sunday morning they all got together and they started forming the Circolo di Montefalcione which was *i paesani* and *gli amici ro paese* (friends from the same village) and they used to meet and there they had meeting and discuss like somebody wanted to come over and they need money and they didn't have the money to pay for the trip, they would loan the money and come over. And the next thing they became a fraternal organization among themselves. Actually they started, what, 1910–1911. They started before that to come over. And the next thing they were all congregated in the corner here. And the next thing they wanted to start something, they were all paesani, they were living all over these streets. Next thing they rented a store and they used to meet on Sunday morning for coffee, pastry, stuff like that. They met once a week, then the next thing they wanted start like in *paese*, they wanted to do a feast, because the other societies were doing feasts. Next thing they started they wanted to run the feast well . . . they couldn't afford this or that so, for instance, this Amoreo (pointing at an old picture on the wall) was a carpenter and who was an electrician, who did this, who did that they got together the boxes, they strung the lights, they came home from work, strung the lights.. And the next thing they got like a city band, boxes around this block and this is how they started the feast.

According to this narrative, the societies were first of all a place where migrants used to gather together, for many reasons: to bring together people of the same origin. This is probably the first and most important reason for founding a society: to reestablish the equivalent of the village, using the religious icons as primary display of identity; helping people of the Italian village following the pattern of chain migration; holding a feast. This can be seen as a manifestation of campanilismo, or, better, of declared local identity.

The first two aspects can be observed through the analysis of secular activities of the societies and the structure of membership, while the analysis of the feasts will be more specifically the object of the next chapter.

Secular Activities

Even if they declare themselves to be "religious" the societies can also be seen in terms of secularization above all if we underline the social activities of the club. For example Vivian, a member of the Saint Lucy Society, described these activities in the following way:

> Now the society has eighty-eight members. You never see them, even at the meetings. There are always the same people, a bunch of us volunteering and doing all the work you know. I can say we are ten to fifteen active members. We have a meeting once a month, the second Wednesday of the month. We try to do different things, we play bingo, we have guest speakers, we had a woman coming here talking about AIDS and we raised two thousand dollars. We try to have social activities, we go to Mohegan Sun, the casino! We do a lot of fund-raising, we have in October a Halloween party, we have a Christmas party or Mother's Day party and we do it for charity, we donate whatever we make. We have a raffle, and again we do it for charity. And when June comes we start discussing the feast.

Along with these social activities involving a high degree of organization the clubs also gather informally. Almost every day, in the case of the Saint Anthony and Saint Lucy clubs,[13] members gather together to watch TV, play cards, drink coffee or just to chat. Around the many tables of the club people sit down with their friends and acquaintances. I did not notice any specific patterns of aggregation in these informal periods, but they were evident in the formal period of meetings, where authoritative roles were not only set and declared but also reaffirmed by members clustering together in patterned fashion. In these cases age and status hierarchies become important variables. Gender is another fundamental distinction: Saint Lucy members do not attend the Saint Anthony meetings and vice versa.

Saturday morning is the most important moment of the social activities in the Fishermen's Club on North Street. Members meet to play cards and have a light breakfast or lunch, and they always talk with each other. As in the previous example, in this case too patterns of aggregation seem to be very casual and do not follow status hierarchy or age, or even gender, which are affirmed during official meetings.

The binary opposition suggested by the terms formal/informal, while describing the surface of the society's life, does not offer an adequate heuristic tool to analyze this complexity. I wish instead to import, albeit on a different, smaller scale, the notion of *disemia*.[14] Focusing on representations expressed by the social life of the club a double register is evident: an official self-representation unfolds in the meetings or the structured activities, bearing the official declaration of roles; this official form of representation alternates with an ordinary, casual, apparently uncoded and introspective practice of gathering together. The exceptionality of the official self-representative moments faces the ordinariness of every day club life in a relationship of dynamic play: the official register can be used in both directions toward the society itself and toward the external surroundings to claim and declare the society's self-determination and distinctiveness. The introspective and informal practices, providing more malleable boundaries between roles, allow the group to present itself to itself with the image of homogeneity, apparently in contradiction with the official register. But binarism is implicit to the disemic code and enables the definition of the group identity: both registers contribute to the narrative's construction regarding the group again toward self ascription, and toward its ascription by others.

It is the disemic tension, along the specific religious contents, that characterizes the societies of saints as social organizations. The mode seems to be the highly structured formal code visible in the official register, as the expression of a declared Gesellschaft, in dialogue with an apparently unstructured practice, which is the expression of an imagined Gemeinschaft.

Membership

The membership was, at the beginning, highly selective: the only way to become a member of the society of St. Anthony of Padua of Montefalcione was to be born in Montefalcione.[15] This is the stated basic characteristics of the societies of the saints in Boston's North End. How did the structure of membership evolve over the years? I will start my analysis reporting Jerry's words:

> Augusto: At the beginning the society was just for Montefalcionesi? And when did they start to open the membership to people from somewhere else?
>
> Jerry: At first the society was strictly Montefalcionesi, they started to open around World War II, let's say '44, '45. We had a Genoese for president and now the president is Sicilian! The only thing I didn't see yet is a president from North Street! [North Street is the "main" street of the Sciaccatani] At that time the members were going, a lot of them

had died in the war, I say maybe they were about 45–50 members. We never been more than 60–65 members. Before they were only Montefalcionesi so you had a small membership. And the only thing is if you were the son of a Montefalcionese, if you were a son of a member, you could have got in that way. That's why I got in here, so that's how Frank got in, Jas got in. And that was it but they managed to run the feast three weeks after the war was over and I'll never forget the amount of money they made: seven thousand dollars. They made money to pay the expanse for the two bands, the made money to pay for Matarazzo's work, the decoration, everything. In those days you didn't ought to pay for the police. James Mayor Curley would give you the police, ok? We never worried about cleaning the streets. So the next thing the feast started growing, they started bringing member, if you had a daughter, she marry a Montefalcionese, all right away they put them up as members, the group grew up to seventy-five members. Now the parade started getting bigger and bigger and we would go further the ring of the North End, but we never used to hit North St. because it was a thing that the Fishermen were never come down here.

In the second and third generations this exclusivism became less rigid. Thus, sons of Montefalcionesi could be members, and even someone who marries a Montafalcionese could be eligible for the membership. The lines for eligibility were lines of kinship.

In 1988, at the time of Mary Jo Sanna's interviews,[16] there was still a strong feeling that members should be descendants from the original village in the home country. For instance only Sciaccatani, descendents of immigrants from Sciacca, could be admitted into the Fishermen's Society, the Madonna del Soccorso Society. But the process of inclusion of different origins was evident even for them: Jimmy and Ray Geany, leaders of the club, were half Sciaccatani and half Irish, although they identify themselves more closely with their Italian ethnicity.

Nowadays membership is open to almost everybody, as it is possible to see in the Constitution of St. Anthony Society, article 2, section 1:

Membership: Men of good moral and intellectual standing with an interest in promoting devotion to our Patron, Saint Anthony, shall be eligible for membership in this organization. A candidate must be at least 21 and not over 50 years of age.

The question of membership loosening up over time was reaffirmed by one of my consultants, who said:

When the books are "closed" no new members are admitted. When you open the books, you screen them.[17] He, as a member, can name so and so and needs two more men to endorse his candidate. They hear the name at three meetings, specify who he is, where he comes from. The members hear the name. And if they ok it the third meeting, he's got a very good chance in getting in. If there's a flaw about him, they'll throw the vote down, if there's something wrong with the guy. In that case, we have a closed ballot. You write yes or no on the ballot. Years ago it was-n't that. Years ago we used to have little round balls. Black balls and white balls. All they had to do was throw three balls and you were com-pletely out. It was terrible . . . just a lousy three. I thought it was very embarrassing. . . . I didn't want none of that black ball stuff because they throw one of my friends down, from now on I start to throwing black balls. They throw one of your friends—nobody gets in. A closed ballot where you write yes or no, that's how we started getting members in. Broke the tradition. The old-timers didn't like it, but we thought it was a good idea. The old-timers were actually fading away. They're old. We needed a lot of help—there weren't that many of us. We started to try to put members in, so we got rid of the black balls.

In the contemporary scenario of what many consultants referred as de-mocratization of the societies,[18] with less rigid geographic restrictions and few residual feeling of exclusivism, becoming a member of voluntary associations in America is still not an easy process, as Weber noted in his analysis of sects (1985, 9). For instance, to join a society in the United States is a voluntary choice, made by the applicants. But the society makes a choice as well, scruti-nizing the purity of the member not only at the beginning but also during the membership. This is fundamental for the sake of maintaining the ethic of a "chosen few." Therefore moral aspects of membership are fundamental, as dis-cussed in sections 6 to 12 of the constitution):

- Section 6: The eligibility of a new member is to be decided by the conscience of each member voting on the new member's acceptance;
- Section 7: The candidate for membership shall be required to com-plete an application for membership. The application shall include personal information of said candidate and questions regarding the candidate's intentions for joining the society. The application will be read to the membership during the second reading of the candidates names;
- Section 8: Application for membership shall be signed by at least two members in good standing, and must be submitted to the Secretary prior the start of the meeting. Said application must then be read by the secretary to the organization and presented to the membership, which in turn, shall investigate the character and the eligibility of the candi-date for membership. Nomination of membership in this organization

shall be within a three month period. First month: application is submitted; Second month: the application shall be screened; Third Month: applicant for membership shall be voted upon;

- Section 9: For the first and second reading of the candidate, at least one sponsor must attend. However, for the third and final meeting both sponsors must attend;
- Section 10: An application may be withdrawn by either sponsor at any time prior to action by the membership;
- Section 11: An applicant for membership is not present during vote;
- Section 12: Two-thirds of the members present shall be sufficient to elect him a member. The vote of a candidate or candidates shall be by secret ballot.

Voluntary, exclusionary, geographically based, associations of individuals gathering together for moral and, specifically, religious reasons, these seem to be the main characteristics of the societies of the saints in Boston's North End. The "moral reasons" are especially fundamental for the quality of membership and are specifically requested by the constitution in the preamble:

We, the members of the San Antonio Di Padova Da Montefalcione, Inc., incited by the indomitable desires of our moral, physical and social advancement and to derive such benefits for ourselves and our community as are gained by the friendship and many activities of an organization. . . .

It is worth comparing the San Antonio constitution with the Statuto (charter/statute) of Maria SS. Di Anzano Degli Irpini (this is the formal name of the S. Maria di Anzano Society). The Statuto della Società Cattolica Italiana di Mutuo Soccorso e Beneficenza S. Maria di Anzano degl'Irpini di Boston, Mass. was approved on January 3, 1905. The society was formally founded three days earlier by Marco Mastrangelo, Gaetano Moriello, Antonio Staffieri, Luigi Leone, Vito Chirichiello, Luciano Pagliarulo and Antonio Sciaraffa. Giuseppe Paglia was the supervisor of the committee for the charter. The Preamble, written as the whole charter in the Italian language, declares the mission of the society and, as in Saint Anthony's case, sets out mutual help, morality and social improvement as the goals of the association.

Lo scopo è di riunire gli onesti cittadini italiani o figli di italiani e cooperare al benessere materiale, morale e intellettuale dei membri.

[The mission is to involve honest Italian citizens or sons of Italians to cooperate for the material, moral and intellectual good.]

More specifically the first paragraph lists the responsibilities of the society: members could count on economic help in case of health problems (medical support by the society's doctor and seven dollars a week, for ten weeks, reduced to three and a half for the following ten weeks),[19] the funerary expenses for dead members, and assistance for family of dead members in need. Through the analysis of the formal charter, the characteristics of membership are evident: the association is voluntary, exclusionary, geographically based, collective of individuals who gather together for moral reasons, carrying the name of the patron saint.

However, the situation changed over the years, raising questions about the problematic nature of relationship between the religious societies in the North End, now more disposed to at least occasional collaboration, and to a less rigid and mandatory exclusiveness of the membership

Relations between the Societies of Saints

It is usual to see members of different societies attending different feasts. The festival is always a moment of entertainment, of intensified social interactions and display involving the entire neighborhood. Therefore for many inhabitants of the North End,[20] it is practically impossible not to participate. People, such as tourists, neighbors and of course members of the other societies simply gather around during a festival. In other words, this kind of casual participation does not directly require any formal identification with the club conducting the festival. But often it is possible to see important members of different clubs. They are clearly recognizable not only because of their popularity in the North End, but also because they perform formal and recognizable actions during the feast. Attending the feast in groups in order to be recognized as a delegation from another society (often pinning money on the statue, therefore paying respect to the saint) is an expected and predictable homage from another society. Sometimes this donation is given by members wearing the uniform of their own club. This performance declares the presence of the other club while fully respecting the specific festive authority and setting.

Societies communicate but also remain exclusive. In the entire history of the Italian settlements in Boston's North End the societies have worked together toward a formal and common goal only on two occasions: a) for the fund raising after the tragedy of September 11, 2001, b) for the rally against the closure of the Sacred Heart Church in April 2004 (as discussed in the previous chapter).

Jason A., of the Saint Anthony Society, remembered the first event in this way:

> September 11 was on a Tuesday so we had the vigil and it was planned very quick so we called Bosco,[21] Saint Agrippina and we were four hundred people at the vigil. The night we marched with candles to the fire station, and we sung patriotic songs like God Bless America, and we had coffee together. Bosco was talking with my cousin Joe who is the

president of my club saying "we should do something, we should do it together." So my cousin Joe said "This can be a great idea why don't we get together." So we had a first meeting and we called everyone, everybody say yes, just Madonna della Cava said no, they wanted to do their own thing. Everybody say yes. East Boston too say yes, they came for the vigil and they talked to Bosco. Some suggested to do something waiting until Saint Lucy's Halloween party, a costume party. Some people didn't like that, they didn't want a costume party, you know some can show up as an Arab, so we said "What we want to do, we want a raffle? do we want to have just an auction? do we want do a walkathon? a banquet? So we all decided to do . . ." Why don't we have some fun? something casual, we are fifty to hundred people each club so eight clubs that's four hundred people, so we said well why we don't have a party?"

So we had few meetings so to make more sense we said "Why don't we elect a chair people?" They voted my cousin Joe as a chairperson, we decide a name first and we decided "North End East Boston Italian for America" so Joe was the chairperson, I became treasurer, and then we had a committee: Bosco was in charge of the food and preparation for the hall, Gennaro, Mark and some other people for decoration, the Saint Lucy Society for the raffle, Jo Ann for the T-shirt, the bar was run by Saint Agrippina. And we had another meeting and we said we want a DJ, so Bosco was in charge of the entertainment too. Luisa from Italia Unita was in charge of media. A complex organization. Then we decide where we want to do the party. We sold 280 tickets before the start. We had meetings discussing everything.

The party was a success, raising a good amount of money to donate to the Boston archdiocese's special fund for Massachusetts victims of 9/11. The ceremony of money donation was held in the Fishermen's Club. All the participating societies were in attendance. Confirming the exclusiveness of the societies and the exceptionality of the event the meeting was clearly separated into two different moments: the first was informal, with everybody friendly, talking and gathering together, with no differences or declaration of group belonging. The second was formal and began when the ceremony started. At that moment the informal general group split, generating small exclusive groups of club members, who sat together around different tables. The societies were again declaring themselves to be exclusive groups.

As mentioned in chapter 2, on March 24, 2004, Father Vincenzo Romano, parish priest of the Sacred Heart's church, called a meeting with the parishioners to inform them about the archdiocese's decision to close the parish. This was the starting point for a series of initiatives involving the North End communities in order to prevent what they considered an abuse perpetrated by the Catholic hierarchy. On April 14, 2004, in North Square, the first rally against the archdiocese decision to close the parish of the Sacred Heart was organized. The leadership of the protest was held by communities leaders such as Bennett and Richard Molinari, of Saint Mark's Society, and other prominent members of religious societies: Jason A., of Saint Anthony's Society, Therese and Sal Diecidue, of Madonna del Soccorso's Society, publicly and openly criticized the decision. But they were not alone: the night of the rally, despite a pouring rain, the statues, the sacred religious icons of the societies, were exposed in front of the Sacred Heart Church. This time, all the societies participated.

Soon after the rally the ephemeral common leadership faded away, leaving the Saint Mark's Society and the Molinari brothers almost by themselves. Thus, although occasionally the societies can join together for common projects, these are still extraordinary ephemeral events. But a new path of formal collaboration seems at least now possible.

Exclusiveness of Membership

I demonstrated that at the beginning being a member of the societies of saints was a choice declaring loyalty to the ethnic enclave as well as showing a sense of belonging to the village of the old country. And it was also strictly regulated. Over time, and due to extensive intermarriage, the regulation became less rigid. Recently a new phenomenon can be noted, involving mostly the "small" societies of saints: this can be called "plural membership." Saint Anthony, Madonna del Soccorso, S. Maria di Anzano etc. are societies that are strong both economically and in membership. Saint Anthony could count at the time of my fieldwork almost 150 members, the Fishermen were numerous as well, S. Maria di Anzano, even though the club was forced to move out of the North End to Somerville in order to sustain an affordable rent, certainly was a "wealthy" club, at least in terms of the attendance at the meetings. But for other societies the situation was not as good. A crisis in membership, with its crippling economic consequences, could become a threat to the survival of the societies themselves. Some small societies do not even have a club, and keep the statue of the saint in private homes (Saint Jude, for instance). For them, running the festival or even just the procession depends on the efforts of a few people, responsible for all aspects and duties. The new phenomenon of plural membership, which provides the possibility of belonging to multiple societies is a way to guarantee the survival of these small collectives. I discovered this strategy when following the festivals. I began to notice people belonging to a certain society but following a different procession. In itself, this is not extraordinary, since it is an expected form of respect between societies and also a social entertainment. But in this case they were wearing the uniform of other societies and, above all, they were carrying the statue of a different saint, showing their belonging to this other society too.

At a first glance plural membership seems to contradict the fundamental aspect of exclusiveness, on which this kind of voluntary association is based. It seems to be in contrast with Weber's concept of sect of a chosen few. But it can be explained as a form of practical essentialism. We have seen the importance of the societies of saints, declaring ethnic enclaves and belonging to a mythical village, thus building a narrative of mythical origin, and a consequent rhetorically constructed group. In this instance, this shifts to a shared declaration of the entire area, the North End, as Italian. As I have noted, identity must be preserved by all means possible, since it is a scarce resource. The North End cannot afford to lose religious societies and festivals, fundamental for an ascriptive definition of local Italian American identity and, more importantly from an economic point of view, for recognition by others, especially by tourists interested in purchasing history and ethnicity. Plural identity allows the maintenance of the all-important festival cycle, despite diminishing numbers.

Societies and Leadership

The issue of plural membership—and of the related relationships between societies of saints—allows me to introduce a more complex problem: the manifest dynamics that is, the visible, often formal and official, power performance within or between religious societies and the group.[22] I suggest a possible typology:

a. groups connected to the declared ethnic enclaves interacting with other groups connected to the same ethnic enclave;[23]
b. groups connected to the declared ethnic enclaves interacting with other groups connected to other ethnic enclaves;
c. groups connected to the declared ethnic enclaves interacting with other local groups, inside the North End, but not connected to ethnic enclaves;
d. interethnic enclaves groups interacting with other local groups, inside the North End, but not connected to ethnic enclaves;
e. groups connected to the declared ethnic enclaves interacting with external (outside the neighborhood) groups;
f. interethnic enclaves groups interacting with external (outside the neighborhood) groups.

Level A concerns the internal leadership of religious societies, formalized by elections and ruled by in-laws. Often clauses are inserted in order to avoid any enduring leadership. For instance the Saint Anthony's in-laws, art. 4, sec. 3 says:

The president cannot succeed himself after serving two consecutive terms in office for the period of one year.

Still formal offices are sufficiently numerous to allow the maintenance of different official appointments by charismatic leaders, and the maintenance of a diffused leadership through the control of appointments. For instance, Saint Anthony's Society has the following officers: president, vice president, recording secretary, treasurer, financial secretary, sergeant at arms, two trustees, and feast, entertainment, and audit committees.

> Every Committee shall consist of four (4) members and a Chairman.
> Except for the Audit Committee, which shall have three (3) members.
> (art. 6, sec. 1)

The more important places of power seem to be the officers and the Feast Committee and it is here that leaders have held offices over the years, sometimes simultaneously. The same situation can be seen in the other societies too, even if with some variants. For instance the Fishermen have a bigger Feast Committee (twelve people). In general the Feast Committee has direct power over the form that the feast will assume year after year, but it must always respect orthopraxy. The possible innovations do not concern the "religious" aspect of the ritual. Naturally orthodoxy is not to be questioned or discussed but orthopraxy is also very seldom questioned. Any innovations are incidental and related more to the "secular" aspect of the feast (sponsors, vendors, shows). This is not unexpected: if the feast declares authenticity, i.e. respect to a declared pure tradition, then the past ought to be respected. The duty is to maintain a "correct" practice, while avoiding any risk of entropy. As I said the loci for changes are in the secular realm. From this perspective the presence on stage of one musical band rather than another may be of extreme importance, but whatever changes occur, they will always remain within general recognizable conditions. In other words, the bands may be different but a heavy metal rock band will not be seen on a North End stage. One example of a successful innovation remaining within the range of the expected was the "Cheese Building Contest" during the Madonna del Soccorso feast. Participants, variously famous, were challenged to a gastronomic cheese-based contest. Not surprisingly the sponsor of the feast was Sorrento Cheese.

Level B concerns what I label as interethnic enclave leadership. The manifest goal of this power relationship is to decide the most influential society and the most important feast. The manifest competition of course refers to another diffuse and pervasive kind of power. For instance, while confirming at a first glance the supremacy of an enclave-based ethnic identity, negotiated power is about the possibility to relate, in different degrees, to the political authorities of the city at large, from the mayor to the representatives, to the speaker of the House. En passant, I would like to remind the reader that electoral votes in the North End were always an ethnic matter (Irish first, then Italian) or at most interethnic (Irish forming alliances with Italians and vice versa). In this general political arena ethnic enclaves have their own importance. I would like to highlight also that this relationship with the authorities never involves the religious sphere. Religious authorities, such as the Archbishop, were never contacted. This is not surprising if we consider the peculiar religiosity connected to the feast and the societies developed in the North End. When, as in the case of Saint Anthony's Society, some clergymen are invited to the feast, it is because they are the chaplain of the society (and so ought to be seen more as members, not authorities) or a priest coming from Italy with a relic of the saint.[24] The goal of any specific presence of the clergy (as confirmed by the numerous talks with the members of the society) was to underline the specificity of their own feast, showing that, in their own words, it was more traditionally religious, and thus superior to the other feasts. The leadership of the interethnic enclave, has been for a long time clearly stabilized around two poles: Saint Anthony and the Fishermen. Yet, other societies too have also had and still have a strong relevance. Nonetheless, the general opinion in the neighborhood as well as outside is that these two feasts are the greatest, at least for in terms of attendance and visibility in the media. This is without any doubt the result of a historic journey where an important role has been played by the ethnic enclave: emigrants from Montefalcione and Sciacca were and are the most numerous and dominant communities among the local settlers.[25]

Level C—representing groups connected to the declared ethnic enclaves who interact with other local groups, inside the North End, but not connected with ethnic enclaves—can be found by looking at local power relationships. I will analyze this aspect through the example of the Italian Council of Boston (ICB). The ICB is a recent organization, formed around the vision of preserving Italian identity. Membership is heterogeneous: Italian American and Italian (often a very difficult coexistence) but also containing representatives of different lobbies (from the economic, like the Italian American Chambers of Commerce, to the institutional, with members formally identifiable and very close to the Italian Consulate, to the religious, with the participation of the present parish priest of Saint Leonard). My presence (I was asked to become a member) at the board of the ICB can be seen as "the scholar of authoritative opinions," serving to characterize initiatives as historically and culturally validated (Cowan 1992, 174–175). More important, and truly authoritative, is the presence of Joe, the actual president of Saint Anthony's Society.

Level D—interethnic enclave groups interacting with other local groups, inside the North End, but not connected with ethnic enclaves—is exemplified by the case of the Sacred Heart. Autonomously formed against the closure of the parish the initial leadership of the committee was represented by the San Marco Society (and specifically Bennett and Richard Molinari). First attempts to widen the leadership were made by recruiting Jason, of Saint Anthony, and Sal, of the Fishermen. Jason especially had a fundamental function of linkage with the political authorities but also, with Sal's fundamental support, of involvement with other religious societies. In this example the relations between societies, referring at least to the imagined ethnic enclaves and with political power, are expressed in an obvious way. The success of the rally was impossible without Jason, Sal and the religious societies with which they were involved. All the societies were thus present, showing not only their shared interest in a common cause (a seeming attack on Italian identity) but also expressing the power relationships between societies and their leaders.

Level E—groups connected to the declared ethnic enclaves interacting with external groups (outside the neighborhood)—represent the relations within the society's various and geographically dislocated leadership. In particular I am referring to groups that represent, even if they do not constitute, an institutional authority. As I said before, a proclaimed leadership in the neighborhood can be used to negotiate relations of power with political representatives. Power relations display various levels of imbalance within the respective ethnic groups. The authorities, for instance, do not participate at every feast, but they will certainly attend whenever the bigger societies ask for their presence. The attendance at the feast of a political authority strengthens the society's power image at the moment of its maximum display. Of course, personal relations are not excluded from these dynamics. Indeed, they can often be very important: Jason, for instance, is a very close associate of Sal Di Masi, speaker of the Massachusetts House of Representatives, while the financial secretary of Saint Anthony is a relative of a city councilor.

Level F—interethnic enclaves groups interacting with external groups (outside the neighborhood)—is seen less often. One example is the collective performance to raise funds after 9/11. The recipient of the amount of money was a charitable association directly connected to the archdiocese of Boston. It does not seem that the initiative had any sort of follow-up. Furthermore, during my fieldwork I did not see any other action at this level. It seems to be practiced on a different informal and pervasive scale. Strategic essentialism in a situation of identity as a scarce resource presupposes exactly this goal: all the societies, pursuing the common target of preserving the local economy through the declaration of an ethnic identity, refer inevitably to a mostly nonresident audience: tourists. Their pervasive influence will be discussed in the next section.

Clergy, Parishes, and Societies

Since these are self-proclaimed religious societies, carrying the name of a saint, it is important to analyze the complex and ambivalent relationship between the societies and the local churches and parishes.

As noted, what Jerry says in this interview is apparently a founding legend of the relationship between societies and churches in the North End:

> Augusto: You told me that the statue was in the church so how could they use it in this way?

Jerry: No, no let me tell you the whole story, this is a long story on this . . . the thing is that they used to leave the statue there [in the church], they left donations to the church, so they could take it out. The next thing they would take the statue on Saturday night, they keep off all Saturday night and they had the mass at the church on Sunday, then they had the procession at two o'clock in the afternoon and they were back by six o'clock, because they didn't to go so far away: Hanover Street, Salem Street and that was it. And the next thing Matarazzo started his look-decorating company.[26] Emilio Matarazzo. And the next thing he was offering the decorating organization, you know, so far a small amount of money, you could decorate half of the North End for one thousand dollars. They used to decorate Endicott Street, all the way to Keaney Square, they used to do on Patrick Court (that's where I lived), part of Prince Street, part of Cooper, north of Margin Street, wherever the paesani lived. And they started getting bigger, ok? The parade started to get extended. Well what happen this way on until 1926 and I guess they were doing very well. So what happened that particular year when they want to take the statue back the priest said "I saw there was a lot of money on the statue and you people should divide the money with me. Actually you should donate all the money to the church." One of the members said, "Who is going to pay for the expenses?" which they couldn't understand. So what happened a little bit of dispute came, the police came so the story was I was told—I have been recently to the library doing research, I tried to find pictures but at that time the library had a flood, they lost a lot of the old papers. I asked for some of the microfilm, I spent this summer doing research—they ended up taking the statue to the police station, with the money, so they ended up going to the judge and the judge said 'They put all the money and they need the money for the expanses, if they wanna give the church a percentage that is another story'. So what happen they brought from the church and they take the statue out of the church and they kept it on Washington Street until 1958.

Augusto: I would like to understand better the relationship between the societies and the church, I mean the local church.

Jerry: The church is a totally separated thing. We are affiliated with St. Leonard, but the priest is not a member, he doesn't come to the meetings, we run the feast totally up to us. The only thing he does, if we invite him, the Friday night, the opening ceremony, he does the blessing. The mass, we have our own chapel, we make a donation to the church. This priest is very nice, we have a very nice relationship, father Michael. But we had problem with the church. I am going to tell you a little story, about father

Whealand. He refused to let us to put the lights near the church. Do you know Casa Maria? Just here? Before was a church, all block used to be a church. And he had a fence, an iron fence, and in the old days we used to put the wires from the pole against the fence, we used to tie it on the fence. He got to the point "No lights." So one year we had no light on Endicott and Cooper, he refuses to sign the permit. And the reason? We used to give donation to St. Leonard Church, we should give him the mass to say. We should do this we should do that. At that time Peter Greco was a fairly new member and he and my father worked together and I think Peter was in the committee. The next thing you know they took off the father and they let him drink a lot wine and the father went back to the church we had to taking back on Cooper Street, it was a little bad for the weather, the only thing before he left we slide a piece of paper on the table and he signed, that was the permit.

This feeling of rejection was mutual. Giacomo Gambera, an Italian priest who also worked in Boston, said in his autobiography:

First of all in a city in which you have a mixture of nonbelievers and those of other faiths, this parading of statues exposed religion to irreverence and derision. . . . In the second place, the promoters of these external feasts were generally not trustworthy individuals, they were not exemplary, they were not practicing Catholics and they were suspected of pure speculation. In fact, without any authorization, they used to solicit offerings from their fellow townsmen in the name of the feast of the parish. Then, when the parade was over, they would strip the statues of the offerings made and not render an account to anyone; at the most they would give an account to their societies as they wished. (1994, 157)

Beyond the economic level, the reason for the controversy clearly seems to be a matter of the control over devotion. Losing the exclusivity of managing religious icons and feasts, priests can lose power and social control over the parishioners. The phenomenon of separation between parishes and societies is quite evident analyzing the Saint Anthony of Padua of Montefalcione Society. The society has a very strong commitment to religious values, as can be demonstrated by the presence of a chaplain of the club during the festival. The first chaplain I met during the festival was Father Michael. He came from Claremont, New Hampshire, and he was devoted to Saint Anthony of Padua: not only he was in charge of celebrating the masses during the festival but he could easily be seen carrying the statue of the saint. After he died another chaplain was nominated: I met the new chaplain, Father Michael from New York City during the festival, after he blessed the statue of the saint. Both the chaplains had no connection whatsoever with the local parishes in the North End. Parish churches and societies were and still are two different and quite separate, things.

Epilogue

In conclusion, Boston's North End societies of saints can be succinctly defined as associations of individuals gathering together for moral reasons, independent from the local churches. They are voluntary, geographically based, and, at the beginning, exclusionary—with the exception of the practical essentialist plural membership. This definition resembles the idea of sect, as defined by Weber (1985) in his seminal article on American voluntary associations. Is it a superficial likeness or can we find a deeper consonance? In other terms, can the religious societies of Boston's North End be studied as sects, in the Weberian meaning of the term? Can a Catholic group, a group of chosen few who declare themselves a religious elite, represent the particularistic formation of the sect, where "the religiosity of the sect is one of the most specific forms of a vital, not just traditional, 'popular' religiosity'?" (ibid., 9) And, if so, what does it mean?

This is not only a matter of choosing a more or less useful theoretical tool. In my opinion this point of view changes the approach to the societies of saints dramatically: as Catholic groups they may belong to the tradition of the old country, as a collective with an embedded sect spirit, they belong instead to the modernity of the new one. It is possible to argue that a Catholic background does not provide members with the powerful signal, or symptom, of the grace of God. And it is also possible to set the distance between church and society in a more traditional anticlericalism, characteristic of the Italian experience of religion. But my suggestion is to study the religious societies of Boston's North End not only as expressions of the "Italian Problem of American Catholicism," looking at them as relics of the past,[27] but also as means for the creation and the claim for a "modern" (even if ephemeral) ethnic identity for Italian American, extended beyond religion. According to Weber "'the sects' importance extends far beyond the religious sphere. Only they give, for example, American democracy its own flexible structure and its individualistic stamp." (1985, 10) Therefore, these voluntary associations can be seen as a secular example of internalized American patterns of manufacturing community within an ideology of equality.

From this perspective the peculiar relationship between the church and societies of saints can be seen as a product of the ecclesiastic communal life in the United States. It becomes an expression of the ambiguous territory between the official constitutional ban on the official recognition of any church and the necessary, compelling private membership in a voluntary association, defined by Weber as descended from the archetypical model of the Protestant ecclesiastic community.

Therefore the relationship between the several societies of saints is not only as a "residuum" of the old campanilismo but also a characteristic example of an

Americans penchant for association. The crux of the matter is here the dichotomy "us/others." According to Hall and Lindholm (1999, 125) membership in voluntary associations is supposed to be based on shared caring, modeled on the ideal relationship between close friends and family and on the covenanted community of believers. And it is common for Americans to refer to one's own group as "everybody." This is exactly what happens in the societies of saints: the group is a declared "everybody."

But if the American group implies "everybody," as Varenne (1976, 95) has suggested, this ideology also implies that "outside of everybody there is nobody," with a consequent demonization of others.[28] If it is true that the tension between the us, the everybody inside the group, and the other, the nobody outside the group, is evident at every level of American culture (Hall and Lindholm 1999, 126), it is also true that this antagonism is not necessarily a threat to the social order:

> On the contrary, it makes it much harder for any group or representative of a group to present themselves as saviours of the American way, and so provides a base for the mundane continuance of a social order based on trust of other American as individuals, along with distrust of them in groups or as leaders. . . . The paranoia that often coincides with belonging may be unattractive, but it simply points out the real fragility of ties made primarily on the shaky grounds of affection. Sociologically speaking, such sentiments are far less harmful to the larger society than would be the case were strong commitments in place. Weak ties may not be heroic, but they also do not inspire fanaticism. (Hall and Lindholm 1999, 127–128)

The dynamic relationship observed in the religious societies of the North End expresses exactly this tension between "us/others," used at first to define the local ethnic enclave "against" other ethnic enclaves. Over the years, through an increasing process of secularization and modernization, with a weakening of the initial "strong commitments" based on geographical origin, the societies of saints still claim declared differences, supposed authenticity and ethnic belonging. But there is nothing "heroic" or "fanatic" about this claim, as plural membership and the changed relationship between societies demonstrate. Instead, proclaimed essentialism is strategically motivated. The goal, beyond the cry for recognition, is the common good of economic improvement, based on performed ethnic identities that are scarcely discernable.

The religious societies of Boston's North End are thus complex institutions, exclusionary sects, with fragile ties, situational and performative, malleable and fluid, both traditional and modern, allowing, like the religious practices, at the peak of their expressions, a continuous negotiation of ephemeral identities. These expressions, beliefs and practices, modalities, performances and processes visible in the feasts are the object of my next analysis.

4

The Festive Practices

The religious feasts I am going to analyze are local celebrations of Catholic saints, patrons of the villages of origin. This simple and very generic definition immediately raises two important issues: the significance of religious devotion to the saints for Italians (especially southern Italians) and Italian Americans, and the transnational character of the feast, displaced between the Old World and the New World. These festivals evoke a variety of patron saints and of local origins: the Madonna del Soccorso, celebrated by the Sicilians of Sciacca; next Saint Anthony of Padua, celebrated by the Montefalcionesi; San Domenico, protector of Augusta; and so on. This attachment to specific areas of origin, so evident in the complex festive practices, reflects degrees of intercommunal differentiation. Such differences in intensity of the degree of differentiation reflect the historical, geographical and cultural distances between originating communities. This premise allows me to approach the feasts of patron saints as symbols and aggregations of symbols, and I will use them as dramatic demonstrations and confirmations of group identity, occurring ritually every year, organized around the display of central religious statues, carried in procession through the streets of the neighborhood or, better, of the ethnic enclaves, claiming a mythical origin in a different, modified landscape, where cultural identities—and people are well aware of the complexity of the problem—are continuously negotiated. Hyphenated identities, ethnic identities, mythical origin and enclave, hybridization and creolization all declined over time in different ways. These and many other questions arise around the religious icon.

I will begin with ethnographic data, and outline a narrative of the festivals. I am aware of the risk implied in this approach, which is to focus above all on texts and narrative structures, losing the fluidity of utterances and the dynamic contribution of agencies. I will suggest that focusing on the performative aspects of the narrative of the feasts is not only a way to avoid this risk but, definitely more important, a way to preserve the complexity of these cultural events as much as possible. Therefore I will follow Galaty's suggestions that the pragmatics of ritual, which I assume as a performative presentation, be contrasted with or, better, be analyzed together with the ritual as text:

> An account of a ritual code cannot exhausts its meaning, since in actual performance it assumes properties of "indexicality," by which contextual factors—the actual participants, pragmatic decisions about its enactment, the expression of emotions—lend to the event (as opposed to the code) a significance of its own. (1983, 364–365)

I will approach the identities negotiated by and through the event of the feast. I assume that the feasts declare the community, or, more accurately, the communities. Therefore the data will allow me to argue against the idea of "*communitas*" (Turner 1978) or the concept of "imagined community" (Anderson 1983) and to propose instead the concept of "ephemeral communities," with malleable and ephemeral identities. I suggest that a model of identities paying more attention to multiplicity, polyphony, and fragmentation, a model framed within a process of never ending constructions, where identities emerge as unfinished and are determined by continuous practices of negotiation, definition and redefinition, should be preferred to any other model of identities. But if it is true that identities are historically and situationally constructed, it is also true that "we need to explore the possibility of a theoretical understanding of social and cultural identity in terms of objective social location.[1] To do so, we need a cognitivist conception of experience . . . a conception that will allow for both legitimate and illegitimate experience, enabling us to see experience as source of both real knowledge and social mystification" (Mohanty 1999, 43). Therefore identity is at the same time socially constructed but not completely arbitrary. It is not self-evident, but is discovered through interpretations of experiences and refers to an epistemic access to reality. From this perspective I will argue that approaching the religious practices as technologies of the self allows us to understand the complex dynamic between groups and self, intentional and situational, as well as strategically proposed essentialist choices. My aim is to demonstrate how each North Ender is engaged in this endless game with "series of move[s] which are objectively organized as strategies without being the product of a genuine strategic intention" (Bourdieu 1979, 72). My aim is thus to propose multiple identities and belongings, analyzing the dynamic game of entrances, escapes and cultural commuting, possible only through the continuous manipulation of symbols.

Last but not least choosing a reflexive approach I will face methodological issues. As I will describe, the problems evoked by the presence of an Italian scholar inside a supposed Italian American community in Boston are numerous and striking: questions of recognizability, issues of emotional distance and excessive proximity, confusions of roles where the dangerous feeling of nostalgia played a major part, just to name a few.

The Festive Practices

An important part of my ethnographic fieldwork was attending and collecting data on the religious festival practices. The feasts begin the first Sunday in June, with the festival dedicated to Santa Maria di Anzano, and end on the second Sunday in September, which is the festival dedicated to Santa Rosalia. Festivals are scheduled every weekend: Saint Anthony of Padua (in June, also known as the "Little Saint Anthony"), Saint Jude, Madonna delle Grazie, San Rocco, San Domenico, San Giuseppe, Santa Agrippina, Madonna della Cava, Madonna del Soccorso, Saint Anthony of Montefalcione (in August, the "Big Saint Anthony"),[2] and Santa Lucia. All of these festivals, with the exception of the Little Saint Anthony, are organized by private voluntary societies, independent from the religious institutions.

Over the years the calendar has changed. Some feasts have disappeared like the religious societies that used to run them. It is still possible to find memories about these lost feasts in newspapers or by talking to people of the North End. For example, memories of San Ciriaco from the Marche, San Giovanni of Messina or Maria Santissima del Buon Consiglio of Candida are also mentioned by De Marco (1981, 67).[3] Seldom the North Enders propose new feasts: during my fieldwork and my bibliographical researches I did not see any new feast connected to different villages of origin or specific ethnic enclaves other than the listed ones. In other words, the feasts in the North End seem in general connected with a specific ethnic enclave, historically formed on the base of the mythical Italian village. Because of the new pattern of migration, and because of the present condition of the North End, definitively no longer the slum where the immigrants used to land, new ethnic enclaves seem difficult to form. Therefore it seems now almost impossible to propose a new feast.[4]

The Little Saint Anthony

I am going to start my analysis of the North End's feasts with the Little Saint Anthony, because it was the first feast I attended and because many of my questions arose that first day. Reading my field notes I can see not only the feast as it first appeared to me, but also in retrospect the trajectory my observations of the festive practices in the North End have taken. This allows me to approach the usual twofold aspect of any anthropological research: "objects" standing in front of observers and observers, as objects of reflexive inquires. The dynamic and reciprocal flow of influences and manipulations, of forces and interferences, agreement and disagreement, as well as fondness and carelessness; the quest for emotional proximities and the quest for emotional distancing; were and still are a continuous stimulus for my reflections and analysis.

I will quote my field notes directly, at least in the first instance, in order to outline a rough draft of this trajectory. I want to state that at the beginning I wrote my field notes in Italian: it was a way to keep myself closer to the object— the religious feasts—that was familiar to me in my Italian experience, and because I deeply wanted to find "Italian" being "Italian" even in a different place. This psychological symbiosis was not easy to identify and very hard to elaborate, and it caused mistakes and misunderstandings, but it was also the necessary premise for my subsequent insights: elaborating the symbiosis that allowed me to finally address the Italian American festival of Boston's North End in a much more appropriate way.

> *Sunday, June 11.*[5] I arrived in the North End around 1:30 P.M. Finding Hanover Street was easy, I learned my way even through the Big Dig's constructions. I still have the impression that the North End is— still?—an Italian neighborhood: stores, peoples, somehow the structure itself of the neighborhood remind me of Italy. More precisely I should say I had the impression of how we Italians imagine an Italian neighborhood in the US. Inevitably the filmic references are quite evident: the Italian American *Godfather*, by Francis F. Coppola, especially the second part, or the Italian *Once upon a time in America*, by Sergio Leone. It is the same impression I had the other times I came here.

The symbiosis I was just talking about is evident here. In these first instances of my fieldwork my need was to not recognize any cultural distance between the field and myself, or to fix my impressions on a recognizable imagery. Evidently it was my way to face the "other" not yet understood or even recognized.

> In front of St. Leonard's Church four or five women sat behind a stall, selling religious objects such as small holy pictures portraying St. Anthony, pins, and rosaries. [See figure 4.1.] I talked to an elderly man, standing near the stall, beside, I think, his wife. I spoke in Italian, asking if the procession was starting from there. The woman answered me, telling me that the procession would start from there around 2:00 P.M. The statue would be brought out into the open outside the church a few minutes before. The woman specified that this was the only feast organized by the parish, the others were organized by private societies. The feast was recently instituted, it seems for economic reasons (*la parrocchia ha bisogno di soldi*—the parish needs money). . . . Another woman began talking to me in Italian (characteristic of the entire day: everybody— EVERYBODY—had been absolutely at ease and comfortable with me as soon as they realized I was Italian, which happened after a couple

FIGURE 4.1   Stand outside St. Leonard Church. (Author's photograph.)

of seconds because of my strong accent). The woman was born in Boston but the family is originally from Avellino. This initial detail has a great importance: furthermore Mr. Greco, a seventy-five years old gentleman from Gaeta, explained to me that even the Little Saint Anthony was organized by Avellinesi, confirming the hypothesis that the feasts are organized on geographical bases.

The information gathered and noted in these few sentences are important: (1) the Little Saint Anthony is the only feast organized by the parish, while the others are organized by private societies. It is recently instituted, for economic reasons; (2) the stall suggests an economic aspect of the feast. Interestingly members of the organizing committee are selling only religious products. This feast is directly run by the parish, and this explains the religious objects for sale, and vendors do not participate because the Little Saint Anthony is not an important tourist attraction; (3) even if this is a parish feast it is still possible to trace a specific ethnic enclave (the Avellinesi) organizing at least the specific cult. The Avellinesi (specifically, from Montefalcione) also organize the Big Saint Anthony, the last weekend in August; and (4) the field notes show also the dynamic of acceptance of an "Italian" by the "Italians" of the North End. Sometime I opportunistically used this dynamic "game" in order to be accepted faster by the insiders. But I was also inevitably setting an image—the Italian studying the Italians—carrying ambiguities and sometimes even confusions. Language was the tool I used to suggest this image of myself: I addressed the people at the feast directly in Italian or sometimes in English while apologizing for my strong accent, in order to be recognized as Italian. Asking in Italian if that was the starting point of the procession provoked not only an answer in the same language, not really important per se, but also recognition as an "insider." Immediately a woman asked me where I was from and when I answered I was from Caserta she burst out laughing: "Allora simme paisane!" [Therefore we are from the same area] because she was from Avellino (a city nearby). This feeling of closeness was emphasized also by questions about my possible acquaintances: she asked me if I knew a guy in Caserta who was the owner of a store downtown, and when I answered: "Yes" she seemed very happy, and used the Neapolitan saying: "U' vi'? simme asciut"a pariente!" [See? We found we are relatives]. And how could I refuse to buy a small article (a little bottle of blessed oil of Saint Anthony) from a quasi-relative when she asked me, in dialect and always smiling: "Mò però t"e accatta' caccosa, a' chiesa ce servone sorde" [But now you should buy something, the parish needs money?] Acceptance has, evidently, its cost! Maria, this is her name, during all the feasts was an important referent for my questions and doubts. With Mr. Greco my approach was different: I first talked to him in English, but immediately apologized for my accent. He looked at me answering "My English is not better than yours, I am Italian too. Where are you from?" And when I answered I was from near Naples he switched to dialect: "I' songhe 'e Gaeta" [I am from Gaeta], again claiming a geographic as well as symbolic proximity. I spoke with Mr. Greco all afternoon, following the procession with him, asking him what I wanted to know about the feast and answering him about what he wanted to know about Italy. Back then I thought that presenting myself as Italian would be a good strategy to be accepted. It was a fast way, but not without consequences. The most negative effect I caused was that interviewees showed me just their "Italian side," and not more their complex identities. They showed up later, after long work in the field. What I gained in fast acceptance and specific information I lost in the slow process to understand the complicated game of identity negotiations.

While I was talking with Mr. Greco, the statue of the Saint was set on the church courtyard. Some ten people were around the statue, adorning it with white ribbons and pinning money on those ribbons. Not far away, a few women were holding small baskets with holy pictures and pins, portraying St. Anthony, giving them to whoever would make an offering.

> It seems to me evident that this is the traditional structure of the *paranza*,[6] with roles and functions easily identifiable: certainly there is a *capoparanza* (Anthony, the *leader* of the group), then the *statue-bearers*, exclusively male roles, and the *beggars*, holding the ribbons,

exclusively women. The presence of the ecclesiastic institution is evident but discreet: the two friars, after the blessing of the statue, followed the procession only for few yards, in order to be back to the church for other services. Afterwards only Father Mattia was present, but visibly at the end.

It is arguable, being a general and generic level of abstraction, that individuating the composition of the group can be a first step to infer social dynamics and how they are revealed during the ritual time of the feast. But some distinctions can be initially deduced: first, a sort of separation between the representatives of the ecclesiastic institution and the rest of the faithful. After the blessing Father Mattia followed the procession but not in a leading position. Two interpretations are possible, and they are not necessary incompatible. On one hand it is possible to see two different, clearly defined, levels of the feast: a liturgical one, controlled by the church, and a secular one, managed by the specific organizational group. The distinction is formally evident, but it does not necessarily mean that the church disappears in the second instance. Simply the church allows the other group to take possession of the feast. In terms of the power relationship the difference is enormous: allowing the secular group to hold the procession is a hegemonic act. It is again a sort of consensual transgression, ritually permitted inside the complexity of the ritual. It is not unusual to see this exercise of power even during southern Italian feasts. On the other hand this is the pattern of the other religious festivals in Boston's North End: the priest is visibly a marginal figure. It does not make too much difference if the Little Saint Anthony is a parish feast, still recognized by the neighbors. As I will show later, the only possibility for recognition is to follow the general pattern. Both interpretations are legitimate and most probably they coexist in this specific practice, as a displaced memory and as a more actual pattern.

Another important separation clearly suggested by the composition of the group is a gender-based one: roles and rules are rigidly established between men and women. At a first glance, this confirmed Gans's (1962) conclusion regarding the West End in the 1950s, namely, that the social structure, based on sexual segregation and marginalization, which the immigrants brought from southern Italy, has changed remarkably little. Social practices, as well as social spaces, are traditionally separated. This could be true for the traditional social groups of southern Italian immigrants, in both the original village and the ethnic enclave, even if more information seems necessary. More precisely these differences refer to different social spaces (home for women/outside for men) and different interest spheres (household management for women/economic gathering for men, for instance) still with embedded female subalternity but in a more complex way. Stereotypically, the male role is seen as strong, tough, and sometime even boasting. According with this stereotype the female role should be seen as subdued, sweet-smiling, and always trying to please men (Boelen

1992, 21). But, as stereotypes, these roles evoke more of a code of performance then a power structure, obviously with all the possible reciprocal influences between the two extremes of the continuum.[7] In the modern urban landscape of Boston's North End—and more in general, as demonstrated by Ruberto (2007) in her analysis of migrant Italian women and the struggles for hegemony in the United States—this stereotype needs to be discussed in depth in order to unfold its complexity: social spaces and interest spheres have changed over the years and the centrality of women for the family as well as of men for earning the economic necessity are diluted. Male and female roles of are profoundly changed, toward more interchangeable positions.[8] But still some manipulations of symbols are practiced, as in the case of the group around the statue of the saint: women and men took different places with different, gender-based, functions. When asked the reason for this distinction—not only during the Little Saint Anthony feast—the answers, invariably, were this is the tradition and this is the Italian way.

These are expected answers but nevertheless they need to be analyzed. In fact saying that this is the Italian way involves the reframing of an ambiguous stereotype: a supposed women's subalternity can be a matter of denigration by an outsider, and surely it is seen as a disparaging value. During several interviews Mary, Vivian and other women involved in the religious societies referred to having arguments with people outside the North End on this topic. For instance, Mary remembered schoolmates teasing them because being Italian and woman meant being repressed. In order to show them how this was not true, Mary decided to bring her schoolmates to a night club one Saturday night. Surprisingly not only easily she could enter the club but it was very clear she was welcome there. "Well . . . I didn't say to my friends that my family was involved in the show business, but they were very astonished that night." Vivian used to argue with coworkers. She referred to an episode about smoking habits: being a nonsmoker her friends considered her, back then, to be scared by possible family reactions. It took a long time to convince them that she did not smoke just because she did not like it, and that her Italian family had nothing to do with this choice: "That was funny! My father used to smoke two packs a day, and my mother too was a smoker!" But at the same time, identifying this as "the Italian way" carries the supposed correlated interest spheres (such as family, sober sexual behaviors, care of relatives and friends, etc.).[9] It promotes the local communities, claiming for them the essential cultural traits. At the same, this is a way to declare through the term "tradition" the specific community (in this case the local parish and, in origin, the Avellinesi) and the community at large (the North End) bonded by and through the implied moral values. The communities declare themselves to be Italian (with less or more adjectives) manipulating not only the feast as a symbol but, metonymically, also the specific symbol.

Another important aspect I noticed almost immediately was the marching band following the procession:

While the group was intent adorning the statue and observing Father Mattia's blessing, on the churchyard the marching band, called Roma Band, was meeting. I spoke for a while with Richard, the band manger, and we will definitely meet again. Meanwhile some of the musicians, becoming aware I was Italian, started to talk with me. At 2:00 P.M. the statue was carried into the street and the procession began. A policeman on a motorbike opened the procession—I saw Anthony, the leader of the group giving him the map of the procession—then comes the statue, carried by the statue-bearers led by Anthony, and surrounded by the beggars. The marching band follows the statue.

The Roma Band is the most popular marching band in the Boston area, invariably present in all the Italian American feasts, not only those of the North End. It is extremely interesting to analyze the repertoire as well as the history and the current composition of the band, as an important moment of identities negotiation, and I will later dedicate a section to this specific topic. The position of the band behind the statue of the saint follows a general pattern that can be also noted in the correspondent Italian rituals. Music is an important component of religious festival, even if for Catholic clergy it ought to be considered a supporting component, an embellishment expected but not vital, and sometimes even reason for arguments.[10] In the North End the clergy is not generally involved in the feast, therefore it has no control on the marching band and its repertoire. The religious society run the feast and often the band is asked to play a specific piece of music for a specific donor when the procession stops by to accept their offers. What remains is the symbolic distribution of the components along the procession, suggesting a subaltern, even if definitely important, role of the marching band. The procession is probably the most important or at least the most evidently important moment of the feast, especially of a small-scale feast like the Little Saint Anthony (see figure 4.2.)

The economic aspect of the feast, besides the offering, was exclusively concentrated on the stall outside the church which was selling religious objects; the entertainment (and it is certain that it is a form of entertainment) was centered on the marching band's performances. Any other religious service, such as mass or blessings, was celebrated in an almost intimate way, with few attendants, in the church and before the official beginning of the feast. The basic function of the procession, and I will come back on this specific point again and again, is to trace the boundaries of the religious community, ritually making them sacred because of the passage of the sacred icon of the saint.

The procession has an economic relevance too: the money offering of the faithful is generally a public one. The statue will stop by the offerer, allowing him or her to pin the money directly on the statue or, more often, to give the money to the beggars and/or to Anthony to do so. The passage of the statue thus is also a reminder to make the offerings. As soon as an offerer makes the offering, the

FIGURE 4.2   Procession of the Little Saint Anthony. (Author's photograph.)

Roma Band plays the so called "Numero 1," or "Marcia Reale."[11] This can be seen at one and the same time as a form of public thanks and also as an acoustic request for other offerings. The public identification of the votive offering implies competition, therefore it is an incentive for other potential offerers.

Continuing the reading of my field notes, I wrote down, at this point:

> It doesn't seem easy to identify the "external" group: on the streets there are not very many people attending the procession. The statue stopped many times in front of private homes, restaurants, churches, nursing homes, and religious societies. Sometimes, especially from the restaurants, people came out with ribbons already filled with money, while I did not see any offerings from the churches or the religious societies. But mainly the procession stopped to receive offerings from individual donors. In order to receive the offering (in general, money) the statue is placed on the ground, the donor gives the money directly or indirectly through the beggars to Anthony, the leader, who then puts the money on the statue. It also happens that the donor may put the offering on the saint on his or her own. It is interesting to observe how the statue-bearers set the statue down when they stop in front of churches,

religious societies or nursing homes. It seems to have something to do with a kind of respect: the statues stops, facing the church, etc. and slightly bows down.

The components of the groups around the icons of the saints distinguish themselves by the use of different uniforms: the priest, with his ritual clothes; the marching band, with (in the case of the Roma Band) light blue and black clothes; the statue-bearers and the beggars (with different nuances, not present in the Little Saint Anthony situation) and the secular authority, the policeman with the official uniform. The uniforms describe the roles and the rules during the performance of the festival, as well as the degree of proximity to the divinity: not wearing any kind of uniform means a noninvolvement or at least an indirect involvement. For example the audience of the feast who do not need to wear any sort of distinctive signal of identification.

The Little Saint Anthony is basically a feast on a small scale, as I said concentrated almost entirely on the procession. Not many people attended the procession, surely fewer than one hundred persons including the organizing group and the audience. On the streets just the occasional passersby and a few parishioners were visible. Nevertheless many people were awaiting the arrival of the statue at home, behind their windows, ready to make their offerings. Countless times the statue stopped by the windows or near the door to allow the faithful to give the money. Often the offerings are just bills; sometimes the money is already pinned to ribbons or other offering sheets of different shapes. The votive offering is a homage to the saint, intimately connected to the peculiar pattern of devotion characterizing the religion of the streets of the southern Italians and the Italian Americans. It is a way to show, most publicly, respect for the saint. But in specific situations it is the icon of the saint who pays respect. This double bond was analyzed by Orsi in the case study of Our Lady of Mount Carmel in East Harlem, New York:

> And so the street theologians proclaimed: that divine and human were in a relationship of mutual responsibility and reciprocity; that the divine needed the human as the human needed the divine; that Christ's redeeming blood established an intimacy between heaven and the *domus*; that the power of the divine was awesome, not always comprehensible from the perspective of the human and to be approached with love and fear; that the divine was bound to behave with *rispetto* (respect) toward the human, that living and dead, holy and human existed together in communion of saints; that what God proposed men and women must respect, though they were also free to entreat the divine for help and support. (1984, 405–406)

In the North End the respect is shown by the group performing the procession to churches, to the institution appointed for the sacred (the religious societies) and to similar groups of interest bound by the same religious and secular goals (the nursing homes and even elder people) thus declaring the importance of their roles for the community, at least during a ritual claiming continuity with tradition and identity.

> The procession broke up, for a few minutes, when it arrived in front at the Madonna del Soccorso's club. The statue of the saint was placed inside the club, just in front of the Madonna. All the *paranza* paid respect to the statue of the Madonna. The President of the society was talking with a woman, who was teasing him about being not completely Italian (English family name). The band has been allocated to the basement were some refreshments were served. I went with Salvi, the trumpeter and I guess the musical leader of the Roma Band, downstairs for a soda. I did not stay long and soon I went back on the street, to talk with some other people. I met again Mr. Greco and I talked to him for a while. He told me about his life, being originally from Gaeta and immigrating to the United States long before World War II. He fought in Italy during the war as an American soldier and it was a sort of paradox because for him Mussolini was and still is a myth, having done so much for Italy, like the draining of the Pontine marsh and the building of the city of Littoria, now Latina. I tried not to comment on his ideas, but of course I told him I was in a complete disagreement. For sure it seems a feeling that is widespread among older immigrants. Mr. Greco told me that I was attending a very small feast, with few offerings: "the other Saint Anthony's feast is much bigger, the statue is completely covered by money, you cannot see the nose of the statue." While I was talking to Mr. Greco the Roma Band reassembled to continue the procession, and before to starting to walk, they played for me "Mamma." I did appreciate it, it was very kind.

The break that the procession had in front of the Fishermen's club raises the issue of the relationship between religious societies and, more in general, with clergy and faithful. As I said above, these relationships are very complex, covering the complete range from irreducible distance to indifference to formed alliances.[12] This case showed a personal friendship between the president of the society and members of the other groups (revealed in the colloquial speech used by the speakers). The statue was placed in front of the Madonna del Soccorso, formally paying respect to the "other" society, while the group informally appreciated the refreshment offered by the Fishermen inside their club. This kind of support is a way to help smaller societies or, in this case, less formal groups to perform their feasts successfully. In this way the calendar can be respected and the North End can sustain a feast every weekend of the summer. The Little Saint Anthony is, as Mr. Greco stated again, a small festival, considering the attendance and the amount of the offerings. Clearly the money pinned on the statue is not so great an amount since can still see the face and the nose of the saint under the donated bills, but the importance of the feast in a more general perspective is fundamental, contributing to declare, and to negotiate through the expressed symbols, the cultural identities of the North End.

A last remark: the discussion with Mr. Greco—at that time very natural to me, even if somehow disturbing because of the profoundly different political positions—reopens the question of being Italian inside an imagined Italian community. And the Roma Band, manipulating highly symbolic musical objects, did the same, by recognizing me and declaring itself as Italian, in the middle of the street of Boston's North End and during the performance of the feast. Why did Mr. Greco feel the need to discuss Italian political issues with me, and why did I feel it so natural to accept the discussion? Why did the Roma Band dedicate a song like "Mamma" to me?[13] The problem goes beyond the importance or eventual reciprocal interests of the issue or the music and it most probably has to do with the roles that we, Mr. Greco, the Roma Band and I, had performed during the feast. Attending the feast, being recognized as Italian because of my need to be recognized as Italian and because of their need to declare themselves as Italian, we set up an imagined stage playing respectively rhetorically determined roles. Hyperbole is probably the figure of speech we used most: Mr. Greco dealt with one of the most stinging Italian political problems; the Roma Band, proposing a song with the symbolic aura of a maternal love—another classic stereotype intimately connected with a possible Italian cultural identity—and immediately recognizable by all in attendance as an Italian song; and myself, declaring not only my ethnicity but also the reason for my presence there, as an Italian scholar interested in what they were doing. All these things were not without consequences for focusing the moment of observation. Again, to me it was evidently important to recognize the object of my observation reshaping it into an already established theoretical frame. Naturally I was aware of this risk before the beginning of my fieldwork. Nevertheless, it was not easy to recognize this very artificial approach and it took some time. I think that two main factors were involved: on one hand, the problematic and dangerous, even if very human, feeling of nostalgia, and, on the other hand, my training as anthropologist in Italy. I suppose that everyone experiencing the anthropological field sooner or later, in a tent outside the village or in the middle of an urban landscape, must confront this feeling. It is an effect of dealing with "others" in a different, other, space. Somewhat paradoxically, the more the space and the otherness are distant the more a rapid elaboration is possible: perceived distances as well as perceived differences become psychological tools that allow the ethnographer to face, sustain and go through the experience of fieldwork. I do not claim any necessary distancing and separation between a supposed observer and a supposed observed. I merely suggest that an important moment during the fieldwork is the elaboration of these ambiguities in order to validate the observation. This ambiguity does not help set a clear, correct, fruitful relationship between the characters performing the ethnographic experience.

The methodological issue concerning my former Italian training can be sketched here in the following way: I come from a scholarly tradition (De Martino, Cirese, Lombardi Satriani, Gallini, Signorelli, just to name few of the important Italian scholars, with Gramsci as primary inspiration), who paid attention to a different object of study, subalternity, than American anthropologist. This is in a dynamic relationship with hegemonic strata of the society. The "exotic" becomes an internal object, definable and recognizable by class positions. Distance is not a geographical or linguistic issue, but a social one. The main problem was, therefore, to deal with apparently familiar objects like subalternity, religiosity and folklore, dislocated in a totally different setting. The desire to do so, without taking into consideration the problem of dislocation was unconsciously very alluring to me. I needed time to elaborate the issues, but first it was necessary to recognize them. As I will say shortly there was a specific moment when I realized how differences and distances, the consequences of dislocation, were vitally important.

Saint Jude

Devotion to Saint Jude is relatively recent in the United States where it was established in 1929 in Chicago (Orsi 1996).[14] The most popular shrines dedicated to Saint Jude are in Jersey City, Chicago, and Baltimore.

> As soon as I arrived in Hanover Street I looked for the place from where the procession would start. I went inside Saint Leonard's Church but I already knew that I could not find the statue there, since the feast was organized by a private society. In fact, it was not there, but as soon as I was out of the church I noticed a stall with a woman setting the baskets with religious medals and small holy pictures. On the stall there was a painting, not very big, with the image of Saint Jude.

The feast of Saint Jude was the first feast organized by a private religious society that I attended. By the time of the festival my fieldwork was already started so I did gather information about that specific ritual. I already knew that the church was certainly not involved in the feast; nevertheless, I wanted to check if any institutional event was going on. But the visit paid to Saint Leonard's Church confirmed the noninvolvement: the church was empty; not a single ceremony was celebrated; the priests were probably somewhere else. Not too much further down Hanover Street, I noticed the stall. That was the starting point of the procession, just as in the case of the Little Saint Anthony. Another similarity was that the objects for sale were religious items, this time concerning Saint Jude: little statues, votive candles, medals, pins and small holy pictures. I noticed a painting, with the icon of Saint Jude, placed on the table (see figure 4.3).

The function of this painting was not immediately clear to me, but it became evident during this feast and later I saw this pattern in the other rituals. The painting was not carried in procession but it was left there, on the table, with a few of the faithful around. Two interpretations are possible and, again, they do not seem mutually exclusive. The pragmatic, economic, interpretation is that leaving a ceremonial image near the club allows even passersby, not directly involved with the procession, to pin money on the ribbons. The symbolic interpretation is that the saint does not "completely" leave his specific residence: the procession will take place along the streets of the North End, the statue will be carried all over the neighborhood, but the starting point, his place, is clearly marked. Implicitly the painting, or, as I will show for other feasts, a more elaborate temporary chapel, suggests the idea of the return of the saint to the initial point. The icon of the saint belongs to the members of a specific society: publicly placed in the temporary chapel, often just outside the club, the statue, as participants pointed out during the interviews, marks the center of the ethnic enclave, which is not the parish as in the Italian case but the voluntary society.

Near the stall Salvi, the Roma Band's trumpeter, was talking with somebody. As soon as he saw me he waved at me so I went by and we started to talk. He scolded me because I did not join the Roma Band at the party offered by Benito, the previous Sunday, after the Saint Anthony

FIGURE 4.3   The icon of Saint Jude, placed on the table. (Author's photograph.)

procession in East Boston. A few laughs later, I asked Salvi where the statue was, because we were in the middle of Hanover Street, surely very close to the point where the procession would start. The platform was there, but no trace at all of the statue. Salvi escorted me to near the main door of a building, a few steps away from we were talking before. There, he introduced me to the president of the society, the organizer of the feast, who told me that the statue was upstairs, at his house.

The feeling of intimacy Salvi's friendly welcome provoked was even more consistent than before because his waving was not only a communication to me but also to the other people around, showing the closeness of the bond that had formed between the two of us. It was the spoken scolding that showed and proved the intimacy of the relationship: only between friends is such a performance allowed.[15] Salvi helped me to find out the reason for the absence of the statue. The presence of the platform clearly demonstrated the starting point of the procession but the statue was missing. Peter, the president of the society explained to me that traditionally he had sheltered the statue at home: the society was not rich enough to open a club and the relationship with the local clergy were not as good as it might be. Therefore the club and statue were accommodated in his private house. Even though I was already aware of the private character of the feast it was a surprise to me to find out where the statue was actually located. In my previous experiences I had often seen sacred corners set aside in private homes. These spaces are generally filled with sacred images, votive candles and flowers. I have also very often seen sacred images pinned up in different parts of the house, or even outside in barns and sheds, with a clear protective function for people and animals. But this was the first time I had heard about a statue, destined to be carried in procession, being hosted inside a private house. There was an initial moment of perplexity: the frame I was trying to set up as an interpretative model was being very quickly destroyed thanks to what at the time I though was an oddity. The statue of a saint in a private house did not fit at all into the pattern of "Italian" ritual, directly or indirectly pervaded by the Catholic hierarchy who owned, if not the feast, surely the official religious icons. It seemed strange to me, therefore, to see the saint getting down from the stairs of the tenement, but it was a salutary shock, a first step toward a disambiguated approach.

On the street the platform was ready to hold the statue and all around the group of statue-bearers and beggars was forming. Nearby two young boys were standing with a banner. As I could note, on the banner there was not only the name of the society, dedicated to Saint Jude Thaddeus, but also two important pieces of information: the foundation date (September 13, 1983) and the private, legally established, character of the society (Inc.). The society is definitely very young, at least with respect to other centenarian societies, and follows the pattern of voluntary and private associations, typical of the other religious societies in the North End.

What are the implications of the relative youth of the society? At first, the society is not directly based on any ethnic enclave either in the neighborhood nor in the old country. Secondly, since it is not geographically determined the ties binding together the group are specifically devotional. It so happens that devotion to Saint Jude is typically Italian American, more than Italian. Not surprisingly therefore if a new feast is proposed it will involve an "American" devotion.

The statue finally was posed under the platform and the group began to decorate it, pinning money on the ribbons. The behavior of a middle-aged woman was especially striking to me. She directly placed her ribbon and hugged the statue, very tight and for long time. I noted later that she was the mother of a disabled teenager. She told me, during the procession, that she is really devoted to Saint Jude, as is her son.

I spoke for a while with an old member of the society. He was very proud of belonging to the society and of having a function during the procession which allowed him to always stay very close to the statue.[16] He said he was too old now to carry the statue, but in that way he could be helpful.

At 2:00 P.M. the procession started, opened by the banner held by the two children . For the first time I heard the order "On the shoulders." The statue-bearers at the command lifted the statue to their shoulders and the procession began. At this point the Roma Band played Shubert's "Ave Maria," one of the rare religious pieces of its repertoire.

As I had noted previously, the church is absolutely extraneous to the ritual. I did not notice a priest even blessing the statue. Nevertheless the first stops that the statue made were in front of Saint Stephen and Saint Leonard churches to pay respect to the Catholic institution.

The procession, escorted by a policeman, was basically analogous, in its general practice, to what I had already seen. However, I noticed a more complex organization of the group around the statue: the leader did not hold a fixed position; rather he moved all along the procession, maybe for better recognition. The opening position in front of the statue was held by another member, near the banner held by two young boys, whose main purpose was to speed up or to slow down the walk. The statue-bearers were helped by two members holding the platform's poles, in front and in back, to better balance of the statue. Around the statue women were holding the ribbons with the offerings or carrying baskets with the religious images to give to those making offerings.

The main function of the procession was the sanctification of the particular spaces to which the group of faithful belong. and at which the statue stopped, along the way. The statue received homage (cash, but also checks, sometime in memory of deceased faithful) and was paid homage. As I observed for the little Saint Anthony, the statue paid respect to Saint Stephen and Saint Leonard churches, to other societies, to nursing homes, and to the memorial plaque for the War Heroes, in Paul Revere's Mall. I expected these procedures: they belong to a familiar pattern I have seen many times in Italy. But during the procession a small event occurred, almost unnoticed, but which was very enlightening to me: the statue stopped to pay respect in front of the firehouse. After the first oddity of seeing a statue of the saint held inside a private house, I now saw what was for me at that time another oddity. Why should the saint pay respect to firemen? It did not make any sense to me: respect is due to churches, religious societies, elderly people, war heroes, but why firemen? Later I realized that this is because regard for them is simply different, profoundly different, in Italy than the United States: in Italy firemen are regarded as merely workers, but in the United States firemen are much more. They are heroes, with a mythical aura,[17] and are therefore worthy of the highest respect, the respect that comes from a saint. Now I was certain that I was not in Italy. I was not attending an Italian religious feast. I was not dealing with objects familiar in my observation. In spite of all my efforts to grasp superficial similarities, supported by the people I met for complementary reasons, I was a stranger in a strange land. It was at this point that the ethnographic work, now disambiguated, could finally start.

Feast of San Domenico, Patron of Augusta

Like the Avellinese, the Sicilian ethnic enclave in the North End is not a homogenous whole. It is fragmented into different sections, probably more distinct in the past than now. The North End was and still is in the declared perception of the neighbors an archipelago of ethnic enclaves, based on the village of origin. All the consultants stated this point very clearly. As I already demonstrated, it is correct to speak about Abruzzese, Avellinese, Sicilian etc. sections in the neighborhood, underlining a regional belonging. One can also assume distinctions between Sciaccatani, Palermitani, people from Augusta, etc., all Sicilians but from different villages, from different campanili. This inner differentiation, probably visible even in the geographical distribution of the spaces in the past, now become evident only during the feast: again, the feast declares the ethnic community around the icon of the patron saint.

    The feast of San Domenico started from North Square. The society's members met in front of the Sacred Heart Church. San Domenico's Society is a small society and does not own a club. According to several members of the society, for this reason, and despite the general trend in the neighborhood as societies hold the icons of the patron saint in the club and even at home, the statue of San Domenico is held in the Sacred Heart Church. When I arrived people were already in line, behind the banner, to stat the procession. Three things were immediately apparent: the presence of a banner with the image of the Saint, with the sign: "S. Domenico Protettore di Augusta"; a more formally evident uniform, worn by the members; the Italian and American flags, as an opening element of the procession.

    Banners are not exceptional along the procession of Boston's North End feasts, but in this specific case there is a specific reason to take note of it. In Augusta, the Sicilian city from where the migrants came, the feast is celebrated on May 24 to remember the transfer of San Domenico's body to the new sepulcher and the miracle in 1594 of the apparition of the saint in the sky above Augusta to throw the Arabian invaders out of the city.[18] But the celebration used to start forty days before May 24 and the signals were specific music played on the drum and the transport of the banner, called *"Bibidibì,"* through the city's streets. The banner in Augusta is and, like the Bostonian one, portrays the saint riding a white horse.[19] In Augusta, this banner is an important symbol of the feast, signifying the initial moment of the celebrations. In the North End the symbol seems to have lost its original meaning. If asked the reason why they carry the banner, people again would answer that it was tradition, often without any more specific memories and meanings and only seldom recollecting the original function.

I felt again—and this feeling was very often with me during the feast—that I was observing not only the event per se but an event telling me the story of another but similar event, already told somewhere else and in a different time. The people from the North End were performing a ritual that at the same time was celebrating the topicality of the present and the memory of the past. The feast, from this point of view, is a dislocated performance: the banner of San Domenico in the North End does not tell the story of the miracle. Indeed it tells the story of another banner, the Sicilian one, proclaiming the miraculous event. This is not a matter of the geographical distance between the Italian village and the actual ethnic enclave only. It is a different narrative practice. An indirect evidence of this difference is the necessity to inscribe on the Bostonian banner the sign explicitly designating, in the Italian language, the saint as patron of the Italian city. The Sicilian banner does not need any such specification. The narrative can be told and listened to without any specific sign: everybody in Augusta knows what the narrative is about. In Boston instead not only the iconic representation of the event (the saint, the horse, the sword) is necessary, but a caption too is also necessary.

The second point of interest is the display of a more formal uniform: in general members wear a white shirt and black pants or skirt. Members also have on a medallion with the image of the saint, not present in the Italian feast. But the uniforms suggest also an internal gender based difference (while women have a medallion with a white ribbon, men have a tricolor ribbon, red, white and green as the Italian flag) as well as another difference, of hierarchical nature: the "important" male members do not wear a white shirt but a grey one.

The other interesting element I noticed at the beginning of this particular feast was the contemporary presence of the Italian and American flags (see figure 4.4). There is no reason for me to be surprised at this in light of the "enlightenment" that had occurred during Saint Jude's procession. The feast celebrates San Domenico, the patron of a Sicilian city, but the procession walks through the street of Boston's North End. The members of the group are devoted to the saint who freed Augusta from the Arabian invaders, but they mostly

FIGURE 4.4 Italian and American flags, during the procession of San Domenico. (Author's photograph.)

speak English. Few of them speak the Sicilian dialect and even fewer the lingua franca, the Italian language.

Still the presence of symbols evoking different cultural identities must be highlighted. The two flags standing at the beginning of the procession communicated without any hesitation or doubt the participants' simultaneous membership in both American and the Italian groups. It was a declaration of a hyphenated identity as Italian Americans. But the flags were not the only symbols of this negotiation of identity and the identities symbolized by the flags were not the only ones declared. The feast as a symbol and as an aggregation of symbols began to unfold in an endless game of ethnic and cultural belonging which I now only began to understand.

Another element of plurality and dynamism can be seen in the banner, opening the procession, which unlike the Bibidibì portraying the saint and describing him in the Italian language, bore an English script with the name of the society. As I already noted (see the feast of Saint Jude), the banner with the symbol of the society functions to open the procession. This pattern seems to be very common for Boston's North End feasts. While the structure itself of the procession is self-evident and easily recognizable both for the neighbors and for the tourist attending the performance, the organizers still need to be specified. The banner explicitly and immediately declares what society is performing the procession. This manifest function is important, but it is not the only function. The overall pattern itself is relevant because it suggests the specificity of the religious feasts in the North End. Therefore another cultural identity (the North Ender) is implied. This is not to say that banners are not used in other Italian American processions or in American parades in general but rather to state how banners are used in the peculiar case of the North End: the feast is a display, therefore it ought to be recognizable in all its components, above all in the specification of its organizers.

In the North End around the platform two important things can be noted: the statue is not carried by any statue-bearers but by members pulling the cart (in Augusta they pull the platform with ropes) and the ribbons, not present in the Sicilian feast, are held by men. It is definitely possible to see at the same time a persisting tradition (the platform pulled by men) but with elements of the new context (the ribbons). The cultural identities negotiated through these religious symbols are multiple, from the Sicilian to the North End. Another difference can be noted: the money pinned on the statue in the North End, again respects a local, contextual, tradition in the United States.[20] San Domenico, no different in this regard than the other saints in the North End, not only receives but also pays respect: for example to the Madonna del Soccorso's Club, and to a nursing home, at the North End Community building.

I will propose now another comparison between the two feasts, concerning the leaders of the feasts. I have observed that both were wearing emblems of the authority: the gray uniform for the procession leader in the North End, and the tricolor ribbons indicating the role of mayor, for the Italian leader. But there was another signal, present in both the situation: the two leaders were holding a bell. The original meaning of the bell is to announce the passage of the procession, so every faithful can attend it in an appropriate way. But now the presence of the bell seems to be more iconic rather than pragmatic. Quiet interestingly the Italian American leader was holding the bell in one hand and in the other hand a cellular phone, a more modern and useful tool of communication. Again a tradition is performed but in a new modernized landscape.

San Giuseppe di Riesi

With this feast,[21] generally celebrated about at the end of July, more complex practices begin in the North End. First of all, the feast is no longer concentrated in just one day but it last three days, from Friday to Sunday. Actually the seventy-fifth anniversary feast was preceded by a barbeque on Thursday night, in front of the outdoor chapel, where a picture of Saint Joseph was placed, but the event had a more private characteristic. The banquet recalls another important social event organized by the society: the annual banquet, held generally on March 19 (Saint Joseph's Day on the calendar of the saints):

The founders of the Society were grateful for the blessings in their lives and one means of expressing such gratitude was through the Saint Joseph's day gathering of family and friends on March 19th and the establishing of a table with bread and food to be distributed to the immediate community. Traditional prayers and a young male representing Saint Joseph giving the Saint Joseph prayer are important components of this traditional, nearly forgotten, gathering. Society members, today, strive to keep these traditions and ceremonies vibrant and alive. During the annual banquet it is hoped that at least some of those attending will bring some canned goods as practical alternative to bread and fresh food. In the absence of a communal village, as in the Riesi of 1925, or a tight knit ethnic community, as in the North End of 1925, the canned goods are distributed to a local service agency, Aid to Boston Community Development (ABCD) for distribution to the elderly of the North End.[22]

The San Giuseppe di Riesi Society was founded in 1925 and the mutual aid functions are evident even in a different urban scenario. Not only is there a feast but also a social gathering, originally limited to members of the community, now to social agency.

It is important to state that, since the feast lasts longer than previously, a specific section of the neighborhood was closed to traffic and many stalls, selling mostly food and memorabilia, found places in that restricted area. The faithful and tourists could gather out of danger for the entire length of the feast. The banner welcomed participants to the festival. A signal of different, more complex organizational and economic level, can be seen in the presence of a sponsor for the feast (Heineken Beer). An economic element was evident in the other feasts too but, as I demonstrated, the importance was clearly circumscribed to a small stall selling religious objects. Now I see about a dozen big stalls with a business flow of considerable dimensions. Saint Joseph Society is a "strong" society (in membership, organization and funds) and it can afford a three-day feast,[23] luring many more tourists than the previous ones. Vendors are more interested on a "long" feast because, as I was told by many of them, they can better amortize the cost and make more money because of the tourist influx. The feast, as public event, started on Friday evening, when at 7:00 P.M. the statue of Saint Joseph was carried out of the club and adorned with ribbons already covered by dollar bills.

The procession was preceded by the traditional group photo, in front of the society's club (see figure 4.5).[24]

The picture supplies much information: the society is wealthy enough to have a private club (on Charter Street, at the corner of Hanover Street); members of the society wear a sort of uniform. Women use white shorts and white pants or skirts. Men wear white shirts and light brown pants. Still a gender-based difference can be noted. Men and women have a tricolor button

FIGURE 4.5   San Giuseppe di Riesi, traditional group photo, in front of the society's club. (Author's photograph.)

(recalling the Italian flag) with Saint Joseph's image. The hierarchic difference is evident only for the president of the society, who uses a tricolor band; at the center of the group is situated an old man, a very important member in the past. The society is paying respect to him in this way; just behind the elderly member stands his daughter, at the moment an influential member of the society, and at her right, with a blue suit, the mayor of the Italian village, Riesi. Because it is an official presence he wears the tricolor band designing his office. The transnational character of the feast was confirmed.

While members were adorning the statue, the priest, Father Vincenzo of the Sacred Heart Church, came for the blessing, escorted by two members, two young flag bearers, holding the Italian and the American flags, and by the Roma Band. The blessing was the first of two events managed by the clergy: the second one, an outdoor mass in front of the outdoor chapel, happened on Sunday morning. But the blessing was also a moment of official display of the secular authorities attending the feast, namely, the mayor of Riesi and the mayor of Boston, Thomas Menino (see figure 4.6).[25]

Outside the club a temporary chapel was built, and the statue was posed there for the adorning. On the ground another statue, in a smaller scale, and a painting portraying the saint, were ready to be placed inside the temporary chapel as soon as the procession started. The temporary chapel had the function of hosting first

FIGURE 4.6   The mayor of Riesi and the mayor of Boston, during the feast of San Giuseppe. (Author's photograph.)

the official statue: symbolically, for the ephemeral time of the feast, the saint does not belong to the private sphere of the religious club but is publicly displayed. But the saint still needs an adequate site: in Boston's North End this is the function of ephemeral building, used as a provisional host for the statue of the saint and, when the statue is carried out for the procession, for the smaller icons (see figure 4.7).

On Friday evening the procession is short, lasting about one hour and a half. The composition of the group carrying the statue in procession follow the usual pattern of Boston's North End feasts: statue-bearers, assisted by a hierarchically more important members holding the platform's poles to balance the statue (for Saint Joseph's feast too these seem to be a male functions); beggars, holding ribbons (again, this is generally a female function); other members are around the statue, ready to replace the bearers when they become tired; at the back, the marching band has its place. On Friday night the statue was carried only through the streets adjacent the club, and about 8:30 P.M. the statue was placed in the temporary chapel. Finally the evening entertainments can start. If for the previous feasts the marching band alone constituted the entertainment (and it is questionable if this can even be considered entertainment since it comprises part of the ceremony of the ritual), in this festival the entertainment becomes more varied and complex.

All of Saturday is dedicated to musical performances by the marching band—now emancipated from ritual parading—and popular bands. For the seventy-fifth anniversary of the feast, a dance contest also took place. Sunday is generally the climax of the feast, beginning with a mass celebrated in front of the statue near the outdoor chapel. This is the second, and last, moment of clergy presence at the celebration of the saint. Immediately after the mass, around 11 am, members and guests gathered together for a private brunch, just before the procession.

Around 1:00 P.M. the procession begins, lasting until 8:00 P.M., with the saint displayed over and over in the area. At the same time DJ's play recorded music, on the smaller stage, and bands alternate on the bigger stage. The little statue and the painting took their place inside the outdoor temporary chapel, replacing the statue. Members of the club stood nearby to help the faithful and tourists, sometimes answering questions about the saint, the society, the village or the feast, but more often accepting money offerings, repaid with holy images and pins.[26] The procession was opened by the banner with the name of the society, held by women. Immediately after the Italian and the American flag were carried by two young boys. In the small space between the banner and the flags several ephemeral identities could be identified and understood through different symbols: the American and the Italian identities were represented by the display of the national flags; the local

FIGURE 4.7   The statue of San Giuseppe is carried out for the procession. (Author's photograph.)

identities (Riesi and Boston's North End ethnic enclave) were proclaimed by the banner belonging to both the original and present membership, as well as the pins worn by the banner-holders and by their position at the beginning of the procession, known and recognized as the usual pattern in the neighborhood. The composition of the group around the statue is the same as the Friday procession, but one notices a larger participation by the general public. The presence of many people attending the feast justifies the presence of many beggars around the statue, each holding a little white basket with religious items and asking for offerings. The presence of two marching bands was another signal of the importance of the Saint Joseph feast: the inevitable Roma Band, followed by the North End Feast Band

All along the streets, I could notice another important element of the feast, an element not yet explored because it was not present in the previous, smaller feasts: food. Food ought not to be seen only at the economic level, even if this is definitely relevant: business between the society, vendors and tourists plays a fundamental entry of the feast budget. But if food plays an economic role the symbolic economy of the feast can be seen in the food as well.

One of the many stalls, for instance, was offering fried calamari (squid) and ravioli. The stall was painted in red, white, and green like the Italian flag. It was also possible to see other kinds of food offered: chicken fingers and fries. If calamari and ravioli, linguistically and gastronomically, evoke Italian food, chicken fingers and fries suggest other culinary scenarios, just like the chicken with ziti and broccoli, a combination of both "flavors." But the situation is more complex than it appears. For instance, ravioli is a food traditionally more from northern Italy, not often sold during the feasts, but fried calamari is a popular Italian American dish, seldom sold as a ritual food. Chicken fingers and fries are American fast food, often related to different kinds of more secular rituals, like football parties..

Saint Agrippina di Mineo

The feast of Saint Agrippina was celebrated in Boston's North End for the first time in 1914 and

> every year the Saint Agrippina feast in Boston's North End is packed with tradition, entertainment, food, music and more. Throughout the days and nights families and friends gather to celebrate throughout the neighborhood. The members of the Saint Agrippina di Mineo benefit society would like to welcome you, your friends and families to come celebrate the 91st anniversary of this great tradition. Come and see the procession, eat some food, play some games and listen to the music. We hope to see you there—VIVA SAINT AGRIPPINA!!![27]

Interestingly, but not surprisingly, the general advertisement for the Saint Agrippina's feast does not place too much stress on religion. Beside the name

FIGURE 4.8   Sicilian and American flags, during the procession of Saint Agrippina. (Author's photograph.)

of the saint, only the procession is mentioned, hoping an audience will come. The focus is on social activities like tradition, entertainment, food, and music. The possible questions raised by the advertisement concern secularization and/or religiosity. And a first, superficially, the answer is that the feast has lost the original religious character, replacing it with other aspects relatively connected to the sphere of the sacred. This answer may seem incomplete and misleading. What the advertisement indeed suggests is a sort of separation between actors and audience along the performance of the ritual. Actually the audience is asked to come and see the procession, implicitly but clearly suggesting a separation between the members of the society, appointed to perform the procession, and the audience, seen as guests who are allowed just to see it. The idea of hospitality with the double meaning of participation and separation is present in the auspicious welcomes. The religious aspect of the feast therefore seems to belong to the society and the members. The guests can enjoy the other aspects such as entertainment, food and, in general, fun. This is not to say that changes toward secularization are not present in the ritual itself, but they are very slow and unpredictable.

I underlined for previous feasts the simultaneous presence of the Italian and the American flags, with the evident purpose of claiming a national belonging. The Saint Agrippina's feast shows an interesting variation: the presence of the red and yellow flag of Trinacria, the old name for Sicily (see figure 4.8).[28]

The presence of the Sicilian flag, carried as usual by a young boy, shows a different level of nationalism, a level that can be formally called regionalism. Sicily by law has a special regional constitution but even if Italy is slowly reaching a peculiar federalism the island is still formally an Italian region. Historically Sicily often claimed independence[29]—this explains the making of a flag—and certainly the flag is a symbol claiming regional identity, a regional identity situated near the imagined national and the declared local identities.

On a more local level is situated the banner with signs, written in the Italian language and bearing (1) the name of the saint (Santa Agrippina) and the locality (di Mineo), above the icon; (2) the corporate name of the society, being formally incorporated in 1940, in Boston, Massachusetts, below the icon; and (3) the type of the society: Società Femminile (Women's Society). For the first time I observed a formally organized female participation at the feast. If in origin female presences in the societies were often disallowed by charter, then this is not unusual, but small societies in general do not have enough members to justify inner differentiations, gender based or otherwise, allowing a sort of diffuse membership.[30] Therefore, what is performed during the procession is not a direct representation of a social order, as a superficial abstraction can suggest, but the utterance of a stereotype. This is what Bob, a friend from outside the neighborhood who loves to attend the festivals, said to me: "Don't you see? Here you are not allowed to be anything else but Italian, especially during the feast! Otherwise how do you think all these restaurants can be still in business? Augusto, this is a tourist trap, a nice one, but still a tourist trap." Conceptualizing what Bob told me, stereotypes are used toward a tactical, strategic and rhetorically informed essentialism.

On Friday the statue of the saint took its place in the temporary chapel in Battery Street. Dislocating the saint from the private club to the public display is the formal initial moment for every feast in the North End. An undifferentiated audience can at this point see the saint. In Saint Agrippina's case the initial exposure of the statue happens in two steps. First, the statue is placed on the platform outside the club. The statue's face is covered by a red veil, and one cannot see it; and, second, the statue is unveiled during the ceremony of the blessing, performed by the priest. The veil is an ancient tradition in the Mediterranean area connected with many nuptial rituals: in pre-Christian rites the groom used a mask or temporary drawing to cover his face while the bride wore a veil, often red, in order to exorcize negative spirits or to protect against the omnipresent evil eyes threatening the wedding. It is not my intention to claim a cultural continuity with ancient rites of Mediterranean area.[31] I am more interested on continuity and changes of the ritual connected with migration. I asked father Nunzio Valdini,[32] parish priest of Santa Agrippina's Church in Mineo, information about the ritual of unveiling the statue (see figure 4.9). He told me that in his seven years of experience in the parish he has never seen the ritual, and from what he could remember he did have not direct or indirect knowledge.[33] This raises the question of cultural continuity and changes with the Italian feast at the end of the nineteenth century, the time of Mineo's migration. Even if I have no direct evidence it is very possible that the immigrants brought the specific ritual, with the patron saint: this is at least what informants told me. And it is very much possible that this ritual was a distinctive trait of the Saint Agrippina's feast, therefore of the specific ethnic enclave. The distinctiveness seems to be now supplanted by a more general respect of correct practices, diffused all over the North End, for every feast. The ritual of unveiling the statue, still present but without explanation or interpretation, is one of the few characteristics referring to a specificity. The rest of the feast, instead, matches the festive pattern generally visible in the neighborhood.

Unveiling the statue allows one also to see the object votive offering pinned on her mantle. If the votive offering denotes the specific relationship between the faithful and the saint, invoked in a sort of private agreement to plead with God on behalf of the faithful, asking for some kind of grace, it also carries other meanings when seen on the statue. First of all, the votive offerings together adorning the mantle claim the greatness of the saint: Saint Agrippina is a powerful saint, as is shown by the many votive objects. This is a recurrent discourse I have heard many times during the feast: people I have spoken with highlight the miraculous protection and help Saint Agrippina continuously offers them. Oral tales of great

FIGURE 4.9   Unveiling the statue of Saint Agrippina. (Author's photograph.)

and small miracles are told along the procession, and the objects on the mantle indicate the power of the saint. This leads to the second aspect. The objects ought to be recognizable if not by the audience at large at least by those who made the offering or by members of her or his family or close group. The miracle needs to be remembered and, through the miracle, the special attention that the saint gave to the specific kin. Therefore the objects are shown always in the same position: actually they are pinned on the mantle and they are not supposed to be dislocated. In this way those who see the statue can recognize the specific votive offering. Memory and recognizability are two fundamental dimension of the votive offering, and refer to a more general use of the past and of the history of the group visible in many aspects of all the feasts, that I will analyze in the conclusive comparative part of this work.

The area of the feast is adorned by lights and festoons. In this case the lights look like Christmas decorations (the angel and the comet) and the festoons recall the crown of Saint Agrippina. The lights are expensive items for the feast—for an arc it is possible to spend around a thousand dollars—but they indicate also the importance of the feast itself and of course the wealth of the organizing society. And since it attracts tourists, it indirectly contributes to feast revenues, but for members and faithful lights and festoons are a way to compare their own feast with the other ones as well as to compare the present feast with the others in the past. For instance, Saint Anthony's Society members tell with evident pride that their decorations were made by the Matarazzo's family (a very famous decorator, coming from Avellino): it was and it is still a sort of trademark, being accurate and showy, therefore expensive.

Saturday is the part of the feast dedicated to entertainment: music is offered from stages or on the streets with the marching bands. Sunday is the climax of the feast. The procession starts around noon and does not return until many hours later, at night, when the statue will be returned to the club, and the feast will be over. The beginning of the procession is announced by firecrackers, a memory, even if in a small scale, of the tradition Italian fireworks, but still indeed another important aspect of the feast.[34] The small scale of fireworks in the United States is explained by participants in the ceremony as a consequence of the strict regulation on security.[35]

In general Saint Agrippina's procession follows the pattern of all other Boston North End religious feasts, with the icon of the saint carried by male members of the society while female members hold the ribbons. The statue stops in front of everyone donating money, while the marching band plays the "Marcia Reale." The donors often prepare the money in very different ways: they pin the bills on veils with neckbands to put directly on the statue. Sometimes they wait by the window and when the statue stops nearby they throw long ribbons with the offerings, and the process of votive offering takes a great deal of time. Paying respect to the saint is on one hand a private action, intimately connected with personal faith and respect to the saint, following the southern Italian pattern of peculiar, reciprocal and familiar relationship with the divine, but on the other hand it is a public event, publicly displaying the devotion and wealth of the faithful and their family or group. From this point of view, not surprisingly, the procession becomes a sort of public arena where power and wealth are the communicated values. Often the big offerings are not individual but collective, such as a familial effort.

Again, the saint too pays respect stopping at different places. Beside churches, nursing houses and other societies, Saint Agrippina also stopped to pay respect to the memory of a deceased member, affixing a garland on the pole indicating the place name.

Looking at the groups around the icon of the saint one notices a peculiar aspect: the statue-bearers are unusually numerous and generally young, twice as many as the bearers of Saint Joseph statue, for instance, even though the platform does not seem heavier. This is related to a specific form of devotion shown during the procession, generally if front of churches or in large spaces. It does not seem to be related to any specific form of respect while it is definitely connected to a specific form of bodily mortification: the statue-bearers not only walk the platform along the streets but also they sometimes stop and literally dance while carrying the statue.[36] Movements of the platform become faster (the bearers run) and unusual (the bearers walk diagonally or they jump). It is a difficult performance, requiring skills and strength, though the fundamental function of the members in front and in back of the platform is to hold the poles and balance the weight.

Madonna della Cava, Patron of Pietraperzia

Sicilian settlers, coming from the city of Pictraperzia, near Enna, during the big wave of Italian migration at the beginning of twentieth century, clustered in Boston's North End mostly on Battery, Charter, and Hanover streets, and on Salutation Alley. Following the pattern of other southern Italians they founded a religious society and began celebrating the patron saint. As usual, at the beginning the Madonna della Cava Society only allowed people from the original village in Sicily as members. Now, after the first generation passed away and the second and third generations moved out of the neighborhood, the society has almost ninety members who are not only from the North End but also from the suburbs where they settled in the 1970s and 1980s. The Madonna della Cava, as in the case of Saint Agrippina, also has a female section, very active in social activities, and clearly present during the feast. In the 1950s the society, erected a private chapel on Battery Street. This was renovated in the late 1980s with the addition of a lower room for social activities, such as banquets, Halloween and Christmas parties, etc.

The second week of August the society holds its feast, at the same time as the feast in the Italian village. At first, the banner with the image of the Madonna della Cava is moved outside the private chapel in the club (see figure 4.10). I already pointed out the common custom of carrying banners of various natures during the procession, but the exceptional part of the festival of the Madonna della Cava within the whole complex of festive practices of the North End is that members do not carry any statue, the usual icon of the divinity.

After the blessing of the banner, a short procession is performed. When I participated, the procession started around 7:30 P.M. One hour later the banner was back and situated in the temporary chapel just outside club. Meanwhile another icon was placed in the temporary chapel. As usual Friday night is dedicated to entertainment and to the first of three raffles. The raffle is another normal element of the North End feast, in general held on Sunday, the last night of a feast. The Madonna della Cava's Society places a great deal of stress on raffles, run by the female society, and sponsored by important labels (in this specific case by Budweiser—an important American beer brand—and Birra Moretti—an important Italian beer brand in a sort of different declination of

FIGURE 4.10   Banner with the image of the Madonna della Cava. (Author's photograph.)

ethnicity and food, but still claiming the double—Italian and American—aspect). Prizes are considerable, quite different from the past when, for instance, before World War II the prize was a lamb. Music is performed every night of the feast, provided by a DJ and from the stage.

Sunday shows again the aspects of religiosity, with the 10:00 A.M. mass celebrated at the Sacred Heart Church. The Madonna della Cava Society, although a private and secular organization, has a good relationship with the local parish, at least with the Sacred Heart Church.[37]

The procession at the time of my fieldwork started around 1:00 P.M.. The banner was moved out from the temporary chapel, and given to a member. In general the carriers of the banner are the same people, year after year. I asked why certain members wanted to carry the banner and I was told "because it is devotion" or "because it is my personal votive offering," assuming therefore the form of a prayer. Sometimes it is not even a personal devotion but a familial one: faithful carry the banner because their fathers used to, and so pay respect not only to the saint but also to the memory of their elders. The banner is not as heavy as a statue but still some skill and strength is needed, and there are always some other members ready to help the bearer when the weight becomes unendurable. Therefore the procession stops many times, not only for the usual reciprocal offerings of respect, but also to let the new bearer take the place of the tired one. By the end of the procession dozens of bearers have alternated on carrying the banner. Around the icon, the group was arranged in the usual way. Members wore a vague sort of uniform (white shirt and black shorts, with leaders in long white or black pants) , while female members, wearing long white and blue dresses, held ribbons or, walking through the audience, carried baskets with religious images or buttons to give to those offering donations. But the uniform seemed to be not too exclusive: some bearers carried the banner but were not wearing any kind of uniform and some beggars too wore casual dress. As usual while money offering is the general form of respect shown by the faithful to the Madonna, stopping by churches, other societies' clubs and other important points in the neighborhood is the way for the saint to show respect. The procession was accompanied all the way by three marching bands. showing how important the society and the procession are.

The banner went back to the permanent chapel around 11:00 P.M. after the last concert on the stage and the final Grand Raffle. The area, delimited by fences, was overcrowded by stalls, mostly selling food.

As I mentioned previously, the food sold during the North End's feasts can be considered a ritual symbol manipulated by negotiated ethnic identities. Items are specific, and generally belong to an Italian American tradition, such as calzones, chicken ziti and broccoli, and eggplant parmesan subs. Other food refers to some other ritual like the zeppoli (English spelling for the Italian *zeppole*) which are ritual pastry, generally made for Saint Joseph's day. The question implicitly raised by these observations pervades this feast and all the other feasts: the question of declared authenticity, and I will try to answer in the next chapter.

Madonna del Soccorso, Patron of Sciacca

On September 15, 1910, the Sciaccatani (or Sciaccadani, if pronounced following the Sicilian dialect) of the North End founded the Madonna del Soccorso Society of Boston, Inc., in honor of the Madonna del Soccorso (Our Lady of Perpetual Help), patron of their original village in Sicily, near Agrigento. One year later the society bought a replica of the original statue of the Madonna so that the fishermen could hold their first small feast on the streets where they settled: North Street and Fleet Street.

The feast of the Madonna del Soccorso starts in general on the third Thursday of August with an opening ceremony at 9–11 Lewis Street in the North End, which is the society club. The statue emerges from the permanent chapel on the upper level of the club after a collective prayer of the members, and is carried to the waterfront for the blessing of the fishing waters.

In the past, when fishing was the predominant occupation of the Sciaccatani, the waterfront was filled by fishing boats. At the end of the priest's blessing all the boats blew their horns and whistles and people went out onto the boats and ate and drank (Sanna 1988, 8). This practice is no longer followed: fishing is no longer the main occupation of the Sciaccatani and those who wanted to fish have moved north to Gloucester, therefore there are very few boats remaining in the North End.

The short procession through the Sicilian section of the North End culminates with the return of the statue to the temporary chapel, situated at the corner of Fleet and North Streets.

Bodily penitence is always present in every procession: carrying the saint is a mortification of the body that is offered to the divinity, and the bearers need to show their suffering and strength to the Madonna and to the audience. This explains the "dance" under the platform (as in the Saint Agrippina's feast) or the sprint over the hill usually performed by the fishermen carrying the saint.

This can be considered a performed prayer displayed to the audience and offered to the Madonna. Sal "Bosco," talking about bearers and bodily mortification, told me that many of them want to carry the statue all the way, and he, as president of the society and leader of the procession, cannot allow them to do so. Dealing with the bearers is not easy and Sal needs to follow traditional rules:

Augusto: The people that go under the statue, how you decide the order?

Sal: The guy that carries '*a Maronna* is usually a seniority, like Mark, he's thirty-three, and has been doing so for seventeen or eighteen years. He started in the back where someone else went out and can be passed from father to son, from uncle to nephew. And then I use a lot of discretion. The guys at the front have been there for a while, the same four guys. And I call them because they were with me when I started, at the back. Then I moved. It is not to be more respectful but the guys in front get the pictures taken!

Augusto: When do you decide it is time to change the guys carrying the statue?

Sal: During the procession? It is up to them. A lot of guys want to do it all the way, on one shoulder, a lot of guys can't do that now. So half way I say "You ought to switch shoulders." Sometime they have to go back home so it is up to them to find out somebody who will take that spot because when he comes back he wants that spot back. The captain is different.[38] The captain stays as captain until he says I don't want to do it anymore, but if an old captain wants to come back, just to do it for. . . ten minutes, the old captain just taps the guy on the shoulder and he takes his place. . . someone else can't do that. An old captain always has the right to carry the statue.

Temporary chapel seems to be an American innovation, and the reason is evident. Basically, the feast in Italy is church-centered, the statue always returns to the shrine inside the chapel. As I previously mentioned, in Boston's North End the church and the clergy make their appearance only in few specific moments, and narratives stress the distance between societies and local parishes. The statue belongs to the society and is hosted inside private chapels in private clubs. Therefore there is no need to bring the statue back to any church. Still, why does the statue not come back to the ordinary chapel inside the club? A first answer is that because the feast is not an ordinary time, extraordinary symbols are not only allowed but also desired. It is also possible to see the temporary chapel as a "common sharing" of the statue, which is usually viewed only by the members of the society in the private chapel. And naturally, because of the presence of the larger community, an economic aspect is also present: tourists can pay respect by pinning money on the statue more easily if the statue is displayed on the street, rather than hidden in a private room. But there is another reason too: I repeatedly asked many people during the feast about the outdoor temporary chapel, and the common answer was "because it looks like a chapel." This is a simple answer, but it carries many potential meanings. Even if the relationship with the saints, for the southern Italian religiosity of the streets, is a kind of personal issue, even if Boston's North End religious societies make the distance from the local ecclesiastic hierarchy clear, even if the presence of formal clergy is confined to few moments, still the feast has an important religious aspect. The saint must be respected; therefore the solution lies between two opposite poles: on one hand the private space of the religious society and on the other hand the public but clearly institutional space of a church's chapel. The tension between public/private and institutional/associative is settled through constructing the compromise of the outdoor temporary chapel. The likeness to a church's chapel guarantees that the institutional sacred and the secular both belong to a private religious society, paradoxically—but not excessively—guaranteed by its public dimension, since it is built in middle of the street. But the likeness is ephemeral and lasts only for the period of the feast. In the past temporary chapels and bandstands were built by a famous *paratore* (decorator) of the area: Emilio Matarazzo. Matarazzo was a decorator in the Avellino area before migrating in the United States. Again, it ought to be said that in southern Italy a paratore is involved more with lights and bandstands, while in the North End he also designs and builds the temporary chapel. Most of the temporary chapels in the North End were made by Matarazzo, his sons or his apprentice, Mario Picardo, and are still in use. In the 1980s, as reported by Sanna (1988, 10) the temporary chapel was designed using the front door of the club's building and decorated in the same structural space year after year. However the bandstand, designed and built by Emilio Matarazzo and Mario Picardo, was temporary. At the peak of the popularity of the feasts, in the 1960s and 1970s, the temporary chapel was newly built every year, but economic reasons and a lack of craftsmen presently make replacement very difficult. Nowadays, the temporary chapel is located outside, as I said, at the corner of Fleet and North streets.

While the procession is going on vendors attract tourist to the feast area and entertainment is offered from the stage. The economic level is extremely important but presently much of the income is provided by sponsors. In the case of the fishermen the Sorrento cheese company sponsors the feast, just as they sponsor the San Gennaro feast in New York City.

Often during the Fishermen feast contests of various natures are organized, such as the children's pie eating and the celebrity cheese building contests. Local prominent people such as representatives and congressmen are invited to the contest and are willing to participate. Musical entertainment is also offered during the feast, as is true generally.

In the Fishermen's feasts I have attended, entertainment is mainly Italian American songs and comedy: Danny and Tony the Italian Strollers, Tony Pace, Johnny Maestro and the Brooklyn Bridge, Frank Zarba Orchestra, Johnny Pizzi and the cast of *Maria's Comedy Wedding* are just few of the performers alternating on the bandstand.

Since the Madonna del Soccorso feast is organized on four days, instead of the usual three days, some differences in the schedule occur. Friday (instead of Saturday) is dedicated exclusively to entertainment, while Saturday sees the celebration of the mass at the Sacred Heart Church, followed by performers on stage. Sunday at noon the procession of the Madonna begins at the temporary chapel, through the streets of the North End.

I attended the preparatory meeting of the society just before the beginning of the procession: members were tense so Sal made a speech about tradition and memories, stating that the way to carry the statue was important. Other members spoke quickly, shouting "Viva la Madonna di Sciacca" (Hurray for the Madonna of Sciacca), and then the crew was ready to start the procession.

During the procession the pattern I have found for the other feasts is respected. The icon of the Madonna is carried out through the streets and occasionally stops to receive homage and to pay respect. Being a statue-bearer was a male prerogative; no women were allowed to carry the statue. They have important function during the feast: they beg for money; they hold the ribbons; they can even be the president of the society. But they do not carry the platform. In my fieldwork I saw just two exceptions to what seems to be a rule of respect of southern Italian traditions: the first is the Saint Lucy procession, and the reason is self evident, since Saint Lucy is an exclusive female society and since the feast is a ceremony involving only women. The second one occurred during one of the processions for the Madonna del Soccorso. But it was ephemeral: the following year women were not allowed anymore to carry the statue. When I asked Therese, Sal's wife, the reason she told me that because of some unspecified disagreement women no longer wanted to carry the statue, and she gave me to understand that carrying the statue was her idea originally to underline women's presence in a visible way during the feast. Therese was a very influential member, directly or indirectly. Her suggestions, particularly about economic aspects (she obtained the advertising agency for the necessary sponsorships) or concerning entertainment (Therese comes from a family involved in show business), as well as her support for Sal, were precious and made her respected.

But there is one very peculiar and spectacular aspect of the Madonna del Soccorso feast: its climax is on Sunday evening, when the angel flies. As the procession of the Madonna comes close to the chapel, there is a crescendo: in North Square, special fireworks are lit. Thousands of people fill the streets around the temporary chapel. Some prominent individuals, such as the mayor of the city, pay respect to the Madonna. Paying respect is a private gesture, but also a public demonstration of faith and belonging. For a political figure this is the right moment to make the offering. And the angel is ready to fly. This is Sanna's description of the grand finale:

> The most spectacular of these [changes in the feast] is the completely American grand finale of the Fisherman's Feast during which three young girls dressed as angels address the Madonna, chanting a text of praise (in Italian) to the saint. Two of the children declaim their text from balconies on either side of the street, but the third is "flown" over the middle of the street and lowered in front of the carried Madonna, addressing her face to face. The girls, who have been for a numbers of years mostly members of the same family, are trained for weeks ahead by ex-angels. This extraordinary performance is known to be a part of only one feast—that of the Madonna del Soccorso in America. The finale was also part of the feast as celebrated by the Sciaccadanis of

New York, and it is not clear to anyone whether the tradition began in New York or Boston, but it is now only practiced here in the North End. In the past, in conjunction with the angel's flight, doves were released from a small wooden fishing boat also suspended above the street, but a hitch in the proceedings which resulted in a threatened law suit terminated this practice. (1988, 9)

Sanna's description is accurate, but not her interpretation of this performance as a peculiarly American phenomenon: the flight of the angel (*volo dell'angelo*) was and still is a practice common in southern Italian feasts (Ottaviano and Somma Vesuviana, near Naples, but also Villafrati, in Sicily, to provide just few examples).

The way the flight is arranged is simple. Not too far from the temporary chapel wires are suspended between two buildings. On a balcony at the second floor the first angel starts her prayer, on the opposite side of the road, the second angel answers the first one. The dialogue continues for about ten minutes, and ends when the third angel is ready to fly.

The choice of the angels is not easy, and it depends on the president's preference. Since it is the most important moment of the feast, as well as the most visible element of the entire feast, being chosen is considered a sign of pride and honor. Sal, the then president, told me that it was a very difficult matter, and that he used to receive a great deal of pressure to select girls from various families. Immediately after the end of the feast I asked him when these pressures would start, and he answered: "Right now."

The angels are now trained not by ex-angels but by a member of the female society. Rehearsals, held in the upper room of the society club, are frequent, especially during the days immediately before Sunday. The three girls learn the poem, written in Italian, which is basically a long prayer to the Madonna. They memorize the words by the sounds, not the meanings: this is quite evident from their pronunciation.

In front of the Madonna, the third angel recites her poem, accompanying the recitation with gestures. At the end of the poem, the angel flies back to the balcony and confetti is thrown from the buildings.

The end of the feast is now near. What remains is to pose the statue in the temporary chapel. But it is also the time for the members hold each other in a long embrace in a gesture of communitas. This experience of ecstatic unity is as ephemeral as the feast itself, but just as memorable.

Saint Anthony of Padua, Patron of Montefalcione

Augusto: What does the feast means for you?

Jerry: You know, for me when he (Saint Anthony) come out the Friday night I think back to my parents, when they were all alive and they were here for. It brings a lot of memory back, my grandparents they are all gone.

My friend Jerry was talking about his parents and a very small procession of the beginning of the twentieth century that over the years became, along with the Madonna del Soccorso, the biggest feast in Boston's North End and probably one of the most important in the United States. Attendance at the Big Saint Anthony can number in the thousands, as people gather around Endicott Street every last weekend of August.

Changes occurred gradually. According to Abruzzi whose narrative coincides with Jerry's tale, for the feast of the last Sunday of August 1919 a main concern was to illuminate and decorate the area of the feast:

> It was decided that they would purchase strings of lights and the members would do their own decorating. For a week prior and after a full day's work, members would work through the night stringing and wiring these lights. (2004, 4)

After contracting the Roma Band, on Saturday night the members went to saint Leonard to bring the statue of saint Anthony in procession through Hanover and Parmenter streets, Salem to Cooper streets and finally to Endicott Street where, near the society's club, "a city makeshift bandstand was decorated, as was an extended storefront, which was to house the statue overnight" (Abruzzi 2004, 4). Sunday, after the mass in Saint Leonard Church, the procession started, again through the same itinerary of the night before but with the addition of Prince to North Square, to Moon Street, onto Fleet to end again in Endicott. "This route continued for nearly forty years. North Street was never part of the parade because of some petty feud with several members of other organizations, as to who had the larger feast."[39] The procession gathered almost a thousand dollars and some jewelry. At 10:00 P.M. the statue was returned to Saint Leonard. According to Abruzzi, but also to other members' memories, the feast continued in this way until 1925, with increased votive offerings particularly in jewelry, pinned on a cape and a bridle (2004, 4). At the end of the 1920s a first change was necessary because of the profound disagreement with the new pastor who wanted all the money gathered during the procession to be donated to the church.[40] The question was resolved in favor of the society but afterwards the pastor refused to host the statue any longer. The statue, as well as a new one, was kept by a member in North Washington Street until 1958.

> As the 1930s approached, the feast was growing and was attracting several vendors who sold tonic, balloons, ice cream, and light refreshments. (2004, 4)

The economic growth of the feast was inevitably stopped because of World War II. No feasts were held between 1942 and 1944. But in 1948, after facing organizational problems of membership, which was now extended beyond the Montefalcionesi, the feast was again expanding. Abruzzi describes that feast in this way:

> The sight of 10,000 yellow and red roses illuminated the streets of the North End. It seemed to turn Endicott Street and all its companion streets into a false daylight. This was the first year vendors had traveled from New York, via trucks, to this little town to celebrate the feast of Saint Anthony. Younger members added their own flair to the feast with their famous snowballs. Tons of paper and streamers came flying from rooftops on both sides of Endicott Street. (2004, 4)

After the success of 1948 procession, the society decided to extend the length of the feast, starting not on Sunday but on Friday. In 1958, the procession finally ended at the present club, at 203 Endicott Street, thanks to the donations and work of members who remodeled an old pool parlor and hall. Another economic effort occurred in 1985 when the society purchased the gold and amber lights with the images of Saint Anthony and Saint Lucy that can be seen now during the feasts (see figure 4.11).[41]

Aspects of change can be seen in the differences over the years about the number of vendors and the kind of goods sold. At the present time there are more than a hundred vendors selling a great variety of products, from T-shirts to Henna Tattoos and an oxygen bar. But food is the main product. According to Mary Jo Sanna the only food sold before the expansion of the feasts was hard candy, seeds and nuts.

> Everyone's door was open and the people shared the traditional foods which had been prepared for weeks ahead of time. Whiskey, beer and wine were available, but no one got drunk. Although these open houses still go, they are only for those who know and there are far fewer of them. The vendors who supply the vast number of tourists have been operating for about the last 20 years; there is some speculation that the idea first came from New Yorkers who came to the Boston feasts to sell sausage and fried dough the local picked it up from them. Now, along with the food, T-shirts, hats and souvenir trinkets are sold, games of chance are available, and it is possible to have your picture taken with a cut-out of the Pope or the President. (1988, 8)

This has been replaced in recent years with stands that allow one to be photographed waiting for the statue from an adorned window.

FIGURE **4.11**   Gold and amber lights with the images of Saint Anthony and Saint Lucy. (Author' photograph.)

The economic aspect of the feast has grown with the feast itself: if at the beginning of the twentieth century the cost of the small feast was relatively unimportant because of the voluntary effort of many members and votive offerings of about one thousand dollars, a century later figures are completely different. Asking about the cost I was told that a feast like Saint Anthony now can cost between forty thousand and sixty thousand dollars: marching bands, entertainment, municipal fees for the rented bandstand and the clean-up of the streets after the feast, ribbons, candles, pins, confetti, flowers etc. have a cost and they have to be contracted early. Income is not directly generated from the tourist flow, which basically effects the vendors, but by donations, gathered from members during social activities over the year, and, most importantly, from sponsors, who are a recent phenomenon, and from votive offerings during the feast. If the weather conditions are good the statue of Saint Anthony can come back to the club with more than fifty thousand dollars in money pinned on the ribbons.

The numbers and variety of vendors offering a variety of goods to attract more and more tourists, the heavy presence of sponsors advertising their products, the entertainment that is now omnipresent and constant all over the feast, might seem to indicate a transformation toward a more secular ritual. Still many narratives illustrate that the religious aspect remains very important. Joe, a very influential member of the society, told me:

Saint Anthony is a religious feast and we are very devoted to the saint. For us the procession is a way to express our devotion. I have been in New York City for San Gennaro—did you ever been there?—that's just a business, people don't even pay attention anymore to the procession and the saint, it's a parody. Of course we need stalls and vendors, and we need sponsors as well, because the feast is a lot of money, and even if we collect many offers along the procession it is not easy to afford. We have a lot of expenses and we have to find the way. But the central point, at least for us, is the devotion to Saint Anthony and to pay respect to the memories of our grandfathers and fathers. Carrying the statue, we carry our saint and our traditions. We are not the only one with our saint and our tradition but sometime they look too much at the commercial aspect of their festival.

Joe's narrative confirms the many tales of devotion to the saint that can be heard during the procession. Tales of small, private miracles are told alongside the charter legend of the saint and tales of other miracles, involving the entire community. Thus, I heard people telling stories of their healing from desperate diseases, of being spared from breast cancers, surviving difficult surgeries, getting out of economic struggles, or getting married. Narratives of personal miracles are endless. In this context, I want to quote Sanna again. She reported the following narrative of a Saint Anthony devotee, Danny, which in my opinion illustrates the broad magnitude of the private sphere of the relationship with the saint.

Saint Anthony represents God, God, Buddha, and all that, ok, you know, eastern, northern religions, whatever. But it's a belief, ok. Personally, I am willing to tell you, he granted me a miracle. I remember crying for three years since '84 and this year my ex- wife and children, it's been two weeks now, they stayed in my house for 8 days. They just left last week. She was very angry, with the divorce and all this stuff but the fact is, the miracle did occur. She stayed in my house, my children stayed around me. We were a family for 8 days. It wasn't my expectation, but it happened, ok. It's true. . . . I think it's important. . . . You'll find in this particular neighborhood in this particular area with Saint Anthony and with the feast, there are some serious believers, and we are not talking about miracles that make the sun come down and kiss the earth, It's miracles of the heart, miracles of passion, miracle of love, and a miracle of life, ok. (1988, 1)

The feasts I observed (from 2001 to 2004) began on Friday night, following a pattern that now seemed to me to be usual.

The statue of the saint was carried from the private chapel, located in the club. The ceremony, like many secular American rituals, was preceded by the

American national anthem sung by a young girl, surrounded by the crowd. American and Italian flags as well as the Massachusetts flag, were carried by members of the society, seamen and policemen. The statue, decorated by some of the leaders, was celebrated by the crowd and soon, after a shower of confetti, moved to the temporary chapel made by Emilio Matarazzo on the other side of the street, just in front of the club.[42]

The Friday procession is again short, opened by young boys holding a banner with the corporate name of the society, San Antonio da Padova di Montefalcione, Inc. A little statue was placed in the temporary chapel.

Another banner, with the image of the saint is also carried in procession. A male member of the society holds the banner while female faithful hold the ribbons, where money will be pinned.

Statue-bearers are located under the statue, in the typical uniform (white shirt and black pants).[43] On Friday night not too many devotees followed the statue. Shortly, after a walk around Endicott Street, the statue came back to the temporary chapel. This is the general pattern in Boston's North End feasts, but in the Saint Anthony feast something occurs that is very common in southern Italian ritual, but is rarely seen in the North End. The banner, coming back to the temporary chapel, stops and pays respect to Saint Anthony, bending toward the statue.

Friday night after the return of the statue, as well as Saturday, is dedicated to entertainment. Marching bands, performing singers and bands on stages and music by DJs occur every time the saint is in procession or on Saturday. It is not unusual to see a small band performing Italian American music and dance. That time this band announced its performance by saying "And now let's play some Italian music" and started to play Dean Martin's hit "That's Amore," a very popular Italian American song. The use of a tricolor hat and what looks like a traditional costume, as well as shaking tambourines, together evoke a stereotypical image of Italian folk music, while songs and context suggest something much more American. A complex mix of stereotypes, history and memories play a major part during the entertainment's performances.

In contrast to the general pattern Saturday was also an important religious occasion, with an outdoor mass, celebrated on the bandstand by the society's chaplain and followed by the blessing with the relics and the distribution of the *pane di Sant'Antonio* (Saint Anthony's bread). These small loaves of bread are blessed on the feast of Saint Anthony and given to those who want them—a traditional ritual during any celebrations dedicated to the saint. The mass was also a display for authorities, including, as usual, the city's mayor.

The big procession started on Sunday at noon. Devotees from the morning paid respect to the saint, who had been guarded all night long by members of the society. The all-night vigil is a member's duty, comparable to the bodily mortification of the statue-bearers. Money is not left on the statue, but the saint wore the golden votive offering. The form of respect is as usual the votive offering, pinning money on the statue or giving it to the guardians, and receiving back a religious image of the saint or a button (see figure 4.12). Many young boys (Saint Anthony's is always holding the Infant Jesus and the infant Jesus is traditionally their saint's patron, as the charter legend of the bread seems to confirm) gather around the statue, paying homage to the saint.

The first band (in 2005 seven marching bands were hired for the feast) approached the temporary chapel playing "God Bless America" and "America the Beautiful." But the conductor walked side by side with a different figure who held a pole and moved it rhythmically. He could be taken for the drum major of a band, and is very close to a traditional southern Italian figure, the so-called *pazziariello*, who is joker teasing the authorities.

The procession followed the usual pattern: statue-bearers carrying the statue, beggars holding ribbons or basket with religious images. The statue-bearers in general try to have the same position under the platform, year after year, as I already suggested for the Madonna del Soccorso. Carrying the statue is a matter of personal votive offering or even familial tradition, but in general the leader of the procession tends to respect the wishes of the bearers.

FIGURE 4.12   Votive offering during the procession of Saint Anthony. (Author's photograph.)

The Sunday procession walked the streets of Boston's North End for many hours, coming back to the club only around 11:00 P.M. As I mentioned before the votive offerings on the statue are very munificent and, as Mr. Greco told me during the little Saint Anthony feast, it was not easy to see the nose of the statue because it was so completely covered by dollar bills, pinned on the ribbons held by women and gathered by beggars, rewarding the donors with the image of the saint. Also on the so-called calendar are pinned on the statue but. According to Sanna:

> In the weeks prior to the feast many people stop by the societies and request a "calendar" stapled to a piece of ribbon. According to Jimmy G. this is strictly a North End innovation. The "calendar" is actually a glossy colored picture of the saint, beautifully printed in Italy (in case of Saint Anthony, a standard iconographic representation . . . No one seems to have any idea why they called calendars, although speculations suggests that the idea of keeping track of time by pinning money on the attached ribbon each day would be a reasonable explanation. These pictures of the saint, to which people add more and more ribbons and more and more money, are then, during the procession draped around the neck of the statue by the jubilant giver who must be lifted up by the members of the society to accomplish the task. (1988, 10)

It is probable that this name comes from the tradition of bringing home a real calendar with the image of the saint, but definitely the function of keeping track of the offering is valid. It is not an imported tradition from the village of origin, and in my knowledge does not seem to occur outside the North End. Another seemingly unique North End tradition, also reported by Sanna is "pinning money onto long rolls of ribbons which are lowered from upper story windows" (1988, 10).

Reciprocal respect is shown during the votive offering from the windows as the statue approaches, with the bearers lifting the statue to the window, bending the platform to allow the faithful to caress the saint, or stopping by a little boy, who is lifted by his father to kiss the statue.

With the return of the statue to the private chapel of the club, whit the faithful holding candles, the feast is over. It will be necessary to wait another year to see the saint in procession again. And then again. The feast is a repetitive tale, with few changes over time and few differences between similar feast in the neighborhood. But this is its strength, providing the potential to be told and retold, almost immutable. The reassuring function of the ritual resides in its dual nature as ephemeral and yet repetitive.

Saint Lucy of Montefalcione

With the return of the statue to the private chapel of the club in Endicott Street, the feast of Saint Anthony is over, but, as it happens in Montefalcione, this is also the beginning of another feast, this time organized by a uniquely female society: the feast of Saint Lucy. It is important to state that the Saint Lucy Society is not a female section of the male society, but a specific society devoted to their own saint and therefore with their own feast, even if they share the club and many of the social activities with the Saint Anthony Society. The feast itself is organized with the help of members of Saint Anthony, but it is a matter of reciprocity, since Saint Lucy members also help the organization during the progress of the "male" feast.

The tradition to feast Saint Lucy on Monday immediately after Saint Anthony came from the Italian village of Montefalcione, where this specific pattern is traditionally performed. But in the United States it was not always this way: at the beginning only Saint Anthony was celebrated. In 1928, after the embarrassment with the local priest about the ownership of the funds generated by Saint Anthony feast, a new charter was approved for the organization (with the name changed from Circolo di Amici [Circle of Friends] to Saint Anthony of Padua of Montefalcione) and statues of Saint Anthony and Saint Lucy were commissioned. The annual feast for Saint Lucy was started in the 1930s but only when the Saint Anthony weekend concluded on Sunday immediately before Labor Day. Being a vacation day, the Saint Lucy feast could then be performed. The eventuality occurs every six years. According to Mary, an influential member of the society, it was impossible to have the feast on Monday "because people ought to work" and also because "there was a misunderstanding too with this other lady, she had Saint Lucy she used to take it out, you know some sort of conflict, but we solved this little problem too." After World War II Saint Lucy became a night-time celebration on Sunday, and a day feast every sixth year. According to Abruzzi (2004) the huge success of the feast suggested that they constitute a specific society, formed by children and wives of the Saint Anthony Society members. The tradition of the nighttime celebration on Sunday, is still evident during the long weekend of the feast. According to Vincenza A., many women, often because they came to the Saint Anthony feast with their husbands, came to pay respect to the saint on Sunday night, pinning their offerings on the statue inside the chapel. In recent years finally the Saint Lucy Society started their feast on Monday. Vincenza told me "We tried to change the day but the men said no, we tried to change to Thursday but they said that Saint Anthony ought to be first." Of course this demonstrates the unbalanced relationships of power, but also the proximity, between the two societies. As Vincenza said "They [the members of the Saint Anthony Society] helped us a lot, they pay for almost everything, for the entertainment and for the band, and we do not pay the rent here in the club. And two of the members help us by carrying the statue, one on the front one on the back, they always did that."

The procession of Saint Lucy started on Monday around 2:00 P.M., after a mass celebrated in Saint Leonard Church. The opening is always a banner, carried by young girls, in declaration of belonging. Immediately after the banner the Italian and American flags are paraded. It can be noted from the banner that the Saint Lucy Society is not formally incorporated. The statue is moved from the permanent chapel in the club to the temporary chapel outside. This is done by members of both societies. The statue then is moved out from the temporary chapel, ready to start the procession. Members of Saint Anthony have a prevalent rule in this case.

The initial decoration of the statue is a duty that belongs to the women of Saint Lucy. The statue is then ready to be carried in procession, and the groups of statue-bearers and beggars are formed. The platform with the statue is not particularly heavy but still carrying it is a matter of physical effort, and is made more difficult because of its unstable balance. The function of members—in this case male members of Saint Anthony, as Vincenza said—is holding the poles of the platform to stabilize the weight for an easier procession. The group of members, recognizable by white shirts and black pants with a pink band, is divided between statue-bearers and beggars holding the ribbons. Division in not, of course, gender-based but age-based. Age is an important variable in Saint Lucy feast: statue-bearers are generally teenagers (now the undeclared limit is sixteen years), while beggars holding the ribbons are younger. Little girls, as I said, carry the opening banner and a decorated sheet with Saint Anthony and Saint Lucy names embroidered on, it while young teenagers hold the flags.

Older members are not without functions during the procession. Some help balance the platform, others help the little girls with the decorated sheet, the prominent member such as the president superintends the procession and manages the procession stops.

Just after the opening banner a few little girls hold a decorated sheet, helped by adult members. The original function of this sheet was to catch the coins offered to the saint, often thrown from windows. Now the function of the sheet is decorative, evoking memories and history.

The procession stops when the faithful pay respect to the saint. This is not just a completely unforeseeable event but also a preorganized action. Days before the feast members of the society gather around the neighborhood to discover in advance who will make an offering and where it will be necessary to pick it up. The president—and this is true for every feast—already knows if not all at least most of the stops of the procession (see figure 4.13).

People wait for the passage of the statue by their windows, ready to lower their offering. Even for Saint Lucy, ribbons with dollar bills are already made. It is not unusual in the specific case of Saint Lucy that the offerings come from Saint Anthony members. The offerings are not gender-based but mostly territory-based: women are not the only ones paying respect to the saint, while Montefalcionesi are expected to show their devotion. As Vincenza said "Saint Lucy is more North End people, it is small. Some people from other towns come up here but not too many. Some come on Sunday night to see Saint Lucy. Years ago used to be more of Montefalcione, because most of the people who lived here were from Italy, but now there are not so many left here. Endicott

FIGURE 4.13   Procession of Saint Lucy. (Author's photograph.)

Street was all Italian." Indirectly Vincenza underlines one of the most important characteristics of the feasts: the pilgrimage. I explained previously the
demographic changes in the neighborhood have pushed many original settlers
out of the North End toward suburban areas. For them the feast is the most
important occasion to come back to the neighborhood. They may have lost their
territory but certainly not their territoriality, the feeling of belonging to a place.
During the feasts I met people from Boston's greater area, but also from Michi-
gan and Pennsylvania, New York and Rhode Island, all of them performing
their ephemeral, but highly symbolic, return. A different kind of pilgrimage can
be considered the transnational one. As I pointed out for Saint Joseph often
authorities from Italy can be seen during the feast. I underlined the presence of
the mayor of Riesi, but this is also the case of one of the leaders of Augusta's San
Domenico committee who came to Boston to help organize the feast, or of
priests who came from Padua with a relic of Saint Anthony or from Anzano, on
the occasion of the centenary of the feast. Beside authorities who have been
invited by the local committee to set a sort of cultural bridge between the original village and the ethnic enclaves, ordinary people also travel between Italy and
United States for these festivals. In 1988, for instance, two charter flights were
organized by the Saint Anthony and Saint Lucy clubs to attend the tercenten-
nial celebration of the feast in Montefalcione. The same thing happened to the

Fishermen Society, who organized a special trip to Sciacca to participate in the feast. Also trips by individuals are frequent: I personally met people from the North End while I was attending the Saint Anthony and Saint Lucy feasts in Montefalcione as well as people from Montefalcione during the North End ceremonies in Boston.

Another form of contact between the Italian village and the communities of emigrants abroad can be seen in a ritual performed in Montefalcione. Before the procession the official speaker reads in church the names of faithful offering money for the local feast. They can be collective or individual, and they come from many parts of the world: Boston and Chelsea, Massachusetts; Brooklyn, New York; South Orange, New Jersey; and Maplewood, California; as well as Montreal, Toronto, and Calgary, Canada; Geneva, Switzerland; Bedford and Peterborough, England, are some of the locations I have heard named during the ritual. The links between the two countries are, more than ever before, reinforced by the ease of transportation and availability of communication. However, not many pilgrims attend the Saint Lucy's feast. Vincenza and other members of the society explained that this is because their feast is a small one and it is held on Monday, certainly not the best day for people to join the ritual. But still the votive offerings are remarkable. At the end of the day the statue is covered by dollar bills.

Each time a donation is made all the three marching bands (and this is not a small expense for a small society) play the "Marcia Reale," the number one tune. The omnipresent Roma Band, with the North End Feast Band and the Lawrence Band, walk the streets of the North End again, behind the saint, supporting the festivals of the saints with their music. This is a fundamental contribution that is locally perceived to be the hallmark of the Italian feasts of the North End.

Santa Rosalia, Patron of Palermo

The feast of Santa Rosalia is the last one of the North End calendar and occurs the first (or second) weekend in September, after the big event of Saint Anthony. Santa Rosalia is the patron saint of Palermo, Sicily and the Italian feast is celebrated in July, from the ninth to the fifteenth, and also September 4, the day of the death of the *Santuzza*, as she is familiarly called in Sicilian dialect. The exceptional length of the ritual and the fact that the ritual is celebrated not even two months after the previous one, gives us an idea of the dimension of Santa Rosalia's Sicilian cult.

In Boston's North End the Santa Rosalia feast does not have nearly the magnitude of the Italian celebration. It is important to remember a few things that explain its small scale. First of all, southern Italian migration, above all in the late nineteenth–early twentieth century, is mostly a rural phenomenon, only rarely involving urban population. Emigration from Palermo, the biggest Sicilian city, proportionally had a less important impact, while the numbers of farmers and workers from the inlands are simply more impressive. Nor was Boston even the first target of *Palermitani*, who usually preferred to remain in New York City.[44] Settlers from Palermo came to the North End relatively late and the foundation of a religious society in 1939, at least twenty years later the other societies of the area, is a sign of their small impact compared to other ethnic enclaves on the neighborhood social landscape. The absence of the society's club is another consequence of the reduced number of the Palermo settlers. The statue is left all year long at the entrance to the Sacred Heart.

The relatively small scale of the society and competition with other societies to celebrate the feast in the middle of July is probably why the to the choice was made to celebrate Saint Rosalia close to September 4, the day of the pilgrimage (often barefoot) to Mount Pellegrino in Sicily, a tradition still remembered by the Palermitani in Boston. To again demonstrate a transnational aspect to these feasts, I quote a report of the pilgrimage to Mount Pellegrino performed by Rita Giambrone, from Boston:

> Every time I come home my first visit is to go to the Santuario Santa Rosalia have been there many times, it is a beautiful and peaceful place. (I love this Santuario, very peaceful full of love and peace a place to pray and feel the holy spirit come upon me. Thanks to Santa Rosalia). I have come to the Santuario on foot, the path is absolutely beautiful, praying at the station of the cross. have attended MASS at the plaza of the Santuario, have walked the entire Santuario, seen all the gifts of grace received by Santa Rosalia. How wonderful Santa Rosalia is. God Bless you all in Jesus name. your Friend Rita . PS please pray for my father that Santa Rosalia will restore him all new organs in his body, deliver him from Cancer.[45]

Although the feast does not reach the dimensions of the Sicilian celebration, nonetheless devotion is still fundamental.

The members of the society gather near the church and adorn the statue with ribbons, money, and calendars.[46] The pattern of Santa Rosalia is like that of the other feast: group members, wearing white shirts-light brown pants, with brown handkerchiefs around their necks, carry the statue on the streets, focusing on the Sicilian section. A marching band is ready to play the "Marcia Reale" for devotees offering money to pin on the statue. Offers are made by faithful and collected by members, and pinned on the ribbons held by women, around the statue of the saint.

Santa Rosalia is a small feast, with a short procession, like the feasts of June and the beginning of July and like that of Saint Lucy, which immediately precedes it. It reveals a decrease in tension after the climax reached during the big feasts of Madonna del Soccorso and Saint Anthony.

Saint Mary, Patron of Anzano

The feast of Saint Mary, patron of Anzano is celebrated on the first weekend of June. It is the first feast of the long summer's festivals in the North End. The charter legend of Santa Maria is connected with the discovery of an image of the Madonna in a small village, Anzano, four centuries ago. A young farmer was herding his cow to the pasture when he noticed a light under a shrub. Moving the shrub, he found an image of the Madonna. He ran back to the village and told everybody what he found. The townspeople then decided to make a statue in honor of the Madonna. When the statue was ready, people attempted to move her to Trevico, a town nearby, but the wagon could not move. Thinking that the statue was too heavy, they added more bulls to pull the wagon, but not even nine bulls could move the statue. Interpreting this as the Madonna's wish not to go to Trevico, they tried to move the wagon to another town, Zungolo, but again the wagon could not move. It was a clear sign of the Madonna's will to stay in Anzano. So the faithful built a church to host the statue and since then the Madonna di Anzano is celebrated in Italy every Pentecost.

It is important to understand the charter legend to understand the Italian ritual based on the symbolic trip to the different towns made by the statue on a decorated wagon pulled by bulls.

In Boston, as I said, the feast is celebrated the first weekend of June. But even if the date of celebration has changed, the idea of the trip has survived. It must be mentioned that the Society of Santa Maria Di Anzano, one of the oldest religious societies in Boston, founded on January 3, 1905, moved out from the North End and settled down in Somerville for economic reasons. The feast, while celebrated in the North End, also includes ceremonial events in the Somerville club.[47] The dislocation has only partially affected the society and its activities per se. The society is still very active, regularly holding meetings the first Tuesday of every month and organizing social events, such as the trip to New York City for the San Gennaro's procession. Two of the characteristics of the Society of Santa Maria di Anzano are (1) the important presence of women and (2) the continuous switching back and forth between English and Italian, or more accurately a variant of Neapolitan dialect.[48]

Women are an especially important part of this society. A basic reason is because of the importance of a specific female figure in the history of the club. Interestingly the initial page of the society's official web site is dedicated to this woman:[49]

This page is dedicated to the loving memory of Concetta (Immaculata CERASUOLO) Giampapa. Born Dec 8th, 1898 in Anzano Di Pugia Di Foggia, Italy, died Sept 30th, 1984 Boston. Founder of the Santa Maria Di Anzano, Female Society and past President for 37 years. Concetta's father's name was Rocco CERASUOLO, Rocco died 1917 in America, her mother's name was Maria and she died in italy. She also had a brother Gennaro who was a postman and a sister Plinia. She also has another sister which is being research. One of her sisters lives in Canada, near the Toronto area, where relatives worked in a cheese factory. Concetta's husband, Charles came from Catania, Sicily.

Women's presence is even now still fundamental and evident during the procession and throughout the club's life. For instance, when I attended the meetings of the society, I noticed active participation by women. More formally, two important offices are held by women: the chaplain is Tina De Crescenzo and the trustee is Marion Marciello.

The opening position, characterized by the banner with the name of the society, traditionally belongs to the female section of the society. An icon of the Madonna di Anzano is hosted in the club but the statue is blessed before the procession in Saint Leonard Church, at the corner of Hanover and Prince streets. If it is true that any procession has the fundamental function of sanctifying the physical space of the community, in this case this is even more important. The North End's area is a space that belongs to the memory and to the symbolic imaginary of the group. The ephemeral performance of the ritual is situated on an ephemeral area, kept alive in the memory. Inside the church a Franciscan friar blesses the statue. Again, I noted women's presence. They are in charge of the initial decoration of the statue. Then the statue is carried out. The priest walked with the faithful, throughout the procession, occupying a very prominent position. This is the only time this happened in my experience in the area, In other words, the priest walked in the procession as he would have in Italy: wearing sacred vestments and leading the group of statue-bearers.

Members of the society start to adorn the statue inside and immediately outside the church. Although women's presence in the society and during the procession is relevant, the devotees' group around the statue is gender based: the usual four statue-bearers are men and the beggars, holding the light blue ribbons are women. If, as well known, the dislocation of roles and rules in side the ritual reflects the social structure, it has to be said that the stereotype of a male-dominated community is stereotypically displayed during the procession.

Respect, as usual, is the fundamental value expressed, following the usual patterns. The North End tradition of the statue waiting by the window is, again, confirmed, with the marching band ready to play the "Marcia Reale." Money and the so-called calendar are offered to the Madonna, demonstrating at the same time a private devotion and a public display.

The end of the procession does not coincide with the end of the feast, since a concluding event is held at the club. The members, and I again emphasize the importance of women's presence, have a social gathering there in Somerville to celebrate their patron saint. The symbolic territory sanctified by the procession necessarily includes not only the historical settlement in the North End but also the new club, in a different town. The ritual of the Madonna di Anzano feast establishes the tension between territory and territoriality as geographic and symbolic area of belonging year after year.

San Rocco and Madonna delle Grazie

The calendar of festivals in the North End cannot be considered complete if I do not analyze, even if briefly, two other feasts: San Rocco and the Madonna delle Grazie. My information about these two is not as complete as it is for the other cases, but these feasts confirm the prevalence of a pattern in the local festive practices, as I have already demonstrated.

The feast of San Rocco was established in the North End by Italian immigrants from the village of San Nicola Baronia, Avellino Province, in 1921. According to his *Acta* and his *vita* in *Legenda Aurea*, San Rocco was born in France in 1295. He is considered the saint of miraculous recoveries from pestilence and in general incurable diseases because during an epidemic of plague in Italy "he is said to have effected many miraculous cures by prayer, the *sign of the cross* and the touch of his hand."[50] The saint is represented as a mendicant pilgrim (he was a follower of Saint Francis), near a spring of water, with a dog, in memory of his withdrawal into the forest following his illness. The water bubbled out miraculously and the dog supplied him with bread. His cult spread through Spain, France, Belgium, Italy, Germany and more recently into the United States. San Rocco is celebrated on August 16 in San Nicola Baronia, but in the North End in 2004 the feast was held on July 16.

San Rocco is a small feast. I was told by my consultant,[51] that the society does not have enough money to run a bigger feast, as it used to be in the past:

> Now you need at least twenty-five thousand dollars to make a big feast, and we don't have it. But still we have mass on Sunday morning and the procession. This year [2005] we hired two marching bands, the Roma Band and a Portuguese one. They did a very good job. The society is still organizing the banquet on March 4 to raise funds for sick children and the statue is still in Saint Leonard Church. In the past the feast was bigger but now the old members are gone . . . some died, some left the North End. Now we have many American members. (interview with Carmela, member of San Rocco Society)

The pattern is the usual one, with statue bearers carrying the icon of the saint in procession. Women and children hold the ribbons where the money offerings will be pinned. The procession is short lasting three to four hours, basically walking around the Saint Leonard Church. Another sign of the reduced scale of the feast is the absence of a uniform. Only cockades distinguish members and leaders. But even if on a smaller scale, San Rocco contributes to the calendar of festive practices in the North End, respecting the neighborhood's pattern.

The feast of Madonna delle Grazie (Mother of Grace), often misspelled Madona del Grazie, is organized by the homonymous society, whose members are original to, or rather, claim a common origin with San Sossio Baronia, Avellino Province. The society is one of the oldest, founded in 1903, but now, like the San Rocco Society, it is going through a difficult period, suffering a crisis of membership and organization.[52]

The memory of a great past, with a three day feast competing with the Fishermen and Saint Anthony for the biggest celebration of the neighborhood, is still alive. But now the club is closed and many members are deceased or, as in the case of Lina, have moved to the suburbs. The society is still formally active, but meetings are not held regularly and the organization of the feast is handled by the president and few other members. Actually the feast is concentrated on one day, in general the second Sunday of July, after the celebration of the fourth, and as with the San Rocco example after mass the icon is carried in procession. In the Italian village the feast is a three-day feast that occurs on July 2 and again, on August 8. The North End feast shows the usual pattern around the statue: male members, some of them in "uniform," wearing a T-shirt with the image of the Madonna, bear the platform. Women and children hold the ribbons with the votive offerings on them. Following the procession, beside a crew of paesani, is the Roma Band.

Madonna delle Grazie, even if no longer the important feast it used to be, holds an important role like the San Rocco feast, since it confirms the practices prevailing in all the festivals in the North End.

My ethnographic account of Boston's North End feasts is at its end: similarities suggest a common pattern, while differences underline specificity and multiple voices. My comparison allows me to conclude that even if the icon of the saint is the same on both sides of the ocean an original belief has been transformed to a diffuse practice in the North End. The data concerning the festive practices of the North End suggest to me an initial double reflection: (1) the homogeneity of the North End's festive practices cluster around a specific performative pattern; and (2) the heterogeneity of the Bostonian feasts with regard to the analogous rituals in the villages of origin.

From Correct Belief to Correct Practices:
On Similarities

As I have shown, the festivals have two different patterns: the one-day feast or the three-day feast. Saint Anthony (in June), St. Jude, Madonna delle Grazie, San Rocco, San Domenico, Santa Lucia and Santa Rosalia follow the one-day pattern. San Giuseppe, Santa Agrippina, Madonna della Cava, Saint Anthony of Montefalcione, the three-day pattern. There is just one exception, the Madonna del Soccorso (also called the Fishermen's feast): is a four-day festival, starting on Thursday and ending Sunday.

The one-day festival concentrates on procession and entertainment. The entertainment consists of the band that follows the procession as well as the stalls selling mostly religious objects. This is a matter of organization and a lack of wealth. Often members of the stronger societies also become members of the weaker societies to help them survive. The three-day festivals are, naturally, more complex. They start with a short procession on Friday. Saturday is almost completely dedicated to entertainment. On Sunday the statue of the saint is taken through the streets in a grand solemn procession. During all three days of the festival the entire area is full of stalls for material exchanges, economic transactions and also to manipulate symbols such as ethnic foods (Italian and/or Italian American).

Inside the festive practices one can discern a narrative sequence and narrative invariants that concur to define the orthopraxy of the festive practices. Synthetically the repetitive practices are the following:

1. *The preparation of the statue* is always the starting point of the ritual. Normally members inside the society's chapel get the statue ready to go outside to meet the faithful. For instance, Sant'Agrippina and Saint Anthony are covered with the golden offerings of the past years. Year after year the gold must be set exactly in the same position, indicating continuity with the past (see figure 4.14).

2. *The statue is carried out* and placed on a temporary platform: sometimes fireworks and confetti highlight this moment.

3. *The statue is blessed by a religious figure.* This is the only moment of the clerical presence during the festival. In the three day model there is, on Sunday, a mass celebrated for the saint (see figure 4.15).

4. *Authorities pay homage to the saint.* For example the mayor of Boston (an Italian American from Grottaminarda, Campania) and the mayor of Riesi (Sicily) both made a short speech in honor of San Giuseppe di Riesi. Political relationships are very prominent at this time.

5. *Near the statue, members go on duty.* Under the supervision of the leader (usually the president of the society) members put ribbons on the statue. Later, dollars will be attached on these ribbons. The ribbons are held almost exclusively by women, and in a few instances by children. Other women (and sometimes men) bring baskets with religious images. They will be given to the people who offer money during the procession. A duty of the men is to complete the setting

FIGURE 4.14   Preparation of the statue: *Little Saint Anthony.*
(Author's photograph.)

FIGURE 4.15   The statue of Saint Agrippina is blessed by a friar.
(Author's photograph.)

of the statue. Even before the start of the procession many people offer money that will be attached to the statue. Sometimes parents allow children to give the donation. Other members stay continuously in touch with the policemen waiting for the authorization to start. Appointed members are ready to carry the statue, but they need the order of the *capoparanza*.

6. *The procession starts* when everything is set: the policemen is first, followed by banners and flags (usually both Italian and the American, but I also saw the Sicilian and the Vatican flags), accompanied by dignitaries (see figure 4.16). Then the capoparanza orders the men under the carriage to lift the statue (sometimes the order is in English sometimes in dialect) and to walk. This is the aspect of bodily mortification. The number of participants can vary, depending upon the weight and the shape of the statue. Usually two members, one in front one on the back, provide balance during the walk. In general, only the members of the society, which is made up exclusively of men, can carry the statue. The exceptions are: Saint Lucy, because it is a women's feast and Madonna del Soccorso, because the society has a women's section.

7. The procession is very slow because the statue stops each time somebody wants to make an offering. This is the begging by the members, which is answered by the symbolic offerings of the faithful.

FIGURE 4.16   Saint Anthony: The procession starts. (Author's photograph.)

Every time someone gives a donation, the band that follows the statue plays the "Marcia Reale." The statue also pays homage in front of churches, nursing homes, firehouses, police stations, and even to some members (the elders, the authorities, etc.). At the end of the journey the statue comes back to its starting point. In the case of the one-day feast the statue is returned to the society's chapel. In the case of the three-day feasts a smaller statue is set in a temporary chapel on the street. After the collection of money a continuous protective guard is mounted, day and night. On Sunday the solemn procession takes place after the mass.

Persistence in respecting and imitating what are regarded as the historically correct practices is the fundamental characteristic of the festive performances in the North End. Orthopraxy now definitely seems to prevail over orthodoxy, which, while still present, is relegated to second place. I am proposing two examples concerning control of orthopraxy and illustrating the resistance to changes. The first example concerns a change proposed for the Santa Maria di Anzano's feast on 2003, that is, the introduction of a cart hauling the statue in procession. With this innovation, the statue was no longer carried but dragged. This change, even if respectful of the original charter legend (in the Italian village, Anzano, the statue is on a cart) involved indeed a substantial modification of the recurrent symbolism. The following year the correct practice of carrying the statue was reintroduced. The failure of the proposed change was fairly predictable, since it was in clear contrast with orthopraxy in the North End festival cycle. It is necessary to add that in a roughly extended local area, examples of processions where the saint is located on a cart do appear. For instance, in Cambridge, a town very close to Somerville where the Santa Maria di Anzano Society's club is active, the cart is used during the feast of Saint Cosmas and Damien, and it is plausible to assume that members of Anzano's Society have been in touch with this group. Finally, the cart is used during what can be considered the archetypical, and certainly still one of the most important, southern Italian feasts in the United States, that is, the feast of San Gennaro in New York City. In this case Anzano's leadership's regular attendance at the New York's feast was confirmed by a recent episode. I was attending the San Gennaro feast in the middle of a very crowded Mulberry Street when Dale, Elio and other prominent member of the society crossed the street and stopped by for a friendly chat. This episode indeed confirms their knowledge of the specific festive form. Apparently, the pattern of the saint dragged by a cart, seems to be diffused in a wide area. And it is necessary to recall that this pattern surely refers to the American "authentic tradition" of parades, where displays are placed on carts or truck beds. This is exactly the crux of the matter: if the reference to a mythical, historical past or to the local present prevails then the statue of the saint will be still carried on the shoulders. If, instead, the model proposed by other feasts performed in a greater geographical area is the main term of reference, then the use of the cart may be admissible. The latter choice is surely possible. Yet, its chances of success are few due to the weight of orthopraxy in the North End festival complex.

The other example regards the attempt of the women's section of the Fishermen Society to carry the statue of the saint in procession. In general, the North End's feasts clearly enact a gender-based division of roles and rules. This is contrasted by the women of the Fishermen Society, whose resistance while carrying the icons of the saint led to a situation in which they ended up occupying a nontraditional, exclusively male, position during the performance of the ritual. But when I consider why women's resistance was unsuccessful, despite the fact that nowadays the gender-based distinctions within the groups are weakened, the answer can be found in the tension between inheritance and invention.

The dynamic approach I am pursuing cannot be completed if I do not take into account the transnational perspective, that is, bringing in touch the feasts performed in Boston's North End with the feasts of the original Italian villages. The transnational perspective leads to my analysis of the transformations and continuities of these religious festivals.

My first comparisons were of the festival of Saint Anthony of Padua, then the Madonna del Soccorso in Sciacca and the Santa Maria in Anzano. I observed the southern Italian festival in Montefalcione, near Avellino, in the summer of 2001 and the one in Boston's North End in the summer of 2002, the Madonna del Soccorso in Sciacca in 2004 and in Boston from 2001 to 2004, the Santa Maria in Anzano in 2004 and in the North End in 2002 and 2003.[53]

On Differences: Saint Anthony

To make the comparison as clear as possible, I will here restate some material covered in the previous pages of description. To begin, every festival, being a ritual, has a founding narrative. Saint Anthony's feasts are no exception. This will be the first element of comparison:

Boston's North End

Actually they started, what?, 1910–1911. They started before that to come over. And the next thing they were all congregated in the corner here. And the next thing they wanted to start something, they were all paesani, they were living all over these streets. Next thing they rented a store and they used to meet on Sunday morning for coffee, pastry, stuff like that. They met once a week, then the next thing they wanted to start like in paese, they wanted to do a feast, because the other societies were doing feasts. So they ended up and turned around and they said "we will buy a statue in Italy" which they did. And the next thing they sent somebody to Naples to buy a statue, from the same place that made the statue of Montefalcione. I guess they waited a couple of years they made the statue. When they finally got it here they kept in one of the members house. (interview with Jerry).

Sundays, after church, people would gather at the corner of Endicott and North Margin to discuss their week, their lives and renew
friendship. In 1909, a large group of these newfound immigrants all
got together and rented a store, a stone's throw away from where they
would congregate. That was the birth of Ciciolo de Amici di Montefalcione.[54] The pack numbered thirty-five, but this number would soon
grow as another paisani would come to America. In 1910, after much
discussion of bringing some old world home to their new homeland,
the group wished to have a feast for their patron St. Anthony. They
raised the money among themselves and had a statue cast in Naples by
the same people who created the statue in Montefalcione, but at three
quarters the actual scale. (Abruzzi 2004, 4)

Montefalcione

Nell'Archivio Diocesano di Benevento si legge che nel disastroso
terremoto del 6 giugno 1688 una vera ecatombe di vittime colpì tutta
la Regione: e se Montefalcione sfuggì alla cieca falciata del flagello,
subendolo in minima parte, ebbe ad attribuire la causa alla potenza di
S. Antonio. Da ciò in atto di gratitudine, nell'agosto successivo,
i superstiti Montefalcionesi supplicarono il Sommo Pontefice di
benignarsi proclamare S. Antonio speciale patrono di essi. La grazia fu
concessa e notificata al parroco nella seconda quindicina di agosto
dell'anno medesimo 1688. (Baldassarre 1982, 2)

[In the Diocesan Archive of Benevento it can be read that in the dis-
astrous earthquake of June 6, 1688, a true massacre of victims wounded
the whole Region: and if Montefalcione escaped the blind violence of
the scourge it is because of Saint Anthony powerful mercy. For this
reason and as act of gratitude the following August the survivors im-
plored the Sovereign Pontiff to gracefully proclaim St. Anthony their
special patron. The grace was granted and the parish priest was noti-
fied the second fortnight of August of the same year 1688].

From this account, it is clear that for the Italian villagers the main reason
to pay respect to St. Anthony was a votive offering of thanks while for the North
Enders it was a matter of copying the local feasts of other societies (as Jerry
suggests in his interview) or a matter of preserving memories of the old world
in the new homeland (as suggested by Abruzzi).[55] Often the founding narrative is reinforced with subsequent tales. In May 1931 the archpriest of
Montefalcione Antonio Pagliuca wrote:

Questa data storica segnò la celebrazione di un patto di alleanza tra
il Santo di Padova e Montefalcione, dove il primo si offriva nostra rocca

di difesa nei dolorosi frangenti della vita, e il secondo impegnava la parola ad amarlo sempre ed assai a preferenza di tutti gli altri beneficati. . . . In questa nostra cittadina sino ad oggi e cioè nel periodo di tre secoli furono frequenti le scosse telluriche, ma per la nostra patria non si ebbero danni materiali, nè perdite di persone. Per la mancanza di acqua ed igiene, sul nostro orizzonte spesso si addensarono morbi epidemici come il colera del 1836, quelli del 1884, il Lupus Spagnola del 1916, il terremoto del 28 luglio 1930 e mentre dappertutto apportarono sterminio e morte, per noi non fu segnalato danno di qualsiasi sorta.[56]

[This historical date marked the celebration of an alliance between the Saints of Padua and Montefalcione,[57] the first offering himself as a fortress against the painful situation of the life, the second promised to love him forever and more than the other. . . . In our village until now, that is for almost three centuries, we suffered many earthquakes, but no material damages, neither loss of human life nor for our country. Because of lack of water and hygiene, epidemic disease gathered on our horizon such as cholera in 1836 and 1884, Hispanic Lupus in 1916, earthquake in July 28, 1930 and meanwhile everywhere they brought death and slaughter, we had no damage of any sort.]

Another tale of devotion can be seen in the following article of Franco Baldassare, Il Ponte, August 25, 1984:

Il morbo asiatico (colera), fulminante a volte non offre la possibilità di distribuire sacramenti, di assistere al ben morire. . . . La morte fulminante alimenta sentimenti religiosi, di rifugio nel sacro, di ricorso al potere taumaturgico di S. Antonio.

[The Asiatic disease (cholera) as it spreads does not allow for the possibility of celebrating the sacraments to assist the wellbeing of the dying. . . . Spreading death foments religious feeling, a need for shelter in the sacred, turning to the thaumaturgic power of St. Anthony.]

In Boston's North End narratives about devotion connected to the thaumaturgic power of the Saint have lost the aspect of communal belonging, fading into more individual narratives. Mary Jo Sanna wrote:

By far the majority are private miracles, when the saint directly influences one's own life by interceding in relation to sickness, personal danger, punishment or general well being. During the course of St. Anthony feast I was told dozens of these stories by, for example, a woman who had been spared additional cancer, a woman whose husband had returned from World War II, by another who had breast cancer twice, 20 and 12 years ago, but not since, and by a man whose divorced family had been returned not in the way he expected, but in a way that he believes is the beginning of a reconciliation . . . We're not talking about miracles that make the sun come down and kiss the earth, It is a miracle of the heart, miracles of passion, miracles of love, and a miracle of life (interview with Danny Puopolo). (1988, 15)

Naturally, even these small miracles (I assume present also in Montefalcione) affect the devotion to St. Anthony, since they are extraordinary in ordinary life.[58] But, again, the more general sense of belonging to the group seems to be lost: the alliance between the Saint of Padua, the fortress against the painful situation of life, and Montefalcione, where the whole population promises to love him forever, operates on a different and more personal scale in the new world.

Differences and similarities can also be seen during the performance of the ritual. Two important similarities appear obvious. Both festivals run Friday through Sunday, thus each can be placed within the three-day pattern. In both festivals we see the same constants, which are, I repeat: processional structure, bodily mortification, begging and symbolic offering, material exchanges and economic transactions. Beside structural resemblance, some peculiarities can be observed. Comparing the programs of the festival I note that in Montefalcione Friday and Saturday are dedicated to secular performances such as concerts and variety shows,[59] meanwhile Sunday concentrates on the religious aspect such as the mass and the procession, which is the climax of this narrative. In Boston's North End the narrative seems to proceed in a different way: Friday, the religious blessing of the statue and the small procession, and Saturday dedicated instead to concerts and shows. Sunday has both aspects, the religious, with the big procession, and the secular, with other concerts.

The narrative sequence of the procession is the following:

The Preparation of the Statue
Boston: A) It is the starting point of the ritual. B) It happens inside the society social club. C) The statue of the saint is covered with the golden offerings of the past years. The officiant is an important member of the society, such as the president. D) Members of the society can pay homage to the statue, inside the club. Usually they pray and put money on the statue.

Montefalcione: A) It is the starting point of the ritual. B) It happens inside the church. C) The statue of the saint is covered with the golden offering of the past years. The officiant is a member of the feast committee. D) Parishioners and faithful pay homage to the statue inside the church. Usually they kiss the base of the statue. No money can be put on the statue, just on two poles, located at the sides of the canopy.

The Auction

Boston: No auction. There probably was one in the past.[60]

Montefalcione: Crucial point of the ritual. It is held inside the church. The auction has a preface, with a member of the committee reading a list of donors (mostly immigrants). Three different phases: auctions for the privilege of carrying the gold, the poles with the money and the statue.

The Statue Is Carried Out

Boston: The statue is placed on a temporary platform outside the club.

Montefalcione: The statue remains inside the church.

The Statue Is Blessed by a Religious

Boston: The society's chaplain blesses the statue.

Montefalcione: The parish priest blesses the statue during a brief ceremony.

Authorities Pay Homage to the Saint

Boston: Authorities are usually the first to pay homage. The president of the society becomes a sort of intermediary between the saint and political, military or economic authorities.

Montefalcione: Authorities are usually the first to pay homage. The priest becomes a sort of intermediary between the saint and political, military or economic authorities.

Members Go on Duty

Boston: Members of the society approach the statue, ready for the procession. Under the supervision of the leader (usually the president of the society) members put ribbons on the statue. Later, dollars will be attached to these ribbons. Women, and, in a few instances children, hold the ribbons. Other women (but occasionally men) bring baskets with religious images that will be given to the people who offer money during the procession. A duty of the men is to complete the setting of the statue. Even before the start many people offer money that needs to be attached to the statue. Sometimes parents allow children to give the offering. Other members will stay continuously in touch with the policemen waiting for the authorization to start.

Montefalcione: After the priest's order the parishioners leave the church, waiting outside. The priest takes his place in front of the statue, the auction's winners approach the statue, ready for the procession. Authorities take their places behind the statue.

The Procession Starts

Boston: Policemen first, followed by banners and flags (usually both Italian and American), and important authorities. Then the leader orders the men under the carriage to lift the statue (sometimes in English sometimes in dialect) and to walk. This is the aspect of bodily mortification. Usually two members, one in front one on the back, provide balance during the walk. Only the members of the society (only men, because the societies are exclusively male based,) can carry the statue.

Montefalcione: The priest leads the procession. As soon as the statue is outside the church, fireworks and music played by the marching band start. Beside the statue are the two poles with the offered money. The winners of the auction and their relatives and/or friends carry the statue. Behind the statue come the authorities, then the marching band. At the bottom, the faithful.

Begging/Symbolic Offering
Boston: This double aspect is represented by the offering of the money that the faithful put on the statue. But also the statue pays homage: in front of churches, nursing homes, firehouses, and police station.

Montefalcione: This double aspect is represented by the offering of money that the faithful put on the poles.

The Statue Finds a Place in a Temporary Chapel
Boston: At the end of the procession the statue is set on a temporary chapel.

Montefalcione: No temporary chapel. The statue comes back to the church.

Second Procession
Boston: The small Friday procession is followed by the second and bigger procession on Sunday, with the same structure.

Montefalcione: No second procession.

In general the narrative structure seems to be analogous, but it is possible to underline important differences in the location of the ritual, the (main) officiants of the ritual as well as specific elements in the particular form of devotion. For example the statue of St. Anthony is located inside the club, the private club of the private, voluntary association called Saint Anthony Society, in Endicott Street, Boston's North End; the statue of Sant'Antonio is located inside the parish church (more precisely, the sanctuary) of Montefalcione,[61] dedicated to the saint. The main officiant of the American ritual is the leader of the society, assisted by the other members, especially the committee, who is democratically elected almost nine months before the feast during a plenary session of the association. For instance, the president of the society (or a delegate) puts the golden offering on the statue, the president orders the member to go on duty. The president, again, decides where and when the statue ought to stop because somebody is going to pay homage and give a money offering. Finally, the president (or a delegate) accepts the offerings, putting them on the statue, declaring himself as the symbolic *trait-d'union* between the group and the saint. The chaplain of the society blesses the statue; he seems to be more a particular delegate of the president (because he has the unique qualification to perform the blessing) rather than a representative of the religious power. In contrast, the main officiant of the Italian ritual is the parish priest, helped by the so-called *Comitato Festa* (Feast Committee), supposedly open to everybody who wants to contribute to organizing the festival.[62] The priest is the superintendent of whatever is formally and informally performed around the religious icon inside and outside the sacred space. The priest is the intermediary between the faithful and the saint. Even when others perform some parts of the ritual such as the auction, the priest is the main point of reference. It is significant that the president of the *Comitato Festa* is the priest, and that the position is not only honorary, but also a position of control. Thus, in the two cases, the roles of power and authority are reversed: in Boston's North End the secular society controls the feast, with the religious institution occupying a place of secondary importance. In Montefalcione, it is exactly the opposite, with no doubt at all about the priest's authority.

Another moment of power and control is related to the specific donation of the offering. As I said before, in the North End the procession is very slow because the statue must stop every time somebody wants to offer money. The president gives orders to stop, the statue is turned to the offering, the money is pinned on the statue,[63] the president orders the marching band to play the ritual song for the offering (the "Marcia Reale"), and finally he orders the procession to continue.

In Montefalcione, like everywhere else in Italy, it is impossible to pin money on the statue of the saint: many different deliberations of Conferenza Episcopale Italia (Italian Episcopalian Conference) prohibit performing this act. This is not the place to discuss the money offering as a form of popular religion and, in the final analysis, as a kind of peculiar devotion, but it is important to underline how the church controls the ritual, manipulating its form. The money can be pinned on the two poles beside the statue, but absolutely not on the saint. This form of begging and symbolic offering is of secondary relevance, because the function is carried out in a different, highly formalized, moment of the ritual: the auction. As I said before, inside the church and under the supervision of the priest everybody can bid to gain the honor of carrying the saint, the poles for the money and the golden offering. Often family or friends put together enough money for a big bid so they can have more opportunity to win, and it is possible to regard this as a vague and momentary informal association. But it is far from the formal, voluntary Bostonian society, which has a specific membership ruled by a legal constitution. This contrast determines a fundamental difference in the process of deciding who can become a protagonist in the procession carrying the statue: in Boston's North End only the members of the society can have this honor. In order to become a member of the society—the elected few, using a sectarian terminology—must prove they are a first-, second- or third-generation immigrant from Montefalcione,[64] so this performance reinforces the ethnic enclave and its ethnic identity in front of the other ethnic enclaves and their members. Furthermore they are also regulated by the approval of their fellows. In other words, there is a consensus of the association, whereas in Italy it is a matter of recognition by the church. In the Italian village the apparently democratic auction does not aim for any formal or informal identification, because, as I already demonstrated, there is a more important power that demands submission, which is the power of the church. In other words, while in Saint Anthony's procession members declare cultural and geographical belonging through the members' devotion to religious icon, in Sant'Antonio these things are taken for granted and what remains is a declaration of faith to the saint and, above all, to the ecclesiastic institution.

On Differences: Madonna del Soccorso

I will start again comparing the charter legends. This is the Boston's North End's one:

> In 1910, Italian immigrants from the fishing town of Sciacca, Sicily, founded the Boston chapter to preserve the memory of their ancestors and to honor the patron saint of the fishermen. In 1911, a replica of the original statue of the Madonna del Soccorso was constructed and the fishermen held their festival on Fleet and North Streets in the North End. The early festivals were primarily religious, commemorating the Blessing of the Fleet of fishing boats in Boston Harbor, the parading of the statue of the Madonna through the streets of the North End and former West End, and the Flight of the Angel. Today, these events are still the main stay of the festival.[65]

On the same page of the booklet was presented the picture of the founding member and their names.

The legend of Sciacca is:

> In the year of our Lord 1300, an Augustinian monk by the name of Nicolo Bruno lay ill in bed with severe fevers and a broken neck. One night he received a vision of a woman of radiant beauty, who said to him, "I am The Madonna del Soccorso di Sciacca (The Lady of Help of Sciacca). I have come to your town of Sciacca to aid and assist the people." She then told him to get up from bed and spread her message to the people of the town. Miraculously the monk rose from his bed free from fever and healed of a broken neck. Nicolo Bruno spent the rest of his years telling his story and spreading the message of the Blessed

Virgin. Nicolo Bruno was not without his critics however, many attributed his "vision" to his high fevers. No one could explain though the miraculous healing of his broken neck. As the people acceptance of this story grew their devotion to the Madonna also grew, as result more miracles were attributed to the Blessed Lady. One such miracle took place when a six-year-old boy misbehaved for his mother. The boy, like most six-year-olds, was full of energy and getting on his mother's nerves. In a rage, the mother shouted to her son "go to the devil you little pest." Suddenly the devil appeared and grabbed the boy. The mother realizing what she had done and truly sorry called on the Madonna del Soccorso to rescue her son from the hands of Satan. Miraculously the Madonna del Soccorso dressed in a white and gold robe and carrying a wooden club appeared. In one sweep of the club the Blessed Lady hit the devil and knocked him to the ground. The boy now released ran not to his mother but ran instead to Madonna del Soccorso, under whose cape he hid. The Blessed Mother with the boy still under Her cape walked over to the Devil and stood on top of him. She then turned to the boy's mother and said, "Put your trust in Madonna del Soccorso for I am the protector of Sciacca." Then releasing the boy to his mother She said "Fear not my children for I shall never abandon you." Another miracle took place one day when the Blessed Virgin visited upon a thirteen-year-old girl suffering from paraplegia. The Blessed Lady said to the girl "I am the Madonna del Soccorso di Sciacca, rise from your bed and tell the town I am here to help them always." The girl then told the Blessed Lady that she was paralyzed and could not get up. The Madonna then told her to touch her belt and she would be able to walk. The girl did as she was told and miraculously went out to tell her story. The townspeople of Sciacca realizing how lucky they were to be in the good graces of the Mother of God decided to show their gratitude and devotion to her by commissioning a statue to be built in her honor. Using the description of the Madonna given to them by the monk, the mother of the six-year-old boy, and by the thirteen year old girl, the town created a painting of the Madonna and gave it to the sculptors commissioned for the statue. In the year 1492, two sculptors by the names of Guliano Mancini and Bartolomeo Birrittaro went to Palermo to build the statue of solid marble.[66]

Again, miracles and devotion are the basis for the Italian charter legend while memories and respect are the founding reasons for the Bostonian feast. There are also other important differences between the two festive practices: for instance, while the Italian feast occurs twice a year (in February and in August), in the North End it is performed only in August. It is worth recalling the unsuccessful attempt to initiate the feast of San Calogero, the other patron saint of Sciacca. More importantly, the flying angel seems to be a Bostonian peculiarity, probably imported from New York City. Other differences that can be seen are in Sciacca the fundamental role of church and Catholic hierarchy is evident: the statue always leaves the basilica preceded by the priest. The statue is different, according to the charter legend, and while it is possible to see the votive offering situated on the icon, money is clearly pinned on the platform's foot. Bodily mortification is evident: the weight of the statue is enormous and many bearers are necessary to lift it and to walk the procession.

The feasts, even in the Madonna del Soccorso case, are substantially different.

On Differences: Santa Maria di Anzano

The charter legend of the Santa Maria talks about the discovery of a sacred image of the Madonna in a small village, Anzano, four centuries ago. A young farmer was herding his cow to the pasture and he noticed a light under a shrub. Moving the shrub he found an image of the Madonna. He ran back to the village and told everybody what he found. The townspeople then decided to make a statue in honor of the Madonna. When the statue was ready people attempted to move her to Trevico, a town nearby, but the wagon could not move. Thinking that the statue was too heavy they add more bulls to pull the wagon, but not even nine bulls could move the statue. Interpreting this as a Madonna wish not to go there, they tried to move the wagon to another town, Zungolo, but again the wagon could not move. It was a clear sign of the Modonna's will to stay in Anzano. So the faithful built a church to host the statue and since then the Madonna di Anzano is celebrated in Italy every Pentecost. The charter legend is important in understanding the Italian ritual based on the symbolic trip to the different towns made by the statue on a decorated wagon pulled by bulls. The procession is headed, again, by priests. The statue is adorned inside the church with the votive offering, then is carried in procession toward the other village.

When the procession meets the faithful of the other village they replace the bearers: bringing back the Madonna to the Sanctuary. The bishop is heading the procession. The symbolic journey between the two villages is fundamental for the Anzano feast, a characteristic lost in the New World.

Another difference concerns the day of the feast: while in the North End the feast is the first weekend of June, in Anzano the saint is always celebrated the day after the Pentecost. Furthermore the program of the feast shows these two elements, religious and secular, of the ritual. The religious element seems to be more central, and this is not surprising, since the church and the priest serve as the "guardian" of the feast, as I already stated for Saint Anthony and Madonna del Soccorso. This of course does not mean that entertainment is not present: marching band and merchandise stands are active during the whole feast. Again, the feast in the Italian case seems profoundly different from the American one I am studying, while the latter seems to conform to the local pattern of the North End.

Orthodoxy and Orthopraxy

Differences between the festive practices of the original villages and similarities between the feasts in the North End, which seem to follow a specific pattern. I am arguing here that there are evidences of a dislocation from an original orthodoxy, the correct belief or the "conformity to an official formulation or truth, esp. in religious belief or practice,"[67] toward the creation and perpetuation of ritual forms "considered" as correct, a level that can be called orthopraxy.

The anthropological debate about the supposed dichotomy between belief and action,[68] reductively defined as an interiorized state of the actors juxtaposed to a performative act, has a long history, as Catherine Bell (1992) has illustrated.

It is not my intention, therefore, to go back over this important question. However, I would like to state that in this long and vivid discussion the relationship between orthodoxy, the "correct belief," the ritual character, the correct practice or the body of practices accepted and recognized as corrected, and orthopraxy, the creation and perpetuation of ritual forms considered as correct, seems confined to other fields of study.[69]

The term orthopraxy is predominant in theological studies, often related to Orthodox Judaism and some Islamic sects. It is also used in the Christian world, referring to the *Imitatio Christi*,[70] that is, the emulation of Christ's approach to poverty and oppression, and to the Eastern Christian Orthodox Church. From a more sociological and anthropological perspective the seminal account of Wilfred Smith (1957) highlighted differences within Islam concerning more what is good (or, better, right) than what is true. Another fundamental contribute to the study of orthopraxy was made by James Watson (1988; 1993). His analysis of the uniform structure of funerary rites in late imperial China demonstrates how cultural homogenization can be expressed in performance and practices. According to Watson the sequence of the funeral rites displayed an impressive uniformity:

> [T]he proper performance of the rites, in the accepted sequence, was of paramount importance in determining who was and who was not deemed to be fully "Chinese." Performance, in other words, took precedence over belief. (1988, 4)

The Boston's North End festive practices I am studying display likewise the extraordinary uniformity seen in the case of Chinese funeral rites, certainly historically constructed. The two are not completely similar: for instance Watson (1988, xi) suggested that the normative structure of the Chinese ritual was produced by the complex interaction between actual practices and the written codification of earlier customs that were recorded by the literate elites. In the Boston's North End festive practices the interactions are not so clearly vertical but rather tending to the horizontal: no literate elites writing about past forms are involved in the process of codification. Instead what is at stake is an intense mechanism of imitation and control. In this study, therefore, I am proposing a more complex and dynamic model of orthopraxy. It is indeed the combination of the official discourse about the feast with the vernacular one that makes possible the correct practice in its moments of proposal, performance, control and reproposal.[71] This dynamic suggests a disemic aspect (see Herzfeld 1980; 1997a),[72] permeating these festive performances. From this perspective, and following the suggestion of Michael Rhum (1993, 801), orthopraxy can be considered as a statement that acts as indicator of motivations, a nonlinear model of orthopraxy seems very dynamic and becomes the privileged ground of expression of the asymmetric relations of power expressed inside and by social groups. As Herzfeld (1997a) suggested, it is important not to see the polarization official/vernacular as a radicalized opposition between, on the one hand, hypothetical authorities or authorized discourse provided by the political and social power, and, on the other, subaltern or disempowered strata, (which are hypothetical as well). Even the latter category, the so-to-speak "ordinary people," retain power and know how to use it, no matter how agency can remain opaque.[73] They know how to compare symbols and their use, and convey their consent or dissent to the actual leadership, which is, in any case, part of the local collective and therefore not greatly differentiated from the "ordinary people." This is the microcosm of religious societies, ultimately deciding the festive practices. Here the dialectic between leadership and groups is evident but not exasperated. Practices are not imposed, but proposed (mainly by the leadership) and controlled (not only by the leadership but also by the group in general). I analyze now just an example, the meetings at the society's club concerning the organization of the feast. Generally it is possible to see two different moments in meetings like these: one, that is, before and after the formal meeting which is often this discussion is confined to other fields of study a rather casual and friendly one and where a vernacular version of the feast's discourse can be stated and proposed. And a second, that is, the official meeting, where roles and rules are officially displayed and performed. The vernacular idiom in the latter moment is almost entirely absent. In this second moment the institutional (if I intend for insti-tutional the idiom enunciated by the leadership) prevails, yet the relationship between the two moments suggests a diffuse control rather than an autocratic one, even if this takes places within a broader scenario of asymmetric relations of power.

Correct practices are also signals of, and instruments for, the neighborhood's integration. The ritual of the feast reaffirms solidity of the ethnic enclave through the procession, but the times of rigidly bounded communities are definitively past, so that procession can trace symbolic borders not at all coinciding with the original ones. The boundaries of the ethnic enclaves are now blurred if not completely dissolved. At the same time each procession, in concurrence with the other processions, strongly reaffirms the remembered boundaries of the neighborhood. The dimension of heterogeneity (the different and historically formed ethnic enclaves) and homogeneity (the neighborhood) is expressed by the festive practices.

To better illustrate my argument I will quote Bestor's comments about communal identification and religious rationale:

> [I]n part the religious rationale of the *mikoshy* processions is to enable the tutelary deity to inspect and bestow blessings on its territory. Thus they serve as compelling markers of a community's boundaries and identity. (1989, 240)

This is exactly what happens in the North End (and everywhere else, I suppose, since it is a structural characteristic of every procession). But it is important to suggest a particular aspect: I have demonstrated that processions tendentially mark out the original territory of the ethnic enclaves. I have also shown how the course of the processions have changed and for what reasons. I have also suggested that processions skim, but do not cross, the perceived boundaries of the neighborhood. Historically speaking, one exception to this "rule" can be traced. Traditionally, the Fishermen's feast (I remind the reader that the ethnic enclave was established around North Street, North Square and Fleet Street, the southeast area of the neighborhood) used to trespass on the West End. This is because a second wave of Fishermen immigrants did not find room in the North End, and therefore they settled on the neighboring West End. For this reason the procession extended the course out of the North End. Naturally, when the West End was razed to the ground in the late 1950s by urban development (see Gans 1962) with the further and consequent diaspora of Sciaccatani, the procession began to be performed within boundary of the North End.

It seems evident that orthopraxy of the festive performances signals the decreasing importance of the ethnic enclaves and of the specific ethnic identity (even if this is continuously declared) in favor of a claimed local identity which is however also based on the whole neighborhood territory. I have already shown how the meaning of an ethnic enclave has been blurred, just as its own boundaries have been weakened, but this is not the case for the whole neighborhood. Although with the conclusion of the Big Dig it has lost its identity as the Island of Boston (and not for the first time in its history) it still continues to practice a symbolic defense of its borders, tracing them through the processions and the festive practices.

In conclusion, comparison between the festive practices in the North End and a transnational perspective suggested a transformation away and dislocation from the correct belief and worship of the patron saint of the village of origin, which I called "orthodoxy," toward performances of ritual forms perceived as correct, which I called by the term "orthopraxy." The Italian feasts seem to be strictly controlled by the clergy, who respect charter legends while maintaining a hegemonic relationship with faithful. The festive practices in the North End have tended over the years to be more egalitarians and toward aesthetic reduction (Garcia Canclini 1988, 479), a mechanism that I will call "stylization" in the next chapter.

5

Ephemeral Identities

I have introduced in the last chapter the concepts of "orthodoxy" and "orthopraxy," promoting them as the fundamental heuristic tools in order to understand both the changes and the continuity in the North End rituals. In this chapter, I will argue that a process of stylization is the foundation of the idea of correct festive practices, criticizing Nestor Garcia Canclini's (1988, 479) idea of "double reduction." He proposes that popular forms move (1) from the rich ethnic diversity of the regional to the unified national, and (2) from the flux of social process to that of codified object. The specificity of the North End and the risk of "nostalgia" implicitly evoked by reduction suggests to me a less controversial term, that of "stylization."

But first, in order to better address my analysis of the North End's festive practices I will situate it in a more general anthropological debate about the analysis of rituals and performances. I am arguing here that the legacy of Durkheim, Gluckman and Turner still influences both the ethnographies and the theoretical approaches to feast and rituals. I am proposing instead a model of ritual as a performance that dynamically responds to contemporary historical and social realities and bears a reflexive quality for participants and ethnographers. Following Abner Cohen (1993), rituals and performances are fundamental for the analysis of the dialectical relationship between power and symbolism.

I will discuss another quality of ritual, very often proposed as a break in time, or as a threshold or limen. I am arguing that the traditional distinction between ordinary time in everyday life and extraordinary time in ritual is less rigid than it is usually supposed. Ritual appears to be the climax of actions, narratives and social dynamics that extend beyond the ephemeral festive moment. I will suggest as well that the feast is a dynamic social construction dialogically formed (or at least informed) by intertextuality, that is, the relations between discourses historically produced and completely integrated in a social landscape, and by the production of meaning through multiple voices engaging in debate within the utterance of the performance. From this perspective, I define "ritual," the feast and performance as discrete locations, using a spatial metaphor rather than a textual one.

I will then reintroduce the concepts of orthodoxy and orthopraxy, promoting them as fundamental heuristic tools for understanding both change and continuity in North End rituals. Furthermore, I will analyze how North Enders select, debate and use memory, past and myths for strategic essentialist reasons, and how these essentialist constructs can also be used to represent unbalanced relationships of power between groups (related to ethnic enclaves) both inside and outside the North End. Finally I will propose a model of performative identity based on hypertextual theory. This metaphor appears more dynamic than the already established models presently used in the scholarly work on hybridity and creolization. I will entitle this model by a term I have used throughout this book: "ephemeral identity."

Feasts, Rituals, Performances

From the very beginning of scientific interest on the subject of feast, ceremony and ritual (terms intimately related but not completely overlapping) scholars have been debating about the nature, meaning and definition of these categories. And the debate is still going on: the transformative aspects of ritual, its significance as a public display, the assumption that feasts are both symbols per se as well as aggregations of symbols, are among the few general points having received a diffuse agreement of opinions. The legacy of Durkheim (1915, 237–238) who proposed rituals as the main, if not the only available, means to communicate group solidarity, has the characteristic of *long durée*. While considering the social group during rituals as more aware of itself, actively expressing collective consciousness and its celebration, Durkheim suggested that the group, through the ceremonial practices and the elaboration of symbols, renews itself as well as providing individuals with a stronger sense of belonging, affecting not only the level of interpersonal relationships but also the intimate and reflexive aspects of the self. Following this approach, Max Gluckman (1963, 110–136) stressed the basic function of ritual as a mode for displacing social conflicts. The ritual, in other words, is the symbolic locus where conflicts can be declared and expressed, allowing the harmonic unification of the group. According to this scholarship Turner (1969) derived his concept of "communitas," meaning the modality of social interactions, basically unstructured or rudimentarily structured and relatively undifferentiated, emerging in the liminal period of the ritual, a "moment in and out of time" taking the place of a suspended daily time. The legacy of Gluckman and Turner, as well as Durkheim's, still permeates the ethnography of feast and rituals.

Of course, these are not the only well known approaches to the subject. Many authors have, for instance, proposed more conflictual interpretative models, suggesting that the feast can be seen as a dramatization performed during the transient period of social conflicts in which a specific group may be involved. The feast is a performance, a public display of the economy, authority relations, identity and culture of a social group, offering various degrees of representation and inevitably influenced by the historic-cultural context in which it takes place. Thus, since conflict is a fundamental component of society, it is the conflict it-self that is displayed, through different modalities and patterns. For instance, the carnivalesque (an underlying dimension of every feast according to Bakhtin, 1968, 1–58) is a celebration of a temporary liberation from the prevailing and established social order, therefore implying a new state of becoming, change and renewal. The ritual transient inversion effects the official hierarchy and the actual social power structures (such as crowning a fool as a temporary king). It degrades and subverts authority. However, being, in the last analysis, a codified transgression, this inversion, while mocking authority nonetheless confirms the social order. Notwithstanding this, it also constitutes a way for marginalized social groups to express themselves and so has a rebellious potential.[1]

An example of how feasts perform social conflicts can be seen in the French ceremony of *charivari*, a custom of Latin origin diffused in many areas.[2] Origi-nally a wedding serenade, a sarcastic and ironic mocking of both bride and groom through the mechanism of inversion, this ceremony later became a more general way to mock unpopular people. The charivari was forbidden by the Council of Tours at the beginning of seventeenth century, but still lingers in some areas, and it was introduced, where it is called Chivaree,[3] in the United States, in Louisiana, by the French and the Canadians. An even more explicit display of local social tension is the Palio di Siena (Dundee and Falassi 1975). This is a vi-olent horse race, performed twice a year, on July 2 (for the liturgical calendar of the saints this is the day dedicated to the Madonna delle Grazie) and August 15 (Madonna Assunta), the *palio* embodies the differences and tensions between the city's neighborhoods and between social classes. Another example of how a festival can express social conflict is reported by Sabina Magliocco (2006). In-terestingly Magliocco discussed the transformation of the two Sardinian festivals she studied in Monteruju as reflecting the struggle between a socialist public ad-ministration (with a progressivist political agenda), and an emerging center-right coalition, which claimed a political identity stressing the values of local tradi-tions and authenticity. According to Magliocco (9), from this point of view fes-tivals can be seen as important for the enactment of social conflicts and for the airing of political dissatisfactions. Yet, as she points out, not all festivals enact or display conflict nor is conflict the only aspect of social life displayed and paraded in the festival. For understanding the meanings of conflicts as expressed within the festival she suggests observing them as displays bearing symbolic and ephemeral inversion of everyday norms of behavior and hiding symbolic mean-ing and significance (for a parallel see Geertz 1973 on "deep play").

Among other scholars, Theodore Bestor promoted the view of festivals as expressions of social order in the Miyamoto-cho neighborhood in Tokyo:

Although it is a momentary punctuation in the year's activities the festival illustrates many of the themes that suffuse Miyamoto-cho's mundane social life throughout the year: the hierarchical structure and the egalitarian ethos that permeates many resident's conceptions, tensions between internal and external definition of the community; Miyamoto-cho's assertion of its identity and autonomy through local events and activities that are self-consciously seen as parts of the neighborhood life. (1989, 224)

What Bestor individuated in Miyamoto-cho's feast is not the display of an explicit conflict but a more blurred and flowing social dynamic that enacts hegemonic tensions between different parts of the group.

Years later and in a different geographical area, that is, Venezuela, David Guss analyzed different festive forms and approached them as cultural performances to be read not as simply "texts:" "a discursive approach recognizes that they are dialogical and even polyphonic. They are fields of action in which both dominant and oppressed are able to dramatize competing claims" (2000, 10). From this perspective festive forms become performances dynamically responding to contemporary historical and social realities and not static texts (23). This idea of performance retaining a reflexive quality for participants and anthropologists alike, can be also seen in Baumann:

They are cultural forms about culture, social forms about society, in which the central meanings and values of a group are embodied, acted out, and laid open to examination and interpretation in symbolic form, both by members of that group and by ethnographer.[4]

Analogously, my experience with Boston's North End feasts allows me to say that, rather than looking for binary oppositions it is heuristically more productive to try to analyze the flux of social dynamics involved that contain the richest insight and implications (even if structurally these dynamics can usually be clustered around the dichotomy hegemonic/subaltern).[5] In other words I have chosen to approach the observed social group in terms of asymmetric relations of power, arguing that members within do not simply oppose each other but rather are dynamically intertwined and continuously both struggling and cooperating with each other. From this perspective, and following Williams (1976, 115–120),[6] the feasts, and traditions in general, are symbolic tools that instantiate the hegemonic naturalization of these asymmetric relations of power. According to Guss (2000, 15) canonized official tradition and rituals are visions imposed by some dominant groups of specific versions of history and the past. But, again, this imposition is an expression of dialectical tensions rather than a direct social clash. Even if dominant groups are identifiable and even if their hegemonic tendency is identifiable too, the subalterns are not passive objects or recipients. Instead, they are actively committed in this process, through social practices such as Bakthinian inversion or the construction of strategic essentialisms or, in general, through pragmatic claims for cultural intimacy. Here I will discuss how these dialectical tensions express themselves during the performance of the feast in the North End. I will do this after having unfolded the relations between power and symbols on a more general and theoretic aspect.

Abner Cohen (1993), analyzing the Notting Hill Carnival, suggested the presence of a dialectical relationship between power and symbolism. As Cohen notes, power pervades all human actions as well as all symbols. Power can be symbolically expressed, and symbols can carry power. Often power uses symbols to present itself not only as authoritative but also as an authoritarian, indisputable and totalizing force. Yet, at other times, it also claims compliance and collusion, for consent and acceptance of social hierarchies and rules. The concept of "hegemony" expresses this asymmetric dimension in relations of power. It is important to state that hegemony is a concept that must be contextualized every time we use it. This is particularly important when the social context under study claims to be egalitarian. Even if this is only a claim rather than a pragmatic and realistic peculiarity self-defined egalitarian societies remain different from the historically hierarchically stratified European realities. But even in the United States, and even if in need of contextualization, hegemony is still a powerful heuristic tool. Thus, no matter what kind of coloring power assumes and no matter what kind of symbols are used, a dialectical relation between power and symbolism can be traced: power informs symbols, but the process of symbolization is never without new and ambivalent effects.

To individuate the intertwined relations between power and symbols is important when we discuss how to represent reality. It is a basic requirement for every discourse on ritual, ceremony, festive forms, feasts, or whatever name I prefer while discussing performances.

Bailey (1993) observed how representations of reality enacted through performance bear a paradox: performance is real and imagined at the same time. Indeed, it is real in its effects. Yet, by being also imaginative it allows performers and audience (a distinction that also must be discussed and contextualized) to exercise a freedom of invention and interpretation certainly different from a wholly structured and positive reality. The question is not only about freedom and the creativity of performance, but about whether social reality must be distinguished from its representation. I completely agree with Parkin (1996, xix) who argues for the indissolubility of the two terms: event and its representation as different aspects of the same reality, influencing each other in an endless mirror game.[7] Power and symbols are embodied in the ritual, or in my case the feasts, in what Cohen (1993) called performative and transformative aspects.

It is not only the boundaries between events and performances that are blurred and malleable. I am proposing here that even the traditional—another long durée concept—three phases of the ritual, drawn from Van Gennep's (1938, 1977) notion of the rites de passage and the aspects of separation, margin (or limen, "threshold" in Latin), and aggregation, and reaffirmed in Turner's (1957, 1969, 1974b) model of liminality and communitas are not rigidly separated from each other and are more dynamic than what has conventionally been thought. An argument tending in this direction was provided by Goffman's (1959) analysis of what he called the "region," consisting of team (described as a group of individuals cooperating in performance), performance (the mode of presentation employed by actors, shaped also by audience and setting) and audience (which is inevitably an active participant and not a mere passive object). The idea of region allowed Goffman to introduce the concept of front, back and off "stage" regarding the relationships between actors and audience in the performative play. Beyond and behind the official stance visible in the "front-stage," the team performs a different type of performance. The "backstage" performance is apparently more "truthful" because it is enacted without any pressure or responsibilities, except the absolute responsibility to act as one is expected to act in informal, offstage settings. Outside the stage is located what has been called the "audience segregation" indicating the regulation of access to the performance by the team. Indeed, Goffman's approach goes far beyond a rigid allocation of exclusive modules, but an emphasis on structures is still visible: the performance region proposed by Goffman is still separated by conceptual and dramaturgically contingent boundaries.

From my perspective ritual is never a temporal break disconnected from the temporal and geographical context in which it is performed. Rather it is the climax of actions, narratives, social dynamics that extend themselves beyond the ephemeral festive moment. The separation, very often pronounced in anthropological scholarship, between ceremonial and everyday time is artificial; instead there are significant extensions of the everyday into the ceremonial (for instance, familial relationships or power relationships) as well as extension of the festive time into the everyday (for instance, the daily pressures that the president of Fishermen Society receives in order to pick the "right" flying angel). Ritual is conceived, imagined, discussed, structured and destructured, felt and lived, rehearsed and imagined both before and after the actual performance, continuously influencing and transforming the social life of the group. And if the pervasiveness of ritual inside everyday life can be seen diachronically, at the same time ordinary time pervades the limen synchronically: the ritual does not set apart moments of everyday life while it is taking place. In other words the immediate pragmatic context of production of the event is not the only reference for the feast.[8] (8) Perhaps I should add to my discussion the more dynamic term "discourse," but even discourse is not an antiseptic term. For instance, behind the dynamic appearance of Foucault's notion of discourse, defined as a field "made up of the totality of all effective statements (whether spoken or written) in their dispersion as events and in the occurrence that is proper to them" (1969, 27), it is possible to see the immobility of the text. Nevertheless, discourse is a term I am going to use, while being aware of this risk.

I am proposing an idea of the feast as a social construction dialogically formed (or at least informed) by intertextuality, that is the relations between discourses historically produced and integrated in a social landscape, and by disemia, as a production of meaning through multiple voices engaging in dialogue within the utterance of the performance.

This idea of intertextuality comes from Julia Kristeva (1986), who proposed text as three-dimensional. Writing subject, ideal reader, and exterior texts concur to provide the definition of textual space. Since I am not comfortable with the reduction of the complexity of the ritual to text, my use of Kristeva's concept is, again, more oriented toward a thorough analysis of the social dynamics of asymmetric relations of power. For instance the use of the past in order to reconstruct orthopraxy is not only a proposed link to determined cultural forms but a social dynamic where dominant groups, promoting their hegemonic posture, converse with subaltern ones.

It is fundamental to augment this idea of intertextuality with the concept of disemia, meaning the tension between official and vernacular cultural forms (Herzfeld 1997a). Disemia not only expands the narrowly linguistic frame of diglossia (ibid., 14), but also the Bakhtinian idea of heteroglossia (also a linguistically oriented idea): "it does not ignore language, but contextualizes it as part of a semiotic continuum that includes silence, gesture, music, the built environment, and economic, civic, and social values." And rituals too, I add.

From this point of view ritual, feast and/or performance can be seen as discrete locations, suggesting a spatial metaphor rather than a textual one. While my debt to Goffman's scholarship is evident, my definition differs from his idea of region because it stresses not a framed setting but a continuum, where locations are not rigidly bounded, if they are bounded at all. Multiple locations are continuously available on the general landscape related to the feast. Some of them are more official, such as the ephemeral space and time of the feast per se, and can be seen narratively as a climax reached following a mechanism similar to *gradatio*, or in the sequence of meetings at the religious societies. Some are more casual, even unpredictable, such as daily encounters at various social places at the bars, at home, in the streets etc. where gossip, less formal but surely not a less important as a form of social regulation, takes place.

The feasts of the North End, in my case study, become a symbolic, pragmatic and performative location, discretely differing from a surrounding historical, social and cultural landscape, heterogeneous because it is scattered into multiple discourses spreading beyond any stable boundaries.

Discrete locations are characterized by degrees of localizability, a term with which I explore how kinds of cultural forms are actively selected by the social group to provide the discourse of the ritual. It is easy to see a disemic aspect of this enunciation. Official and vernacular accents are both present, again in various degrees, and characterize the different locations. During the performance of the feast the maximum degree of official form is reached. In the following section dedicated to orthopraxy I will explore this aspect, debating the idea of correct practice and its distance from orthodoxy, the correct belief. An example is the malleable boundaries of the ethnic enclaves marked by the procession of the icons, which recall a traditional pattern but which nowadays have been deprived of their original function of sanctifying a specific territory. Another official form produced during the feast is the distinction between the male statue-bearers and the female beggars. In origin the structure of the group surrounding the icon of the saint was an image of the social structure based on gender distinctions. This distinction is no longer as dominant within the group, but nevertheless it still pervades all the feasts.

During the feast vernacular forms are also practiced but they have been dimmed by the official forms and become therefore less visible. For instance the barefoot believers walking in the procession are now seldom present during the feast (I did not directly observe this devotional behavior, I was only told that somebody showed up barefoot at the procession I was attending) but they surely enact a memory of the group's past.

This use of memory is what makes the vernacular forms not only present nowadays but also fundamental: the correct practice in the present is observed and regulated by continuous comparisons with the past. As Herzfeld (1997a) suggested, it is important not to see the polarization official/vernacular as a radicalized opposition between, on the one hand, hypothetical authorities or authorized discourse provided by the political and social power, and, on the other, subaltern or disempowered strata, (which are hypothetical as well). Even the latter category, the so-to-speak "ordinary people," retain power and know how to use it. They know how to compare symbols and their use, and convey their consent or dissent to the actual leadership, which is, in any case, part of the local collective and therefore not greatly differentiated from the ordinary people.

In the North End's feasts the disemic process is not expressed at the level of formal doctrines of the state concerning culture and pragmatic actualities. Nevertheless I can point out the negotiations of power taking place between groups or individuals. In other terms even in such a small scale and where power is muted by an egalitarian ideology and a relative absence of objective status differences, it is still possible to discern the dialectic between dominant/subaltern groups. It is this dialectic moment that seems to me absent in Goffman's (1959) analysis of stages: in his work, performance relies on a distinction between actors and audience. In my view instead, the audience is not separated from the stage by any kind of border and is very much active in the performance itself, influencing the contemporary ritual through comparison with past performances and oriented toward the performance of future feasts.

To show how localizability is expressed, I will consider the reaction toward the closure of the Sacred Heart Parish which took place in April 2004. At the rally in protest of the closure, all the societies participated, carrying the statues of their saints in a short procession. Some of these statues (Santa

Rosalia, for instance) were preserved in that church, and they made a round trip tour around North Square. I could approach this rally as a specific, ephemeral, occasional ritual, and as far as it goes, this would be a correct way to approach the event. Implicitly, if I do so, I am using a bracketed vision of what is going on. But the rally was also about the feasts. The official form of the feast was metonymically restated through the short processions. Everything was represented according to the correct practice: statue-bearers under the statue carrying the saint, beggars around the people, this time not asking for money but for ideological support. Moving on a more symbolic level the protesters were representing the collective unity of the neighborhood, through the different representation of the different ethnic enclaves. The usual play of strategic essentialism claiming an identity was performed just as in the summer's festivities. Vernacular enunciations about the feast were also present: during the rally I spoke with many participants, members of the societies or neighbors who were purposely attending the event, or just passers-by, and the usual tales about the charter legends of greedy priests looking for the society's money collected during the feast were told once again. Being symbolically more aggressive and conflictual, the vernacular ideas of the festival, supplemented by memories of the past, differed from the official presentation. In this exceptional but grounded case based on everyday life of the North End, both vernacular and official forms of symbolic expression were marshaled against an external threat. The specific instance was a ritual which talked about other rituals and about the everyday reality of the parish. It was indeed exceptional and ephemeral but it also blurred into the quotidian.

Another location, showing similar ambiguities and dialectics, can be found in the fund-raising activities following the September 11th attacks. On that occasion, all the societies gathered together. The saints did not personally arrive at the banquet and dance. Yet, their presence could be discerned in the diversification of task and duty, organized according to memberships. Saint Agrippina's members took care of the food and beverages at the bar, the Fishermen were in charge of the entertainment; Saint Lucy's fellows were in charge of the decoration and cleaning. No feast, apparently, was named during the event, at least not officially. But this separation, evident to the insider as well to the outsider, vernacularly speaks about perceived essential traits of the society's members. Saint Agrippina's people are considered to be the "funniest" and the "nuttiest": the bar was considered the perfect duty for them. The Fishermen, mostly because of Sal and Therese's capability, were acknowledged as very good at organizing shows: their feast is believed in general to be the most efficient from this point of view. Saint Lucy's members could take care of decoration adding a female look. Again, the festive collectives are not named but are immanent at the event. This location, therefore, is even more discrete: as an event, it is indeed exceptional, but it is also pervaded by mundane influxes of cultural forms, intertwined with those related to the feast.

To further explore the disemic aspect of the rituals of the North End, I am going to analyze now the meeting at the society's club concerning the organization of the feast, participating in what Goffman would call backstage.

Generally it is possible to see two different elements in meetings like these: one, that is, before and after the formal meeting, more casual, and more friendly. This is where a vernacular version of the feast's language can be stated; and a second, that is, the official meeting, where roles and rules are displayed and performed. Vernacular language in the latter moment is almost entirely absent, and the institutional (if I intend for institutional the language enunciated by the leadership) prevails. The official language is at the same time the idiom as well as the target of the leadership, and it reproduces itself.[9] To be able to control the form of the feast, and this is the core of these meetings, entails a degree of control over the society and the group connected to it.

These are just examples, and many others can be proposed. My fieldwork experience allows me to state that by looking at the importance of the feasts in the neighborhood it is likely that there is no location excluding ritual discourse a priori. Localizability is therefore immanent and pervasive, even if it is not always expressed.

The spatial metaphor (with all the limits that a metaphor can have) leads to two important consequences:

1. To see ritual, feast and performance not only as exceptional but also as rooted within the social group expressing them. This allows me to look for asymmetric relations of power as expressions of the feast (what the feast is talking about) as well as expressed by the feast (how the feast is talking) and as expressing the feast (who is talking about the feast) on both synchronic and diachronic directions. It seems to me an expression of the approach that Herzfeld called social poetics, "the play through which people try to turn transient advantage into a permanent condition in the socially comprehensive sense. It links the little poetics of everyday interaction with the grand dramas of official pomp and historiography in order to break down illusions of scale" (1997a, 26).

2. To be more respectful of emic definitions and interpretations of the event. North Enders see the festivals as climax, as pivotal point of a pervading phenomenon formally bracketed in the ephemeral time of the ritual but also continuously permeating the social group beyond these temporal barriers. According to Sal, Therese, Jason, Joe, Dale, Ezio and all the people attending the feasts, the feast truly comes to its end when the statue comes back to the permanent chapel. Yet, according to all of them this entrance also marks the beginning of the new cycle, and even this is a conventional sequence narrated for the sake of the reduced and

reductive mutual understanding between supposed observer and supposed observed.

I would not claim that this perspective should replace other scholars' approaches. Rather I see it as complementary and as a means to offer ground for an extended analysis of the feast. Recognizing the ephemeral time of the feast is the first, and not eliminable, step for understanding its pervasiveness in the social group and, its importance. With this I am not questioning the invaluable importance of Erving Goffman's (1974) suggestion that performance is "framed" or "bracketed," nor Turner's assertion that the first phase of social drama and ritual process is breach: "signalized by the public, overt breach or deliberate non fulfillment of some crucial norm regulating the intercourse of the parties" (Turner 1974a, 38). Rather I am emphasizing the porousness of these frames, brackets and breaches that make possible the continuous negotiation of the pattern and content of the performances.

Having clarified the perspective I am using in general I can now approach issues of definition. I have purposely made my argument continuously shift from the bracketed notion of ritual to the twin concept of performance. But I also used terms such as feast, festival, ceremony, festive forms or social drama and cultural performance in a nearly interchangeable way. The terms are not equivalent; they are chosen by scholars, therefore historically determined or incidentally proposed. They are adventures and consequences of ethnographic insights. They have multiple meanings, some beyond the dictionary meaning of the words. Ritual can be (1) the form for conducting a ceremony, (2) a ceremony or body of ceremonies, and (3) a procedure customarily or automatically repeated (*Webster's II New Riverside University Dictionary*). The ambiguities involved in these definitions highlight problems of form and procedure. Definitions of ritual also carry a semantic halo deriving from their use in specific debates within specific discipline. I will start this concise illustration with Turner:

> A ritual is a stereotyped sequence of activities involving gestures, words, and objects, performed in a sequestered place, and designed to influence preternatural entities or forces on behalf of the actors' goals and interests. Rituals may be seasonal, hallowing a culturally defined moment of change in the climatic cycle or the inauguration of an activity such as planting, harvesting, or moving from winter to summer pasture; or they may be contingent, held in response to an individual or collective crisis. Contingent rituals may be further subdivided into life-crisis ceremonies, which are performed at birth, puberty, marriage, death, and so on, to demarcate the passage from one phase to another in the individual's life-cycle, and rituals of affliction, which are performed to placate or exorcise preternatural beings or forces believed to have afflicted villagers with illness, bad luck, gynecological troubles,

severe physical injuries, and the like. Other classes of rituals include divinatory rituals; ceremonies performed by political authorities to ensure the health and fertility of human beings, animals, and crops in their territories; initiation into priesthoods devoted to certain deities, into religious associations, or into secret societies; and those accompanying the daily offering of food and libations to deities or ancestral spirits or both. (1974a, 1102)

Two main characteristics can be seen in Turner's definition of ritual: (1) the religious, or at least mystical, features of the ritual; and (2) the tribal context. While the religious rituals are the expression of tribal societies, the secular ones are expressions of modern societies. Gluckman's (1963) idea of ceremony, which basically restates Turner's ideal typical construct, reaffirmed this concept: rituals are religious and mandatory, while ceremonies are secular and optional. Many scholars followed the path traced by Turner and Gluckman but many others strongly disagreed.[10] Mary Douglas (1978, 36–38) for instance suggested that rituals should be studied not because they refer to some supernatural phenomenon/entity but because they express the dynamics and the structures of a social group.

Recently Guss (2000), in order to escape the immanent dichotomy presupposed by definitions of ritual, proposed the term "festive forms." According to him this term can encompass "a wide range of public events, including parades, carnivals, concerts, fairs, funerals, patron saint and feast days, caroling, sporting contests, civic commemorations, and even political demonstrations and trials" (173). Guss's definition allows us to highlight the main aspect of festive behaviors: they are a public display, while other kinds of distinctions become blurred.

In the feasts of Boston's North End it is certainly possible to find a religious aspect, not only declared but also practiced, performed and, above all, lived. Still the borders between the "religious" and the "secular," as I have already shown from the analysis of the local religious societies, are extremely malleable. Devotion and entertainment become codes reciprocally contaminating each other.

What is fundamental to analysis is not a matter of definition or of classification but an issue of social conditions of production, representation and use of the feasts. This is what Bestor, Guss and myself privilege.

More precise information is necessary in order to clarify the terms performance and social drama. They are similar but, again, not overlapping. Briefly, social drama was a term first proposed by Turner (1957). Influenced by Gluckman's dialectical perspective of social life and by Marxist theory he saw it as processual and against the more static suggestions of classic structural-functionalist scholars who were looking for "states" rather than dynamics. Turner developed the idea of social drama as a public event with ritual characteristics and a performative emphasis (see Parkin 1996, xviii). He suggested the following pattern for social dramas:

1. a breach of regular norm-governed social relationships between persons or groups of a social unit;
2. a crisis or extension of the breach, unless the conflict can be sealed off quickly;
3. adjustive and regressive mechanisms brought into operation by leading members of the social group;
4. reintegration of the "disturbed" social group or social recognition of an irreparable breach or schism. (Turner 1957, 91–94)

Influenced by social psychologist Kurt Lewin (1949) and his idea of "fields" where individual dramas are acted out, Turner suggested that social conflicts can be expressed "in terms of customarily acceptable disagreements, but which hid their ultimate irreconcilability" (see Parkin 1996, xviii).

In the United States, in contrast, the more influential concept of cultural performance was developed. First proposed by Singer (1959), cultural performance has been seen as based in observable units, having specific time and structures. It is a cultural production fundamentally mimetic in the Aristotelian sense of the term, metaphorically representing everyday moments of everyday life. The essentially non-Marxist American approach, not necessarily interested in social conflicts and contradictions, comes to a postmodern declination through Jon McKenzie:

[L]ike discipline, performance produces a new subject of knowledge, though one quite different from that produced under the regime of panoptic surveillance. Hyphenated identities, transgendered bodies, digital avatars, the Human Genome Project—these suggest that the performative subject is constructed as fragmented rather than unified, decentered rather than centered, virtual as well as actual. Similarly, performative objects are unstable rather than fixed, simulated rather than real. They do not occupy a single, "proper" place in knowledge; there is no such thing as the thing-in-itself. Instead, objects are produced and maintained through a variety of sociotechnical systems, overcoded by many discourses, and situated in numerous sites of practice. (2001, 18)

As I said previously, fragmentation, multivocality and dialectic relationship between reality and its representation are the theoretical frame of my approach to cultural performance. Nonetheless I am also in debt to Abner Cohen's idea that the Boston's North End feast are ceremonialised ways to name and resolve social contradictions, in a social landscape dominated by asymmetric relations of power. I am following Abner Cohen's (1993) idea that rituals have without any doubt a performative as well as a transformative aspect. They are at one and the same time signals and producers of change; they are witnesses and agents; they create and are created by knowledge in an endless play among performers and audiences.

Rituals, in their symbolic aspects, in their doxa and praxy, in their inevitable ephemeral character, still belong to the out-of-the-ordinary, the odd, as Cohen would say. But the ritual does not speak only of its exceptionality: it is an expression and effect of the social dynamics surrounding it. Rituals are about perpetuation and transformation, they are ahistorical and historically determined, they live inside a context and they are expressions and contaminations of the context itself.

This indeed has methodological consequences. From this point of view what Goffman's (1959) notion of the "critical case-study" is correct. It supplies, according to Parkin (1996, xxxviii) the same amount of possible considerations as a study based on more classical methodologies, through its language, use of symbols and activities on human agency, knowledge, justification and representation. Again, Cohen is right saying that it is the odd that reveals the mystery behind the routine. This was my starting point when I decided to approach the ephemeral ethnic identities expressed by the North End's rituals as a "meta-model" to give a sense of human experiences, and I still believe in the correctness of my initial choice. But, as I will show later, this theoretic and methodological position needed to be born out of the field experience. And this is what I did, questioning my field experience through itself. In other words, I am not denying the validity of this approach; I am only suggesting a more complex and fluid image of rituals and cultural performances that will expand their complexity beyond analytical brackets imposed more by the scholar rather than the agents, and therefore implying a different methodological approach. From this perspective it will be important to trace the relationships between the actual feasts with their past, as well as with contemporary festive forms.

Selecting the Past in the North End

The origin of Boston's North End feasts ought to be seen:

1. in the mythical past of the village of origin;
2. in the historical past of the ethnic enclave in the North End, indicating a diachronic dimension;
3. in the historical present of the continuous confrontation between the contemporary festive performances of the neighborhood declaring on one hand the microdifferences between ethnic enclaves and, on the other hand, performing the specific pattern of the broader social group. In this case, a synchronic dimension is indicated;
4. in the eventual comparison with the contemporary feasts in the Italian villages—this highlights the transnational perspective of the feast that I have already suggested;
5. in the eventual comparison with analogous feasts (religious and not) outside the neighborhood.[11]

The first source seems to be, by definition, nonhistorical. In other words, the festive performance is situated along a metahistorical horizon, populated by ancestors not only never known (this would be an inevitable condition for a discourse with a long history), not only belonging to a cultural and geographical elsewhere (this can even be a desirable condition in a transnational perspective) but also characterized by a mythic halo. It is, according to De Martino (1977, 240), the myth of the origin, repeated and renewed by the ritual, reabsorbing the historic proliferation of the mundane becoming and representing the world always again following the exemplary power of the first time when the world began by the will of the gods. To sustain the world, and life, means to ritually repeat the founding myth. The feast celebrates not only the divinities, through worshipping their icons, but also the genesis of the group, who have left an imagined land, which is worshipped as well, like a biblical Eden, even if with more ambiguous connotations.

The rhetorical mechanism evident in this analysis of the feast is definitely the metaphor, or, better, the metaphors. In other words the real term evokes the imaginary one: as the icon of the saint protected the village so the icons of the saint will protect the ethnic enclave; as the Italian villagers used to perform the ritual so do the Italian American, and so on. I am suggesting that this first source is more directly related to an official forms of belief than aimed at the maintenance of the cult of the local patron saint. This officially correct belief is of course especially important in producing the historical discourse of the ethnic enclaves. Yet, over the years it has given way, replaced by a stronger interest in the accuracy of the performance, which must always follow a common pattern.

The second source for the festive performances in the North End is the historical past of the neighborhood. This dimension is intimately connected with the formation and maintenance of ethnic enclaves. The feast is connected in this case with the historical memory of the group, and with the historical development of the specific feast. Notably, during the feast of Saint Anthony and of Madonna del Soccorso, a flyer with the history of the feast and of the society was distributed. As I will analyze later on, a fundamental figure in this case is the founding member of the religious societies, particularly relevant in the United States where this heroic idea has a specific tonality, emphasized more than in other locations where mythologies have longer and more consolidated histories located in territory and blood.

The immanent rhetorical figure expressing the relationship between the feast and its historical past seems to be the metonymy (if I assume metonymy to express a degree of contiguity and/or proximity, and to stress shared belonging). Continuity is the fundamental category for understanding the historical development from an original form which I assume was specific and connected with the imagined and mythical past, to the present one, which is an expression of the broad group's history. Over the years the feast has progressively lost its original characteristics and assumed new and diffused ones, repeating the common patterns developed in the neighborhood. A source for the historical aspect of the feasts is Whyte (1943) who gives an account of these performances at the beginning of the 1940s. Whyte's focus is on the social organization of what he called the "street corner gangs." His account is accurate, but incomplete:

> The annual *Festa* of the patron saint reveals not only the nature of religious beliefs but also the outlines of the social organization. Until the summer of 1940 the *paesani* of each town which had a sufficient population in and about Cornerville banded together for this celebration. Each *Festa* committee set aside a particular week end every year and selected a location for the construction of a street altar and poles to hold strings of colored lights over the surrounding area. There were band concerts on Friday and Saturday nights, but Sunday was the day of the real celebration. In the morning the *paesani* attended a special Mass in honor of their patron. The Mass represented the only direct connection of the church with the *Festa*. While it formed a part of the general religious life, the *Festa* was entirely a people's ceremonial. (269)

Whyte described a feast that is very similar to the contemporary festive practices, yet with a few differences. For instance the committee does not decide (and it never did) the day of the feast autonomously but always in agreement with the committees of the other societies. This is important in order to highlight leadership and power relationships. Moreover, the street altar (or temporary chapel) was constructed on a specific location, and was never changed over the years. This is an important aspect of the North End tradition: the ethnic enclave selects a specific area to be sacred as well as a church. Whyte observed the distance between the church and the faithful, pointing out the performance of Masses as the only moment of contact. The situation is probably more complex, with the priest also blessing the statue or the water (as in the Fishermen's feast), but the basic pattern is the same as the one outlined by Whyte.

Furthermore, Whyte outlined the presence of children's band, fife-and-drum corps of the Italian churches, little children dressed as angels and carrying bouquets of flowers, women marching with lighted candles, some of them barefoot. All these are symbolic practices no longer in use in the North End, and are signs of a movement toward a more general stylized model.

Similarities can be found in these other traits:

> To the canopy above the statue of the saint were attached streamers on which contributions of money were pinned. Several of the women carried a large flag or sheet stretched between them to catch change thrown from windows. Others circulated through the crowd lining the streets to solicit donations. In recognition of the larger contributions, the professional band faced the house of the contributor and played the Italian

national anthem. Upon passing each of the churches the procession halted and the statue was turned toward the church, but no ceremonial followed. (Whyte 1943, 270)

The pattern seems to be the same for the contemporary feasts, with the exception of the large flag, or sheet, to catch the coins, which has vanished since the coins no longer are a valuable donation. Also, surprisingly, Whyte did not understand the importance of the statue paying respect to churches: there is no further ceremonial because that is the ceremonial and he confused the "Marcia Reale" (the hymn of the Italian royal family) with the national anthem. This is just a small detail but it is important if we reason in terms of ethnic identity.

Some practices are definitely no longer evident in the North End. It is still true that the climax is the return of the statue to the temporary chapel, but I did not find any evidence of pigeons imprisoned in decorated boxes suspended over the center of the street and released at this moment.

Another difference, which I already commented upon, concerns the entertainment aspect of the feast: in 1940 vendors and concerts, even when present, were not of the same kind of those to be seen today. Concerts were performed by the marching bands and vendors used to sell ice cream, "while the local ballrooms and restaurants were filled with friends and relatives celebrating the occasion. All members of a family gathered in one house to eat and drink together" (Whyte 1943, 270). The familiar aspect is now replaced by a more "tourist" dimension.

Whyte's descriptions are of fundamental importance because they make a historical comparison between the contemporary feasts and their historical sources possible. What becomes evident in this comparison is the process of stylization toward the contemporary correct practices.

The third source, that is, the synchronic confrontation with similar feasts of the neighborhood, constitutes the historical present of the festive practice as a whole. From this point of view each specific feast can be considered as a synecdoche illustrating the general through the particular or vice versa.[12] I am suggesting that this third source is the most central in the development and the stabilization of practices seen as officially correct and seldom violated. Here, every feast becomes an expression of all of the feasts.

The fourth source is less evident, since it is occasional. Only few examples can be traced: members of Saint Anthony of Padua's Society have been in Montefalcione, so members of the Fishermen's Society as well as some Anzanese have seen the contemporary feast in the village of origin (Sciacca and Anzano), and it does not seem to have produced significant effects. This source is even the more ambiguous to define from a rhetorical point of view. The possible rhetorical figure seems to be, by extension, the diaphora, assuming this is a repetition of a common name allowing performance of two different logical functions. In the case of the feast the different functions illustrated by the diaphoric mechanism are related to the different context therefore referring to a transnational perspective.[13] Trasnationalism is not a new concept (the idea of migrants as birds-of-passage is an early example of the concept) and does not illustrate a new form of connection between sending and receiving locations. However, it surely indicates a different degree of communication and economic as well as cultural exchange. The transnational source of the feast has not (so far) affected the orthopraxy but is rather situated on a level of officially correct belief. The saint is the common name, repeated on both sides of the ocean, but the feasts, as well as their functions, are different.

The last source is the comparison with other feasts, not necessarily religious, taking place outside the neighborhood. Like the previous dimension this one too is occasional and can be seen regularly. I will further explore this source, analyzing the possibility of transformation of orthopraxy. For now it is sufficient to say that this comparison is also based on the diaphora. Different functions and different practices of the feast, according to the diaphoric mechanism, are related to different contexts which may be occasionally, but increasingly, in contact. Therefore diaphora is imminent in this kind of comparison.

Today, the cultural performance of the festive rites in the North End tends more towards orthopraxy than orthodoxy. I can add, following Lewis (1982), some conclusions about rituals.[14] People in the North End know how to correctly perform rituals, but they do not necessarily know their meanings, or at least they cannot explain directly what is expressed or symbolized. Belief (officially correct belief, of course) is present, and significant, but it is relegated on a secondary level.

First evidence of this dislocation can be seen in the problematic relationship with the local and superlocal clergy. I already have talked about the tale of the priest who was greedy to get the money of the saint's statue as a charter legend establishing the autonomy of the societies and their ownership of the feasts. The clergy did not lose the power of official worship but it has been excluded from the festive practice or else relegated to specific and marginal moments. The astonishment of San Jude's faithful at a local restaurant's owner refusal to pay respect to the saint had little to do with officially correct belief. The transgression concerned the officially correct practice of respect that has to be shown to the saint and to the members of the society. Another example occurred when the Madonna della Cava Society closed their club door at the passage of Saint Agrippina. The officially correct pattern is for the statue to pay respect to the other societies by stopping by their club. The members of the other societies in response pay respect to the saint in procession with money and/or food donations. Again, the transgression was not at the level of officially correct belief but at the level of the correct practice. These examples allow me to introduce the discourse on orthodoxy and orthopraxy but they also provide the cue to remember the fundamental dimensions of the Bostonian feasts: the practice of respect, codified in a pattern (i.e., the money pinned on the statue) and the respect of practice, codifying a pattern.

The orthodoxy level is based on a mythical past and it is useful to evoke the common belonging to an ethnos, declared as isomorphs, that is territorially bounded and believed to be distinct at both the level of the imagined land of the village of origin and within the historically determined areas of the ethnic enclaves that are ritually reaffirmed and sanctified by the procession. Nowadays the geographical areas of the ethnic enclaves are still recognizable but, as I have repeatedly shown, their borders (and the processions' journey confirm this) are blurred and claim a territoriality rather than a territory. The ethnos evoked by the commonly held officially correct belief evokes solid, as well as temporally ephemeral, groups. It is important to state that the correct belief is determined not only by devotion to the saint and the related icon, but by everything connected with them: for instance, the charter legend of the Madonna del Soccorso is used to establish a strong moment of social cohesion based on class and specific job niches (the fishing business). In the past in the North End, as well as in the contemporary Sicilian village, this cohesion has been fundamental for forming and maintaining the ethnic enclave of the Sciaccatani. Nowadays (and this is another evidence of the necessity to move to the orthopraxy level) a similar social cohesion is simply obsolete, because the fishing business moved away from the North End. A historical example of how cultural performances can be used to rethink the ethnic enclaves and, consequently, to rewrite the neighborhood history, is the renegotiation of Sciaccatani/Montefalcionesi borders. The already presented narrative of the presidents of the two societies coming back from World War II areas on the same ship and discussing new opening for the respective procession is a strong example of Bakhtin's argument (1968, 211) that feasts are powerful tools to grasp reality. The feast takes note of the new social reality and ratifies it, performing and ratifying transformations. Another example is the collective performance to raise funds after 9/11 where a new social reality became evident and was confirmed by the feast.

It is interesting that the orthodoxy dimension is activated and also sustained by the observation of the diasporic character of the specific social group. It is no longer sufficient, from a transnational perspective, to share devotional symbols. Devotional practices are not static but a historically determined product. They are dynamic and they vary in the different contexts. If at the beginning of the feast it was enough to represent the icon (and it is worth noting that many charter legends of the North End's feasts state that their statues are exact replicas of the originals in Italy) or to remember the same prayers (such the cheer: Viva la Madonna di Sciacca) today novel symbols are displayed during the feast. This is one reason behind the growing presence of many Italian authorities (mayors, representatives or priests from the Italian villages),[15] during the processions, walking next to relatives or friends of the immigrants. This diasporic aspect can also be seen during the feast in the natal Italian village in the presence of pilgrims from abroad or tourists from other Bostonian ethnic enclaves. The representatives sent from the North End are the leaders of the religious societies. Besides the obvious expressions of official and unofficial power in these voyages the correct orthodox belief is confirmed, and the immigrant ethnic enclave as well as the village of origin are confirmed as well.

But if we look at the North End's ethnic enclaves not as confined but rather as multistranded and open-ended locations, where distinctive traits have declined into the past, orthopraxy becomes a necessary strategy for the protection of a restricted territory—the neighborhood—that is threatened. This is even more the case now with the disappearance of the physical barrier of the Big Dig. Maintaining the officially correct practices of the feasts maintains symbolic boundaries within a market economy where cultural identity, not only as an Italian but specifically as a North Ender, is a scarce resource that is now more important than ever. Therefore orthopraxy refers to a type of discourse necessary for maintaining the perceived authenticity of rituals in North End.

But before I unfold the specific issue of authenticity I would like to focus on the mechanisms activated in order to achieve what I called the officially correct practice. The process is at first characterized by "aesthetic reduction" and "cultural objectification." In his analysis of Venezuelan festive forms, Guss (2000, 13–15) analyzed the transformation of local forms into national ones. Following Nestor Garcia Canclini's (1988, 479) idea of double reduction he reaffirmed that popular forms move (1) from the rich ethnic diversity of the regional to the monolithic unity of the national, and (2) from the flux of social process to the solidification of a codified object. Of course, in the North End there is no national tradition to reinvent, invent or defend. The North End is just a neighborhood that is smaller than Disneyland's parking lot. But the necessity of a strategic essentialism is very important for the survival of the local economy. I underline again that over the years the performance stage, the neighborhood, has transformed itself from an area of ethnic confrontation to a more complex place of ethnic identification and tourist attraction. Therefore the claim will not be for state unity but for a distinctive "authentic" particularity.

The possibility of misunderstanding is generated by the term reduction and objectification. Both, even if in a very different degree, carry a semantic and, more important, theoretical halo that on the long run risks invalidating their application in the North End's case. While objectification is a more reflexive term, reduction presupposes an aesthetic process of losing important characteristics. But the scale and the context that make hegemony a concept to be calibrated inclines me to the use of a less normative term. I propose instead the term stylization as a more appropriate tool within the general frame of orthopraxy. This allows me to underline two aspects: the creation of a style (in this case a pattern of practices) and conformity to a style (in this case respect for officially correct practices). Since aesthetic stylization is not necessarily a process of loss, but rather often a process of gain, the concept avoids the dangerous issue of nostalgia. Rather than thinking of a past to be regained we can consider the political and economic processes involved here. After all, formerly subaltern classes have increased their status and opportunities and actually are profiting by presenting themselves today as a community that was once marginalized and dispossessed.

Therefore, stylizations, like objectifications and aesthetic manipulations in general, are far from nonideological; the act/practice of selecting features or building up patterns is not antiseptic. They are produced by (as well producing) socially determined choices and asymmetric relations of power.

Stylizations and objectifications, as preludes to orthopraxy, are neither linear nor solid. Instead they are generated by tensions and conflicts between and within the different groups organizing the feasts. It is once again a matter of the enactment of asymmetric relations of power.

Debating the Past in the North End

In the North End history is a story. This is not a claim for a determinist narrative approach to history but simply to underline, following Guss that

> the growing awareness that histories (and not merely Histories), are more than simply static traditions inherited from a neutral past parallels an equally significant realization that the most common subjects of anthropological study (that is, oral-based tribal cultures) actually possess historical consciousness. (2000, 24)

This allows Guss to state, recalling Appudurai (1981), that the debatability of the past not only concerns talking about traditions but changing them. And debatability is not a pure process; it reflects relations of power. Acknowledgment, as well as denial, of the past has little to do with the accuracy of memory, but, instead it has very much to do with social relations.

Guss points to a very important argument but surprisingly does not refer the debate that historians, such as Lucien Febvre (1933), have developed since the 1930s around the review *Les Annales*. Febvre criticized the notion of document that was in use in those days. In opposition to historians like Fustel de Coulanges, he argued that history can be made only through texts, and questioned the passivity of historians dealing with historical documents. As historian Jacques Le Goff (1978) reminds us, this is not a matter of a critique of the sources, (which was already in use ever since the positivist approach of the Ecole des Chartes) but of examining the notion of document itself. More explicitly March Bloch (1941–1942, 74) commented provocatively that documents do not just show up here and there by the will of God. Their presence or absence in an archive or a library depends upon human activities which are open to analysis in many different ways. Thus even the problems connected with their transmission are matters of historical interest. These issues were presented in all their importance by Foucault (1969), who expressed his perplexity about the notion of the document as an inert matter through which historians reconstruct what other people have said or done. Instead he promoted the idea of a documentary texture where it is necessary to insulate, to assemble, to make relevant, to relate and to cluster a multitude of elements. History transforms documents into monuments, as suggested by Le Goff (1978). But the document is not neutral. It is the result of conscious or unconscious constructions made by history. The document, from this point of view, is an attempt by those in the past to impose on the future a certain image of themselves. According to Le Goff, therefore, every document is a lie. This is why it is necessary to deconstruct the document as a cultural artefact in order to analyze the nature of its production. Similarly the process of selecting a particular version of the past is a transformation of document (etymologically from *docere*, to teach) into monument (etymologically from *monere*, to admonish). This selection is a datum, enforced within multiple possibilities.

If the selection of the past is a matter of power relations between and within groups, and above all a struggle of the dominant against the subaltern, a level of hegemony can be assumed. For instance the nowadays largely taken-for-granted narrative that the push factor for southern Italians emigrants was local condition of extreme poverty does not have any dramatic confirmation in historical analysis. Rather, according to Mangione and Morreale (1993), mass emigration resulted from an intricate relationship between a complex cluster of social, psychological, political, and economic factors. Choices existed even in the most remote village. In most cases the emigrants were not simply pushed out by crippling disaster. Alternatives existed, they suggest. Moreover, those who migrated often viewed emigration as a means of assisting those who remained behind, most often family members. This relationship between temporary migration and familial goals has long been recognized. To be sure, many villagers conceived of migration as a way of obtaining money in order to increase the family's landholdings in the paese and acquire the status accorded to property owners. This is basically the meaning of being "birds-of-passage."

But all this complexity is suppressed in the local narratives concerning a perceived past. For instance, very seldom are memories of somebody returning to the old country ever told. Sometimes the stories of those who left the United States to go back to Italy are told, but only to emphasize of coming back again to America. Surely this selection has to do with making a standardized narrative, seen and understood as "true" of personal, familiar or groups experiences. Emigration is narrated, on the one hand, as inevitable and, on the other hand, as a success. This interpretation reflects the attitude of a dominant class that had an interest in promoting this specific narrative. A class, especially a working class, that perceives itself as running away from desperate conditions and lands in a new country where the streets are not paved with gold, but where a job, even if an unskilled one, is nonetheless possible to find, is easy to control.

The process of conferring meaning to the experience of emigration through a selective use of the past, seems to have clear traits of hegemony, although I repeat the necessity of contextualizing this concept in the United States where dynamics between individuals and social classes are peculiar and, above all, where social hierarchies, even if present, are less visible. I also must point out that the situation of the early immigrants was harsh: southern Italians were used as unskilled laborers, employed as low-paid substitutes for other ethnic groups.

This seems to reinforce the idea of the Italian immigrant's "in-betweeness,"[16] uniting "intricate and spurious associations of race, strikebreaking and lack of manly pride." (Barrett and Roediger 1995, 27). The process of becoming white was a process of identity formation, where the competition for wage labor and citizenship were the central issues. In other words, white identity, and the formation of a working class went hand in hand. This is the central thesis of the new-labor historian David Roediger's seminal work *The Wage of Whiteness* (1991). Citing American Exceptionalism, Roediger criticizes the way Marxists address the relationship between race and class in the United States. According to Roediger, white workers (he studied especially the popular perception of Irish workers in the late nineteenth century and the early twentieth century as the "white Negroes") received not only a monetary wage for their labor, but also a psychological wage of whiteness attributed to them by the public and obtained in contrast to black laborers who were perceived and discriminated against as "others."

Yet, the assertion of hegemony always implies its alter: alongside a hegemonic relationship of power there are inevitably elements of resistance among the subaltern classes. This is what Gramsci called a process of counterhegemony. In the North End's case, at the time of early immigration, the selected narrative for counterhegemony was the feast.

I am not talking here about class-consciousness because opposition does not appear at the political level but remained at the level of nostalgic emotion. The feast initially had this function: to declare a different identity and way of belonging in resistance to the asymmetric relation of power face-to-face with the dominant "WASP" classes. The feast does not only express religious devotion, but the remembrance, the memory, the history as well as the story of the village of origin and of their inhabitants. Carrying the saint in procession is the narrative of resisting hegemonic pressure, of a different identity that proclaims its past as well as a narrative of a past claiming its identity. In sum, the early feast, however much it was metonymically associated with the original village social structure with its symbolization of hierarchic relations, gender-based distinctions, and assertions of power, was nonetheless the ideal instrument for resistance against a demand for assimilation. In this case the feast was not only a performance of nostalgia but also of resistance.

Over the years, with the arrival of second and third generations, the feast gradually became referential and then self-referential: the feast celebrates a past that is now mythical as well as the historic past of the ethnic enclaves. This is, as I demonstrated, a memory that places itself on more ambiguous and nostalgic levels or, better, on a metahistorical level—a level that belongs to myths and charter legends. This is no longer a memory of a group's actual arrival and past, but the memory of a memory. In this historical process, the counterhegemonic potentiality decreases, transporting the feast from an ideological level toward a more aesthetic level.

Selecting the past and selecting festive practices thus are not antiseptic choices. They are ideological and reflect social dynamics, and many actors and agencies are deeply involved in this ongoing process, as I shall discuss in the next few pages.

Selecting the Festive Practices: Changes and Continuity

North End feasts were discovered by a general public in the late 1960s. As Cowan (1992) argues for the Hellenic carnival in Soho, the tourist interest in the feasts was in general the starting point for competitions that are internal to the local communities and that concern the control of celebratory activities. But this is not the case in the North End. I have already demonstrated that these tensions in the neighborhood that are highlighted, though not caused, by the feasts, are intimately connected with the constitution, at the beginning of twentieth century, of the ethnic enclaves and, later, with the inner dynamics arising within the various enclaves. However, the external perception of the neighborhood was and is that it is homogenous. This homogeneity was at the beginning based on class and ethnicity but later on—and this is certainly an effect of a "whitening" process of the Italian American and gentrification of the North End—it was based on the locally declared shared identity as North Enders. But in fact, heterogeneity was the main characteristic of the North End groups, which had many inner confrontations and conflicts within the profoundly different enclaves.

One similarity with the Hellenic carnival can be seen in the use of tradition to legitimate local controversies. But I am arguing here that different arguments for "authentic" tradition, as expressed by all the societies, have the goal of a better negotiation of power, within or outside the neighborhood, rather than direct control of the officially correct practice. For example, groups often accuse one another of letting the feast become too business-oriented, losing its characteristics of "purity" and "religiosity." The opportunistic nature of this accusation is demonstrated by the declarations of the economic success that are formalized in many official report of the feasts. For instance, Saint Anthony's program-book of year 2002 declared that "over 100 vendors hawked their wares: and everything from food to clothing and furniture sold out." Or, on the Madonna del Soccorso program-book of year 2003 we read that "the early festivals were primarily religious" or that during the feast there will be "continuous entertainment programs for 4 days at the beautifully decorated outdoor bandstand, and Italian food of all varieties."

In other words, tradition and authenticity seem to be useful shibboleths, useful to give a sense of belonging, connection and solidity, as Lindholm (2008) suggests, which have been completely interiorized to the point that any kind of opposing evidence is simply ignored. Discourses on tradition and authenticity are articulated not only by societies but also by external authorities. For instance, Sal Di Masi, a representative of the House who later would become its Speaker, together with Mayor Thomas Menino, State Auditor Joe Di Nucci, Representative Scapicchio and Senator Robert Travaglini, greeted and wished the best for the performance of the feast. Often these personalities would thank the society for "continuing a great tradition" (Saint Anthony program-book 2002).

"Continuing the tradition" is the most significant slogan of Saint Anthony's Society. It is reported in their own presentations of the feast as well as in the speeches of the authorities. Naturally, an electoral issue is more or less directly involved : politicians are looking for consensus and votes and declare their support to the celebration following the accepted slogans. Through similar declarations, the authorities gain direct access to the specific society performing the feast, but also become visible to all the societies and to the whole neighborhood.

Tradition is continuously declared, since taking possession anew of the past is seen as a way to legitimate the present. This is the function of the constant quoting of the first settlers in the specific ethnic enclaves. For instance, in the message to the participants at the Saint Anthony's Feast Committee, in 2002 we read:

> [O]n this most festive occasion we remember our founding members and their families, who bought their love of faith and family to their new home in America. Today we continue our great tradition.

The Fishermen's program-book listed the names of their own founding members, showing them in an early photograph. As I said before these displays have a legitimating function for the statements relating to tradition and authenticity expressed and performed throughout the feast. Furthermore, the analogy (at least on a semantic level), with the American charter legend of the founding fathers, must be noted.

Transforming the Festive Practices

Authenticity, tradition and orthopraxy inevitably seem to refer to a discourse where changes and transformations of the pattern are difficult if not impossible to enact. Of course, even the most rigid claim for a officially correct practice allows, at least indirectly, the possibility of transformation. Certainly an apparent contradiction between a ritual orthopraxy (tending to immobility or at least to very slow transformation) and the realities of a living social group, can be noted. To reconcile this contradiction and to understand how changes are carefully introduced in the ritual, I use the metaphor of the wheel, with a rim, in this case the group, and a hub, in this case the ritual. The two are intimately connected. Yet, the movement is much more evident along the rim rather than on the hub. What happens on the rim effects the hub, but in a less evident way.

The correct question, therefore, is not if but how changes are allowed.

My experience in the field seems to indicate a pattern that can be called by paralogy. According to Lyotard (1986), paralogy is basically a movement against an established way of reasoning. What seems to be fundamental in paralogy is its transgressive or unconventional character: changes become possible through inventions outside the norms or through new language games or new games. I am referring here to a philological use of the term useful for the local phenomenon: changes are possible beside and/or beyond reason.

The first thing that needs to be analyzed is "where" these paralogical changes are possible. The feast, as I said before, has at least two performative moments: devotion and entertainment. I remind the reader that these two aspects are not only not in conflict but are also hard to disentangle. If we assume, for instance, that the concert on stage is part of the entertainment, what happens when the singer eventually performs Shubert's "Ave Maria"? Moreover, even if the procession has a self-evidently devotional character, many other elements are more ambiguous. For instance, fire crackers or fireworks are surely playful and a moment of entertainment, but if I relate them to the original meaning of exorcism through fire and noise against evil spirits, they become legitimate devotional instruments. These ambiguities are even more evident if I take into consideration the music of the marching bands which I discussed in the last chapter. The devotional aspect is clearly evident during the performance of sacred hymns (which, to tell the truth, are not very numerous), while other "secular" songs seems to belong to the entertainment level. Therefore, I prefer to use terms like devotional and secular only to exemplify my argument, keeping in mind the ambiguities related. Here and now, during the performance of the feast, the act of playing Shubert's "Ave Maria," the "Marcia Reale" or "Amapola" all respect the correct practice.

With this caveat in mind, we can still say that transformations do occur, even if their occurrence is limited. One example of this is the appearance of vendors around the end of the 1940s who came from New York City, where they already had experienced economic benefits during the great feast of San Gennaro, or the recent innovation of sponsors, assuring that expenses are covered. Interestingly (and perhaps paradoxically), local societies, while stressing tradition, authenticity and religiosity, are today sponsored by Foxwoods Resort Casino, Budweiser and by one of the most important Italian beers, Birra Moretti. For a fervent Catholic this may be experienced as an ambiguity if not an outright blasphemy.

Transformations at the "religious" level seem occur with less frequency and with much more restraint. Besides the already mentioned example of the

women's section of Fishermen Society carrying the statue, I would also remind
the change proposed for the Santa Maria di Anzano's feast on 2003, that is, the
introduction of a cart hauling the statue in procession.[17]

With this innovation, the statue was no longer carried but dragged. This
change, even if respectful of the original charter legend (in Anzano the statue
is on a cart) in a sort of example of decreolization, involved indeed a substantial modification of the recurrent symbolism. The following year the correct
practice of carrying the statue was reintroduced. The chance probably threatened two main points of the feast: authenticity and tradition. Resistance to
change demonstrates the importance of reiteration and orthopraxy during the
festive performance and also suggests information about the modalities of
change. I am arguing here that the charter legend, which following—
and stretching—Lyotard's interpretative model of legitimation can be assumed
to function as a metanarrative, is the base for the feast's orthodoxy and also for
the procedural/formal aspect of the performance, the orthopraxy. The divinity
chosen to protect an *ab origine* specific village (then, by extension, the ethnic enclave) is ritually recalled through the performance's symbology: the icon's sacral-
izing journey metaphorically renews the enclave's privileged relationship with
the patron saint. The transportation of the icon is often a fundamental part of
the charter legends: there is not only a territory to be sanctified but also the
bodily mortification of the statue-bearers to show. Manifestations of respect,
such as pinning the money on the statue, recall the original narrative of gratitude performed by the faithful.

This general ritual form—shared by most southern Italian feasts—has different local manifestations, allowing the individuation of specific festive forms.
I will offer an example gathered from Santa Maria in Anzano where the involvement in the ritual of solidarity is, at the same time, also a legitimation of
a social hierarchy of three communities: Trevico, Zuncolo and Anzano. The
charter legend narrates that the Madonna refused to stay in Trevico and Zuncolo, and preferring Anzano instead. The performance perpetuates the legend.
The procession starts from Anzano, walks for a mile, meets faithful of Trevico
and Zuncolo, then comes back to the sanctuary in Anzano.

The same ritual is obviously not possible in the North End. Yet, the original charter legend belongs to an ethnic enclave that is supported by another
narrative of foundation. I have already shown how when tradition is claimed, the
reference is about the founding members of the society and of the feast. It is the
memory of the first settlers that legitimate the authenticity of the feast. If orthodoxy relates more to the original charter legend, orthopraxy is connected
more with the other narrative.

The tendency to homologation of the festive pattern is explained by:

1. the pragmatic impossibility of a reiteration of the original feast in
   the ethnic enclave;

2. the aesthetization of the feast privileging stylized aspects—this is the process that Garcia Canclini called "double reduction" (from local to global and from flux to code) and that I named "stylization";
3. the necessity in this moment of ambiguity for a strategic essentialism in order for the event to be better recognized as ethnic, and, therefore, to improve the economic available resources.

This does not mean that feasts are authoritative texts, legitimated and legitimating some sort of metanarrative, but rather that they are historically and culturally determined performances, tightly connected to the contemporary social realities. The stylization toward a common pattern, beyond the declared different ethnic enclaves, for strategic reason confirms this perspective.

Changes do not occur through slow innovations but though traumatic, disruptive and paralogic legitimization. Innovations inaugurate the new aspect of the festive forms Only after their stabilization (and, as I showed, it is not an even process), and after they are incorporated within an imitative process, can they be recognized as components of the officially correct practices. The selective process of incorporation of new elements in orthopraxy is extremely unpredictable. And so is its persistence. After all it is a substantially contradictory process that contrasts with the essence of the festive practices developed in the North End, which are in turn more inclined to follow the officially correct practice.

To reiterate, festive forms and their performances and practices, are far from static. Changes are possible, but the general tendency is the respect of practices that are considered to be correct. Authenticity and tradition, regardless of it or how they are imagined, are the unquestionable values inherent in the festive practices in the North End. Some of the problematics of these values is the subject of my next section

Transformed Landscape and Authenticities

It is ironic, according to Parkin (1996, xxviii) that while anthropologists have tried to remove essentialism from their own vocabulary, members of various social groups kept continuously proclaiming their peculiar and exclusive traits of authenticity. Of course I am not talking about antithetical positions here. Again the two poles suggest a dynamic dialogue rather than a dichotomous opposition. On one hand, constant reference to a metahistorical past inevitably influences and limits the choices of symbols and their expressions and, on the other, there remains the necessity of creating or recreating symbols in order to declare a historic present. This is what Parkin (ibid.) calls the tension between the inherited and the invented.

As I have already noted, in this case the concepts of orthodoxy and orthopraxy are epistemologically useful even though they included other religious and the devotional aspects such as music and food, which have often been relegated to a ceremonial level. Orthodoxy is a concept that can be recalled not only by icons and prayer but also by songs and food. From this perspective, for instance, performing the "Marcia Reale" or eating the traditionally Sicilian rice balls (*arancini*) is a moment of orthodoxy, referring to a mythical past, as well as the historical past.

Using—as I will do henceforth—a linguistic metaphor, orthodoxy shifts to the concept of decreolization, claiming and referring to an original form of language. In both cases, elements of authenticity can be claimed. They were cultural performances acted in the original village, and now they are visible in the North End during the feasts. On the same level, I find that eating fried calamari or performing "Amapola" or "God Bless America" are aspects of orthopraxy.[18] Even though they may be considered as entirely invented performances now they have become historically recognizable in the festive practices in the neighborhood. Therefore, they may be considered authentic as well. But, we may ask, authentic in respect to what? For the history of the North End fried dough is an authentically ritual food. It is to be found at every feast and people come to the feast with the purpose of eating it. And although fried dough can be at the same time reminiscent of the Navajo fried bread and of the Italian *pizzelle*, this is just a peculiarity, or oddity, of the tension between "the inherited" and "the invented."

According to Clifford (1987, 126), authenticity is conceived now by scholars as hybrid and creative activities immersed in a local but interconnected cultural world system. The contextualization of this net of meanings, inherent in this concept of authenticity, leads me to opt for a usage of the term in plural (authenticities) rather than in singular. For example, as I wrote before, we may state that the southern Italian religious feasts are dislocated in a different environment. While being at the beginning the chosen identity—as an expression of the subaltern ethnic enclaves—the feasts were also involved in an entirely different system of the conditions of production. Thus, at the beginning, the feast was authentic insofar as it resembled the original Italian feast. Orthodoxy—in this case the correct belief in the patron saint—was here evident, while orthopraxy could be pursued only through the mediation of memories. Afterwards, the feasts became authentic because they resembled the other feasts of the neighborhood. Orthopraxy—in this case the correct practice of the performance, codified in and by shared local patterns—was fundamental, while orthodoxy continued to survive in a blurred declaration of origins and perhaps in some of the religious aspects of the performance.

Both factors can thus be said to be still present. On one level, there is the authentic arancino, "Marcia Reale" and the icon, brought to bear when the saint is portrayed. On the other level though, another kind of authenticity is expressed by "Amapola," "God Bless America" and the icon, which portrays the original icon of the saint.

In other words, authenticities, as displayed during the performance of the feast, place themselves on a transformed cultural landscape (Guss 2000, 3) where the local, the national and the global converge and collide. I am suggesting that even these definitions should be contextualized in order to make more complete sense. Local, national and global can be understood in different ways: for instance, what kind of locality am I talking about? The village, the ethnic enclave, the neighborhood or the city? And what kind of nationality? Italian and/or American? "Global" too is not a static or unitary term: direction, weight, influence of the phenomenon, etc. are determined by the context where the term is used. The gradient, the texture of the phenomenon is completely different if lived out in Boston or in Sciacca. From this perspective authenticities are malleable as well as situationally determined and performed. They are, ultimately, negotiable, being a product of the dynamic interaction not only between people or group but between histories or, stressing the narrative aspect, between stories.

The Reductive Aspect of Performance

I have assumed, following a well-established tradition, that rituals with a performative and transformative aspect display the asymmetric relationship of power pervading the group that is enacting them. I am aware that sometimes rituals not only express the social group's identity, but also express mystifications, such as the gender division performed during the feast. The latter is in fact closer to what I have labeled a strategic orthopraxy than a direct representation of the group's identity. This variety depends of course on the different condition of production of the feast. Therefore, inevitably, the feast has assumed peculiar forms and narratives: the rules and roles of clergy and authorities, for instance, were and are expressed in different ways. In the Italian villages the priestly rules and roles were and are much more central and evident, expressing all the dynamics along the hegemonic/subaltern axis of cleric/worshipped. This is true also for gender relationships: it is extremely probable that the distinction between statue-bearers and beggars was at the beginning a mirror of a social condition, where at least in the public arena the fundamental rules were acted by men. The performance of the procession is an even more explicit metaphor of what can be seen at the surface. It expresses the crypto-matriarchal southern Italian society at large: men perform in public actions of bodily sufferance and physical support. At the same time the economic control, as in the household, is performed by women: they literally have *i soldi in mano* (the money in their hands).

In different, capitalistic and modern social conditions of production, the feast assumes new forms. Probably, and this is again an example of decreolization, the feast will reaffirm the correct practice, but the meaning will be determined by a different context. In this tension lies the mystifying aspect of the feast. I will explain this crucial point with an example, that is, the attempt of the women's section of the Fishermen Society to carry the statue of the saint in procession. Using Bailey's (1996, 8) model of cultural performance, taken from his work on Shiva's birthday ritual in Bisipara, India, I suggest likewise that the two levels of expression of a social hierarchy and resistance to hegemony are both performed in the North End. In general, the North End's feasts clearly enact a gender-based division of roles and rules. This is contrasted by the women of the Fishermen Society, whose resistance while carrying the icons of the saint led to a situation in which they ended up occupying a nontraditional, exclusively male, position during the performance of the ritual. But when I consider why the women's resistance was unsuccessful, despite the fact that nowadays the gender-based distinctions within the groups are weakened, the answer can be found in the tension between inheritance and invention. Women as statue-bearers undermine not the unquestioned level of orthodoxy but the level of orthopraxy.

Of course, mystifications are always possible during the performances, and this is another reason why one single critical case study must be supported by a more extended research in the field. Mystification is just one of the many concerns a researcher must take account of while analyzing a cultural performance. I already mentioned the question of reality and its representation. Reality is a questionable notion, and it may be suggested that event and representation are different aspects of the same reality. Still, cultural performance is a simplification of reality, or better it is a rhetorical reduction—mostly based on an iconographic process, meaning the construction of a sign not yet connected to the specific object but suggesting an intuitive understanding—ultimately producing stereotypes. According to Bailey:

> [P]erformances assert a truth: something removed from the instability of time and the variation of particularity so as to make it authoritative. (1996, 3)

Hence, being inevitably assertive they should be simple, uncontested and permanent. But they are not.

This bears upon another concern, also expressed by Bailey: cultural performances are unreal but they must also try to make viewers and participants believe they are not unreal. "A play has actors, who pretend to be what the audience knows they are not" (1996, 3). In order to believe the reality behind what is performed, everybody—and not only the audience as suggested by Bailey—must suspend the distinction between the real and the unreal, accepting the unreal as real, but only during the ephemeral time of the performance. Bailey suggests, following Goffman (1974), an approach to cultural performances as "framed." As I declared at the beginning of this chapter I prefer a more blurred model, and this is the reason why I am using the term, and the concept, of ephemeral time, as more appropriate to designate the time and the locations of the performances.

Reality is, therefore, celebrated through performance. Yet, being performed it is, inevitably, an imagined reality reflecting an imagined group, and also the brute facts of the real expression of power. There is no need to accept the Turnerian idea of communitas (not easy to substain, at least in my fieldwork experience) or the Geertz's warning (1980, 103) about the risk of exegesis in order to see more in things than there really is, and reducing the richness of particular meanings to a drab parade of generalities. But it is not, as Bailey (1996, 13) ultimately suggests, that there is more in things than can be seen. My point is, rather, to be aware that performance is not an isolated break in time and that whatever the proposed imagined reality is, it has a counterpart or a match in the "real" world. In my case this counterpart is to be found in the asymmetric relations of power immanent to the group. In other terms cultural performances are the climax of a generalized narrative telling us about social and cultural dynamics, and, foremost, talking about power and its vicissitudes and levels. How this occurs is the topic of the following pages. I begin with a discussion of insiders and outsiders.

Performance of the Feast: Insiders and Outsiders

I will now discuss how the festive practices in the North End show a tension between the local, the national and the global. The terms indeed need to be discussed and contextualized. "Local," "traditional" or, even more, "authentic" often suggest a sort of binary opposition: global, modern and contaminated seem to be the inevitable terms to cope with. A dichotomy is generally supposed when introducing the discourse about insiders and outsiders. This dichotomous view can be useful. For example, if I look at the feast as situated in a global market, then the distinction between insiders and outsiders can be an important heuristic tool. As Guss (2000) noted for the Venezuelan case of San Jose and Magliocco (2006) noted for the two Madonnas of the Sardinian village of Monteruju, the North End's feasts are under the spotlight of a supralocal attention. The feasts provide a motif of attraction for emigrants who come back to the neighborhood for the specific occasion. They respect a modern pattern, probably already transnational, which attempts to demonstrate that the caesura of relations with the original social group did not happen or has been rectified (at least within the symbolic level performed by the feast).

In a modern, diffused, global market the attention toward the local implies on one hand the necessity of a stylization (in order for the local to be more easily readable and interpretable), and on the other hand, a claim for authenticity and exceptionality. Tourists are urged to attend the feast because the feast is typical, authentic and heterogeneous. Yet, the tourist also must be allowed to recognize the festive form. On the stage of the feast, stylization and in general aesthetization generate the tension between homogeneity and heterogeneity. In this condition, the audience is ready to participate at the performance.

Similarly, a dichotomic opposition between insiders and outsiders, at least in the case of North End, hides a complexity. I am arguing here that instead of a binary model we should try to apply a pattern based on a continuum.

Looking at the festive practices of the neighborhood "insider" seems to be a complex term, including among other aspects:

1. Members of the religious society involved in the organization and performance of the feast. Indeed even this is a reduction, just as any other sorts of categorization are ambivalent and ambiguous. In fact a constant complaint during the numerous talks with members of any society was about the lack of any active participation of some members. Often they pay the contribution in order to maintain the membership but they are basically outside the society life. However, on the day of the feast they show up claiming their rights of membership.

2. Nonmembers of the society, but belonging to the same ethnic enclave, may attend the feast in various ways, according to a recognizable spectrum that goes from indifference to individual devotion (such as following the procession barefoot). Sometimes even nonmembers are allowed to carry the statue, if they are sponsored by some members.

3. Nonmembers of the society and of the ethnic enclaves but still active subjects of performances constitutive of the feast itself. This is the case, for instance, for anyone who pays respect to the statue of the saint pinning money on it, playing the game between the intimacy of the devotion and the spectacle of the performance.

Outsiders can be:

1. Emigrants coming back for the feast and claiming, like the insiders, a shared local identity performed in and proclaimed by the feast. And even here multiple distinctions are possible. Those who left the village or the neighborhood to migrate to Montana, Wyoming or New York likely will tend to claim the imagined identity of the original village. Those, first or following generations, who left the North End for the suburban area of Boston, and have often maintained close relationships with the neighborhood, tend to identify with the mythical village and with the ethnic enclave and practice the ambiguous game between territory and territoriality.

2. Guests, who are located on the border. For instance, during the Fishermen's feast, Sal, the president of the society, gave to me a cockade with the sign "Madonna del Soccorso Society—Guest." The cockade at the same time made me identifiable as insider, accepted, on a temporary basis, by the society and the feast, and as outsider, as the term guest ontologically bears.

3. Authorities, who attend the feast officially. In this case, at least formally, these may become insiders, being sometimes directly involved in the festive performances (like the politicians participating in the Sorrento Cheese contest), or outsiders but always maintaining a functional recognizability related to their representation of the relationship to external power.

4. Journalists or scholars (and what about the ethnographer, the eternal participant-observer?), who are by definition outsiders. Their visibility, along with their function of publicizing the performances, is an integral part of the feast from a perspective of globalization.

5. Tourists, who come to the feast because they have heard about it somehow. Even in this case the category is ambiguous. For instance many of them, besides "consuming" the feast, follow the procession, perhaps paying respect to the saint too. In other words the degree of their participation can change widely.

To unfold this complexity is not a simple exercise of categorization but shows the complex and pervasive relation between those who supposedly organize and perform the feast and those who supposedly constitute the audience. There is no logical separation between insiders and outsiders but a continuous integration, shaded perhaps in different degrees. In other words, in a global perspective, the feast is not a monodirectional process (for instance the tourist, as active subject, knowing about the feast, as a passive object) but bi-directional (for instance the religious society which organizes the feast appealing to, even through the use of professional agencies, the possible tourist market). From this perspective the outsider is not just the occasional costumer of a performance from which she or he is extraneous. She or he is an integral part from the same initial moment of projecting the performance itself.

Therefore the opposition insiders/outsiders, as presented during the performance of the festive practices, should be discarded in favor of a model suggesting more blurred boundaries. Again, and again, the festive practices of the North End's religious societies demonstrate how emic categories are displaced on a continuum rather than structured on dichotomies.

Choosing a model based on displacement and dislocation rather than dichotomy does not deny the existence of differences between categories. Of course both perspectives carry ideological implications. But while an oppositional model tends to reify and basically to reduce social complexities, it is perhaps useful to illustrate tensions such as global vs. local, a more pervasive model of continuums can reveal far more clearly the social strategies illustrating dialogic and dynamic relationship of power.

Performing Ethnicities

The claimed tradition, in the specific case of Boston's North End, can be discussed within the polarizing framework of the global/local tension. For instance, the Venezuelan feasts studies by Guss (2000), as well as the Sardinian two Madonnas analyzed by Magliocco (2006), are situated in what the latter describes as the threshold of globalization. In Magliocco's words:

> [T]he old world of peasants economies and value had not disappeared, but the global economy and consumer capitalism were already at the door. Globalization and its twin, localization, were just emerging as discourses on the public stage. (xiii)

The festive practices I am studying in Boston's North End are actually produced within a geographic, economic and cultural reality that sees itself, and is often perceived from outside, as the center of globalization (if we intend global to be synonymous to Westernization or Americanization). In this case there would be no threshold to cross, there would be no doors still closed in front of an incumbent global economy. From this perspective globalization is not an emergent and contested discourse. However, according to Appudurai (1990, 295), the process of globalization is not a one-way movement of culture from West to "the rest." Therefore it is not possible to observe through the festive practice tensions of urban/rural or center/periphery, nor a sort of postcolonial emergency. The specific trajectory of global/local dynamics allows the discovery and performance of different cultural and ethnic identities. Specific local identities, in both senses of imagined community (the village of origin) and of proclaimed community (the ethnic enclave), are performed during the feasts. But also generic superlocal identities are ratified, from regional (referring to the "Old Country" in the case of clusters as Sicilians, Avellinesi, Abruzzesi, and to the "New Country" for "Bostonian" or "North Ender" identities) to the national (Italian and American).[19] The mechanism of aesthetic reduction, as I have shown, can be seen as a process of homogenization toward a model approachable by the global market (i.e., a product of Americanization).

What is performed is at one and the same time a claim for heterogeneous identities firmly rooted in the ethnic enclaves and in the original village. The two aspects should not be seen as competitive but as cooperating for the procurement of economic goals. Visitors and tourists, but also investors, businessmen and yuppies are attracted by the offer of specific authentic traditions, staged through the year in the neighborhood (restaurants, ethnic shops, but also a community-style life based on the perceived idea and preformed representation of the Italian village) and reaching a climax during the festive practices. What is manufactured in fact is a product resulting from previous and continuous negotiations: food, music, and performance have reached, in terms of the model of orthopraxy, a level of homogeneity that allows consumption on a large scale while preserving an appealing level of heterogeneity. This dynamic of homogeneity/heterogeneity is complex and not linear. The basic push factor is certainly the strategic essentialism which aims toward the consolidation of the neighborhood's economy. Yet, an aspect of reclamation, perhaps of specific counterhegemonic nature, is also undeniable,. For example, when Big Lou, the owner of Caffè Graffiti in Hanover Street, replies, almost offended, to the request of a friend (an ironic request since she is Italian) for a "regular American coffee" that at the Caffè Graffiti only espresso is served, he claims a local (Italian) specificity he sees as authentic but also as heterogeneous (not American). On the other hand, I have invited a friend for a tour in the North End by stressing the "local" aspect, making a contrast with other sites that are implicitly considered "less authentic."

The tension between homogenization and heterogenization can be also described in terms of hybridity and creolization in order to highlight cultural traits produced by the encounter of different cultures. These terms for instance are used not only by Bakhtin (1981) in his linguistic approach to hybridity, but also by Garcia Canclini (1995), analyzing strategies for "entering and leaving modernity," by Hannerz (1987), suggesting the limits and the complexity of creolization, but also by Korom (2003), who uses the opposite concept of 'de-creolization' in his analysis of rituals in Trinidad. Both terms are continuously critically revisited but still commonly used by scholars, especially those focusing on postcolonial or cultural studies.[20] According to Favero:

> Always maintaining the metropolitan "West" as the natural point of reference hybridity has, in these contexts, been used to address situations in which actors are consciously aiming at representing and coming to terms with controversial identities (often their own) and to reflect upon personal experiences regarding to the position of group or society. (2005, 125)

I am arguing that creolization and hybridity are metaphors in need of a better unfolding in order to be completely useful.

According to Hannerz (1987; 1992; 1996) creolization is a linguistic metaphor indicating processes of cultural confluence within a more or less open continuum of diversity, stretched out along a structure of center-periphery relations which will extend transnationally, and which is characterized also by inequality in power, prestige and material resources:

Creolization is a *root metaphor as many in capturing the quality* of those processes in which meaning and meaningful forms are shaped and socially organized between center and periphery. (Hannerz 1992, 39; emphasis added)

Hannerz is indeed well aware that:

1. creolization is just a metaphor;
2. creolization can be replaced with other metaphors;
3. creolization is a useful term in capturing quality of process.

If I assume that metaphorical construction is always a process of replacement,[21] therefore incomplete and ambiguous, I appreciate even more the intellectual honesty of Ulf Hannerz, who is aware of this limit in using metaphors. This is the reason why creolization is a root metaphor. In a later work, Hannerz) stressed on the multiplicity of the term:

Anyway, here we are now, with hybridity, collage, mélange, hotchpotch, montage, synergy, bricolage, creolization, mestizaje, mongrelization, syncretism, transculturalism, third cultures and what have you; some terms used perhaps only in passing as summary metaphors, others with claims to more analytical status, and others again with more regional or thematic strongholds. (1996, 13

Every one of these terms has its own history and inevitably, being less or more frequently used by scholarship, it carries a semantic halo; but according to Hannerz, despite these implicit or explicit differences, it "perhaps does not matter much which of these concepts one chooses"(1996, 14). This declaration of flexibility is somewhat disingenuous and needs to be questioned. What quality of the cultural processes can be captured by the idea of creole? Like the creole language, this kind of culture can be seen as contaminated, impure, not bounded, not homogenous. This reaches an important target: to gain distance from an old anthropological tradition that has too often built cultural analysis on the assumption of closed societies. If Malinowski's Trobrianders indeed had few relations with an "outside" world, the Nigerian people studied by Hannerz, and even more so the Bostonians in my research, are completely integrated in a globalized world economy.

The theoretical question is no longer if there are communications between cultures or not, but what kind of communication there are, what kind of relations of power are implied, what kind of dynamics and dialogical confrontation are possible. Talking of the *Global Ecumene*, with emphasis on the process of globalization of culture in the twentieth century as product of center/periphery relationship in ordering cultural process, a relationship that is dialectical, bearing diffusion but also differentiation, not simply homogenization, Hannerz (1992, 264) suggests that Creole cultures are "intrinsically of mixed origin." Like Creole language, these cultures are made at "the confluence of two or more widely separate historical currents" in interaction. Furthermore, this interaction is not merely the constant pressure of the center toward the periphery, but a much more creative interplay, where the periphery can "talk back" (265).

Ethnicity exists in this kind of dialogical situation. Even before an emically declared purity, bearing political meanings we will have to deal with these "hybridizing webs of meaning" (Hannerz 1992, 265).

According to Korom (2003), the term "creolization" has a questionable colonial history, but it can be accepted because, on one hand, it is a concept well established in the sociolinguistics scholarship, and, on the other hand, "it is commonly used by creole makers themselves."[22] Creolization emphasizes a social process of cultural mixture. Creolization is a concept that speaks

> of the convergence of distinct cultural practices perpetuated by different ethnic group sharing the same geographic, economic, and political landscape within a context of unequal power relationship. (Korom 2003, 196).

Interestingly, Korom suggests a dialectical process for the understanding of these complex forms of culture, seen as a production of a synthetic process of convergence. Beside creolization, where it is possible to notice aspects of acculturation and accommodation of the dominated culture (in linguistics, the substrate, the subordinate language) to the dominant culture (in linguistics, to the superstrate, the dominant language), we can also see the convergent, necessarily complementary, phenomenon of decreolization as a form of resistance to creolization. According to Korom:

> [C]reolization always implies decreolization: hence resistance can be accomplished through creative accommodation. What I mean by creative accommodation is that what might be seen like acculturation on the surface may simultaneously be a valid form of resistance to total cultural absorption. (2003, 13)

Let me try to clarify this point with an example from my ethnography.

The religious societies in Boston's North End were made in order to sustain the ethnic enclave, as equivalent in the new world to the original Italian village (for instance, people from Sciacca gathered together around the Fishermen Club). Every year, in the summertime, they carried the statue of their patron saint in procession in the new neighborhood. Over the years these religious societies set a distance with the local church, becoming more or less American voluntary associations described by Weber and Toqueville. Every year, in the summertime, the members carry the statue of their patron saint in procession in the neighborhood. If I try to approach the societies and the rituals as replicas of the original situation in Italy, I will miss the complexity of the problem, deriving from the contact situation: why does the marching band play "God Bless America"? Why does the statue of the saint pay respect to the fire station? Why do I not see any priest following the procession? Why do they eat fried calamari as ritual food? These examples, and others I have mentioned already, allow me to assert a phenomenon of creolization (and we can see also accommodation and acculturation, using Korom's terms). Two cultures are confronting each other, producing something new, but I can also see a moment of "creative accomodation" if I interpret this supposed blending as a way to resist to a total cultural absorption.

There is perhaps also an instance of decreolization, for instance, in the use of English for the name of the Fishermen Club, and, above all, in the secular direction of the religious societies. The societies become in this view, thus, traditional cultural forms moving toward assimilation in a dominant culture. But it is a dynamic process of complementary and interactive influences. In order to complete the dialectical process of culture-making, a third element of the process should be added. As many scholars point out creolization and decreolization ought to be complete with recreolization. In a postcolonized community the language may turn inward toward its linguistic and cultural center to survive a hostile postcolonial environment. This occurs when the fishermen from the North End return to Sciacca to celebrate the Madonna, and also when the prior of the sanctuary of Saint Anthony in Padua is invited as superintendent for the festival in Boston.

Hybridity too is far from a neutral term. Despite a clear biological flavor this metaphor became famous within the social sciences and the humanities with Bakhtin:

> We call hybrid construction any utterance that belongs, by its grammatical (syntactic) and compositional features to a single speaker, but that actually contains *intermingled* within it two utterances, two manners of speaking, two styles, two "languages," two semantic and axiological horizons. (1981, 118)

We need to contextualize Bakhtin's idea of hybridization in its more general frame, that is, as the representation of discourse, expressing the "encounter with the other." From an initial description of paradigmatic and syntagmatic relations, referring to heteroglossia, as multiplicity of voices, diffused in the authorial discourse, Bakhtin suggested different degrees of the dialogic encounter: the full presence (or explicit dialogue), the unrealized presence (no material corroboration but the other's discourse is summoned forth, because it belongs to the collective memory of the social group), and the hybrid construction (see Todorov

1984, 73). Finally hybridity, from this perspective, can be expressed in an "organic" and "intentional" way. Organic hybridity can be defined, according to Favero (2005, 126), presenting his analysis of middle-class Indians in New Delhi,[23] as an unconscious integration of new images, words and objects while intentional hybridity is the conscious play performed to communicate a particular position within the hybrid context. In Favero's case the capacity to switch or, better, to instrumentally commute within different dimensions of hybridity is between the categories of traditional and Westernized. In the North End the case is even more complex because of overlapping levels. The traditional is an intentionally claimed dimension, referring to imagined communities, while the organic level is the Western world (or American, or Bostonian?)

From this perspective hybridity is not only a space between two zones of purity where we can distinguish two discrete species with the hybrid resulting out of their combination. Rather, hybrid is analogous to syncretic, indicating something in between (Bhabha, 1994). And it is not only a continuous processes of transculturation (see for instance Clifford's, 2002, idea of "travel trajectories" and "flow"), with two interacting cultures. This in fact would end up resembling a physiological status, leading to the impossibility of any purity or authenticity. Even Garcia Canclini's definition:

> [T]he sociocultural processes in which discrete structures and practices, that existed in separate form, combine themselves to generate new structures, objects and practices is a reduction. (1995, 14)

Hybridity (as well as creolization) should move from a descriptive level, regardless whether it is a less or more complex one, to a functional level, where it represents a mechanism of social negotiation often intentionally performed by social actors (such as in the case of strategic essentialist claims for identity). The only possibility for terms such as hybridity and creolization to be powerful heuristic tools that can be used to understand the everyday experiences of identities is to give them back their own complexity.

In any case a fundamental issue is inherent in the use of the terms: the supposed purity. Hutnyk sets the question of to what degree hybridity relies on an anterior pure, a proposition of nonhybridity preceding mixture: "the descriptive use of hybridity evokes, counterfactually, a stable and prior nonmixed position, to which 'presumably it might one day be possible to return'" (2005, 82). Inevitably the term Creolization also carries a static essentialist dimension.

Identity, especially ethnic identity, is now far from an essentialist concept based on a sort of innate, fixed, unmodifiable characteristics, persisting over the time because they are fundamental for group and personal identity. Identity is not fixed and stable, but malleable and situational. Ethnic boundaries are continually revisited, negotiated, and redefined according to the interests of the actors. According to Barth (1969, 6) ethnic identity is a matter of self-ascription, and ascription by others in interaction. The ongoing process of identity (and many scholars are proposing the more processual, active term "identification") is characterized by incompleteness.[24] Endlessly making "others," as well as building boundaries, is a process defining itself that through differentiation and juxtaposition.

This continuous negotiation of ethnic identities, suggesting both organic and intentional hybridity, is well expressed through the following statements proposed by North Enders.

Frank, a member of Saint Anthony Society, speaking about ethnic identity, said:

> My grandfather was from Palermo: he was Italian. My mother was born here in Boston: she is Italian American. I am a third generation: I am American Italian.

In the following interview with Kevin, of the Fishermen's Club, a symbol of regional Bostonian identity even appears:

> Kevin: Coming back on what we are saying, we are born in United States, we are Italian Americans. But during the [soccer] world cup everyone of us dress in *azzurro*.[25] (25)
>
> Augusto: Yes, but now you are wearing a Bruins T-shirt![26]
>
> Kevin: Because Italy does not have a hockey team! Look, Gus, after September 11 attack we were all American, if the World Cup happens we are Italian, when the feasts came we are Sciaccatani.

I asked Jason, a prominent member of Saint Anthony Society, how he could define himself, in terms of cultural identity. He said to me:

> I feel I am from Montefalcione when I carry the statue of Saint Anthony, I feel Italian when I fight against the Irish or when we watch the soccer games on TV, but I only speak English and I had never been to Italy. Maybe I will go someday and I will be a tourist.

Statements like these show the complexity of ethnic identity. Identity is shown basically as oxymoron because it is related to the idea of permanence (Melucci 1995) and at the same time to the idea of multiplicity, malleability, instability according to the situational and contextual approach I am following here (see, for instance, Okamura 1981). Identity is inevitably a matter of continuity and change, of singular and plural, of reification and processes. The quotes I heard are rationalizations, solicited in a interview setting, but during the festive practices (such as the feasts themselves) symbols of identities are continuously displayed and displaced, suggesting, (according to Gans 1979) the visibility and authority of a symbolic ethnicity.

Multiple identities are also expressed through the music repertoire of the Roma Band in a dialectical game between creolization and decreolization,[27] that is between the dynamic and creative process of blending different streams of distinct cultures elements into something new and the interpreted reanalysis or reinterpretation of preexisting forms to suit contemporary needs (Korom 2003, 198).

As I have noted, the Saint Anthony feast begins with a girl holding the American flag and singing the American national anthem, immediately before the blessing of the statue.[28] This seems to me a clear example of creolization, where the contemporary presence of different cultures appears as a dialogue, creating a complex ongoing narrative about ethnicity. Other moments like this occur in other festivals as well: during the procession, in Boston, one can hear the Italian national anthem played by the marching band. This, in my opinion, can be seen as an instance of decreolization: the Italian national anthem "Inno di Mameli" is played in a different context than it is in Italy.

The marching bands in Italy also play religious hymns, sometimes opera arias, but very seldom do they play the "Inno di Mameli." There is no reason to do so: the festival, again, belongs to the church.[29] Thus, in the North End a symbol of a nation (and here Anderson's, 1983, notion of imagined community is definitely appropriate) is used to declare a hyphenated ethnicity.

I will list a few examples of the repertoire of the marching bands in the North End festival to show the dynamic of creolization and decreolization: (1) "Vitti 'na crozza," (2) "Faccetta Nera," (3) the theme from the *Godfather*, and (4) "When the Saints Go Marching In."

The last piece is an American religious song, or gospel song, belonging to a different Christian tradition but now assimilated to a general "American" musical tradition and to the Mardi Gras in New Orleans.

The first piece, "Vitti 'na crozza" (I saw a skull), is a Sicilian folk love song, probably proclaiming a regional identity. Other songs can claim village and regional Italian identities for those whose ancestry may be traced to specific localities. For example, classical Neapolitan songs such as "'O Sole Mio," and "Santa Lucia" are always played for the Saint Anthony and Saint Lucy societies because the two societies were originally established by immigrants from Montefalcione, a village near Naples. More recent songs from Naples such as "Mamma" and "Malafemmena," became popular in the United States after World War II. As Caputo (2004) pointed out "Mamma" is always played for elderly Italian and Italian American female residents of the nursing home in the North End.

"Faccetta Nera" (Little Black Face) was a popular song of the fascist era that describes the Italian invasion of Somalia and Ethiopia. Why it is still played? There are two interpretative possibilities. One is that the music is linked with the near-contemporary period of immigration. This interpretation seems to me rather forced. An analysis of the immigration waves during the fascist era reveals that the mass movement, typical of the previous decades, slowed down because of two restricting factors: the 1921 Immigration Act and, more importantly, the National Origin Act of 1924 (with its discrimination against eastern and southern European nations). Simultaneously the fascist regime prohibited all but a few from leaving Italy for another country.[30] Therefore, the song probably does not speak to any personal, direct experience and memory.

The second interpretation is linked with the fascist effort to build a sense of the nation, using the metaphors of Roman Classicism, which were expanded to justify the imperialistic invasion of those African countries. From this point of view the song has a reason to be played, as a symbol of a nation-building moment, in the past and even now as a marker of ethnicity.

The third characteristic song is the theme from the *Godfather*, now used as a kind of anthem of Italian American ethnic groups. The popularity of the movie as an Italian American saga was and still is enormous among Italian Americans.

The Roma Band also recognizes a more general Italian identity through its repertoire. According to Caputo (2004) if an elderly Italian or Italian American male approaches the saint, Salvi Puglisi, the leader of the band, may decide to play "Bersaglieri" (Italian soldier's march) if the elderly man served in the Italian army. As noted, an older piece, apparently played for the Italian king during the late 1800s and early 1900s, called "Marcia Reale" (Royal March), is the song played every time someone donates money. Since it is played during the feast scene in Francis Ford Coppola's movie, *The Godfather Part II*, "Marcia Reale" may display more than one identity—a general Italian identity and a Hollywood version of Italian American identity.

A hyphenated Italian American identity is also demonstrated through songs that were made popular in the United States by Italian American singers such as Jerry Vale, Dean Martin, Al Martino, and Frank Sinatra. "Oi Mari'," "Volare," "Arrivederci Roma" and "That's Ammore" are just a few examples.

The Roma Band also performs songs related to American patriotism. When the procession stops to honor fallen soldiers at the Veteran's Memorial in Paul Revere Park, Salvi Pugliese plays "Taps" and the band typically follows with the "Star Spangled Banner," "God Bless America," or "America the Beautiful." The "Marine Hymn" or similar pieces representing the Armed Forces are also often played as well as the "Battle Hymn of the Republic," and "Stars and Stripes Forever."

Another example of creolization and Americanization is the use of the song "Deep in the Heart of Texas," as analyzed by Caputo (2004, 4):

> [T]his piece began simply as another song in the Roma Band's repertoire, but it has been transformed into a sort of theme song for one of the saint societies. A few years ago, the Saint Agrippina Society inserted the words 'Viva Saint Agrippina' in place of 'Deep in the Heart of Texas'

during the chorus section of the song. Since then, the Roma Band has been expected to play that song frequently during the procession for Saint Agrippina. The Saint Agrippina Society is the only society in the North End that has taken a completely secular American song and turns it into a Catholic saint's theme song.

Like the festive practice as a whole the Roma Band's performances exemplify multiplicity and polyphony of identities negotiated in the North End. The continuous manipulation of symbols, like music, facilitates this dynamic game of entrances and escapes, cultural commuting, multiple identities and belonging as well as excluding.

The Roma Band's music not only embodies the identity of the North End, but also influences both the internal and external view of the neighborhood. The complex multiple identities and histories prevalent in Boston's North End are publicly displayed each year in the local saints' day celebrations. Because the Roma Band and many of its members are deeply embedded in the North End community, the group has and will continue to have the ability to perform and form the history and identity of the neighborhood through its musical repertoire.

All these symbols I have presented evoke what Hall (1996, 4) called the "phantasmatic imaginary," that is, the interpretative framework used by social actors to position themselves in contemporary society. According to Ivy (1995, 4) the elements of phantasm lying at the basis of national-cultural communities cluster around (1) Benedict Anderson's (1983) imagined communities (for the modern nation-state), (2) Cornelius Castoriadis's (1987) "social imaginary" (the codified ground for the social production of meaning), (3) Claude Lefort's (1986) "imaginary community" (linking modern ideologies with the rise of mass media), and (4) Jacques Lacan's (1975, 1976) "imaginary" (the phantasmatic basis for the early, presymbolic identification with the image). Being related to the process of representation and identification of the self or the group toward a perceived sameness "phantasmatic imaginary" is one of the fundamental characteristics of ethnic identity, but not the only one.

The absence of purities, inherent even in the scholarly metaphors of hybridity and creolization, the performance of phantasmatic image of any ethnic identity, the dialectic between a supposed organic and intentional perception of the self and the group, and the impermanence and pliability of all processes making claims for situational definitions of belonging, all these allow me to prefer the term ephemeral identities as a heuristic concept for grasping religious practices in Boston's North End. In other words I do not see any kind of purity, stability or authenticity in claims for identity. Identities are intentionally chosen, through mechanisms of self-ascription and/or labeling processes by others,[31] within a limited range and utilizing traits, symbols and elements already stereotyped as organic. Fragmentation and transience are thus fundamental categories for understanding identity and its performance.

The debate concerning the instability of identity and especially of cultural and ethnic identities is so widespread and even longwinded that Stuart Hall's (1996, 1) question, "What is the need of a further debate about identity?" is well-taken, even though it remains a fundamentally rhetorical question.

While scholars stress malleability and multiplicity, assuming a process of endless strategic and positional negotiations for identity, not too much attention has been paid to the process itself. I argue that we must consider not only if identities are social constructs, but also analyze how, when and why they are constructed. I argue further therefore for the importance of approaching the technology of ephemeral identities' production, where the self is the fundamental center.

Ephemeral Identities and the Technology of the Self

Underlying the technological aspect, there are two fundamental aspects: first, the self is embedded in relationships of power, technologically informed. It is evident that, in Foucault's terms, "we have indirectly constituted ourselves through the exclusion of some others" (1990, 146); and second, the self is expressed by self-conscious moments of behavior, technologically informed. In Foucault's terms "we directly constitute our identity through some ethical techniques of the self which developed through antiquity down to now?" (ibid.)

According to Foucault (1990; 1997; but also Martin 1998, 18), it is possible to individuate four major types of technologies: (1) technologies of production, concerning how to produce, transform, or manipulate things; (2) technologies of sign systems, about using signs, meanings, symbols, or signification; (3) technologies of power, which determine the conduct of individuals and submit them to certain ends or dominations, (an objectivizing of the subject); and (4) technologies of the self, which permit individuals to effect by their own means or with the help of others a certain number of operations on their own bodies and souls, thoughts, conduct, and way of being, so as to transform themselves in order to attain a certain state of happiness, purity, wisdom, perfection, or immortality. The four types of technologies hardly ever function separately, although each one of them is associated with a certain type of domination.

In the previous chapters I have stressed the first three types, approaching the festive practices as sign system, and as privileging the feast as location for the analysis of unbalanced relationship of power. My historical approach also showed how technologies of production are situated at the base of social, cultural and symbolic changes in the North End. Here, I will stress the fourth type, privileging the self rather than the more collective perspective, which I think refers to the other types.

Foucault exemplified the development of the hermeneutics of the self only in two contexts: Greco-Roman philosophy and early Christian spirituality (as it was expressed in monastic principles). But it is also well known that Foucault (1990, 19) intended to develop a history of "how an individual acts upon himself" through technology, in the sense of real activity to care for himself, a *technē* (activity) in order to achieve *ephimelnsthai sautou* (the concern with the self).

From this perspective I have no doubt that the North End festive practices can be considered technologies of the self. What I have observed in my fieldwork are a series of "real activities" (Foucault 1990, 24) performed by interacting individuals using their own bodies, souls, thoughts, conduct, and ways of being. Concisely, the feast can be approached as a metaphorical location where in dialogic, dynamic and polyphonic ways participants actualize a stylized pattern of practices. Stressing again the dialectic insider/outsider, not as binary opposition but as a continuum characterized by different commitments of varying degrees and shades, participants perform different routines, and disciplines and intentional activities toward a recognized positive transformation. From the attendance to the feast, seen as degree zero of commitment, to the bodily mortification of the statue-bearers, situated at the opposite point of the continuum (at least if I consider the body the most salient variable), participants actively work on themselves to achieve a desired state of being. It is not, of course, a quest for immortality, as in early Christian spirituality, but it certainly is an attempt to obtain happiness, purity, wisdom, perfection or, in general, an improvement. Or, in other terms, it is a discipline that allows the participant to claim and experience an identity seen as happy, pure, wise and perfect.

What kind of technē of the self is displayed during the North End's festive practices in order to directly constitute this desired identity? Foucault (1990, 26–45) analyzed different technologies of the self, changing over time: (1) The Socratic notion of "taking care of oneself" in relation to the political life, and, more generally, to knowing oneself. (2) The Stoics effort to "retire into the self and stay there," achieved through memories, dialogues and writing. (3) In Greco-Roman time, the Stoics' concept of *asknsis* (ascesis) was affirmed as a progressive consideration of the self and a way to access the reality of the world became increasingly important. (4) The principle of self-examination, fundamental for Christianity: "Christianity is not only a salvation religion, it's a confessional religion" (ibid., 45). The two main forms of disclosure of the self in early Christian times were *exagoreusis* (practices of the body based on absolute obedience and contemplation) and *exomolognsis* (rituals of recognizing oneself as a sinner and penitent that later in the medieval period immediately precede reconciliation with God). Notably, according to Foucault, "*Exomolognsis* is not a verbal behavior but the dramatic recognition of one's status as a penitent" (ibid., 41). Thus, from this perspective, dramatization, self interrogation and recognition, penitential behaviors, as technē of self-revelation were necessary conditions for reconciliation with God and the achievement of a sense of salvation.

The charter model of exomologēsis is martyrdom, that is, the refusal and destruction of the self to establish a new identity.

We find traces of these different technologies for the disclosure of the self in the North End's festive practices: for instance, the use of memory and of the past, as I have demonstrated previously, is a fundamental aspect of the feast. Even a sort of exagoreusis can be seen, especially in the ethic of respect, intrinsic to the festival, and expressed toward the saint but also toward a clear hierarchic leadership, from the society's leader to elderly, to secular and sacred authorities present at the feast. Respect is a way, in this case, to dramatize the self through acts of contemplation and obedience. All these technologies are obvious during every feast.

But the most evident technology for the constitution of subjectivity seems to be the exomologēsis, which is not surprising because "exposé is the heart of exomologēsis" and festive practice are performances and expositions. Performing the festive practices allows the participants a self-revelation, in terms of ethnic identity, through a process of self-recognition. The officially correct festive practices dramatize ethnic belonging as a revelation: through the penitential behavior individuals can claim, again, a belonging and a sacralized self-recognition.

This form of self-recognition is a way to restore an original identity, using myths concerning the village of origin. It is also a way to restore one's historical identity as North Ender, using memories of the past concerning the ethnic enclaves. Such self-recognition is a dramatization that "must be visibly represented and accompanied by others who recognize the ritual" (Foucault 1990, 42). Notably, being a visible dramatization which needs to be recognized by others, the ritual has to be disciplined and stylized. In other words: while orthodoxy provides the ultimate rationale behind self-revelation, orthopraxy is the technology that powers the process of recognition. Self-recognition, finally, must affect and transform the body. In this sense, the procession can be seen as a manifestly penitential behavior: the statue-bearers, again, represent probably the most evident of these bodily mortifications. But also money donations, the walk behind the statue and even simple attendance at the feast can be interpreted, in different degrees, as forms of public dramatization and orientation of the self.

Beside the similarities, some differences can also be noted between the exomolog sis of early Christianity and the festive practices I am analyzing here: while in early Christianity the primary target was the refusal or the breaking away of the self with the establishment of an individual identity only as a consequence (Foucault 1990, 43), the festive practices of the North End stress the quest for identity as fundamental, as a process possible only through a self-destruction prior to a self-revelation. I believe that this inversion is related to the modern journey toward secularization that set the distance between the two example: reconciliation with God is the basic or, better, the only target of any disclosure of the self in early Christianity; reconciliation with a supposed essential identity is the target of the disclosure of the self during the analyzed festive practices.

My analysis of identity as technology of the self cannot be considered concluded if I do not take into account the pluralistic character of the term. I have illustrated here how festive practices allow the disclosure of the self, that is, the declaration of a specific belonging to a specific ethnicity and collectivity. But this is just one of the possible, situational, symbolic, convenient, ephemeral, or whatever-similar-adjective-I-would-use identities that can be claimed. Commuting and negotiating identities is an unquestionable characteristic of postmodernity. If this is so, can I still propose a model of technology of the self even in this fluctuating situation?

I argue that one of the technologies of the self suggested by Foucault (1990, 45–46) can be an important heuristic tool for the model of ephemeral identities I propose here. In his references to the permanent contemplation of God and related self-examination in early monasteries, Foucault stressed a concern with thought rather than with action. In order to describe this specific technology he used the pejorative Greek term *logismoi* (cogitation, reasoning, calculating thought). For the monk, the state of perpetual mobility of the spirit, is a weakness. Self-examination is the endless method used to immobilize the restless movements of the spirit, which turn the self away from God.

In a situation where God is not the ultimate target of a disclosure of the self, but identity itself is, the restless mobility opposed by logismoi among monks will be expressed and negated instead within the endless game of entrances and escapes into and from ephemeral identities. Any efforts to immobilize this tension must end in an inevitable failure. But this ought to be seen in a nonnegative way. First of all, this dynamic, even if necessarily costly in terms of energy, avoids essentialism, which is affirmed only for strategic reasons. Mobility through identities inevitably undermines their supposed respective authenticities for the actors. Last but not least, not only should the actor's control over perpetual mobility toward and away from different desired identities be considered a technology of the self, but so should the perpetual mobility in itself. If choosing an identity (therefore controlling mobility) can be considered the product of intentional actions performed by an individual, then mobility itself is a technē, a product of intentional performances. Both constitute the process of commuting, with travels and stops, between a continuum of overlapping ephemeral identities. In these terms, ephemeral identities is a plural concept characterized by perpetual mobility and momentary stasis. And in this tension, the self is expressed, experienced, and disclosed.

Ephemeral Identities: From Text to Hypertext

My proposed model of ephemeral identities moves from a textual to hypertextual metaphor. This complex representation allows me to achieve a more flexible and adequate representation of the multivocality and multilinearity of the performances of identities, highlighting a vision of performances that is antihierarchical, where author and reader (metaphors from literary critique) are no longer separated but intimately intertwined. The model I recommend comes from Landow's (1992) approach to new forms of narratives, the hypertexts. Hypertext is a term coined by Theodor Nelson (1992) in 1965 to describe a nonsequentially linked electronic text conceived for editing and publications based on "new" technologies and now possible because of the spread of computers.[32] The metaphor of the interconnected textual web was at the base of Xanadu, the system of documents allowing the reader to follow her or his own interests and creativity while approaching the whole network. The World Wide Web was strongly influenced by Nelson's ideas.

Following Nelson's approach, a basic definition of hypertext is nonsequential writing—text that branches and allows choices to the reader; it is a series of textual chunks connected by links which offer the reader different pathways. This basic definition contains two fundamental dimensions: (1) the linking of different parts and (2) the reader's choice. If the first evokes complexity and multivocality, the second refers more directly to situational intentionality, involving power and status relationship (see for instance the author/reader relations, which are now completely reexamined). These are also the main characteristics of ephemeral identities.

The hypertext model is a response to the necessity of conceptualizing a text that poststructuralists would define as "open" (Barthes 1970).[33] Talking about lexias (blocks of texts), Barthes describes an ideal textuality as one in which:

> the networks are many and interact, without any one of them being able to surpass the rest; this text is a galaxy of signifiers, not a structure of signifieds; it has no beginning; it is reversible; we gain access to it by several entrances, none of which can be authoritatively declared to be the main one; the codes it mobilizes extend *as far as the eye can reach*, they are indeterminable . . . ; the systems of meaning can take over this absolutely plural text, but their number is never closed, based as it is on the infinity of language. (1970, 5–6)

Barthes focuses on nonlinearity and readability of the text and likewise Michel Foucault (1969) conceives of the text in terms of network and links, arguing that the frontiers of a book are blurred and never clear-cut because the text is caught up in a system of references to other books, other texts, other sentences: it is a node within a network. Other authors, for instance, Bakhtin's dialogic approach (1984) and Deridda's discussion of the *mourceau*, bite and/or bit (1972), also insist on polyphony and intertextuality and the irrelevance of inside/outside opposition within a particular text.

I am assuming, focusing of course on the festive ritual performance of my case-study, that ephemeral identities and the performances expressing them, are tendentially based on hypertextual technologies of the self. Here in fact, to paraphrase Bakhtin (1984, 29) the dialogical and polyphonic aspects do not allow the totality and centrality of a single authorial tyrannical and univocal voice, of a single conscience, but rather the complexity and totality of interaction of various consciences, with no hierarchy on both levels of intratextual and intertextual. This is what Landow (1992, 87) calls the "erosion of the self," that is, the transfer of privileges from the author to the reader, evident in the multilinearity of the text with increased autonomy for the reader. The organizational principle of hypertext is decentralizion, and therefore this kind of text is much more dynamic than a conventional linearity-based text. In other terms hierarchy and organization are a reader's choice. He or she can choose this or that starting point and pathways, with the freedom to change along the way. Perspective, absolutely static in the text, in the hypertext becomes dynamic with a center that still exists but is chosen as a function not essentialized as being. According to Landow the hypertextual model undermines notions of:

1. a preorganized sequence;
2. a predetermined beginning and end;
3. the broadness of narrative (hypertext is basically an endless combination);
4. the idea of unity (or whole) of text associated with these concepts. (124)

From this perspective ephemeral identities are strategically chosen, just like the links for a hypertextual navigation. Again I have to make clear that the term must be understood in a neo-Durkheimian sense (that is, related to collective actions) and not as a rationalist Weberian concept (in the sense of an instrumental action). From this perspective, strategy does not mean (at least not usually) a coherently organized political practice, in the broad sense, but more often is an inevitable (though also never wholly predictable) manifestation of a power unbalance. Intentionality is certainly fundamental in the choice of an icon or another symbolic practice to situate the self inside the frame of a perceived ethnicity, but it is not necessarily a "rational" process. Choosing a symbol and therefore negotiating an ethnic identity can be a matter of consciousness but more often people know how to correctly perform the negotiation, they know how to recognize innovation, transgression and choices, but they do not necessarily know their meaning. Or at least they cannot explain directly what is expressed or symbolized by their use of symbols, though they do experience their power subjectively and can be passionately attached to them. Paraphrasing Clifford's idea of ethnography (1987, 6), identities themselves are constructed narratives. They are fictions, because they cannot reveal or report on the whole account of the reality. Identity's truths are not only "constructed versions" but also partial and incomplete.

Other points ought to be underlined in my model of ephemeral and hypertextual identities:

1. ethnic identities are chosen within a range of available identities—this is a limited choice;
2. it is possible to individuate different degrees of importance subjectively granted to available identities;
3. unlike the model of hybrid and creole identities, there are no claims or implications of fundamental authenticity in the process of negotiation of ephemeral identity.

In the context of my research the limitations are self-evident. Italian Americans of the third generation can negotiate their Italian identity carrying the statue of the saint or declaring their "Americanness" through language and other symbolic practices. They can also claim a local and regional identity. It is not unusual to see T-shirts joking about Bostonian accent (*I pahked my cah in Boston*—I parked my car in Boston—for instance), on sale on the window of many stores in Hanover Street. And it is the case another store in Hanover Street, also drawing attention on the local dialect: the *Connah Store* (The Corner Store).

But the range of choice is limited. Yet within its limited range, the combination of choices is nonetheless endless, always changing, and continuously played upon by the North Enders. And, as I have shown, it is a game showing, as well as hiding, a hierarchy of identities: I can declare to be Sciaccatano, but during the festival what I really state is my identity as a North Ender. I can claim to be Italian, but my language will announce me as an American, and so on. Ethnic enclaves are gone, a national identity as Italian is a phantasm, and probably so is an American identity. What seems to be strong and effective is hyphenated ethnicity and local identity. But these ephemeral hierarchies too are destined to change over time.

My next point is more controversial: the hypertextual metaphor makes it possible to imagine the negotiation of identities as similar to electronic browsing, as the user actively highlights hyperlinks denoting the possibility of a choice. Icons and symbolic practices can be considered hyperlinks useful to move from identity to identity. But these hyperlinks, and the related symbols, are not authentic in any way: the hypothetical symbol through which I can claim a specific identity is not an essential trait, but a perceived and claimed essential trait, therefore a cultural construct informed intertextually by other symbols and dialogically inserted within a complex context. The symbol is historically and culturally determined. For instance, the icon of the saint, as I have demonstrated, is not only a symbol of a specific ethnic identity, but a polyphonic sign, changing over time, from the symbol of the original village to the icon of an ethnic enclave to a sign of the neighborhood's need for a collective identity, switching from regional and local identities while also making claims for national and hyphenated identities.

In other words, unlike the hybrid and creole model, I do not assume the icon, the symbol or the symbolic practice to be a datum, statically representing the products of different as well as pure preexistent signs. Rather it is a dynamic process of stylization where it is not possible to see any kind of purity since this would be formed from other impure signs. Cultural markers are thus far from being authentic, they are products historically determined in situation of contacts between cultures and/or changes over time. They are phantasms, evocations, ephemeral entities that inevitably can generate only phantasms, evocations and ephemeral identities. The only claim for authentic ethnic identity is a strategic cry, a cry which is fundamental for the economic good of the social group and which is intentionally shouted during the festive practices. Identity is a performance, reaching its climax during the procession of the saints, but always immanent in the lives of the neighbors and effecting their lives. Everything is ephemeral during the festive practices of the North End.

More than ever then, the North End, as well as its identities, is a state of mind, surrounded by water.

Notes

Introduction

1. In March 2008 Caffè Graffiti moved to a different location, but is still in the North End.

2. I use the term "Italian American" regarding the North End because this is the stereotypical idea in the collective imagination of Boston, but of course it is my intent to discuss this label and its historical development. Here, in this introduction, I want just to give the impression of the general feeling concerning the North End.

3. Again, I am using stereotypes to depict the imagery. Stereotypically an American bar is a place to socialize (the American TV series *Cheers* is probably the most famous portrayal of this stereotype), different from the Italian bar where, stereotypically, people spend time for a quick drink or a snack.

4. I was speaking with Guild Nichols (Web master of www.northend boston.com), waiting for Rita Susi (member of Fieri Society, a voluntary society of young Italian Americans). It was not a formal interview but, as I said, a more friendly moment of parting.

5. This sentence is a clear example of code-switching. It is important to point out at least how code-switching can be connected with situational identities, above all when the words or the sentences directly refer to cultural institutions, in this case *comparaggio*, *feast*, or both. "Code-switching provides a means of formulating the relevant social identity to be invoked. But though the languages are symbolic of these identities they are, in accord with their complex associations with these groups, quite multivocal" (Kroskrity 1993, 200).

6. Many scholars have studied ritual kinship. See, for instance, Herzfeld (1986), working in Creta; Pitt-Rivers (1976), studying Spain and the Balkans; and Gudeman (1971), analyzing the *compadrazgo* in Latin America.

7. Symbols, commonly used to switch between multiple identities, are everywhere: we can analyze food, language (as I suggested before), stereotypes, memory, and naming (including personal names, nicknames, and the names of roads and squares). The list is almost endless.

8. I will provide a transnational perspective through comparisons.

9. "Since I must then begin the game/Why, welcome be the cut, and in God's name!/Now let us ride, and hearken what I say."/And at that word we

231

rode forth on our way;/And he began to speak, with right good cheer,/His tale anon, as it is written here.

1. The North End

1. Kathleen Howley, *Boston Globe* correspondent, is the author of this stereotypical description of the North End (November 21, 1998).

2. Montefalcione is a small town in Campania, about twenty miles from Napoli. Sciacca is city-by-the-sea in Sicily, not far away from Palermo. Immigrants from these places constitute the two bigger ethnic enclaves in Boston's North End.

3. According to sociologist Raimondo Strassoldo (1977, 84) it is possible to argue for a distinction between boundary, border and frontier. Even if all indicate the end of a system, a border is zonal or areal, while a boundary is a line. A frontier is a dynamic place where system and environments confront each other (also quoted by Langer 1999, 2). This distinction, not often present in anthropological scholarship, seems to be more appropriate on the macrolevel of nation-states confrontation and more useful for sociopolitical and geopolitical investigations. Arguing the malleability and negotiability of the borders on a microlevel, between a neighborhood and the surrounding city, I assume border as areal, including a dynamic dimension, with the boundary as its icon. Maps are always, according to Herzfeld (1997a, 64), an "important icon of territorial integrity." Therefore, while I am not using the term "frontier," I consider "border" and "boundary," for the specific case of Boston's North End and the microlevel involved, interchangeable terms.

4. The bibliography on anthropology of the border is extensive. See Renato Rosaldo (1985; 1994), Michèle Lamont and Virág Molnár (2002), and Hastings Donnan and Thomas M. Wilson (1999).

5. Geertz defined primordialism in the following way: "By a primordialist attachment is meant one that stems from the '*givens*'—or, more precisely, as culture is inevitably involved in such matters, the *assumed givens*—of social existence: immediate contiguity and kin connection mainly, but beyond them the giveness that stems from being born into a particular religious community, speaking a particular language, or even a dialect of a language, and following particular social practices" (1973, 259).

6. Krieger and Cobb state that "by 1795 the area of Boston peninsula had been increased, primarily by 'wharfing out'—the process of constructing wharves outward from the shore and later filling the slips between them" (2001, 16) An example of "wharfing out" is the progressive filling of the Town Cove, leading to Faneuil Hall and the markets construction areas.

7. *The Book of Possessions* recorded the ownership and transfer of properties. It was published in the Second Report of the Record Commissioners of the

City of Boston, by William H. Whitmore, as quoted in Whitehill and Kennedy (2000, 9).

8. The ridge ran along the track of the actual Causeway Street.

9. The Second Church was the church of the Mathers: Increase, Cotton and Samuel were the pastors. If it is true that their names are widely known because they were intimately connected with witchcraft fear (this is the case of Increase) and Salem's witchcraft trials (Cotton), the Mathers were influential members of the Boston community at large. Increase was the president of Harvard College and Cotton, like his father, was a prodigious author and he was offered the presidency of Yale. Cotton's son, Samuel, became pastor of the Second Church in 1731, but in 1741, following contrasts and profound disagreements with Reverend Joshua Green and being accused of improper conduct, he was dismissed. Samuel left the Second Church with ninety-three of his previous parishioners and founded the Tenth Congregational Church on the corner of North Bennett and Hanover streets. After his death in 1785, with the new parish Reverend John Murray, it became the First Universalist Church (see Todisco 1976, 4).

10. Hudson's Point got its name from Francis Hudson, innkeeper and ferryman (Todisco 1976, 4).

11. As an example of this change I propose Paul Revere's house in North Square, built probably in the 1680s.

12. The contemporary Faneuil Hall, doubled with and a third story, was made in 1805 by Charles Bulfinch.

13. As Rutan (1902, 29) reminds us, toward the end of the eighteenth century six of the wealthiest men of the town were bakers, three of whom (John White, Edward Edes and Deacon Tudor) lived in the North End

14. In 1743 Boston's population was of 16,382 inhabitants, with a slow trend of growth. In 1790 the inhabitants were still only 18,038 (quoted in Whitehill and Kennedy 2000, 47).

15. The filling of Mill Pond started, formally, in 1807, after a long debate and controversies. Only in 1811 could the demolition of the top of Beacon Hill and the filling of the pond be effectively begun.

16. Author's note: The buildings were called Quincy Markets.

17. The "Island of Boston" was connected with the rest of the city, in a complete way, in 1868 with the final dredge of the Great Cove.

18. Epistemologically, my starting point is a postcolonial approach. From this point of view boundaries are determined by the dialectic negotiation between a dominant group and the subaltern ones, where hegemony inevitably plays a fundamental role.

19. The homogeneity of the group ought to be seen not only based on the common religious ground, but, according to Bernard Bailyn in *The New England Merchants in the Seventeenth Century* (quoted in Whitehill and Kennedy 2000, 13), also on the same social and local origins. "Once in America they *(the Puritans)* sought to recreate the life they had know at home. . . .

The list of property owners on Cornhill between Milk and Dock Streets during the first decade reads like the roster of expatriated tradesmen and shop-keepers of the old business district. . . . The settling together of friends and the use of old street names were fragments of the settlers' never-ending attempts to make the wilderness of America familiarly English." Also, quoting Rutan, "that earliest society had a certain ideal character despite its grim defects. The settlers were largely artisans, but they were artisans of unusual quality and intense religious convictions, whose chief ambition was to make homes and establish an ideal state where 'magistrate and minister walked hande in hande, discounte-nancing and punishing sin in whomsoever, and standing for the praise of them that do well'" (1902, 17).

20. As I mentioned before another artificial border was built almost at the same time, in 1643–1644, along the north shore. It is the fortification called the North Battery, also called the Battery Wharf. The functional need for pro-tection from attackers coming from the sea does not overcome the symbolic claim for a specified area, and the consequent identity.

21. *Topographical and Historical Description of Boston*, Massachusetts His-torical Society, Collections, III (1794), 241–304.

22. See http://www.vintagevolumes.com/halloween.html (accessed Feb-ruary 14, 2005).

23. See http://www.massturnpike.com/bigdig/background/history.html (accessed October 16, 2004).

24. Ibid.

25. Ibid.

26. The project, in its whole, expected to redirect the local traffic using the elevated Central Artery, and the through traffic using the Inner Belt, circling Downtown Boston from the South End and Back Bay across the Charles River to Cambridge and Charlestown (ibid.).

27. Ibid.

28. See also Todisco 1976, 52.

29. William F. Whyte (1939, 640) refers to a protest against the City Plan-ning Board to build Lafayette Street, connecting the North End to Charlestown, across the Charlestown Bridge, virtually dividing the North End into two areas. It can be considered an early example of unified trial of negoti-ation with the political power. However this specific threat was undermining the imagined whole of the North End, proposing an inner separation. Instead, the Fitzgerald Expressway and the Central Artery project caused a separation with the rest of the city.

30. The West End was drastically demolished between 1957 and 1959 (see Gans 1962), affecting nine thousand people, in the name of urban renewal (my note).

31. A leading member of this group was Frederick Salvucci, considered by many as the "father" of the Big Dig.

32. *The Boston Transportation Planning Review* is available at http://libraries.mit.edu/rotch/artery/CA_1972.htm (accessed October 16, 2004).

33. See http://www.massturnpike.com/bigdig/background/history.html (accessed October 16, 2004).

34. See http://www.thefreedomtrail.org/home.htm (accessed February 28, 2005).

35. In chapter 5, I will analyze the difficulties and problems of "circumscribing" the feast, which pervades not only the specific moment of the ceremonies but the daily life of the neighborhood. Nevertheless a narrative *gradatio* is evident, reaching the climax during the festival.

36. From the Greek *ephemeros* (*epi*, upon and *hemera*, day).

37. See chapter 4, for the description of the feasts.

38. Unless otherwise noted, all translations are my own.

39. I used the *Oxford English Dictionary* as a basic source.

40. *The Encyclopedia of Ephemera: A Guide to the Fragmentary Documents of Everyday Life for the Collector, Curator, and Historian* by Maurice Rickards et al. (London: The British Library, 2000).

41. I should add even the term "ephemerid," referring to insects commonly called mayflies and, as suggested by the name, ephemerally living during the summertime. The analogy with the festive practices are at least superficially very strong.

2. Diasporas, Ethnic Enclaves, and Transnational Perspectives

1. At the end of the eighteenth century the economic and urban expansion of the city outside the North End, toward Beacon Hill, Back Bay and even to areas previously considered remote, such as Roxbury, became possible thanks to the improved transportations. This can be considered an important prerequisite for the transformation of the neighborhood from an attractive place to a slum.

2. According to Rudolfsky, vernacular is "non pedigreed," "anonymous," "spontaneous," and "indigenous" (1964, 1). Interestingly Krase suggests the term "countrified" to indicate that "even in the urbanized of places, vernacular landscape are part of the lifeof communities which are governed by custom and held together by personal relationship" (2006, 3).

3. Dwight Porter was the author in 1889 of *Report Upon a Sanitary Inspection of Certain Tenement-House Districts of Boston*. It is an account of a survey about the tenements in various wards. In the ward 6 he examined 251 tenements. The report is quoted also in Martellone (1973, 238).

4. This had very dangerous consequences. Porter reported the death rate in this kind of settlement was 1 in 41 inhabitants, while in more healthy neighborhoods the index was raised to 1 in 81.

5. Porter quoted the health condition of a sweatshop examined by the police. The report listed seven German Jews, ten Russian Jews, four Portuguese and six Italians: "from careful observation, the most filth and uncleanliness predominated among the Russian Jews, Italian and Portuguese, the Russian Jews being in the ascendancy so far as regards uncleanliness and filth" (1889, 14–15).

6. Quoted by Chandler (1902, 84).

7. *The North End: A Survey and a Comprehensive Plan—Report of the City Planning Board.*

8. For women the rent was cheaper: $0.50 a week.

9. This slowdown occurred because of two restricting factors: in the United States, the 1921 Immigration Act and, more importantly, the National Origin Act of 1924 (with its discrimination against eastern and southern European nations), and in Italy, Mussolini and the fascist regime allowed only a few to leave Italy for another country.

10. A first analysis of the early settlements all along the Atlantic Coast and the migration movements to the Colony of Massachusetts Bay was offered by Thomas D'arcy McGee (1852, 34).

11. See http://www.bostonfamilyhistory.com/ir_1650.html (accessed March 24, 2005). The practice of indentured servitude was common in Massachusetts, in spite of the relatively small number of Irish immigrants. Cullen (1889, 23) reports the following petition accessed to the authorities, that demonstrates the practice of indentured servitude in Boston:

> The petition of Ann Glyn and Jane Hunter Spinterss Humbly Sheweth: That your Peti.rs lately arrived at Boston from Dublin in Ireland in the Briganteen Ann & Rebecca whereof Thomas Hendry is Master That in Dublin aforsd your Peti.rs agreed to Serve the Said Hendry the Term of Four Years he Transporting them to Boston and he aslo agreeing to provide for and give unto your Petitioners each of then a New Suit of Cloaths for all parts of their Bodys which were Accordingly provided in Dublin and brough over here and since your Peti.rs are disposed of the said Mr. Hendry witholds from and refuses to deliver unto your Petirs their Cloaths according to his promise & Agreement. Your Petitioners therefore humbly pray your honours Consideration on the premises and that the said Master Hendry may be Directed to deliver unto your Petitioners their Cloaths according to his promise and agreement. ANN GLYN x signum, JANE HUNTER x signum. (1889, 23).

12. See http://www.bostonfamilyhistory.com/ir_1650.html (accessed March 24, 2005).

13. As Carlson (2002, 16) rightly affirmed the Goodwin children became the benchmark for the outbreaks that followed.

14. In the eighteenth century, the percentage of Irish Catholic emigrants was definitely small. According to Miller (1985, 137–138) only one-fifth to

one-fourth of the emigrants from Ireland were Catholics. The main reason was the extreme poverty of this part of the Irish population: simply put, they could not afford the cost of the trip and indentured servitude was considered too long and cruel. But they were also discouraged by reports of the pervasive anti-Catholic and anti-Irish feelings. Concerned above all about the Jesuits working in Canada, in 1700, the Massachusetts General Court passed a law forbidding any Catholic priest to stay in Massachusetts (O'Connor 1995, 14).

15. The first Catholic mass in Boston was celebrated Sunday, November 2, 1778, by Father Louis de Rousselet, in the old Huguenot church on School Street (D'arcy McGee, 1852, 18).

16. Nevertheless, anti-Catholic feelings were still present in the Boston area. The climax was reached on August 11, 1834, when a fire was set at the Ursuline monastery of Charlestown. According to Shultz (2000) this episode should be seen as one of numerous outbreaks that occurred in the late 1820s and early 1830s and also as an explosion of ethnic, class and gender tensions. The Ursuline convent was first established near the Cathedral of the Holy Cross, built on land purchased by Bishop Jean Lefebvre de Cheverus at the end of the 1810s. The small convent primarily hosted Irish nuns, and the mission, according to the charter of the order, was to offer free education to poor girls, mostly Irish. In 1828, because of the increased need for space, the convent moved to Charlestown. Changing the location caused a substantial change in the type of woman taken in. Judging from the expenses for the education of the girl—more than $125 a year, which was much more than an Irish family could afford—the residents were no longer poor girls, but now upper-class women, mostly Protestant. This change of policy was probably due not only to the new location but also because offering a fashionable, high and refined education to Protestants in Boston could mean a better acceptance of Catholicism. There were more than fifty girls educated in the convent by 1834. But still the convent was surrounded by a strong anti-Catholic atmosphere, springing from lower social classes. The city was already excited about the tales of Rebecca Reed, who reportedly escaped from the convent and narrated stories of atrocities between those walls, later collected in the book *Six Months in a Convent*, rapidly became popular. Another sparking factor was Sister Mary John, a music teacher at the convent. Probably because of her psychological condition, two weeks before the fire she escaped from the convent, finding shelter in Edward Cutter's house where she refused to meet Bishop Fenwick or her brother Thomas. The day after she agreed to meet both and Thomas took his sister back to the convent. Two days later Cutter was not allowed by the Mother Superior to see Sister Mary, who was sick, but he finally did see her later. Sister Mary assured Cutter that she was not a prisoner and that she could leave the convent at any time, but the rumors that she was being imprisoned against her wishes inside the convent rapidly spread, and were supported by the press. The riot exploded on Monday night, August 11, 1834. The mob was of two hundred.

They allowed the nuns and students to escape but they burned the convent down. Concerned about the possibility of a reaction of the Irish population, Bishop Fenway called for an urgent meeting, with the purpose of mitigating the tension, and asked people to wait for justice. Only eight people, and eventually only three, were charged with arson and burglary and were brought to trial where all of them were found not guilty. The trial concluded with only one sentence, to life. The condemned was Marvin Marcy, a sixteen-year-old boy from New Hampshire, surely a participant of the riot (he burned the bishop's books) but he was not a leader of the mob. The bishop and the mother superior pleaded for him, together with five thousand people, and he was released six months later. This event highlights the social turmoil of Boston in the 1830s. It is not easy, and also incorrect, to try to separate religious reasons from those related to ethnicity or gender or from economic factors. The simultaneous presence of all four factors determined the riot. Anti-Catholic feeling, mixed with the rage of the lower classes against new laborers, who were seen as competitors for the same jobs and who came from a country already detested, was enhanced by the strange and unfamiliar all-female convent. These are the inseparable social factors of the Ursuline convent fire, which not surprisingly happened at a moment when the Irish migration of the first decades of the nineteenth century reached its highest point.

17. It was at first a nativist secret organization. The members were not allowed to reveal anything about the society and for this reason the movement became famous as "Know-Nothing."

18. Smith was an amateur sculptor and according to Handlin personally was not an antagonist of Irish and Catholic. He "associated with them in business and executed a fine bust of Bishop Fitzpatrick" (1941, 202).

19. They were unable to pass these measures due to internal contradictions that did not mitigate widespread racial prejudice.

20. Quoted by O'Connor (1995, 69).

21. According to Jensen (2000, 405–429), it is true that these signs could be used in England and Northern Ireland or could spread out during intense anti-Catholic and anti-Irish periods, such as the period from 1830 to 1870, but the overwhelming evidence is that such signs were never publicly exposed. And even journal advertisements like the previous one were extremely rare. An electronic search of the *New York Times*, from 1851 through 1923, reveals only two classified ads with "No Irish Need Apply" (NINA) for men. But "unlike the employment market for men, the market for female servants included a small submarket in which religion or ethnicity was specified. Thus newspaper ads for nannies, cooks, maids, nurses and companions sometimes specified 'Protestant Only.' . . . Intimate household relationships were delicate matters for some families, but the great majority of maids in large cities were Irish women, so the submarket that refused to hire them could not have been more that ten %" (Jensen, 2002, 407). Jensen's thesis is that "people who 'remember' the signs in the 20th

century only remember the urban legend" (2002, 409). An urban legend flourished after that and the NINA slogan was made famous by a popular song written by John Poole in 1862, describing the lament of the discriminated maid and the attitude of the Irish lad, ready to fight. Jensen's analysis, therefore his results, need to be compared for my area of study at least with the Boston local newspapers, in order to support or disprove the hypothesis. But whether the data confirms or not the presence of a legend over a real discrimination the main issue remains unvaried: the Irish were and felt discriminated against. In other words, the construction of Irishness, the development of a group consciousness based on a self-ascribed ethnic identity, became possible because of the individuation of symbolic borders dividing Irish from resident and superior "Others," also stereotypically qualified by their stereotypes against the Irish themselves. From this perspective the NINA slogan, whether real or a legend, is an example of cultural intimacy (Herzfeld 1997a), defined as aspects of cultural identity that are considered a source of external embarrassment but that nevertheless provide insiders with a shared assurance of common sociality. Surely the NINA slogan was a powerful tool for ethnic identity, probably used consciously and hegemonically also by Irish American leadership to reinforce a nationalistic ideal in order to support the making of an Irish American nation.

22. The data I am analyzing are available on line at http://www.cool lessons.org/ (accessed on April 9, 2005).

23. Family units are easily identifiable: Bourke (Michael and Johana, husband and wife, and also John and Ellen, with their five children), Flannery (Denis and Mary, with their two infants), Froste (James and Ann, and their eight children), Hayes (Mary and Nicholas, their six children and a sister), McNamara (John, his wife and five kids), Ryan (Michael, his wife and ten children), Shannon (James and Ellen, and their two daughters), Sullivan (James and Ellen, and eight sons) are with very high probability family units.

24. The wage of a servant was about $0.05 to $0.10 a day, but the job also included room and board.

25. See http://www.coollessons.org/ (accessed April 9, 2005).

26. See ibid. (accessed April 10, 2005).

27. In Fort Hill the situation was even worse: the Irish population was 42.9 percent, with an average of 16.2 persons per dwelling. The death rate by phthisis was 6.09 per thousand and the death rate by all diseases was 26.3 per thousand.

28. The data is derived from Handlin (1941, 256–257).

29. McGinniskin was reinstated temporarily in service but in 1854 was definitively fired.

30. As I will illustrate, the Irish population in the North End began decreasing in about 1880. One century later a similar situation of ethnic identity negotiated around a church was evident for the Sacred Heart Church, the Italian Parish of the North End. This case is discussed later.

31. It is possible to see in Cole's hypothesis a direct reference to John "Honey Fitz" Fitzgerald. His daughter Rose, future Kennedy, was baptized there, as stated by a sign outside the church.

32. Philanthropic aid to the poor in the North End was offered by the Associated Charities Organization, at the end of the nineteenth century, or the Society of Saint Vincent de Paul, religious associations not immediately recognizable as ethnic.

33. Some of the activities of the Irish societies are listed in Handlin (1951, 155).

34. The Parker House in the Financial District was founded in 1855.

35. Interestingly, Cole (1902, 190–192) highlights the activity of Police Division 1, responsible for the North End and the North Union Station, for the 1901 (December 1900/December 1901): the number of arrests in this division was 4,875 (4,300 males and 575 females). Of these, 3,124 were arrested for drunkenness, 306 for assault, 232 for larceny, 37 for breaking and entering into dwellings and buildings, 77 for offense against chastity, 75 for gaming on the Lord's day, 3 for murder and 6 for manslaughter. Two-thirds of the arrested were from outside Boston. Of the remaining one-third, not less than one-half belong to areas outside the North End, only 825 persons, mostly arrested for drunkenness.

36. The Irish were not the only ethnic group in the North End but by and large was the predominant one.

37. Rabbi Wieder's work is the most extensive research on the Jewish community in the North End. I will refer constantly to this work for my narrative.

38. Wieder noted that besides the basket and the "pack-on-back" peddler there were also "tin-peddler" selling kitchen utensils. The goal for all of them was to acquire a "horse and buggy" so they could carry more merchandise (1962, 28).

39. See Michael Ross, *The Jewish Friendship Trail* (2003), quoted in http://northendboston.com/history4.htm (accessed September 15, 2004).

40. Ibid. (accessed September 16, 2004).

41. Before the building of the synagogues in Baldwin Place, off Salem Street, the first Jewish services in the North End were probably held in the privacy of houses, and often for the High Holidays small temporary congregations could hire a hall.

42. According to Mangione and Morreale (1993) it is possible to characterize a colonial period of Italian migration, certainly not as numerous as the next waves but still evident. In the years 1783–1871, almost twenty thousand Italians, skilled and with the intention to stay, moved to the United States. At this time American perception of Italian immigrants was decidedly mixed: educated Americans saw Italians as artists, political refugees, businessmen, and teachers, while American intellectuals had sympathized with the Italian Risorgimento. But also a negative aspect arose. People read newspaper accounts about the padrone purchasing or stealing poor Italian children and bringing them to the United States as enslaved street musicians. American perception, therefore,

was a multifaceted phenomenon: Italy as a friend of America, birthplace of Dante, land of Garibaldi; but Italian people as immoral and decadent.

43. An interesting analysis of the Genoese (and more in general northern Italian) pattern of migration and settlement, in a very different area—San Francisco—is offered by Gumina (1978).

44. In 1848, Luigi Pastene came to Boston from Italy and began selling produce from a pushcart. By the 1870s Luigi was joined by his son Pietro. Their first food shop was opened in 1874 at 229 Hanover Street and six years later it was moved to 87 Fulton Street (De Marco 1981, 21), then the market section of the neighborhood, inside the Genoese ethnic enclave. The business expanded quickly and by 1901 the shop occupied all the space from 60 to 75 Fulton Street. Nowadays the company is internationally known, based in the United States and Canada.

45. The report entitled "Boston: Immigrazione Italiana," was published in the *Bollettino del Ministero degli Affari Esteri* 26 (1889): 45–265. It is also quoted by Martellone (1973, 203–210).

46. The census of 1880 reported 4,718 Italians in the city of Boston, but the figure included only the Italian-born residents, not the second generation.

47. The sentence is quoted by Martellone from Bushee (1897, 10–13).

48. Donna R. Gabaccia (2001) and Fernando J. Devoto (2006) explore linkages between local and class identities in the formation of a national (or Italian ethnic) identity among Italy's earliest migrants. Both point to Latin America, where over half of Italy's migrants lived in 1870, as an important locus for Italian nation building. In Argentina and southern Brazil, early cross-class alliances built a sense of diaspora nationalism that encompassed artisans, merchants, and political exiles. Gabaccia and Devoto confirm what historians of recent years have also argued—that migrant laborers developed national identities more readily in the diaspora, where natives did not recognize regional differences among them.

49. This distinction was made official by the categories proposed in various census reports. For example, the 1910 Dillingham Commission Report, the popular name of the 1910 *United States Senate Report of the Immigration Commission*, according to De Marco (1981, 35–38) did not include southern Italians in the white race: of the 308 households studied from the Hanover Street District in Boston's North End, only 11 were listed as "native-born heads of households," 3 of them were labeled as belonging to the "white race," as for the others, 1 was English, 1 was German, 4 were Irish, and 2 were southern Italian. Distinction under the category of race was also made between southern and northern Italians in all forty-two volumes. What seems evident is the use of regional or local differentiations historically determined for racial purposes in the receiving country.

50. The changes in population can be explained mainly by the centrifugal flight of the Irish toward new locations and above all toward new social

statuses. The flight was also possible because of the accessibility of new communities such as Roxbury, West Roxbury and Dorchester. According to De Marco (1981, 22) the Metropolitan Street Railway Company and the West End Street Railway Company made it possible for those communities to increase from 60,000 people in 1860 to 227,000 in 1900.

51. See Mangione and Morreale (1993).

52. It is also possible, according to Mangione and Morreale, to see in religion a sense of unity: "If there was a sense of unity for those of the South, it came from Christianity. In Sicilian as well as in many other dialects of the South, the word for 'person' was Christian. Someone coming from Puglia or Sicily in 1890 still considered himself a Christian first, then a member of his community or region. He was hardly aware that he was Italian until he arrived in America" (1993, 34).

53. Another catholic institution was the Portuguese church of Saint John the Baptist on North Bennet Street, replacing an old Protestant meetinghouse, the Free Will Baptist Church.

54. According to *Venticinque anni di missione fra gli immigrati italiani di Boston, Mass., 1888–1913*, published in Milano in 1913 (67–68) and celebrating the Scalabrini mission in the area, three-fifths of the society were Genoese members (called Cicagnini, from the name of a neighborhood in Genoa) and two-fifths came from the rest of Italy.

55. The fabbriceria is a particular way to administrate the property of a church (specifically the budget for the building's maintenance and the cult's expenses), by a specific agency, often not belonging to the clergy.

56. According to Martellone (1973, 269), in 1885, the new society consisted of 420 members. Since this figure only includes heads of households, it is possible to estimate that almost two thousand people were involved, directly or indirectly, with the San Marco Society.

57. The events related to what will be called the Sacred Heart Church are intimately related to the Italian communities in the North End and symbolically can represent the beginning as well as the end of the ethnic group, as I will show in my later discussion about the closure of the church.

58. The letter is reported in Mario Francesconi, ed., *Inizi della Congregazione Scalabriniana (1886–1888)* (Roma: Centro Studi Emigrazione, 1969, and quoted by Martellone (1973, 271–272).

59. Rightly, Martellone (1973, 270) suggests a possible Jansenist connotation of Genoese Catholicism, based on communal participation in the rituals, even as officiants. The *fabbriceria* system can also be seen as an example of this tendency.

60. Giovanni Battista Scalabrini (1839–1905), bishop of Piacenza from 1876 to his death, dedicated his life and his mission (evangelization of the poor and of the workers) to the emigrants. His approach to the social question of poor masses of workers leaving their own country, supported—and this will be a

characteristic of the congregations he founded—by a scientific approach to the social phenomena, can be illustrated by a famous sentence: "freedom to emigrate but not freedom to force or to induce people to emigrate." On November 28, 1887, he organized the Congregazione dei Missionari di San Carlo (also known as the Scalabrini fathers) in order to assist the emigrants spiritually and materially. Also politically active, he asked in 1878 for an emigration law and in 1901 the Italian government approved a law banning the so-called *agenti di emigrazione* (brokers of workers and migration). An important figure, very close to Scalabrini, was the already mentioned Francesco Zaboglio, sent by the Vatican in 1887 with the purpose of founding Italian parishes in New York and Boston.

61. The complete sentences is analyzed in Chapter 5.

62. The first newspaper of the Italian colony in Boston was *The Corriere di Boston*, founded in 1893 by Gaetano Stabile. It was centered on chronicles of Italian events.

63. Felicani preserved the Sacco and Vanzetti papers, donated to the Boston Public Library.

64. *Gazzetta del Massachusetts*, III 35, August 19–20, 1905. Also quoted in Martellone (1973, 389).

65. After the murder of Anna Lo Pizzo, killed by the police during the strike, three Italians—Caruso, Ettor and Giovannitti—were arrested. A committee was formed for the defense of the three men but all the Italian community, from Lawrence to Boston, were involved in supporting their fellow countrymen. Even the moderate *Gazzetta del Massachusetts*, generally against the strikes and the unions, supported the defense.

66. The change from a foreign to a bilingual newspaper was necessary because of the increasing numbers of American-born second- and even third-generation Italians, and also because of the general American suspicion of subversion hidden through alien languages.

67. In 1933, the Paul Revere Mall, called the Prado by the residents, was constructed on Hanover Street.

68. In the 1920s, two big events showed the tendency for ethnic declaration: the success of Rudolf Valentino, the movie star from Puglia, and, in 1927, the funerals of Sacco and Vanzetti in the North End.

69. The source is Greater Boston Community Council, *The People of Boston and Its Fifteen Health and Welfare Areas*, published in 1944, and based on the 1940 census.

70. George Simmel, "The Persistence of Social Groups," *American Journal of Sociology* 3 (March 1898): 662–698; 3 (May 1898): 829–836; 4 (July 1898): 35–50.

71. Not only blood ties were important in the idea of family but also the symbolic connections. Symbolic kinship as *Compare* and *Comare* (godfather and godmother) as Campbell (1964) demonstrated, are a strong component of the family, providing care and solidarity to the individual.

72. The spectacular Brinks robbery in the 1950s in Prince Street was a stereotype hard to destroy. Even though the robbers were not from the North End, for a long time the neighborhood continued to be associated with crime.

73. From a juridical perspective, it is interesting the idea of Italian immigrants as "nonvisibly black," suggested by Richards (1999), within the context of European and American racism.

74. Central Boston Data Profile, Department of Neighborhood Development Policy Development and Research Division, 2004.

75. See www.northendboston.com/living (accessed February 25, 2003).

76. The concept of ascriptions as a critical feature for ethnic groups is suggested by Fredrik Barth (1969, 14).

77. The complete text of Archbishop Sean O'Malley's discourse on reallocation and reconfiguration was available at http://reab.org/News/archbishop BCTV040204.html (accessed June 12, 2004).

78. Ibid.

79. The timetable for reconfiguration was available at http://rcab.org/Parish_ Reconfiguration/FAQ.html (accessed June 12, 2004).

80. The cluster meeting "included representatives from each parish: the Pastor, a member of the Parish Pastoral Planning Council, a member of the Parish Finance Council, and a member of the parish staff. The number of representatives from a parish may have varied since many parishes sent a few more than the required number of both staff and lay people. About 1,800 lay people attended cluster meetings and about 340 priests" (ibid.).

81. Fredda Hollander, "Boston's Central Cluster to Recommend Two Churches for Closure," *The Regional Review*, March 16, 2004, p. 11.

82. Boston's central cluster annex was Sacred Heart Church.

83. The complete vivid sentence was "They Want to Close Our Sacred Heart Church. Over Our Dead Bodies. The Italian Community." This was written on one of the many signs protesting the closure of the parish.

84. Saint Mark's Society played an important role in this complex event. In 1890, the society placed Sacred Heart in trust with the archdiocese. And the trust remains intact over the years, until the present situation.

85. Reported by Fredda Hollander, "North Enders Seek to Save Sacred Heart Church," *The Regional Review*, March 30, 2004.

86. Saint Leonard, on the opposite, is no longer an Italian church, officially giving up this status in 1995, it is a neighborhood parish and the priests depend on the archdiocese.

87. The *Post-Gazette* (formerly *La Gazzetta del Massachusetts*) is traditionally the North End's most popular newspaper.

88. See, for instance, Mary Baumgartner, *The Moral Order of the Suburb* (New York: Oxford University Press, 1988) about the phenomenon and its consequences on social interactions.

89. The importance of the ethnic food business in the North End is easily demonstrated. The concentration of restaurants in an area of not even one hundred acres is impressive: at the end of February 2008, eighty-six restaurants, eight bars and pubs, four coffeeshops, seven home delivery businesses, two catering businesses, and eight bakeries were active in the neighborhood. (See www.northendboston.com, accessed February 25, 2008).

3. The Societies of Saints

1. In my fieldwork I worked with many members of several societies. More intensively I had contact with four religious societies: the Madonna del Soccorso (the Fishermen from Sciacca, Sicily), the Saint Anthony of Padua and Saint Lucy (the male and female organizations from Montefalcione, Campania), and the Santa Maria (from Anzano, Puglia). At the time of my fieldwork the societies of saints still active in the North End were the following: Madonna Di Anzano, Society of St. Jude Thaddeus, Societá San Giuseppe Di Riesi (Saint Joseph Society), St. Agrippina Di Mineo Society, Madonna Della Cava Society, Maria delle Grazie Society, St. Rocco Society, St. Domenic Society, St. Lucy Society, The Fisherman's Society (Madonna Del Soccorso di Sciacca), San Antonio Di Padova Da Montefalcione, Santa Rosalia Di Palermo Society.

2. Robert Orsi (1984, xiv) uses the concept of religion of the streets to broaden and deepen the understanding of the phenomenon of popular religion that he saw as narrow and limited. I agree with Orsi about the necessity to fully analyze the concept. I am using the term "popular" here only because I need to contextualize the phenomenon historically and geographically (Italy after the World War II, and the scholarly approach of Carlo Levi).

3. Zemon Davis is not alone in this approach. Analogous positions are expressed also by Schmitt (1976) and Ginzburg (1977), as Zardin (2001, 48–49) reminds us.

4. An approach to southern Italian religious sensibility, in my opinion, should be much more complex. As always, the risk of stereotyping and labelling people and groups is very high. Here, I can only assume the same position, but I hope to do justice to the actual complexity of the situation in another publication.

5. The American Catholic hierarchy attempted to address the "Italian problem" at the Council of Baltimore in 1884, but the Holy See decided on a more informal approach. In 1887, Bishop Scalabrini promoted an order of Italian priests helping Italian emigrants, and in 1888, Pope Leon XIII sent a letter to the American bishops pleading the cause of Italians in America. By 1905, the Scalabrini priests were operating in twenty parishes in the United States. See the previous chapter for more on the Scalabrini.

6. For more information about Conte's mission in Boston see his autobiography (1903).

7. He founded *L'amico del popolo*, a newspaper in English and Italian, criticizing the local Italian *prominenti*, and stigmatizing the well-known "padrone system."

8. The Società per la Protezione degli Immigrati Italiani became the Benevolent Aid Society in 1904.

9. The activities of the Methodist mission in the neighborhood slowed down in the 1910s. In 1920, the church of Salutation Street was inaugurated, but in 1949, after the property was sold by the New England Conference in the same year, the First Italian Methodist Church merged with the First Methodist Church of Temple Street in the West End (Martellone 1973, 461).

10. The first settlement house in Boston was the Andover House in the South End, founded by Robert Woods in 1891. The mission of the settlement houses was a sort of social utopist Christianity, in order to help workers and migrants to be assimilated in the United States.

11. *Report of the Italian Department of Denison House*, 1911–1912, Boston, also quoted in Martellone (1973, 477).

12. An example can be seen in the attacks against the Boston Italian Immigrant Society (BIIS) in 1903. The formal motivation was, according to Martellone (1973, 410), the *umiliazione immeritata* (undeserved humiliation) suffered by the other societies because the manager of BIIS was Eleanor Collection, an Irish woman. But the real target was the almost exclusive economic help supplied by the Italian Consulate to BIIS.

13. Saint Anthony and Saint Lucy, the male and female societies both declaring their common Montefalcionese heritage, share the same place on Endicott Street. Rent and general costs are handled by the Saint Anthony Society, and many of the social activities of Saint Lucy involve the other society, such as barbecues and parties.

14. *Disemia* can be defined as "the formal or coded tension between official self-presentation and what goes on in the privacy of collective introspection" (Herzfeld 1997a, 14). It differs from *diglossia* (linguistic term referring to the two "registers" of a national language: the formal idiom used for official purposes and the ordinary speech of everyday life), expanding its narrowly linguistic frame to a more complex semiotic continuum.

15. I am using the St. Anthony Society as an example. This pattern is evident in all the societies of Boston's North End.

16. Mary Jo Sanna's report was made for the Massachusetts Cultural Council, Folk and Traditional Arts Program. I thank Maggie Holzberg, director of the program, for the opportunity to use the unpublished data.

17. The consultants referred to the procedure for the admittance of new members.

18. For instance, during an interview with Mary Jo Sanna in January 1988, Anthony Abruzzi, a member of the Saint Anthony Society, reported the changes taking place within the societies over the time, described as "democratization" in

the process of running the feasts and the societies. Another member of the Saint Anthony Society, Rocky Papa, talking about another example of supposed democratization, said, "the old-timers used to allow people to bid to carry the saint, which allowed members with money to have a monopoly on this honor" but now they allow everyone who wants to carry to do it, even non members. The bidding is a well known and widely diffused tradition in southern Italy, and it is a very complex festive behaviors. From my fieldwork in Montefalcione in Italy for the Saint Anthony feast in 2002, I can argue that it is certainly true that allowing the bid for the honor to carry the statue of the saint ratifies social hierarchy. It seems inevitable that members of wealthy classes are more likely to win the auction, and to carry the statue with all the social and moral effects that this can produce. But the bid also allows temporary, and sometimes winning strategic alliances between families, peer or friendship groups. So the bid became a social challenge where, through negotiated agreements, it becomes possible to subvert a given social order, if only momentarily and if only during the special time of the feast. In other words, like the carnival, such temporary and symbolic social subversion is possible only during temporal and symbolically framed festive time. It is basically an oxymoronic ritual transgression: being allowed and framed by a revolutionary potentiality.

19. Interestingly, since the society is morally based, in the case of sexually transmitted diseases or if the disease is a consequence of bad behavior or voluntary hazards, members could lose the right for medical benefits.

20. I will analyze, talking about the festival, the different perceptions by Italian Americans and young urban people about the feast.

21. Bosco is the nickname of Sal Diecidue, president of the Madonna del Soccorso Society.

22. I am not exploring here other dynamics, which I assume as present, but as more elusive and subtle, and more related, for instance, to personal dynamics.

23. By group I do not refer necessarily to formally structured cluster, but to more blurred and dynamic aggregations of individual, ephemerally constituted for strategic reasons.

24. A similar example, but of different degree, is the presence of Anzano's priest attending the Santa Maria feast for the celebration of the centenary. More than a religious confirmation the presence of the priest seems to be an example of transnationalism.

25. It is interesting to note how other ethnic enclaves clustered in time around Montefalcione's identity: emigrants from Lapio, Montemarano and other villages nearby gradually "confused" themselves within the Montefalcione ethnic unity, as seen on a major scale. Other neighbor villages such as San Sossio del Sannio or San Michele Baronia behaved differently: both the related ethnic enclaves still run their feasts, even if in reduced scale.

26. Emilio Matarazzo was a very famous craftsman in the North End, building temporary chapels, stands and lights.

27. There is always a risk, as Weber (1985, 7) suggested, to speak about residuum, about survivals existing within a social institution where secularization has still not penetrated deeply, particularly when this supposed residuum remains one of the most powerful components of conduct (*Lebensführung*).

28. The concept of demonization of others comes from Sigmud Freud, *Group Psychology and the Analysis of the Ego* (New York, Norton, 1959).

4. The Festive Practices

1. The term "social location," according to Moya (1999, 70), is a nexus of gender, class, race, ethnicity, sexuality etc. in which every individual exists in the world.

2. Talking about "Big" or "Little" Saint Anthony I am using the local, emic, distinction. It refers to attendances and economic dimension. Arguably the "Big Saint Anthony," with the feast of Madonna del Soccorso, is the most important event in the calendar of the feast not only for the North Enders but also for tourists.

3. The Maria Santissima del Buon Consiglio was a religious society still active in 1981, at the time of De Marco's fieldwork. Some societies, like Saint Rita and Madonna della Provvidenza, are active but they do not perform any procession or feast.

4. An exception is Saint Calogero whose feast can be celebrated because he belongs to an already formed ethnic enclave, the Sciaccatani. The other exception, and I will analyze the specific reasons, is Saint Jude, a society founded in 1983. But as I stated before, the calendar seems to be mostly stable from at least the 1980s.

5. Following the official calendar of the saints, the festivity of Saint Anthony of Padua is June 13, but in the North End the feasts are concentrated over the weekend when people can more easily participate.

6. *Paranza* is a term borrowed from the southern Italian sailors' slang. It comes from the dialect *paro*, which means "couple" and indicates two fishing boats proceeding together and using the trawl net. It also indicates a specific boat, typical of the central Adriatic. By extension the term designates a group of people working together for the same goal. *Capoparanza* is the leader of the group.

7. Luigi Barzini stated that "both men and women know that it is the woman who runs the household and carries the main burden of the moral responsibility. Men run the country, but women run the men. Italy is, in reality, a crypto matriarchy" (1964, 202).

8. The issue of attitudinal change in male/female roles is precisely addressed, in a different context, by Gutmann (1996; 2003) in his analysis of Latin American machismo.

9. This refers to the old sociological tradition from Edward C. Banfield, *The Moral Basis of a Backward Society* (Glencoe, IL: Free Press, 1958). See, just as one of the many critiques, Alessandro Pizzorno, "Amoral Familism and Historical Marginality," in *European Politics: A Reader*, ed. Mattei Dogan and Richard Rose (Boston: Little, Brown, 1971, 87–98).

10. It is not unusual in Italy for the clergy to prohibit or try to control the musical performances during the feasts: an example is the prohibition of the *tammurriata* in front of the religious icon or in the churchyard during the Marian pilgrimages in the Neapolitan area. The tammurriata is a dance based on a rhythm generated by the frame drum called *tammorra*. Musician, dancers and singers used to perform the tammurriata in honor of the Madonna but the clergy often prohibited this cultural institution because it is considered profane and even insulting to the religious ritual. Instead, it ought to be considered a form of folk religiosity. Another example is the *canto a figliola*, a specific kind of song addressing the Madonna directly, in form of a "profane prayer." The songs, whose lyrics often talk about miracles, votive offerings or simply the majesty of the Madonna, were performed inside the church, in front of the main icon. It was and still is a matter of argument between priests and faithful: the priest trying to stop the performance and the faithful insisting on approaching the icon inside the church.

11. The names mean: "Marcia Reale," because this was the march of the Italian royal family, and "Numero 1," because it was the first score in the musical book for the marching band.

12. See chapter 3 for the analysis of these relationships.

13. "Mamma" is a popular song, written by C. A. Bixio and B. Cherubini in 1940 and sung by Beniamino Gigli.

14. Interestingly, Orsi (1996) hypothesizes how the devotion to Saint Jude was peculiarly female. The cult of Saint Jude helped immigrant Catholic women face the difficulties of living in a foreign land at the time of the Depression.

15. This is the reason why I have resisted using the term "informant" in this writing. Many of these people should be termed "friends" or at minimum "consultants." In other words again I am not implicitly or explicitly claiming any supposed necessary distance between components of an ethnographic observation: distance or proximity is a matter between people meeting in the field. Back then my relationship with Salvi was still characterized by my confusion of being (or being seen as) an outsider/insider.

16. He was not the capoparanza (the leader) of the procession but one of the members appointed to hold the poles of the platform to maintain balance during the walk.

17. I had noticed in my first days of fieldwork in the United States the specific attention that media gave to fires and to firemen's conduct. I had dismissed it as a sort of paranoia connected to the ease of fire diffusion, since there were so many wooden houses rather than brick buildings, so usual in Italy. Seldom in

Italy are fires and firemen seen on the front pages of newspapers or as breaking news in television.

18. I thank Luigi Trigilio for his support and information about the San Domenico's feast in Augusta, Italy.

19. The tale of Saint Domenico's miracle says that the saint appeared to the Arabian army galloping on a white horse, with a sword in his hand and threatening the enemies.

20. Money can no longer be pinned on statues during the Italian religious feasts because of a decision made by the Conferenza Episcopale Italiana (Italian Episcopal Conference), prohibiting this form of devotion. Meanwhile pinning money remains an important devotional moment in Boston's North End and it is definitely a common pattern of the local feasts.

21. San Giuseppe (Saint Joseph) is the patron saint of Riesi, a village not too far from Caltanissetta, in Sicily.

22. Letter of John M. Regan, an influential member of the society, received from the author during the feast.

23. The cost of a one-day feast is basically determined by the expense for the marching band (generally one) and by a small amount of taxes. The Little Saint Anthony had a budget of three or four thousand dollars as I was told by the promoters, and the committee expected to raise the money during the procession. A three-day feast is much more expensive, with strong variation. Big feasts like the Madonna del Soccorso or the Big Saint Anthony can cost between sixty thousand and one hundred thousand dollars. Entertainment, several marching bands, and prizes and awards are important expenses. Even if during the procession the saint "raises a lot of money"—this was the expression used by Sal Bosco, the president of Fishermen-Madonna del Soccorso Society—it is not enough. (Sal told me that the procession could "raise" no more than thirty thousand dollars to thirty-five thousand dollars). Sponsors, raffles and vendors were supposed to cover the rest.

24. The picture is the "official" group photo of the seventy-fifth anniversary of the feast. I was asked by Rocco, the president, to shoot the photograph, waiting for the professional photographer, who came later.

25. Thomas Menino, third generation from Grottaminarda, near Napoli, is one of the most important Italian American politicians in Boston's area.

26. The leitmotif of the procession is, again and again, respect and homage paid to and by the Saint.

27. See http://www.saintagrippina.com/ (accessed September 19, 2005).

28. The Sicilian flag has a female face (Gorgona) on the *triskele* (with three legs), representing the three promontories of the island. The flag was used for the first time in 1282 after the Vespri riots and it was formally approved by the Sicilian Parliament in January 2000.

29. The claim for independence started in the thirteenth century riots in Palermo during the ceremony of the *Vespri* (vespers) to more recent struggles

against the Napoleonic regime in the 1810s or the anti-Bourbons insurrection. The most turbulent times were during the unification of the country, when Sicilians fought against Garibaldi's army and against representatives of the newly formed state, and during World War II. In 1943, a political movement began blending left-wing and right-wing positions, and after the mafia involvement, assumed a more reactionary aspect, beginning with an armed insurrection against the fascist regime and the monarchy, then against the republic. The role of mafia in the late separatist movement is peculiar and involves the United States: because they gave direct help to the American army's landing in Sicily at the end of the war, the mafia asked for and expected more support from the United States for their independence. Then, because of the strong connections with Italian Americans, the mafia supported the so-called Sicilia 49th Star movement, a movement aimed at attaining union with the United States.

30. Societies with numerous members (for instance the Saint Joseph of Riesi Society) still seem not to differentiate membership, showing stereotypical differences through roles and rules, above all during the feast (different uniforms, different functions).The San Domenico Society, for instance, is an interesting example of how a nondifferentiated membership can allow on one hand the election of a woman as president, while on the other hand during the procession maintaining the clearly evident gender-based distinctions.

31. As Magrini (1998) recalls, the idea of the Mediterranean as a territory characterized by specific cultural traits (honor and shame, and its related respect), was introduced in anthropology at the end of the 1950s by Peristiany (1966; 1976) and Pitt-Rivers (1963). In this supposed cultural area the dominant "mode of thought" seemed to be based on a binary opposition, gender-based: honor, associated with men; and shame, associated with women. Scholars have argued about the idea of a Pan-Mediterranean area (see Boissevain 1979, 81–82, but also Gilmore 1987, supporting the idea) and, mostly, about the consistence of the honor/shame opposition (Herzfeld 1987; Markus 1987;). According to Pina-Cabral (1989) the concepts do not appear in every country of the supposed area, while they appear in different localities and may sometimes be considered obsolete (Davis 1987).

32. I thank Father Valdini for his courtesy and for his precise explanations.

33. Recently Father Valdini started the ritual opening of the door of the chapel at the beginning of the feast, but any kind of similarity seems to be abstract and generic.

34. Noise and fire are, in southern Italian tradition, two symbolic elements used to exorcise evil spirits.

35. In different interviews I listened to complaints because it was not possible to use fireworks "in the Italian way." The only exception I found is the feast of the Madonna del Soccorso. Near the end of the procession a large amount of fireworks were exploded, from North Square. It was, for what I was told by Sal "Bosco," a reason for pride, because "fireworks make the feast bigger."

36. The stereotypical example of dance with the platform is the *Giglio*, celebrated in Nola, near Napoli, but also in Williamsburg, Brooklyn, in honor of Saint Paolino, a dance performed by dozens of bearers carrying a sort of heavy steeple while the band plays music. The music played for this dance is in general fast and well known, not sacred hymns or religious songs. The faithful try to show their ability in this very specific form of prayer.

37. The Madonna della Cava Society promptly agreed to participate at the rally in 2004 against the archdiocese decision to close the Sacred Heart parish, together with many other societies.

38. The captain is in general a senior member who reached a position of authority in the society. Respect to the captain is shown by junior members but also by the president, respecting his wishes.

39. Abruzzi refers to the Fishermen. I already quoted another interview with Jerry telling the story of the end of the fights (see chapter 3). In 1957 (for Abruzzi, in 1952) the procession started to reach even North Street.

40. In chapter 3 I have already quoted this episode, referred to by Jerry.

41. They were bought in occasion of the invitation by the Smithsonian Institute in Washington, DC, to attend the summer programs concerning the representation of immigrants' ethnic customs.

42. The Matarazzo Italian Company is responsible also for the light and the decorations of Saint Anthony feast in Montefalcione.

43. The uniform was not the same every year: in different years of the feast members wore light brown shirts and pants.

44. In confirmation I underline that Santa Rosalia September feast is celebrated annually also in the *Benson Hurst* section of *Brooklyn, New York*.

45. See http://travel.yahoo.com/p-reviews-2883935-prod-travelguide-action-read-ratings_and_reviews-i (accessed October 2, 2005).

46. The iconography of the saint is fully respected. She appears to the hunter, with the skull (to bring to mind the transfer of her human remains, the book (of knowledge) and the rose (Rosalia was the daughter of Sinibaldo, prince of Quisquinia and of the Roses).

47. Before its move to Cutter Street in Somerville, the society had a club on Prince Street in the North End.

48. At present time Anzano is formally in Apulia, therefore the dialect it is supposed to be Apulian. But this is just an administrative oddity since the town more close to Avellino, not too far from Naples, therefore in Campania. People migrating from Anzano at the beginning of the twentieth century rightly could consider themselves as Neapolitan, and linguistically they spoke (and they still speak) a variant of Neapolitan dialect.

49. A structural, more general, reason women are an important part of the society is because cults about Madonna, especially those developed in the late nineteenth century in southern Italy, assembled and organized the already existing female devotions. Popular cults of different Madonnas spread rapidly and

deeply: new cults, such as Madonna of Pompei or reinvigorated cults such as Madonna delle Grazie, and those of all the female saints saw the growing active participation of women.

50. See http://en.wikipedia.org/wiki/Roch (accessed January 9, 2006).

51. I am grateful to Father Antonio Nardoianni for introducing me to members of the two societies.

52. I thank Lina Ciccone, president of the Madonna delle Grazie Society, for information and data.

53. I have observed the feast of San Giuseppe in Riesi in 2003 and Santa Rosalia in Palermo in 2004.

54. My note: Ciciolo is probably a misspelling or a misprint for Circolo (Circle)

55. Another piece of evidence concerns the liturgical calendar: St. Anthony is generally venerated June 13 (this is the reason why the Montefalcionesi prayed to him during the earthquake of 1688). When I asked why they used to celebrate St. Anthony so far from his dedicated day, many members of the society answered "because it is tradition" and they don't link the date with any hagiographic legend of foundation.

56. The letter is reprinted in the newspaper *Il Ponte* (August 8, 1988).

57. The date refers to the granted grace for the celebration of the feast the last Sunday of August.

58. The following spell—in between magic and religion, surely belonging to a more popular religious behavior—demonstrates how the saint can be prayed to by an individual for an individual purpose: "Sand'Andonie de Paduve/che de Paduve avenite/tridece grazji'a Ddi' cerchiste/tutt'a ttridece l'aviste/Facite 'na grazij'a mmè/pe le cinghe piaghe re Ggesù Criste/" [Saint Anthony of Padua/who came from Padua/thirteen graces you asked God/and you received all/do me a grace/for the five wounds of Jesus Christ/] (Pagliuca and Cuciniello, 1990, 171).

59. I am not comfortable with the distinction between the sacred and profane aspects of the rituals, as I will show in the last chapter of this work.

60. Mary Jo Sanna, interviewing Rocky Papa, in 1987, asked him if people used to pay to carry the statue: "I ask, but people don't pay to carry him. They say years ago they used to do that, but years ago they used to bid for it" (1988, 21).

61. There is no a formal distinction between church and sanctuary, in the ecclesiastic catholic code (*Rituale Romanun, Paoli V pont. max. iussu editum et a Benedicto XIV auctum et castigatum cui novissima accedit benedictionum et instructionum appendix—1894/1898*), even if it is a necessary formal declaration, by the dioceses. The specific character of a sanctuary is connected with a specific sacred space where a specific manifestation of the sacred is performed, such as the pilgrimage. In other words, topography and specific cult are strongly connected.

62. Naturally this apparent democracy needs to be analyzed more deeply. I assume that the membership of this committee is controlled by social norms, rules and roles. At this point of my research I do not have enough information yet to comment.

63. The president does this operation, but often he delegates other members or even the same faithful. This does not reduce his authority.

64. As I mentioned earlier, in recent years this general rule seems to be less fundamental: now the society accepts Italian Americans, generally speaking, regardless of the village of origin.

65. From the booklet *The Madonna del Soccorso di Sciacca Society: 91st Annual Fisherman's Feast, 2001.*

66. See www.fishermen.com (accessed December 12, 2005).

67. The definitions of "orthodoxy" and "orthopraxy" I am using here as a starting point comes from *Webster's Third International Dictionary of the English Language.*

68. The problematic notion of belief has been addressed by many scholars. For instance (and it will be just an illustrative list), Leach (1996), stressing on its metaphoric aspect; Needham (1972), suggesting and arguing the opacity of this experience; Sperber (1997), proposing the distinction between intuitive and reflective beliefs; and Herzfeld (1997a), highlighting belief as ultimately and irreducibly private. More recently, the problem of belief was discussed by Kirsch (2004), showing religious practices as cyclically regenerating a condition of internalized "believing."

69. A few examples of analysis of orthodoxy in anthropological perspective are: the role of writing and standardization in the making of orthodoxy has been studied, for instance, by Goody (1986). Schipper (1985) analyzed the different strategies for the use of written or oral texts in rituals. Furthermore, Gager (1975) suggested the emerging of orthodoxy in a context of challenging and contending set of ideas.

70. More specifically *Imitatio Christi* (Imitation of Christ, also called Following Christ) refers to specific practices of devotions, in accordance to a widely read spiritual book, *De Imitatione Christi*, presumably written in 1418 by Thomas à Kempis. It can be considered a guide to salvation toward a perfect communion with God, through meditation of the life and teaching of Jesus and the practice of self-renunciation.

71. Susan Naquin (1988) illustrates how in northern China the liturgical expertise, defining doxa and praxy, can be undermined by coexisting, not replacing, texts specially printed by nonspecialist member of the public. Staal (1983), in his study of the Nabudiri Brahmins (southwest India), argues the independence of oral and textual tradition. Again, in Boston's North End orthopraxy is produced by the dynamic interplay between official self-presentation and intimate introspection.

72. See for instance Reed-Danahay (1993)—specifically her notion of *debrouillardise*—Abu-Lughod (1990), and Herzfeld (2005).

5. Ephemeral Identities

1. Turner and Durkheim were very aware of the possibility of rebellion in ritual performance. In fact, this is the whole point of Turner's analysis of the sequence of ritual, which may end either in reintegration or in the formation of a new, alternative synthesis. And for Durkheim the ultimate paradigm for collective ritual was the French revolution!

2. Rituals of making noise with drums or any kind of objects was performed to keep evil spirits out in all the Mediterranean areas.

3. See, for instance, Robert Isbell (1996).

4. As quoted by Guss (2000, 9).

5. I feel very close to Leach's (1962) critique of Durkheim's antagonism of sacred and profane, even if he underlined how they are intermingled. Leach's approach to ritual, while underlining the ritual aspects of any kind of action, is a prelude in my opinion to my idea of ritual as discrete locations, immanent every moment of everyday life.

6. See also Guss (2000, 15).

7. See Eco (1996) about the complexity of mirror's games, images and symbols

8. I am taking into consideration not only the formal processes of preparation of the performances, as studied for instance by Korom (2003) in Trinidad for the Hosay performances, especially concerning the building of the *Tadjahs*, the painstaking reconstruction of the tombs, but the informal flux of communication about the ritual.

9. This "official" language can derive also from a larger and characteristic language of meetings and serves mainly to indicate to the group the importance of what they are doing, therefore marking their actions off from the everyday. Still the official language is an instrument of separation between leadership and members.

10. This is the case of Bestor suggesting that the festival he was attending was "examined here less as religious event than as a social occurrence, a secular ritual" (1989, 225).

11. These different sources are traceable privileging an approach that is not only historically oriented but also derived from the direct observation of the actual performances. Again, the feast is an utterance intertextually and polyphonically informed.

12. I assume synecdoche to be referring to the substitution of the part for the whole or of the whole for the part.

13. It is important to state that the two different contexts are still occasionally in contact, even if lately this seems to be an emergent trend.

14. Lewis analyzed puberty rites practiced by New Guinea villagers. His work is also quoted by Watson (1988, 5).

15. In my fieldwork I saw just one exception to this display of local authorities during the Saint Anthony of Padua of Montefalcione's feast. The

priest holding the relic of the saint came not from the village but from Padua, the center of general devotion. It does not confirm a diasporic moment but certainly reaffirms the transnational aspect of the feast.

16. See also Robert Orsi (1992).

17. See http://www.anzanoboston.com/ (accessed October 1, 2005).

18. Or creolization.

19. I have to underline that in my experience of research I did not notice references to further identities, for instance the European. The constitutive process of this political supernational reality seems not to be perceived as yet.

20. A seminal work on the linguistic metaphor of creolization is Drummond (1980), applying the concept of "intersystem" (Bickerton 1975) to illustrate the dynamics of ethnic designations in Guyana. See also Fabian (1978).

21. Basically a metaphor (from the Greek *metaphorá*, from *metaphérein*, meaning to carry, or, better, to transfer) works in order to discover similarity in dissimilar things. This is, roughly, Aristotle's meaning. Traditionally, and following a philological approach more close to the etymological meaning, a definition can be: replacement of one word with another which in a literal sense has some resemblance with the literal sense of the substituted word. Finally, contemporary rhetoric, with scholars like Northop Frye and the so-called Group μ (see Mortara Garavelli 1976), underline the ambiguity of metaphor, or better, its polyvalence.

22. Korom (2003, 11). The supposed emic reason is certainly valid in the specific case and in the specific field—Trinidad—being creole a term coined by Caribbeanist. I doubt if I can use the same justification in a different situation.

23. Rightly Favero (2005, 148) highlights the resonance of organic hybridity with Lotman's notion of "semiosphere" (2001), characterized by an oscillation between identity and alterity in a constant process of reciprocal influence, transformation and coexistence.

24. See, for instance, Brubaker and Cooper (2000).

25. Azzurro (sky blue) is the official color of the Italian national soccer team jersey.

26. The Bruins is the name of Boston's hockey team.

27. "The Roma Band was founded in Boston in 1919 by Italian immigrants. The purpose of the band was and is to play at religious feasts in Boston's North End. The band has played continuously except during the War Years (1942–1945) when the North End was used as a military area and due to the fact that Italy was then an enemy. Rumor has it that most of the players suddenly became Portuguese and simply walked over to the neighboring city of Cambridge. (Portugal was a neutral country.) What makes the band especially interesting is that the feasts held now more mirror the traditional feast once held in Italy during the days of the King. Money is pinned upon sacred icons as it is lowered from windows. A prepared donation is called a calendar which can contain hundreds of dollars. Sometimes money is lowered in rolls while the

band continuously plays hoping inside that the money will end (as their lips tire) while the society hopes it never ends. The band will traditionally play the "Marcia Reale" when a significant gift is offered. This form of feast is no longer performed or condoned in modern Italy. In 1988 the band went to Washington, DC, to play in a cultural event for the Smithsonian Institution" (www.romaband.com (accessed September 19, 2005).

28. This kind of secular blessing can be seen in the United States in almost every event, especially sporting events.

29. This is naturally an oversimplified approach in terms of power because of the strong church-state relationship. More accurately the absence of the national anthem is, in my opinion, another example of hegemony where the separation between the secular and religious power is elicited for purposes of consent. Being devoted to the religious institution, far from being a moment of secular transgression, is a form of subjection to the dominant class.

30. The fascist attitude toward emigration and foreign policy is complex and has changed over the time. It is possible to underline that after a first period of supporting migrations, related to the American Immigration Acts, Mussolini proposed the so called assisted emigration, as a political reason for his colonial project.

31. According to Okamura (1981, 455) sociological discussion on ethnicity focuses on ascription by others, privileging the structural dimension of situational ethnicity invoking and evoking constrains of actor's behavior in the labeling process. But we should also consider the actor's subjective perception of the situation.

32. The concept of "hypertext" was foreseen in 1945 by Vannevar Bush, creator of a microfilm reader based on key word accessing and processing information, a sort of interactive library, called "Memex."

33. Landow (1992, 3–4) recognizes the importance of Barthes's approach to the development of the idea of hypertext.

Bibliography

Abrahams, Roger. 1986. "Ordinary and Extraordinary Experience." In *The Anthropology of Experience*, ed. Edward Bruner and Victor Turner. Urbana: University of Illinois Press.

Abruzzi, Anthony. 2004. "The History of the San Antonio di Padua da Montefalcione Society in the North End of Boston." In *Saint Anthony's Feast, August 23–25, 2002*. North End, Boston (brochure).

Abu-Lughod, Lila. 1990. "The Romance of Resistance: Tracing Transformations of Power through Bedouin Women." *American Ethnologist* 17, no. 1: 41–55.

Alba, Richard. 1985. *Italian-Americans into the Twilight of Ethnicity*. Englewood Cliffs, NJ: Prentice Hall.

Alvarez, Robert. 1995. "The Mexican–US Border: The Making of an Anthropology of Borderlands." *Annual Review of Anthropology* 24: 447–470.

Anderson, Benedict. 1983. *Imagined Communities: Reflections on the Origin and Spread of Nationalism*. London: Verso.

Appudurai, Arjun. 1982. "The Past as a Scarce Resource." *Man* 16: 201–219.

———. 1990. "Disjuncture and Difference in the Global Economy." *Theory, Culture and Society* 7: 295–310.

Ardener, Edwin. 1992. "The Construction of History: 'Vestige of Creation.'" In *History and Ethnicity*, ed. Elizabeth Tonkin, Marion Mcdonald, and Malcom Chapman. London: Routledge.

Aronson, Dan R. 1979. "Ethnicity as a Cultural System: An Introductory Essay." In *Ethnicity in the Americas*, ed. Frances Henry. Paris: Mouton.

Bailey, F.G. 1996 "Cultural Performance, Authenticity, and Second Nature." In *The Politics of Cultural Performance*, ed. David Parkin, Lionel Caplan, and Humphrey Fisher. Providence, RI: Berghahn Books.

Bailey, M. E. 1993. "Foucauldian Feminism: Contesting Bodies, Sexuality and Identity." In *Up against Foucault: Explorations of Some Tensions between Foucault and Feminism*, ed. C. Ramazanoglu. London: Routledge.

Bakhtin, Michail. 1968. *Rabelais and His World*. Cambridge, MA: MIT Press.

———. 1981. "Discourse in the Novel." In *The Dialogical Imagination*, ed. Michael Holquist. Austin: University of Texas Press.

———. 1984 *Problems of Dostoevsky's Poetics*. Minnesota: Minnesota University Press.

259

Baldassarre, Fausto. 1982. "Il grano, la morte, l'oro, i fuochi di Sant'Antonio." *Il Ponte* (October 9): 2–4.

Banfield, Edward. 1958. *The Moral Basis of a Backwards Society*. Chicago: Free Press.

Barrett, James, and David Roediger. 1995. "Inbetween Peoples: Race, Nationality and the 'New Immigrant' Working Class." *Journal of American Ethnic History* 16, no. 3: 3–44.

Barth, Frederick. 1969. *Ethnic Groups and Boundaries: The Social Organization of Culture Difference*. London: Allen and Unwin.

Barthes, Roland. 1970. *S/Z*. Paris: Seuils.

Barton, Joseph. *Peasants and Strangers: Italians, Rumanian, and Slovaks in an American City, 1890–1950*. Cambridge, MA: Harvard University Press.

Barzini, Luigi. 1964. *The Italians*. New York: Atheneum.

Baumann, Richard. 1988. "Performance and Honor in 13th-Century Iceland." *Journal of American Folklore* 99: 131–150.

Bell, Catherine. 1992. *Ritual Theory, Ritual Practice*. Oxford, UK: Oxford University Press.

Bell, R. M. 1979. *Fate and Honor, Family and Village: Demographic and Cultural Change in Rural Italy since 1800*. Chicago: University of Chicago Press.

Bestor, Theodore. 1989. *Neighborhood Tokyo*. Stanford, CA: Stanford University Press.

Bhabha, Homi. 1994. *The Location of Culture*. London: Routledge.

Bianco, Carla, and Maurizio Del Ninno. 1981. *Festa: antropologia e semiotica*. Florence, Italy: Nuova Guaraldi.

Bickerton, Derek. 1975. *Dynamics of a Creole System*. Cambridge: Cambridge University Press.

Bloch, March. 1941–1942. *Apologie pour l'histoire ou le métier d'historien*. Paris: Colin.

Bodnar, John. 1983. *The Transplanted: A History of Immigrants in Urban America*. Bloomington: Indiana University Press.

Boelen, W. A. M. 1992. "Street Corner Society: Cornerville Revisited." *Journal of Contemporary Ethnography* 21, no. 1: 11–51.

Boissevin, Jeremy. 1969. *Saints and Fireworks. Religion and Politics in Rural Malta*. London: Athlone Press.

———. 1979. "Towards a Social Anthropology of the Mediterranean." *Current Anthropology* 20, no. 1: 81–93.

———. 1991. "Ritual, Play and Identity: Changing Patterns of Celebration in Maltese Villages." *Journal of Mediterranean Studies* 1: 87–100.

Bourdieu, Pierre. 1979. *Outline of a Theory of a Practice*. Cambridge: Cambridge University Press.

Bridenbaugh, Carl. 1955a. *Cities in Revolt: Urban Life in America, 1743–1776*. New York: Knopf.

———. 1955b. *Cities in the Wilderness: The First Century of Urban Life in America, 1625–1742*. New York: Knopf.

Briggs, John. 1978. *An Italian Passage*. New Haven, CT: Yale University Press.

Brown, Mary Elizabeth, "Italian-Americans and their Saints: Historical Considerations." In *The Saints in the Lives of Italian-Americans*, ed. Joseph Varacalli, Salvatore Primeggia, Salvatore Lagumina, and Donald D'Elia. New York: Filibrary, Forum Italicum no. 14.

Brubaker, Rogers, and Frederick Cooper. 2000. "Beyond 'Identity.'" *Theory and Society* 29: 1–47.

Bushee, Frederick. 1897. "Italian Immigrants in Boston." *South End House Bulletin* 10: 42–43.

———. 1902. "The Invading Host." In *Americans in Process: A Settlement Study by Residents and Associates of the South End House—North and West Ends Boston*, ed. Robert Woods. Boston, MA: Houghton Mifflin. Reprint, New York: Arno Press, 1970.

———. 1969. *Ethnic Factors in the Population of Boston*. New York: Arno Press.

Campbell, John. 1964. *Honour, Family, and Patronage: A Study of Institutions and Moral Values in a Greek Mountain Community*. Oxford, UK: Clarendon Press.

Caputo, Jennifer. 2004. "Neapolitan, Sicilian, Italian, American or Italian-American? Reconstructing Ethnic Identity in Post 9/11 Boston, MA." Paper presented at OHA Annual Meeting "Performing Oral History," Portland, Oregon, October 1.

Carlson, Laurie Winn. 2002. *A Fever in Salem: A New Interpretation of the New England Witch Trials*. Chicago: Ivan R. Dee.

Carrithers, Michael, Steven Collins, and Stephen Lukes. 1987. *The Category of the Person: Anthropology, Philosophy, and History*. Cambridge: Cambridge University Press.

Carroll, Michael. 1992. *Madonnas That Maim: Popular Catholicism in Italy since the 15th Century*. Baltimore: John Hopkins University Press.

Cashdan, Elizabeth. 1983. "Territoriality among Human Foragers: Ecological Models and an Application to Four Bushman Groups." *Current Anthropology* 2, no. 1: 47–66.

Castoriadis, Cornelius. 1987. *The Imaginary Institution of Society*. Cambridge, MA: MIT Press.

Chandler, Edward. 1902. "City and Slums." In *Americans in Process: A Settlement Study by Residents and Associates of the South End House—North and West Ends Boston*, ed. Robert Woods. Boston: Houghton Mifflin. Reprint, New York: Arno Press, 1970.

Cinel, Dino. 1984. *From Italy to San Francisco: The Immigrant Experience*. Stanford, CA: Stanford University Press.

Clifford, James. 1987. "Of Other People: Beyond the 'Savage Paradigm.'" In *Discussion in Contemporary Culture*, ed. Hal Foster. Seattle, WA: Bay Press.

————. 2002. "Taking Identity Politics Seriously: 'The Contradictory Stony
    Ground . . .'" In *Without Guarantees: In Honour of Stuart Hall*, ed. Paul
    Gilroy, Lawrence Grossberg, and Angela McRobbie. London: Verso.

Clifford, James, and G. Marcus. 1987. *Writing Culture: The Poetics and Politics of
    Ethnography*. Berkeley and Los Angeles: University of California Press.

Cogliano, Francis. 1995. *No King No Popery*. London: Greenwood Press.

Cohen, Abner. 1993. *Masquerade Politics: Explorations in the Structure of Urban Cul-
    tural Movements*. Berkeley and Los Angeles: University of California Press.

Cohen, Anthony P. 1983. *The Symbolic Construction of Community*. London:
    Tavistock.

————. *Self-Consciousness: An Alternative Anthropology of Identity*. London:
    Routledge.

Cohen, R., and P. Kennedy. 2000. *Global Sociology*. London: Macmillan.

Cole, William. 1902. "Two Ancient Faiths" and "Law and Order." In *Americans
    in Process: A Settlement Study by Residents and Associates of the South End
    House—North and West Ends Boston*, ed. Robert Woods. Boston, MA:
    Houghton Mifflin. Reprint, New York: Arno Press, 1970.

Comaroff, Jane, and John Comaroff. 1991. *Of Revelation and Revolution*.
    Chicago: Chicago University Press.

Conte, Gaetano. 1903. *Dieci anni in America: Impressioni e ricordi*. Palermo, Italy.

Cowan, Jane. 1992. "Japanese Ladies and Mexican Hats: Contested Symbols and
    the Politics of Tradition in a Northern Greek Carnival Celebration." In
    Revitalizing European Rituals, ed. Jeremy Boissevin. London: Routledge.

Crehan, Kate. 2002. *Gramsci, Culture, and Anthropology*. Berkeley and Los
    Angeles: University of California Press.

Cullen, James Bernard. 1889. *The Story of the Irish in Boston, Together with
    Biographical Sketches of Representative Men and Noted Women*. Boston,
    MA: Cullen.

D'Arcy McGee, Thomas. 1852. *A History of the Irish Settlers in North America:,
    From the Earliest Period to the Census of 1850*. Boston, MA: Partick Don-
    ahoe. Reprint, San Francisco: R. and E. Research Associates, 1970.

Davis, John. 1987. "Family and State in the Mediterranean." In *Honor and
    Shame and the Unity of the Mediterranean*, ed. David D. Gilmore. Wash-
    ington, DC: American Anthropological Association, 22–34.

De Marco, William. 1981. *Ethnics and Enclaves. Boston's Italian North End*. Ann
    Arbor: University of Michigan Press.

De Martino, Ernesto. 1975. *La Terra del Rimorso: Contributo ad una storia
    religiosa del Sud*. Milan, Italy: Il Saggiatore.

————. 1977. *La Fine del Mondo: Contributo alle analisi delle apocalissi culturali*.
    Turin, Italy: Einaudi.

Deridda, Jacques. 1972. *La dissemination*. Paris: Seuil.

Devoto, Fernando. 2006. *Historia de los Italianos in Argentina*. Buenos Aires:
    Editorial Biblos.

Di Leonardo, Micaela. 1984. *Varieties of Ethnic Experience*. Ithaca, NY: Cornell University Press.

Donnan, Hastings, and Thomas Wilson. 1999. *Borders: Frontiers of Identity: Nation and State*. New York: Berg.

Douglas, Mary. 1969. "Deciphering a Meal." In *Myth, Symbol and Culture*, ed. Clifford Geertz. New York: Norton.

———. 1978. *Natural Symbols: Explorations in Cosmology*. London: Barrie and Jenkins.

Drummond, Lee. 1980. "The Cultural Continuum: A Theory of Intersystem." *Man* 15, no. 2: 352–374.

Du Boulay, Juliet, and Rory Williams. 1987. "Amoral Familism and the Image of Limited Good: A Critique from a European Perspective." *Anthropological Quarterly* 60: 12–23.

Dundee, Alan, and Alessandro Falassi. 1975. *La Terra in Piazza: On Interpretation of the Palio di Siena*. Berkeley and Los Angeles: University of California Press.

Durkheim, Emile. 1915. *The Elementary Forms of the Religious Life*. London: Allen and Unwin.

Eco, Umberto. 1996. *Sugli Specchi ed altri Saggi*. Milan, Italy: Sonzogno Bompiani.

Efron, David. 1972. *Gesture, Race and Culture*. The Hague: Mouton.

Fabian, Johannes. 1978. "Popular Culture in Africa: Findings and Conjectures." *Africa* 48: 315–334.

Falassi, Alessandro. 1985. "Festival: Definition and Morphology." In *Time Out of Time*, ed. Alessandro Falassi. Albuquerque: University of New Mexico Press.

Favero, Paolo. 2005 *India Dreams: Cultural Identity among Young Middle Class Men in New Delhi*. Stockholm: Stockholm Studies in Social Anthropology.

Febvre, Lucien, ed. 1933. *Combat pour l'Histoire*. Paris: Colin.

Firey, Walter. 1947. *Land Use in Central Boston*. Cambridge, MA: Harvard University Press.

Foucault, Michel. 1969. *The Archeology of Knowledge and the Discourse on Language*. New York, Pantheon.

———. 1984 "The Great Confinement"; "The Birth of the Asylum"; "Space, Knowledge, and Power"; Right of Death and Power over Life"; "Preface to *The History of Sexuality*, Volume II"; "On the Genealogy of Ethics"; "Politics and Ethics." In *The Foucault Reader*, ed. Paul Rabinow. New York: Pantheon Books.

———. 1990. "Technologies of the Self." In *Technologies of the Self: A Seminar with Michel Foucault*, ed. Luther H Martin, Huck Gutman, and Patrick H. Hutton. Amherst: University of Massachusetts Press.

———. 1997. "Technologies of the Self." In *Ethics: Subjectivity and Truth— The Essential Works of Michel Foucault (1954–1984)*, ed. Paul Rabinow. New York: New Press.

Gabaccia, R. Donna. 1999. "Is Everywhere Nowhere? Nomads, Nations, and the Immigrant Paradigm of United States History." *Journal of American History* 86, no. 3: 1115–1134.

———. 2001. *Italian Workers of the Word*. Chicago: University of Illinois Press.

———. 2007. "Inventing 'Little Italy'." *Journal of Gilded Age and Progressive Era* (January 2007). Available at http://www.historycooperative.org/cgi-bin/justtop.cgi?act=justtop&url=http://www.historycooperative.org/journals/jga/6.1/gabaccia.html (accessed March 8, 2008).

Gager, John. 1975. *Kingdom and Community: The Social World of Early Christianity*. Englewood Cliffs, NJ: Prentice Hall.

Galaty, John. 1982. "Ceremony and Society: The Poetics of Maasai Ritual." *Man* 18: 361–382.

Gallini, Clara. 1982. "FESTA." In *Enciclopedia del Teatro Italiano*. Milan, Italy: Feltrinelli, 1982.

Galt, Anthony. 1992. *Town and Country in Locorotondo*. Green Bay: University of Wisconsin.

Galvin, John. 1975. "Boston's First Irish Cop." *Boston Magazine* 67, no. 3: 34–37.

Galzer, Nathan, and Daniel Moyhinian. 1969. *Beyond the Melting Pot*. Cambridge, MA: MIT and Harvard University Press.

Gambera, Giacomo. 1994. *A Migrant Missionary Story: The Autobiography of Giacomo Gambera*. New York: Center for Migration Studies.

Gans, Herbert. 1962. *The Urban Villagers: Groups and Class in the Life of Italian-Americans*. New York: Free Press.

———. 1979. "Symbolic Ethnicity: The Future of Ethnic Groups and Cultures in America." *Ethnic and Racial Studies* 2, no. 1: 1–20.

Garcia Canclini, Nestor. 1988. "Culture and Power: The State of Research." *Media, Culture and Society* 10: 467–497.

———. 1995. *Hybrid Cultures: Strategies for Leaving and Entering Modernity*. Minneapolis: University of Minnesota Press.

Geertz, Clifford. 1973. *The Interpretation of Cultures*. New York: Basic Books.

———. 1980. *Negara*. Princeton, NJ: Princeton University Press.

Gilmore, David, 1987 *Honor and Shame and the Unity of the Mediterranean*. Washington: American Anthropological Association, 1987.

Gilroy, Paul. 2000. *Between Camps*. London: Penguin.

Ginzburg, Carlo. 1976. "Stregoneria, magia e superstizione in Europa fra medioevo ed età moderna." *Ricerche di Storia Sociale e Religiosa* 6, no. 11: 119–133.

Gluckman, Max. 1958. *Analysis of a Social Situation in Modern Zululand*. Manchester: Manchester University Press.

———. 1963 "Ritual of Rebellion in South-East Africa." In *Order and Rebellion in Tribal Africa*, ed. Max Gluckman. London: Cohen and West.

Goffman, Erving. 1959. *The Presentation of Self in Everyday Life*. Garden City, NJ: Doubleday.

————. 1974. *Frame Analysis: An Essay on the Organization of Experience*. New York: Harper and Row.

Goody, Jack. 1986. *The Logic of Writing and the Organization of Society*. Cambridge: Cambridge University Press.

Gramsci, Antonio. 1929–1959. "Osservazioni sul Folklore." In *Quaderni dal Carcere*. Roma: Editori Riuniti.

————. 1971. *Selections from the Prison Notebooks*, ed. Quintin Hoare and Geoffrey Nowell-Smith. London: Lawrence and Wishart.

————. 1984. *Selections from Cultural Writings*, ed. David Forgacs and Geoffrey Nowell-Smith. London: Lawrence and Wishart.

Griffith, William. 1971. *The Irish in America, 550–1972: A Chronology and Fact Book*. New York: Dobbs Ferry.

Grimaldi, Piercarlo. 1994. *Il calendario rituale contadino. Il tempo della festa e del lavoro fra tradizione e complessità sociale*. Milan, Italy: Franco Angeli.

Grimes, Ronald. 1990. *Ritual Criticism: Case Studies in Its Practice, Essays on Its Theory*. Columbia: University of South Carolina Press.

Gudeman, Stephen. 1971. "The Compadrazgo as a Reflection of the Natural and Spiritual Person." *Proceedings of the Royal Anthropological Institute of Great Britain and Ireland*: 45–71.

Gumina, Deanna Paoli. 1978. *The Italians of San Francisco, 1850–1930*. New York: Center for Migration Studies.

Gupta, Akhil, and James Ferguson, eds. 1997. *Anthropological Locations: Boundaries and Grounds of a Field Science*. Berkeley and Los Angeles: University of California Press.

Guss, David. 2000. *The Festive State: Race, Ethnicity and Nationalism as Cultural Performance*. Berkeley and Los Angeles: University of California Press.

Gutierrez, Ramon, and Genevieve Fabre. 1994. *Feasts and Celebrations*. Albuquerque: New Mexico Press.

Gutmann, Matthew. 1996. *The Meanings of Macho: Being a Man in Mexico City*. Berkeley and Los Angeles: University of California Press.

————, ed. 2003. *Changing Men and Masculinities in Latin America*. Durham, NC: Duke University Press.

Hall, John, and Charles Lindholm. 1999. *Is America Breaking Apart?* Princeton, NJ: Princeton University Press.

Hall, Stuart. 1996. "Introduction: Who Needs 'Identity'?" In *Questions of Cultural Identity*, ed. Stuart Hall and Paul Du Gay. London: Sage.

Halter, Marilyn. 2000. *Shopping for Identity: The Marketing of Ethnicity*. New York: Schocken Books.

Handler, Richard. 1988. *Nationalism and the Politics of Culture in Quebec*. Madison: University of Wisconsin Press.

Handlin, Oscar. 1941. *Boston's Immigration, 1790–1780: A Study in Acculturation*. Cambridge, MA: Belknap Press of Harvard University Press.

————. 1951. *The Uprooted*. Boston, MA: Little Brown.

————. 1961. "Immigration in American Life: A Reappraisal." In *Immigration in American History: Essays in Honor of Theodore C. Blegen*, ed. Henry S. Commager. Minneapolis: University of Minnesota Press.

————. 1966. *The American People in the Twentieth Century*. Cambridge, MA: Harvard University Press.

Hannerz, Ulf. 1987. "The World in Creolization." *Africa* 57, no. 5: 546–559.

————. 1992. *Cultural Complexity: Studies in the Social Organization of Meaning*. New York: Columbia University Press.

————. 1996. "Flows, Boundaries and Hybrids: Keywords in Transnational Anthropology." *Mana* 3, no. 1: 7–39.

Hansen, Marcus. 1938. *The Problem of Third Generation Immigrant*. Rock Island, IL: Augustana Historical Society.

Harrison, Simon. 1999. "Identity as a Scarce Resource." *Social Anthropology* 7, no. 3: 239–251.

Harvey, David. 1989. *The Urban Experience*. Baltimore: John Hopkins University Press.

Hayden, Dolores. 1991. "The Potential of Ethnic Places for Urban Landscapes." *Places* 7, no. 1: 11–17.

Herzfeld, Michael. 1980. "Disemia." In *Semiotica 1980*, ed. Michael Herzfeld and Margot Lenhart. New York: Plenum Press, 205–215.

————. 1986. *The Poetics of Manhood: Contest and Identity in a Cretan Mountain Village*. Princeton, NJ: Princeton University Press.

————. 1987. "'As in Your House': Hospitality, Ethnography, and the Stereotype of Mediterranean Society." In *Honor and Shame and the Unity of the Mediterranean*, ed. David D. Gilmore. Washington, DC: American Anthropological Association, 75–89.

————. 1997a. *Cultural Intimacy. Social Poetics in the Nation-State*. London: Routledge.

————. 1997b. *Portrait of a Greek Imagination: An Ethnographic Biography of Andreas Nenedakis*. Chicago: University of Chicago Press.

————. 2005. "Political Optics and the Occlusion of Intimate Knowledge." *American Anthropologist* 107, no. 3: 369–376.

Hodgen, Margaret. 1936. *The Doctrine of Survivals: A Chapter in the History of Scientific Method in the Study of Man*. London: Allenson.

Hugues, Thomas. 1998. *Rescuing Prometheus*. New York: Pantheon Books.

Hutnyk, John. 2005. "Hybridity." *Ethnic and Racial Study* 28, no. 1: 79–102.

Isbell, Robert. 1996. *Last Chivaree: The Hicks Family of Beech Mountain*. Chapel Hill: University of North Carolina Press.

Ivy, Marilyn. 1995. *Discourses of the Vanishing: Modernity, Phantasm, Japan*. Chicago: University of Chicago Press.

Jackson, John Brinkerhoff. 1984. *Discovering the Vernacular Landscape*. New Haven, CT: Yale University Press.

Jacobs, Jane. 1961. *The Death and Life of Great American Cities*. New York: Random House.

Jacobson, Matthew Frye. 1997. *Whiteness of a Different Color*. Cambridge, MA: Harvard University Press.

———. 2006. *Roots Too: White Ethnic Revival In Post-Civil Rights America*. Cambridge, MA: Harvard University Press.

Jensen, Richard. 2000. "'No Irish Need Apply': A Myth of Victimization." *Journal of Social History* 36, no. 2: 405–429.

Keller Brown, Linda, and Kay Mussell. 1984. *Ethnic and Regional Foodways in the United States*. Knoxville: University of Tennessee Press.

Kirsch, Thomas. 2004. "Restarting the Will to Believe: Religious Pluralism, Anti-Syncretism, and the Problem of Belief." *American Anthropologist* 106, no. 4: 699–709.

Kivisto, Peter. 2001. "Theorizing Transnational Immigration: A Critical Review of Current Efforts." *Ethnic and Racial Studies* 24, no. 4: 549–577.

Korom, Frank. 1994. "Memory, Innovation and Emergent Ethnicities: The Creolization of an Indo-Trinidadian Performance." *Diaspora* 3: 135–155.

———. 2003. *Hosay Trinidad: Muharram Performances in an Indo-Caribbean Diaspora*. Philadelphia: University of Pennsylvania Press.

Krase, Jerome. 2006. "Italian American Urban Landscape. Images of Social and Cultural Capital." In *Varieties of Urban Experiences,* ed. Ian Michael Borer. Lanham, MD: University Press of America. Also available at http://www.brooklynsoc.org/docs/Krase_ItalianAmericanUrban Landscapes.pdf (accessed February 10, 2008).

Krase, Jerome, and Judith De Sena. 1994. *Italian Americans in a Multicultural Society*. New York: Forum Italicum.

Krieger, Alex, and David Cobb, with Amy Turner, eds. *Mapping Boston*. Cambridge, MA: MIT Press and Norman B. Leventhal Book.

Kristeva, Julia. 1986. "Word, Dialogue, and the Novel." In *The Kristeva Reader*, ed. T. Moi. New York: Columbia University Press, 35–61.

Kroskrity, P. V. 1993. *Language, History, and Identity: Ethnolinguistic Studies of the Arizona Tewa*. Tucson: University of Arizona Press.

Lacan, Jacques. 1975. *Ecrits: A Selection*. New York: Norton.

———. 1976. *The Four Fundamental Concept of Psycho-Analysis*, ed. Alain Miller. New York: Norton.

Lamont, Michèle, and Virág Molnár. 2002. "The Study of Boundaries in the Social Sciences." *Annual Review of Sociology* 28: 167–195.

Landow, George. 1992. *Hypertext: The Convergence of Contemporary Critical Theory and Technology*. Baltimore: John Hopkins University Press.

Langer, Josef. 1999. "Towards a Conceptualization of Border: The Central European Experience." In *Curtains of Iron and Gold–Reconstructing Borders and Scales of Interaction*, ed. Heikki Eskelinen, Ilkka Liikanen, and Jukka Oksa. Aldershot, UK: Ashgate.

Langone, Fred. 1995. *The North End: Where It All Began—A History of the North End the Way It Was.* Boston, MA: American Independence Edition.

Leach, E. R. 1962. *Political Systems of Highland Burma: A Study of Kachin Social Structure.* London: Athlone Press.

———. 1966. "Virgin Birth." *Proceedings of the Royal Anthropological Institute of Great Britain and Ireland* 96: 39–49.

Lefort, Claude. 1986. *The Political Forms of Modern Society: Bureaucracy, Democracy, Totalitarism.* Cambridge, MA: MIT Press.

Le Goff, Jacques. 1977. "*Calendario.*" In *Enciclopedia Einaudi*, vol 2. Torino, Italy: Einaudi.

———. 1978. "Documento/Monumento." In *Enciclopedia Einaudi.* Torino, Italy: Einaudi.

Levi, Carlo. 1945. *Cristo si e' fermato ad Eboli.* Torin, Italy: Einaudi.

Lèvi-Strauss, Claude. 1969. *The Raw and the Cooked.* New York: Harper and Row.

Lewin, Kurt. 1949. *Field Theory and Social Science.* London: Tavistock.

Lewis, Gilbert. 1982. *Day of Shining Red: An Essay on Understanding Ritual.* Cambridge: Cambridge University Press.

Lindholm, Charles. 1996. *The Islamic Middle East: Tradition and Change.* Malden, MA Blackwell.

———. 2008. *Culture and Authenticity.* Malden, MA: Blackwell.

Lloyd Warner, W. 1953. *American Life: Dream and Reality.* Chicago: University of Chicago Press, 1953.

Lotman, Mihhail. 2001. "The Paradoxes of Semiosphere." *Sun Yat-sen Journal of Humanities* 12: 97–106.

Luconi, Stefano. 2001. *From Paesani to White Ethnics.* Albany: State University of New York Press.

Lyotard, Jean Francois. 1986. *The Post-Modern Condition: A Report on Knowledge.* Manchester, UK: Manchester University Press.

Macdonald, John S., and Leatrice D. Macdonald. 1962. "Urbanization, Ethnic Groups, and Social Segmentation." *Social Research* 29: 433–448.

Magliocco, Sabina. 1993. "Playing with Food." In *Italian American Folklore*, ed. Luisa Del Giudice, Logan: Utah State University Press.

———. 2006. *The Two Madonnas: The Politics of Festival in a Sardinian Community.* Long Grove, IL: Waveland Press.

Magrini, Tullia 1998. "Women's '*Work in Pain*' in Christian Mediterranean Europe." *Music and Anthropology* 3. Also available at http://research.umbc.edu/eol/MA/index/number3/magrini/magr0.htm (accessed November 12, 2005).

Mallet, Paul Henry. 1847. *Northern Antiquities; Or, an Historical Account of the Manners, Customs, Religion and Laws, Maritime Expeditions and Discoveries, Language and Literature of the Ancient Scandinavians.* London: Bohn.

Mangione, Jerre, and Ben Morreale. 1993. *La storia: Five Centuries of the Italian American Experience.* New York: HarperCollins.

Markus, Michael. 1987. "'Horsemen Are the Fence of the Land': Honor and History among the Ghiyata of Eastern Morocco." In *Honor and Shame and the Unity of the Mediterranean*, ed. David D. Gilmore. Washington, DC: American Anthropological Association.

Martellone, Anna M. 1973. *Una Little Italy nell'Atene d'America*. Naples, Italy: Guida.

————. 1980. *La "Questione" dell'immigrazione negli Stati Uniti*. Bologna, Italy: Il Mulino.

————. 1995. *Towards a News American Nation? Redefinitions and Reconstruction*. 1995.Staffordshire, UK: EPAI I.

Martin, Emily. 1997. "'You Can't Take the Subway to the Field!': 'Village' Epistemologies in the Global Village." In *Anthropological Locations: Boundaries and Grounds of a Field Science*, ed. Akhil Gupta and James Ferguson. Berkeley and Los Angeles: University of California Press.

Martin, L. H., ed. 1988. *Technologies of the Self: A Seminar with Michel Foucault*. London: Tavistock.

Mazzacane, Lello. 1985. *Struttura di Festa*. Milan, Italy: Franco Angeli.

Mcguire, Meredith. 1994. *Religion: The Social Context*. Belmont, CA: Wadsworth.

McKenzie, Jon. 2001. *Perform or Else: From Discipline to Performance*. New York: Routledge.

Melucci, Alberto. 1995. "The Process of Collective Identity." In *Social Movements and Culture*, ed. Hank Johnston and Bert Klandermans. Minneapolis: University of Minnesota Press.

Miller, Kerby. 1985. *Emigrants and Exiles: Ireland and the Irish Exodus to North America*. New York: Oxford University Press.

Mohanty, Satya. 1999. "The Epistemic Status of Cultural Identity." In *Reclaiming Identity: Realist Theory and the Predicament of Postmodernism*, ed. Paula Moya and Michael Hames-Garcia. Berkeley and Los Angeles: University of California Press.

Mormino, Gary, and Pozzetta George. 1997. *The Immigrant World of Ybor City: Italians and Their Latin Neighbors in Tampa, 1885–1985*. Gainesville: University Press of Florida.

Morphy, Howard. 1994. "The Interpretation of Rituals: Reflections from Film on Anthropological Practice." *Man* n.s., 29, no. 1: 117–146.

Mortara Garavelli, Bice. 1976. *Retorica Generale. Le figure della comunicazione*. Milano: Bompiani.

Moya, Paula. 1999. "Postmodernism, 'Realism', and the Politics of Identity." In *Reclaiming Identity: Realist Theory and the Predicament of Postmodernism*, ed. Paula Moya and Michael Hames-Garcia. Berkeley and Los Angeles: University of California Press.

Namias, June. *First Generation: In The Words of Twentieth-Century American Immigrants*. Urbana: University of Illinois Press.

Naquin, Susan. 1988. "Funeral in North China: Uniformity and Variations." In *Death Ritual in Late Imperial and Modern China*, ed. James Watson and Evelyn Rawski. Berkeley and Los Angeles: University of California Press.

Nash, Gary B. 1986. *The Urban Crucible: The Northern Seaports and the Origins of the American Revolution*. Cambridge, MA: Harvard University Press.

Needham, Rodney. 1972. *Belief, Language, Experience*. Oxford, UK: Blackwell.

Nelson, Theodore. 1992. *Literary Machine*. Padova, Italy: Muzzio.

Newman, David. 2004. "The Resilience of Territorial Conflict in an Era of Globalization." Paper presented at the International Workshop "Globalization, Territoriality, and Conflict," organized by The Institute for International, Comparative, and Area Studies (IICAS) at the University of California–San Diego, January 2003 and January 2004. A revised version of this paper will be published in a forthcoming volume to be edited by Miles Kahler and Barbara Walter. Also available at http://www.sgir.org/conference 2004/papers/Newman%20-%20The%20resilience%20of%20territorial %20conflict%20in%20an%20era%20of%20globalization.pdf (accessed February 26, 2005).

Nolan, Mary Lee, and Sidney Nolan. 1989. *Christian Pilgrimages in Modern Western Europe*. Chapel Hill: University of North Carolina Press.

O'Connor, Thomas H. 1993. *Building a New Boston: Politics and Urban Renewal, 1950–1970*. Boston, MA: Northeastern University Press.

———. 1995. *The Boston Irish: A Political History*. Boston, MA: Northeastern University Press.

Okamura, Jonathan. 1981. "Situational Ethnicity." *Ethnic and Racial Studies* 4, no. 4: 452–465.

Orsi, Robert. 1984. *The Madonna of 115th Street: Faith and Community in Italian Harlem, 1880–1950*. New Haven, CT: Yale University Press.

———. 1992. "The Religious Boundaries of an Inbetween People: Street Feste and the Problem of the Dark-Skinned Other in Italian Harlem, 1920–1990." *American Quarterly* 44, no. 3: 313–347.

———. 1996 *Thank You, St. Jude: Women's Devotion to the Patron Saint of Hopeless Causes*. New Haven, CT: Yale University Press.

O'Sullivan, Patrick. 1999. "A Portable Identity: John Denvir and the Invention of the Irish." In *The Irish in Britain: The Local Dimension*, ed. Roger Swift and Gilley Sheridan. Dublin, Ireland: Four Courts Press.

Paden, John. 1967. "Situation Ethnicity in Urban Africa with Special Reference to the Hausa." Paper presented at the annual meeting of African Studies Association, New York.

Pagliuca Fulvio and Cuciniello, Nicola. 1990. *Storia di Montefalcione*. Foggia: Leone.

Paine, Robert. 2000. "Aboriginality, Authenticity and Settlers." In *Signifying Identities: Anthropological Perspectives on Boundaries and Contested Value*, ed. Anthony Cohen. London: Routledge.

Parkin, David. 1996. "The Power of the Bizarre." In *The Politics of Cultural Performance*, ed. David Parkin, Lionel Caplan, and Humphrey Fisher. Providence, RI: Berghahn Books.

Pascoe, Robert. 1983. "The Fear of Radical Alien: Boston Italians between the World Wars." Lectures at a Charles Warren Center Seminar, Harvard University, April 20. Available at http://www.robertpascoe.net/migration/boston.html (accessed November 7, 2002).

Peristiany, John. 1966. *Honour and Shame: The Values of Mediterranean Societies.* Chicago: University of Chicago Press.

———. 1976. *Mediterranean Family Structures.* Cambridge: Cambridge University Press.

Peristiany, John, and Julian Pitt-Rivers, ed. 2005. *Honor and Grace in Anthropology.* Cambridge: Cambridge University Press.

Piccione, John Anthony. 1980. "Naturalization, Ethnic Intermarriage, and Education as Measures of Acculturation: The Italian-American Community in Boston, 1890–1940." A.B. honors thesis, Harvard University.

Pina-Cabral, Joao. 1989. "The Mediterranean as a Category of Regional Comparison: A Critical View." *Current Anthropology* 30, no. 3: 399–406.

Pitrè, Giuseppe. 1884. *Feste Patronali nella Sicilia Occidentale.* Reprint, Palermo, Italy: Brancato, 2000.

Pitt-Rivers, Julian, ed. 1963. Mediterranean Countrymen: Essays in the Social Anthropology of the Mediterranean. Paris: Mouton.

———. 1976. "Ritual Kinship in the Mediterranean: Spain and the Balkans." In *Mediterranean Family Structures*, ed. John G Peristiany. Cambridge: Cambridge University Press, 317–334.

Porter, Dwight. 1889. *Report upon a Sanitary Inspection of Certain Tenement-House Districts of Boston.* Boston, MA: Rockwell and Churchill.

Portes, Alejandro, ed. 1995. *The Economic Sociology of Immigration: Essays on Network, Ethnicity, and Entrepreneurship.* New York: Russell Sage Foundation.

———. 1999. "The Study of Transnationalism: Pitfalls and Promise of an Emergent Research Field." *Ethnic and Racial Study* 22, no. 2: 217–237.

Primeggia, Salvatore. 1999. "The Social Context of Religious Devotion." In *The Saints in the Lives of Italian-Americans*, ed. Joseph Varacalli, Salvatore Primeggia, Salvatore Lagumina, and Donald D'Elia. New York: Filibrary, Forum Italicum no. 14.

Reed-Danahay, Deborah. 1993. "Talking about Resistance: Ethnography and Theory in Rural France." *Anthropological Quarterly* 66: 221–229.

Rhum, Michael. 1993. "Understanding 'Belief.'" *Man* 28, no. 4: 801–802.

Riccio, Anthony. 1998. *Portrait of an Italian American Neighborhood: The North End.* New York: Center for Migration Studies.

Richards, David A. J. 1999. *Italian American: The Racializing of an Ethnic Identity.* New York: New York University Press.

Roediger, David. 1991. *The Wage of Whiteness: Race and the Making of American Working Class*. London: Verso.

Rosaldo, Renato. 1985. "Chicano Studies, 1970–1984." *Annual Revue Anthropology* 14: 405–427.

———. 1994. "Race and Other Inequalities: The Borderlands in Arturo Islas' Migrant Souls." In *Race*, ed. Steven Gregory and Roger Sanjek, New Brunswick, NJ: Rutgers University Press: 213–225.

Ruberto, Laura. 2007. *Gramsci, Migration, and the Representation of Women's Work in Italy and in the U.S.* Lanham, MD: Lexington Books.

Rudolfsky, Bernard. 1964. *Architecture without Architects*. Albuquerque: University of New Mexico Press.

Rutan, Elizabeth. 1902. "Before the Invasion." In *Americans in Process: A Settlement Study by Residents and Associates of the South End House—North and West Ends Boston*, ed. Robert Woods. Boston, MA: Houghton Mifflin. Reprint, New York: Arno Press, 1970.

Sanna, Mary Jo. 1988. "Miracles of the Heart: A Report on the Feasts of St. Anthony and Madonna del Soccorso." Unpublished manuscript.

Saunders, George. 1983. "Contemporary Italian Cultural Anthropology." *Annual Review of Anthropology* 13: 447–466.

———. 1993. "'Critical Ethnocentrism' and the Ethnology of Ernesto De Martino." *American Anthropologist* 95, no. 4: 875–893.

Scalabrini. 1913. *Venticinque anni di missione fra gli immigrati italiani di Boston, Mass., 1888–1913*. Milan, Italy: Santa Lega Eucaristica.

Scartezzini, Riccardo, Roberto Guidi, and Anna Maria Zaccaria. 1993. *Tra due mondi: l'avventura Americana tra i migranti*. Milan, Italy: Franco Angeli.

Schipper, Kristofer. 1985. "Vernacular and Classic Ritual in Taoism." *Journal of Asian Studies* 45, no. 1: 21–57.

Schmitt, Jean-Claude. 1976. "'Religion populaire' et culture folklorique." *Annales, Économies, Sociétés, Civilisations* 31: 941–953.

Schneider, Jane, ed. 1998. *Italy's "Southern Question": Orientalism in One Country*. New York: Berg.

Schneider, Jane, and Peter Schneider. 1976. *Culture and Political Economy in Western Sicily*. New York: Academic Press.

———. 1996. *Festival of the Poor*. Tucson: University of Arizona Press.

Schultz, Nancy Lusignan. 2000. *Fire and Roses: The Burning of the Charlestown Convent, 1834*. New York: Free Press.

Sciorra, Joseph. 1989. "'O Giglio e Paradiso': Celebration and Identity in an Urban Ethnic Community." *Urban Resources* 5: 510–539.

———. 1999. "We Go Where Italians Live." In *Gods of the City*, ed. Robert Orsi. Bloomington: Indiana University Press.

Seymour, St. John. *Irish Witchcraft and Demonology*. Dublin, Ireland: Hodges, Figgs.

Shaughnessy, James D. 1973. *The Roots of Ritual*. Grand Rapids, MI: Eerdmans.

Shellenbaum, Paola. 1993. "Stereotypes as Cultural Construct." In *Italian American Folklore*, ed. Luisa Del Giudice. Logan: Utah State University Press.

Sherman, Philip. 1904. "Immigration from Abroad into Massachusetts." *New England Magazine* 29, no. 6: 671–681.

Singer, Milton. 1959. *Traditional India: Structure and Change*. Philadelphia: AFS.

Smith, Robert. 1975. *The Art of the Festival*. Lawrence, KS: University of Kansas Press.

Smith, Wilfred. 1957. *Islam in Modern History*. New York: Mentor.

Sori, Ercole. 1979. *L'emigrazione italiana dall'Unità alla seconda guerra moniale*. Bologna, Italy: Il Mulino.

Sperber, Dan. 1997. "Intuitive and Reflective Beliefs." *Mind and Language* 12, no. 1: 67–83.

Spivak, Gayatri Chakravovorty. 1989. *The Post-Colonial Critic: Interviews, Strategies, Dialogues*. New York: Routledge.

———. 1993. "Can the Subatern Speak?" In *Colonial Discourse and Post-Colonial Theory: A Reader*, ed. Patrick Williams and Laura Chrisman. New York: Columbia University Press, 66–112.

Stewart, Charles. 1989. *Demons and the Devil: Modern Imagination in Modern Greek Culture*. Princeton, NJ: Princeton University Press.

Strassoldo, Raimondo. 1977. "Study of Boundaries: A System-Oriented, Multidisciplinary Bibliographical Essay." *Jerusalem Journal of International Relations* 2, no. 3: 81–107.

Swiderski, Richard M. 1984. *Voices: An Anthropologist Dialogue with an Italian-American Festival*. Bowling Green, KY: University Popular Press.

Tager, Jack. 2000. *Boston Riots: Three Centuries of Social Violence*. Boston, MA: Northeastern University Press.

Tak, Hermann. 2000. *South Italian Festivals*. Amsterdam: Amsterdam University Press.

Tambiah, Stanley J. 1989. "Ethnic Conflict in the World Today." *American Ethnologist* 16, no. 2: 335–349.

Thaon Di Revel, Vittorio. 1889. "Boston: Immigrazione italiana." *Bollettino del Ministero degli Affari Esteri* 26: 45–265.

Thernstrom, Stephan. 1971. *The Other Bostonian: Poverty and Progress in the American Metropolis, 1880–1970*. Cambridge, MA: Harvard University Press.

Todisco, Paula J. 1976. *Boston's First Neighborhood: The North End*. Boston, MA: Boston Public Library Duplicating Department.

Todorov, Tzevan. 1984. *Michail Bakhtin: The Dialogical Principle*. Minneapolis: University of Minnesota Press.

Turner, Victor. 1957. *Schism and Continuity in an African Society: A Study of Ndembu Village Life*. Manchester, UK: Manchester University Press.

————. 1969. *The Ritual Process: Structure and Anti-structure*. Ithaca, NY: Cornell University Press, 1969.

————. 1974a. *Dramas, Fields, and Metaphors: Symbolic Action in Human Society*. Ithaca, NY: Cornell University Press.

————. 1974b. "Liminal to Liminoid in Play, Flow and Ritual: An Essay in Comparative Symbology." *Rice University Studies* 60. Houston, TX: Rice University Press, 53–92.

————. 1976. "Symbols in African Ritual." *Science* 179: 1100–1105.

————. 1977. "Variations on a Theme of Liminality." In *Secular Ritual*, ed. Sally Moore and Barbara Myerhoff. Assen, The Netherlands: Van Gorcum.

————. 1978. *Image and Pilgrimage in Christian Culture*. Oxford, UK: Blackwell.

————. 1982a. *Celebration*. Washington, DC: Smithsonian Institution Press.

————. 1982b. *From Ritual to Theatre: The Human Seriousness of Play*. New York: Performing Arts Journal.

Van Gennep, Arnold. 1938. *Manuel de Folklore Français Contemporain*. Paris: Picard.

————. 1977. *I riti di passaggio*. Turin, Italy: Boringhieri.

Varacalli, Joseph, Salvatore Primeggia, Salvatore Lagumina, and Donald D'Elia, eds. 1999. *The Saints in the Lives of Italian-Americans*. New York: Forum Italicum.

Varenne, Hervè. 1976. *Americans Together: Structured Diversity in an American Town*. New York: Teachers College Press.

Vecoli, Rudolph. 1964. "Contadini in Chicago: A Critique of The Uprooted." *Journal of American History* 51, no. 3: 404–417.

————. 1969. "Prelates and Peasants: Italian Immigrants and the Catholic Church." *Journal of Social History* 2, no. 3: 217–268.

Waters, Mary. 1990. *Ethnic Options: Choosing Identities in America*. Berkeley and Los Angeles: University of California Press.

Watson, James. 1988. "The Structure of Chinese Funerary Rites: Elementary Forms, Ritual Sequence, and the Primacy of Performance." In *Death Ritual in Late Imperial and Modern China*, ed. James Watson and Evelyn Rawski. Berkeley and Los Angeles: University of California Press.

————. 1993. "Fighting with Operas: Processionals, Politics, and the Spectre of Violence in Rural Hong Kong." In *The Politics of Cultural Performance*, ed. David Parkin, Lionel Caplan, and Humphrey Fisher. Providence, RI: Berghahn Books.

Weber, Max. 1985 "'Churches' and 'Sects' in North America: An Ecclesiastical Socio-political Sketch." *Social Theory* 3: 7–13.

Weiner, Annette. 1992. *Inalienable Possessions: The Paradox of Keeping-While-Giving*. Berkeley and Los Angeles: University of California Press.

Whitehill, Walter, and Lawrence Kennedy. 2000. *Boston: A Topographical History*. 3rd ed. Cambridge, MA: Belknap Press of Harvard University Press.

Whyte, William F. 1939. "Race Conflicts in the North End." *New England Quarterly* 12, no. 4: 623–642.

———. 1943. *Street Corner Society: The Social Structure of an Italian Slum.* Chicago: University of Chicago Press.

Wieder, Arnold. 1962. *The Early Jewish Community of Boston's North End.* Waltham, MA: Brandeis University.

Williams, Drid. 1975. "Brides of Christ." In *Perceiving Women*, ed. Shirley Ardener. London: Dent.

Williams, John A. 1989. "Italian American Identity, Old and New: Stereotypes, Fashion and Ethnic Revival." *Folklife Center News* 11, no. 4: 4–7.

Williams, Raymond. 1976. *Marxism and Literature.* Oxford, UK: Oxford University Press.

Wood, Robert, 1998. "Tourist Ethnicity: A Brief Itinerary." *Ethnic and Racial Studies* 21, no. 2: 230.

Woodham Smith, Cecil. 1962. *The Great Hunger: Ireland 1845–1849,* London: Hamilton.

Woods, Robert, ed. 1902. *Americans in Process: A Settlement Study by Residents and Associates of the South End House—North and West Ends Boston.* Boston, MA: Houghton Mifflin. Reprint, New York: Arno Press, 1970.

Yans-Mclaughlin, Virginia. 1976. *Family and Community Italian Immigrants in Buffalo, 1880–1930.* Ithaca, NY: Cornell University Press.

Zardin, Danilo. 2001. "'Popular Religion': Historiographical Interpretations and Research Hypothesis." *Memorandum* 1: 41–60.

Zemon Davis, Natalie. 1980. "From 'Popular Religion' to Religious Cultures." In *Reformation Europe: A Guide to Research*, ed. Stephen Ozmet. St. Louis, MO: Center for Reformation Research.

Zukin, Sharon. 1987. "Gentrification: Culture and Capital in the Urban Core." *Annual Review of Sociology* 13: 129–147.

Index